The Color of Angels

The Color of Angels explores the rich symbolism of the senses in Western culture through the ages. In the process, Constance Classen uncovers the gender politics behind such cultural constructs as the 'male gaze' and the 'female touch' and traces the development of an aesthetics of the senses from medieval cosmology to modern art.

The book is divided into three parts – cosmology, gender and aesthetics – and explores topics ranging from the sensuous visions of St Hildegard of Bingen to the gender codes of Renaissance literature and the machine aesthetics of Futurism. *The Color of Angels* compellingly demonstrates the relationship between sensory and gender orders, revealing a crucial but previously unexplored area of women's history. Beautifully written, the book will appeal to students from a variety of disciplines, including gender studies, cultural studies and art.

Constance Classen is a cultural historian whose previous publications include *Worlds of Sense: Exploring the Senses in History and Across Cultures* and *Aroma: The Cultural History of Smell* (with David Howes and Anthony Synnott).

The Color of Angels

Cosmology, gender and the aesthetic imagination

Constance Classen

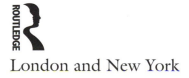

London and New York

First published 1998
by Routledge
11 New Fetter Lane, London EC4P 4EE

Simultaneously published in the USA and Canada
by Routledge
29 West 35th Street, New York, NY 10001

Typeset in Galliard by Routledge
Printed and bound in Great Britain by TJ International Ltd,
Padstow, Cornwall

British Library Cataloguing in Publication Data
A catalogue record for this book is available from the British Library

Library of Congress Cataloging in Publication Data
Classen, Constance, 1957–
    The color of angels : cosmology, gender, and the aesthetic
    imagination / Constance Classen.
        p. cm.
    Includes bibliographical references and index.
    1. Senses and sensation – Sex differences – History. 2. Senses
    and sensation – Religious aspects – Christianity – History. 3. Senses
    and sensation in art – History. I. Title.
    BF233. C56 1999
    152.1' 09–dc21   98–21837
                                                              CIP

ISBN 0–415–18073–2 (hbk)
ISBN 0–415–18074–0 (pbk)

For Jonathan Gabriel

Contents

Illustrations

Acknowledgements

My thanks to the people who have supported my work over the years, including Gregory Baum, Anthony Synnott, Michael Herzfeld, Steven Feld, Roy Porter, Chris Rojek, Mike Featherstone, Londa Schiebinger, Michael Jackson, Lawrence Sullivan, Thomas McIntire, Jim Drobnick, Jennifer Fisher, Susan Ashbrook Harvey, Mari Shullaw and Janice Helland. David Howes has been a continual source of encouragement and advice, for which I am deeply grateful. My thanks also go to George Classen who has tirelessly and skillfully assisted me in preparing my manuscripts for publication.

Part of the research for this book was undertaken while I was a Fellow at the Center for the Study of World Religions at Harvard University and a Research Reader at the Centre for the Study of Religion at the University of Toronto. My work has been supported by grants from the Social Sciences and Humanities Research Council of Canada and the Fonds pour la Formation de Chercheurs et l'Aide à la Recherche.

An earlier version of Chapter 3 was published as "Engendering Perception: Gender Ideologies and Sensory Hierarchies in Western History," *Body & Society* 3: 2 (1997), pp. 1–19.

Introduction

Modern Western culture is a culture of the eye. We are constantly bombarded, seduced, and shaped by visual models and representations, from maps and graphs to pictures and texts. This rule of sight carries with it a powerful aura of rationality and objectivity, even though many of its contemporary manifestations, such as advertising images, seem designed to manipulate the emotions more than to encourage the exercise of reason. The photographic nature of much of twentieth-century representation helps maintain this aura of objectivity by appearing to provide the viewer with direct access to reality, rather than only mediating reality.[1]

The visualist regime of modernity, in fact, prides itself on its transparency: everything can be seen, everything can be known, nothing is withheld from our inquisitive and acquisitive eyes. The microscopic view and the panoramic view intersect to display our world to us inside and out. However, the very visualism of modernity has, so to speak, thrown a cloak of invisibility over the sensory imagery of previous eras. So thick is this cloak that one can scarcely see through it, or even recognize that there might be something worth exploring underneath. When this cloak is lifted, however, the cosmos suddenly blazes forth in multisensory splendor: the heavens ring out with music, the planets radiate scents and savors, the earth springs to life in colors, temperatures, and sounds.

The aesthetic cornucopia of earlier cosmologies was not simply a hedonistic reveling in sensation. The myriad sensory characteristics of such cosmologies, their colors and odors, tastes and temperatures, were coded with cultural values and linked in chains and hierarchies of meaning. The visual was an important element in this construction of sensory meaning, but it was not all-encompassing. If often first in line as the "noblest" of the senses, sight nonetheless took its place alongside the other senses, without subsuming them. The multiplicity of sensory channels of communication meant that one could taste or breathe in the order of the cosmos and society, as well as visualize it.[2]

The cloak spread over the history of the senses in modernity has also obscured other domains of history, notably, women's history. Women have traditionally been associated with the senses in Western culture, and in particular, with the "lower" senses. Women are the forbidden taste, the mysterious smell, the dangerous touch. Men, by contrast, have been associated with reason, as opposed to the senses, or else with sight and hearing as the most "rational" of the senses. The occultation of the sensory underpinnings of Western culture by the modern visual and rational world view may therefore be read as an occultation of certain feminine dimensions of that culture. In order to recover the latter, it is necessary to uncover the former.

The Color of Angels explores the potent sensory symbolism underlying Western culture with the aim of rediscovering the sensory imaginaries of the past and revealing the roots of our contemporary perceptual paradigms. The history of the dominance of vision in Western culture is not a primary area of investigation in this book, for this is a subject which has been treated extensively elsewhere.[3] The emphasis is rather on the cultural *interplay* of the senses and on the social lives of the often neglected "lower" senses of smell, taste, and touch.

The book is divided into three parts – cosmology, gender, and aesthetics – each consisting of two chapters. The first part offers a glimpse at the fertile aesthetic landscape of pre-modern cosmologies by delving into ways in which the cosmos was conceptualized through sensory imagery before the rise of the modern scientific world view. The second part examines how sensory imagery was employed to create and express different gender identities and roles in pre-modernity. The third part of the book looks at attempts by late nineteenth- and early twentieth-century artists to recover and re-invent the "lost" world of the senses. In closing, the book explores how we in the postmodern age may arrive at a new awareness of the multiplicity of our sensory world and create aesthetic alternatives to the reigning sensory and social order.

The unifying theme of *The Color of Angels* is the "aesthetic imagination," with "aesthetic" referring not only to the arts, but to the apprehension and interpretation of the world through the senses – the original Greek notion of *aisthesis*. As Terry Eagleton writes in *The Ideology of the Aesthetic*, the territory of aesthetics "is nothing less than the whole of our sensate life together."[4]

With the "cloak of imperceptibility" removed from our sensory past (and from the multisensory reality of our present) we can discern the operation and transformation of sensory paradigms across cultural fields and historical periods, and come to appreciate the diversity of Western sensory life.

Cosmology

Televangelism notwithstanding, in many ways Christianity would seem to have escaped the visualizing tendencies of modernity and remained a stronghold (or perhaps a museum?) of multisensory iconology. Many churches in the twentieth-century West are still fragrant with incense. Religious services are still held in the time-honored oral fashion. However, if the traditional sensory signs of worship remain in certain branches of Christianity, much of the symbolism which once integrated them into a larger sensory and sacred reality has been forgotten. It is this vanished multisensory cosmic order which provides the topic of the first section of *The Color of Angels*.

The organization of perceptual experience by the five senses served as a basic paradigm for conceptualizing the organization of the world from an early period. Aristotle, for example, concluded that the five senses corresponded to the four elements: sight with water, hearing with air, smell with fire, and taste and touch with earth.[5] A similar arrangement was put forward in the Jewish-Hellenic *Book of the Secrets of Enoch* in which the sense of smell was associated with the wind, sight with the sun, hearing with the earth, touch with the grass, and taste with the dew.[6]

Within Christianity, the senses operated both as a structural metaphor for the cosmos, and as a model for Christian behavior. According to Christian mythology, the fall of Adam and Eve entailed a fall of the senses. Through hearing, Eve was convinced by the serpent of the desirability of the forbidden fruit. Through sight, Eve decided that the fruit was "pleasing to the eye" (Gen. 3: 6). Through smell, touch, and taste, Adam and Eve ate of the fruit and committed the original sin. While the fall of Adam and Eve left humans with a vitiated sensorium, the death and ressurection of Christ (the "fruit of the Cross") offered humanity a chance to redeem its fallen senses.

Such redemption required both a strict control of sensory impulses and an acute appreciation of the cosmological dimensions of perception. Just how acute this appreciation could be can be seen in the sixteenth-century *Spiritual Exercises* by St. Ignatius of Loyola. Consider, for example, the indications given by Ignatius for the contemplation of hell:

> The first [exercise] will be to see with the eyes of the imagination those great fires, and the souls as it were in bodies of fire.
>
> The second will be to hear with the ears of the imagination the wailings, the howlings, the cries . . .
>
> The third will be to smell the smoke, the sulphur, the filth, and the putrid matter.
>
> The fourth will be to taste with the taste of the imagination bitter things, such as tears, sadness, and the worm of conscience.
>
> The fifth will be to feel with the touch of the imagination how those fires touch and burn the souls.[7]

Two characteristics of this sensuous evocation strike the twentieth-century reader. The first is that Ignatius considers it necessary to involve all of the senses in his exercises in order to create the effect of a full-bodied experience. Simply to picture hell is not enough, one has to hear the wailings, smell the stench, and so on. The second characteristic is that Ignatius invests sensory perception with sacred meaning: sensory images form a rosary of spiritual reminders. For Ignatius, and for the pre-modern world in general, perception was a spiritual as well as physical act, and the sensory order of the cosmos was also a moral order.[8]

While the sensory model of the Christian cosmos followed a generally accepted scheme of values (in which, for example, heaven was pleasing to the senses and hell displeasing), there was nonetheless a good deal of historical and individual variation as to the specifics and dynamics of this scheme. Let us take as an example a subject which excited the interest of many cosmologists: the color of angels.

In his influential work *The Celestial Hierarchies*, the fifth-century Dionysius the Areopagite likened angels to red, white, yellow, and green jewels.[9] In typical medieval fashion, the twelfth-century St. Hildegard of Bingen imagined angels as glowing red like fire or shining white like stars.[10] In the seventeenth century, the Protestant mystic Jacob Boehme wrote that angels come in as many varieties of colors as the flowers of the field.[11] A century later Emanuel Swedenborg presented a hierarchy of angelic colors in *Heaven and its Wonders*: from the color of flame for the angelic élite to ordinary reds, greens, and blues for less enlightened angels.[12] Influenced by mystical cosmologies and Romantic aesthetics, the nineteenth-century poet Charles Baudelaire clothed his angels in rich hues of gold, purple, and hyacinth.[13] Each of these "colorings" of angels stood for and within a particular vision of the cosmos and evoked a train of sensory symbols.

"On the Color of Angels" is the title of the first chapter of this book. This chapter examines and compares the sensory cosmologies of three extraordinary visionaries: St. Hildegard of Bingen, Jacob Boehme, and Charles Fourier. These thinkers are singled out for the wealth of sensory imagery in their cosmological designs and for the unique ways in which each engages with the world view of a different historical period.

St. Hildegard elaborates what could be termed a sensory geography in her writings. With medieval precision, she divides the world into five parts and allots to each a different sense.[14] Inspired by Renaissance alchemy, Jacob Boehme invents a mystical "chemistry" of the senses. Boehme declares certain sensory qualities, such as sweetness, sourness, and heat, to be primordial spirits which work together to create the cosmos.[15] The Enlightenment utopianist Charles Fourier combines pre-modern sensory symbolism with modern notions of social welfare and progress. Through his critique of the "abuse" of the senses in the class system, Fourier develops a political economy of the senses.

Remarkably, the role of sensory symbolism in the cosmologies of these three visionaries has never been explored. In fact, the sensory complexity of such cosmologies has often been seen as an obstacle to understanding their "underlying" conceptual frameworks. Hegel, for example, wrote that while he admired Boehme for his "profundity of mind" he found his thought to be "confined in the hard knotty oak of the senses . . . [and therefore] not able to arrive at a free presentation of the Idea."[16] In a similar vein, Marx and Engels praised Fourier for his critique of capitalism while dismissing his "cosmogonic absurdities."[17]

Roland Barthes' well-known comparison of the writings of Ignatius of Loyola, Sade, and Fourier is something of an exception to this trend in that Barthes does take notice of the different sensory emphases of his authors.[18] Ironically, however, the model which he uses for undertaking his comparison is the eminently visual one of the "text." Hence it is not the sensory imagery which is of primary interest to Barthes, but the tantalizing play of written words on a page. The emphasis on the text as a model for understanding culture found in Barthes is found in many contemporary studies.[19] "On the Color of Angels" offers an alternative to such textual approaches by undertaking a *sensual* exploration of the word and world-making activities of earlier eras.

The second chapter in this section, "The Breath of God" investigates the decidedly non-visual concept of the odor of sanctity. When one thinks of the sensory expressions of the religious past, the "odor of sanctity" is perhaps one of the first to come to mind. It is probably also the one which is least accessible to the modern, "deodorized" mind. The term itself seems like a strange juxtaposition of opposites – "odor," with its contemporary connotations of physicality and undesirability, and "sanctity," with its traditional connotations of spirituality and virtue. The result in terms of scholarly interest is that, while major studies have been undertaken on the history of visual imagery in Christianity, the history of olfactory imagery is still largely unexplored.[20]

The divine scent attributed to saints and the evil odor associated with sinners were part of a whole olfactory mythology which depicted heaven and hell, salvation and perdition, in terms of good and bad smells. According to this mythology the initial pristine aroma of creation was corrupted by the stench of sin and then purified by the fragrant blood of Christ. Here all the aromatic references of the Gospels – the myrrh and frankincense of the Magi, Mary Magdalene's ointments, the spices which embalm Jesus's body – come into play, along with a number of legendary additions, such as the conception of Jesus by smell and the redemptive fragrance of the Cross. These mystical odors, like the odor of sanctity, travel across space and time, from heaven to earth and from creation to redemption, binding the cosmos in a sacred network of scent.

The multisensory visions of St. Hildegard, the sweet and sour alchemy of Boehme, the utopian sensuality of Fourier, and the aromatics of heaven and hell were all part of the heady mix of sensory symbols which enlivened the pre-modern cosmological imagination. Chapters 1 and 2 explore how such sensory symbolism constituted a vibrant universe of sense in the centuries before modern scientific philosophy transformed the cosmos into what Alfred North Whitehead has called "a dull affair, soundless, scentless, colourless; merely the hurrying of material, endlessly, meaninglessly."[21]

Gender

When exploring the sensory cosmologies of past eras it becomes apparent that the aesthetic imagery employed in such cosmologies was deeply imbued with social ideologies, as well as with spiritual principles. In different contexts sensory symbols could represent not only the nature of sacred reality, but the categories of gender, class, and race. Part II of *The Color of Angels* is dedicated to investigating the sensory iconology of the first of these social categories – gender.

It is perhaps necessary to underline that I am examining *stereotypes* of the senses and the sexes in this section. Such stereotypes may strike many modern readers as generalizations which fail to take account of historical exceptions and social variations. However, it is the nature (and power) of stereotypes to generalize and to ignore exceptions and variations. Thus, for example, centuries of labor by diverse women as farmers, craftswomen, scholars, and so on, did little to dislodge the traditional representation of women as homemakers.

Chapter 3, "The Scented Womb and the Seminal Eye," considers the ways in which different sensory characteristics were attributed to men and women and examines how such gender distinctions inflected the sensory formation of the cosmos. In so doing this chapter provides an "archeology" of such current sensory constructs as the "dominating male gaze" and the "nurturing female touch." The notion of there being an archetypal opposition between male sight and female touch (as expounded in the work of Luce Irigaray, for example) has become a commonplace in feminist theory.[22] Yet little consideration has been given to the cultural history of this opposition or to its relation to the other senses in the gendered sensorium.

"The Scented Womb" explores how different qualities were linked to the different sexes within each symbolic sensory field. Thus, within the field of sight, men tended to be associated with light and form, and women with darkness and color. Men were held to employ sight for intellectual purposes while women concerned themselves with sensuous appearance. Within the field of touch, men were typecast as hot and hard, and women as cold and soft. Touch as physical aggression was associated with men, while sexual and fostering touch was linked to women.

Such gender distinctions *within* sensory fields notwithstanding, the senses themselves were gender-typed. As mentioned above, men have traditionally been associated with the "higher," "spiritual" senses of sight and hearing, while women have been associated with the "lower," "animal" senses of taste, touch, and smell. Speech – sometimes accorded the status of a sense – had an ambivalent gender status. While its active character made speech intrinsically male, its supposed widespread appropriation by domineering women made speech female.

The sensory and gender hierarchies of pre-modernity were actively enforced by social, religious, and legal codes. "The Scented Womb" proposes that during the Renaissance women's senses – linked with intuition, emotion, and sensuality – came to be seen as dangerous obstacles to the establishment of a modern masculine and rationalist model of the world, and as such were targeted by the ideologues of the sixteenth- and seventeenth-century witch hunts. The obsession with the witch's supernatural sense of smell, her seductive/destructive touch, her evil eye, her gluttonous appetite, and her poisonous speech all evidence anxiety over female sensory powers. When the enthronement of the scientific world view was finally assured in the late eighteenth century, the figure of the witch ceased to threaten the cosmic and social order with her transgressive female sensuality. In a masculine age of reason, the expectation was that "irrational" feminine sensibilities could henceforth be contained and controlled.

The gender-coding of the senses served to explain and legitimate the assignation of different social spheres to men and women. Men's star-set mastery of the distance senses of sight and hearing empowered them to travel, to read and write, to conquer and govern. As the guardians of the proximity senses of smell, taste, and touch, women's place was in the home, cooking, sewing, and taking care of their families.[23] Chapter 4, "Pens and Needles" looks at the relationship between traditional male and female domains of work and traditional male and female sensory domains. The chapter centers on the paradigmatic opposition between writing as a male and primarily visual activity and needlework as a female and primarily tactile activity.

In recent years, the history of writing by women has been the subject of increasing scholarly interest, particularly in relation to women's experience of embodiment.[24] "Pens and Needles" contributes to this growing field of investigation by considering the sensory and gender codes which influenced the practice and reception of writing by women.

Women who read and wrote instead of sewing and spinning often faced wrath and ridicule for transgressing the limits of their gender domain. The intensity of such attacks in the eighteenth and nineteenth centuries indicates that after the Enlightenment, the literary woman replaced the witch in some ways as a focus for male anxiety over disruptive femininity. While women tried to emulate the literary "vision" of men, the argument went, their work was inevitably impregnated with the animalistic reek of femininity. "Study their works, open them where you will! At the tenth line . . . you will smell a woman! *Odor di femina*," exclaimed Barbey D'Aurevilly in 1878 in *Les Bas-bleus.*[25]

Writing, however, would seem to have had a special appeal for women, in that it could be undertaken within the feminine sphere of the household. Thus, while female writers were well aware of the traditional opposition between pens and needles, writing and housework, they also appreciated their similarities. It was such similarities that would make it possible for many female authors, including Fanny Burney and Jane Austen, to pursue their writing under the guise of plying the needle.[26] Usurpations by women of other masculine prerogatives, such as traveling or speaking in public, could hardly have been accomplished so handily.

Aesthetics

A formidable literature has been generated on the subject of the cultural construction of sight in art history. Contemporary scholars of art have explored at great length the visual paradigms expressed in the works of artists from different periods of Western history and analyzed how those paradigms supported the dominant social and symbolic order – or else helped fragment that order into a multiplicity of perspectives.[27] This intense examination of the semiotics of visual representation begs the question of how the non-visual senses may have been theorized and evoked in earlier periods of art.

In the Middle Ages and the Renaissance, the visual arts were often integrated into a multisensory context. Churches were resonant with music and redolent with incense, as well as rich in visual display. The homes of the wealthy united fine arts with fine music and fine cuisine. In the eighteenth and nineteenth centuries, however, these different aesthetic and sensory fields were increasingly separated and relegated to distinct public spaces. Eventually the gallery would become the quintessential place for viewing art, the concert hall for listening to music, and the restaurant for savoring a meal.

Furthermore, the organic, synaesthetic cosmos of pre-modernity within which these different fields were intrinsically (if hierarchically) linked and invested with spiritual significance, was replaced in the eighteenth century by a mechanical and pictorial world view in which different areas of aesthetic appreciation seemed to have no inherent connection and no cosmological significance.

In the nineteenth century many artists, musicians, and writers rebelled against the materialistic and segmented character of modern culture and sought to recover sensory and symbolic meaning in their work. Inspired by the synaesthetic visions of the mystics, such artists declared "that everything, form, movement, quantity, color, odor, both in the spiritual world and in nature, is significant, reciprocal, converse, correspondent."[28] To a disenchanted modern world this vision of sensory correspondences came as a revelation.

Chapter 5, "Symbolist Harmonies, Futurist Colors, Surrealist Recipes" explores the quest for a multisensory aesthetics in nineteenth- and early twentieth-century art – from Symbolism to Futurism to Surrealism – and the relationship of this quest to the perceptual and gender order of modernity. Many of the artists involved in this quest sought to recreate the essential sensory integrity of the cosmos by transposing mystical notions of synaesthetic unity into artistic creations. The proponents of multisensory aesthetics did not, however, simply wish to return to the sensory and symbolic plenitude of pre-modernity – nor could they have had they so desired. The idea of a cosmos alive with sensory interplay had long since ceased to seem natural and could only be resurrected through artifice. Artists who played with the senses in their work were also playing with elements of artificiality and exoticism, as well as employing sensuality to challenge the rationalist principles of modern culture.

As in the case of writing, painting was traditionally a masculine preserve. Craig Owens writes in "The Discourse of Others":

> What can be said about the visual arts in a patriarchal order that privileges vision over the other senses? Can we not expect them to be a domain of masculine privilege – as their histories indeed prove them to be.[29]

In this context the "elevation" of such symbolically feminine senses as taste or smell to the level of art would seem to be a poke in the eye of the male art establishment.

Groups such as the Symbolists and the Surrealists did indeed emphasize the feminine in their work; however, they tended to do so according to masculinist conventions. Women were presented not as agents of their own destinies, but as vessels of primordial forces: passion and death, inspiration and perdition. Female artists within these aesthetic movements had ambiguous roles. When it came to aesthetics women were traditionally conceded to have "taste," but not creative vision – and the latter still held first place in art. Nonetheless, as brought out in the conclusion of Chapter 5, a number of female artists, particularly those linked to Surrealism, engendered highly imaginative sensory worlds of their own through their art.

In a turn-of-the-century critique of Symbolist multisensoriality, Max Nordau stated that "civilized" people perceive the world through the senses of sight and hearing, and not through the "lower" senses.[30] With the dominance of photographic, cinematic, and computer images in the late twentieth century, we have, in a way, achieved Nordau's ideal. Much of our time is spent attending to a world which *can* only be perceived through sight and (less often) hearing. It is as if, in order to bring the world in line with our current sensory priorities, the cosmos has been technologically recreated as a visual spectacle.[31]

The proliferation of technologies of representation in contemporary culture has had the effect of greatly magnifying the role of sight in aesthetics. Is it possible, in a world of such compelling visual imagery, to create, or even imagine, an alternative sensory aesthetics? Chapter 6, "A Feel for the World," responds to this question by examining how the exploration of the sensory worlds of the blind and the blind-deaf may help to open up new dimensions of aesthetic experience in a hypervisual age.

Standard philosophies and psychologies of aesthetics customarily held that the appreciation of aesthetics relies so heavily upon visual perception that the blind can have no real notion of beauty.[32] The argument developed in "A Feel for the World," by contrast, is that our modern understanding of aesthetics relies so heavily on the visual that the sighted are hampered in their appreciation of beauty as experienced through the other senses. To begin to appreciate the subtleties of a scentscape, to feel the power of a music of vibrations, or to experience tactile works of art, the sighted majority must turn for instruction to the aesthetic realms of the blind and the blind-deaf.[33]

There are intriguing similarities in imagery between the sensory worlds experienced by the blind and the blind-deaf in modernity and the sensory cosmologies described in the first part of this book. To give one example, Fourier, in his system of cosmic correspondences, ascribed to melons the quality of "ironic humour." For Barthes this is a perfect illustration of the idiosyncrasy of much of Fourier's thought: "What reader can hope to *dominate* such an utterance – adopt it as a laughable or critical object . . . ?"[34] However this is just what the renowned blind-deaf writer, Helen Keller, would have been able to do. In describing her aesthetic classification of tactile forms, Helen Keller remarks that for her, humor is embodied by the melon:

> The bulge of a watermelon and the puffed-up rotundities of squashes that sprout, bud, and ripen in that strange garden planted somewhere behind my finger-tips are the ludicrous in my tactual memory and imagination.[35]

This convergence of opinion between Fourier and Keller is likely nothing more than a coincidence. Yet would it necessarily be that strange for Fourier, who emphasized the importance of the "lower" senses, to have shared certain notions with the blind-deaf Keller, who lived in a world solely constituted by touch, taste, and smell?

While probing the aesthetic worlds of the blind "A Feel for the World" also examines Western stereotypes of blindness, particularly with regard to gender ideologies. In a society which associates masculinity with sight, the blind are symbolically female, just as women are symbolically blind. The symbolic overlap between the blind and women in Western tradition means that creating a space for the alternative aesthetic experiences of the blind may help open up new domains for the artistic expression of women's experiences. The notion of an art of tactilities or aromas seems to hold, however ephemerally, the tantalizing promise of a medium of aesthetic communication untainted by a history of exclusionary doctrines and practices.

"A Feel for the World" reveals the range of sensory orders and endeavors which are possible even in a hypervisual age. All six chapters of *The Color of Angels*, indeed, are dedicated to challenging the sway of vision over contemporary culture and bringing the multiplicity of sensory experience – with all of its potent symbolic content – to the fore of consciousness. By so doing they invite us to rediscover and re-imagine our senses at the turn of the twenty-first century.

Part I
Cosmology

Figure 1 Hildegard of Bingen, "The Choirs of Angels"
Source: From *Scivias*, New York, The Paulist Press, 1990.

1 On the color of angels

The sensory cosmologies of St. Hildegard, Boehme, and Fourier

The medieval cosmos was an intricate tapestry of colors, sounds, and scents. In heaven saints and angels sang in an eternally flowering garden. In hell, damned souls cried out in a foul, fiery pit. This potent cosmic imagery was reinforced by the sensory dimensions of Christian ritual. Incense, music, vestments, and the savors of feasts and fasts helped to engage participants through all of their senses.[1]

Medieval cosmology was not simply a feast for the senses, however. The medievals held that every sensory image embodied a spiritual truth and partici-pated in a cosmic code of meaning. On the level of popular culture, the basic elements of this code were known by all: doves stood for the Holy Spirit, blue was the color of the Blessed Virgin, incense represented prayers, sulfur was a sign of the Devil, and so on. Such iconography – expounded in church, elabo-rated in folktales, depicted in paintings – formed an intrinsic part of the popular mentality.

On a scholarly level, theologians, philosophers, and alchemists attempted to tease out the more complex and arcane meanings encased in the sensory signs of the cosmos.[2] The scriptural commentaries of the eighth-century English monk, Bede, exemplify this search for the spiritual content within the material form. In a passage in which he comments on the biblical description of Solomon's temple, for instance, Bede transforms all the material elements of the temple – stones, woods, precious metals, colors – into spiritual values, so that the physical building becomes an edifice of morals.[3]

Not only sensory images, but the senses themselves were allegorized by medieval and Renaissance writers. Common tropes were to compare the five senses to the gates of a city or the windows of a citadel. Such allegories repre-sented the senses as avenues for physical and moral good or evil. For example, Peter Damian declared in the eleventh century: "Close then, beloved, these gates of the senses of the body, and block up the phalanxes of the onrushing vices, and open them up for the troops of the spiritual virtues."[4]

This allegorization of the senses had a long literary history. It was customary, for example, to regard every mention of the number five in Scripture as refer-ring to the five senses. Philo, a first-century exponent of Hellenic Judaism, encountered such a wealth of sensory symbolism in Scripture that it sometimes seems that he regarded the Bible as one long series of sensory allegories. For example, the five cities of the Sodomites are said by Philo to represent the five senses as instruments of worldly pleasure, while the three wives of Abraham stand for the three senses of hearing, sight and smell as media of revelation.[5] Seven senses come into play when Philo wishes to break down the sevenfold punishment of Cain into one punishment per offending sensory organ:

> First upon the eyes, because they saw what was not fitting; second, upon the ears, because they heard what was not proper; third upon the nose, which was deceived by smoke and steam; fourth upon taste, which was a servant of the belly's pleasure; fifth upon touch [for bringing about] the seizure of cities and the capture of men . . . sixth upon the tongue and the organs of speech for being silent about things that should be said and for saying things that should be kept silent; seventh, upon the lower belly which with lawless licentiousness sets the senses on fire.[6]

The mystics of the Middle Ages incorporated both popular symbolism and techniques of scholarly exegesis in their writings. At the same time mystics were able to claim a direct insight into the sacred and sensory order of the cosmos. This allowed them to elaborate very personal descriptions of cosmic reality.

It was not always possible, however, to relate a mystical experience using the terms of ordinary perceptual experience.[7] Theologians, in fact, often asserted that there were *two* sets of senses: an external physical set and an internal, spiritual one.[8] Thus a Christian could practice extreme asceticism in terms of the physical senses, and still lead a rich sensory life with regard to the spiritual senses: seeing divine light, tasting heavenly sweetness, and so on. This double sensory life was experienced by many mystics, who would seem to have more than made up for their physical deprivations by the intensity of their spiritual delights.[9]

This preliminary consideration of medieval notions of sensory symbolism serves as an introduction to the three sensory cosmologies examined below. The first is the work of a twelfth-century nun, St. Hildegard of Bingen. The second was developed by a seventeenth-century Protestant mystic and shoemaker, Jacob Boehme. The third was created by the early nineteenth-century utopianist, Charles Fourier. Whereas St. Hildegard produced her cosmology within an established tradition and community, Boehme and Fourier were both lone thinkers who nonetheless acquired significant followings.

As a product of the Middle Ages, St. Hildegard's cosmology most closely exemplifies the symbol-laden thought of that time. However, the cosmologies of Jacob Boehme and Charles Fourier also resonate with traditional notions of sensory codes and correspondences, although tempered with the alchemical theories of the Renaissance in the case of the former, and with Enlightenment ideals of social reform in that of the latter.

These particular cosmologies are considered here because, while all three draw from a common fund of sensory symbolism, each presents a distinct and remarkable understanding of the sensory order of the cosmos. Exploring the different ways in which the senses are elaborated in the writings of Hildegard, Boehme, and Fourier, we discover the extraordinary sensory complexity of earlier Western cosmologies. It is an exploration which initiates us into a cosmos alive with celestial harmonies, multi-colored angels, and planetary aromas, while at the same time revealing the webs of religious and cultural values underlying this compelling imagery.

St. Hildegard of Bingen

Hildegard of Bingen was born in Germany in 1098. She entered conventual life as a child and eventually, at the age of 38, became abbess of her community of Benedictine nuns. Hildegard's abilities were extraordinarily diverse. Aside from her duties as abbess, she practiced and wrote books on medicine,[10] composed liturgical music, and even designed robes for her nuns.[11]

It was Hildegard's mystical visions, however, which brought her the greatest renown. These began when she was a child and were marked by a sensation of strong light. As Hildegard clarified in a letter to an inquiring monk, however, she did not experience her visions through her bodily senses:

> I do not see these things with my external eyes nor do I hear them with my external ears. I do not perceive them through the thoughts of my heart or through the mediation of my five senses. I see them much more in my soul alone . . . [12]

Although accustomed to receiving visions from an early age, Hildegard did not record her mystical experiences until she was 42. At that time, she writes, "a burning light coming from heaven poured into my mind" and "I heard a heavenly voice speaking to me: *Proclaim and write thus.*"[13] Three major visionary books resulted from this prompting: *Scivias* ("Know the Ways"), *The Merits of Life*, and *Divine Works*. Hildegard also wrote hundreds of letters in which she used her visionary knowledge to provide guidance to everyone from popes and emperors to ordinary religious and lay people. Still holding the position of abbess, Hildegard died in 1179.

Hildegard's visions consist primarily of intricate tableaux of supernatural figures and scenes. Each of the elements of these tableaux was held by the saint to encode a particular theological truth. She describes one vision as follows:

> I saw a very great and peaceful brightness which was similar to a flame. This brightness had a lot of eyes in it . . . . Inside this brightness, there was another brightness which . . . had the clearness of purple lightning inside itself. I also saw the earth with people on it. The people were carrying milk in their vessels, and they were making cheese from this milk. Some of the milk was thick, from which strong cheese was being made; some of the milk was thin, from which mild cheese was being curdled; and some of the milk was spoiling, from which bitter cheese was being produced.[14]

Hildegard explains in her commentary that the eye-filled brightness signifies the knowledge of God, and the purple lightning within, "that the knowledge of God has the Only-Begotten [Jesus Christ] inside itself." The milk carried in vessels, in turn, stands for the procreative seed in the bodies of humans (in contrast to the lightning, which symbolizes the "procreative seed" of God). Thick milk – good seed – makes strong cheese – strong people. Weak cheese, similarly, symbolizes weak people, and the bitter cheese troubled people.[15]

The use of evocative metaphors – purple lightning, bitter cheese, and so on – to convey spiritual values is characteristic of Hildegard. Part of the appeal of Hildegard's work consists in the saint's ability to find meaning not only in her heavenly visions, but in the simple experiences of everyday life. A blue hyacinth, for example, is said by Hildegard to be like the Word of God in the way it brightens its surroundings; while water glittering in the sun is said to remind one of pure intentions.[16] Sections of her work with headings such as "Similarities of a Garden, a Sheep, and a Pearl to Humans," and "About the Rain-Bringing Air and the White Skin, and What These Signify" similarly expound the moral messages of the material world.[17] Even as apparently unremarkable an object as a stone is transformed into a revelation of sensory and divine truth once it comes under Hildegard's mystical gaze:

> In a stone there is moist greenness and tangibleness and reddish fire. It has moist greenness so that it may not be destroyed and crushed, tangibleness so that it can be used as a dwelling or for defense, and a reddish fire so that it can give warmth and have solidness from its hardness. The moist greenness signifies God, who never becomes dry nor is limited in virtue. The tangibleness stands for the Word, who was able to be touched and grasped after being born from the Virgin. The reddish fire signifies the Holy Spirit, who is the attendant and the illuminator of the hearts of faithful people.[18]

Hildegard often used the senses or their sensory organs as the subjects for religious allegory. In her song to St. Ursula she writes:

> your eyes are like sapphire
> and your ears like Mount Bethel
> and your nose is like a mountain of myrrh and incense
> and your mouth like the sound of many waters.[19]

Here different sensory organs are associated with corresponding stimuli: the eyes with a bright gem, the ears with Bethel where God spoke to Jacob (Gen. 28: 17–19), and the nose with incense. The mouth, interestingly, is presented not as the organ of taste, but as that of speech, and as such is compared to the sound of water. Each of these associations had a special theological significance for Hildegard. "A mountain of myrrh and incense," for example, was a customary way for Hildegard to refer to good works.[20] The implication is that St. Ursula embodies and communicates virtue through all of her senses.

According to Hildegard the senses "are like precious stones in a person."[21] The soul, the body, and the senses together form what the saint called the "three footpaths" of the human being. The soul gives life to the body and the senses. The body attracts the soul and employs the senses. The senses affect the soul and attract the body.[22] By using vivid imagery in her writing, Hildegard interested her readers in the theological values which informed her metaphors. At the same time she encouraged them to relate to the world of the senses as a world of sacred meaning, and not simply one of physical pleasure or displeasure.

Hildegard's metaphors are occasionally synaesthetic, with different qualities blending together to produce uniquely evocative images. In one example, Hildegard combines smell and touch to write of an odor being "as smooth as gold."[23] In another, smell and sound are united as she tells of heavenly trumpets which blow forth aromatic songs of myrrh and frankincense.[24] Describing how Jesus Christ is present in the Eucharist, Hildegard "whirls around" a variety of sensory impressions until they melt into one overwhelming sensation of sweetness:

> This is the same as if some precious ointment were rolled into some bread and a sapphire were placed in some wine. I might whirl that around into such a sweet taste so that your mouth would not be able to distinguish that bread with the ointment nor that wine in with the sapphire.[25]

Such blending of sensations suggests an underlying unity of the senses which transcends their apparent division into distinct modes of perception. It is evident from the associations Hildegard makes at times among the various senses that she did not separate the different properties of the senses into mutually exclusive categories. She in fact states that "the various senses are never separated from one another. Instead, they strongly cling to one another and illuminate our entire person beneficially . . . ."[26]

The five-fold division of the senses was, nonetheless, of fundamental symbolic importance to Hildegard. In one of the saint's visions, the earth is divided into five areas: east, west, south, north, and center. Each of these zones is associated with a different sense and has distinct sensory and moral properties.[27]

The east is the most beneficial region according to this cosmological scheme. It is bright and green and associated with sight, which, Hildegard writes, "recoils from evil as a result of its knowledge of good."[28] The west, in contrast, is dark and damp and morally ambivalent. It is the region of hearing, which "sometimes announces good fortune and at other times misfortune."[29] The south is balmy and odorous and associated with smell, representative of human longing for the divine. The cold north, tempered by warmth flowing from the east, stands for the discriminating sense of taste, which offers us a foretaste of "heavenly sweetness." The center, finally, moderates and is supported by the influence of the other four regions. Similarly, says Hildegard, the sense of touch lies in the middle of the senses, sharing the powers of them all.[30]

Hildegard, on the whole, presents a very positive or affirming "theology of the senses." She is clear, however, that if the role of the senses is to lead us to God, then if misused they lead us into sin. To illustrate this Hildegard employs the medieval association of poisons with colors[31] to present an image of a demonic worm with five poisonous colors signifying the five senses in a state of perversion. Here green stands for sadness, white for "tasteless irreverence," red for "false glory," yellow for "stinging withdrawal," and black for "lukewarm imitation."[32] Presumably each of these "anti-colors" is associated with a particular sense, although Hildegard does not specify which sense corresponds to which color.[33]

The various zones of Hildegard's cosmos contain their own "sensory hells" where those who have abused their senses are punished. Unlike Philo, however, Hildegard does not seem concerned about matching sensory punishments with sensory crimes. Thus those who have sinned through their sense of hearing are punished not by noise, but by darkness. In the southern region of smell, those who lack "the sweet odor of virtue" suffer from cold in the summer and heat in the winter. In the northern zone of taste, "adulterers, gluttons, and drunkards" are tortured by "stinking dampness, death-causing odors, and smoke."[34]

Hildegard's series of hells is counterbalanced by a sequence of heavens which accommodate the different ranks of the blessed. These heavens are all wondrously bright and fragrant and appear to be distinguished primarily by the different colors of their inhabitants' apparel. For instance, "teachers of souls" have blue garments and gold footwear while martyrs have red robes and emerald footwear. Virgins are clothed in aromatic white and gold robes and have transparent footwear. On their heads they wear musical crowns made of jeweled pipes:

> Whenever the Lamb of God used his voice, this sweetest blowing of the wind . . . touched these pipes so that they resounded with every type of sound that a harp and organ make.[35]

All of the different aspects of Hildegard's heavens have a theological interpretation. The virgins' transparent footwear, for example, indicates the purity of their path in life. The crowns on their heads are a sign of "crowned virginity." The music produced by the crowns signifies that through their chastity the virgins resonate to the voice of God.[36]

Hildegard's cosmos might seem at times to be simply a static and rather artificial ensemble of sensory and symbolic elements. Nonetheless, for Hildegard the cosmos was very much a dynamic, organic entity. "The air lives by turning green and being in bloom," she writes, "The waters flow as if they were alive. The sun lives in its light . . . ." [37] Indeed Hildegard, along with her medieval contemporaries, believed that the human body and the cosmos shared similar structures and functions. Hildegard states, for instance, that the human head corresponds to the curved dome of the sky, the senses to the planets, and the soul to the winds (which in Hildegard's cosmology blow the sky and the planets around the earth).[38]

This correspondence between elements of the cosmos and elements of the body meant that the condition of the former could affect the condition of the latter. With regard to the senses Hildegard notes:

> When the moon is full, our brain is also full. We are then in full possession of our senses. But when the moon is new, our brain becomes emptier so that our sensory powers are injured.[39]

The direct relationship between human health and the cosmic order enables Hildegard to employ her cosmology as a basis for her medical, as well as mystical, works.[40]

The cosmos and the body are animated and integrated, according to Hildegard, by music. She compares the human being, and by analogy the cosmos, to a song: the body is the words and the spirit is the music. The ultimate song is Jesus Christ, in whom music and lyrics – divinity and humanity – are perfectly combined.[41]

In Hildegard's musical cosmogony, all was originally harmonious in the world. Adam, says Hildegard, possessed a voice that resonated with "the loveliness of every musical art."[42] Satan, however, found Adam's singing unendurable. He therefore introduced an element of discord into paradise, causing Adam to fall from grace and lose his melodious voice (which, in turn, prompted later generations to create musical instruments). Nostalgia for this lost paradise of sound is why, according to Hildegard, "sometimes when we hear a song we breathe deeply and sigh."[43]

Hildegard's own cycle of liturgical songs, "Symphony of the Harmony of Celestial Revelations," is an attempt to reproduce the divine harmonies revealed to her in her visions. Nor is Satan forgotten in Hildegard's musical work. The Devil does not have a singing part, however, but a speaking or shouting part, in which he interrupts and critiques the singers – a heckling, uninvited guest at a cosmic concert.[44]

Interestingly, Hildegard's image of a perfected world stands in sharp contrast to her dazzling heavens or to her vision of a living cosmos. She writes that at the end of time, "when all the filth and blackness has been carried away," fire will be temperate, water will be clear and still, and the land will be firm and flat. In an endless day, the sun, the moon and the stars will stand motionless in the sky and shine with a mild red gleam.[45]

This unchanging world of complete moderation may seem dull or even frightening to us today – more an image of a dead world than of a perfected one. The flatness of Hildegard's perfect world, however, represents a return to the world as it was at the time of Creation, when, according to medieval theology, it had a smooth surface unblemished by mountains or valleys.[46] In Hildegard's day, furthermore, the extremes of nature often seemed frightening – rushing rivers which flooded homes and fields, lofty mountains which made travel difficult and dangerous, raging fires which killed people and destroyed property . . . . In one of her medical works Hildegard pictures the world before the biblical flood as having fordable streams and pleasant woods rather than the forbidding rivers and forests of her own day.[47] The stillness and moderation of the post-apocalyptic world, therefore, represented for Hildegard "a state of great tranquillity and beauty."[48]

Jacob Boehme

Jacob Boehme was born in Germany, almost five centuries after Hildegard, in 1575. Like Hildegard, Boehme apparently had visionary tendencies from childhood. Unlike Hildegard, however, Boehme did not become a monastic. As a Lutheran he found his vocation in the life of the world – taking up a trade (shoemaking), marrying, and having children.

Boehme's mystical experiences continued throughout his adult life. At the age of 25 he was thrown into a rapture by gazing at sunlight shining in a burnished pewter dish. After this experience he found that he could see the inner nature of whatever he looked at, even the plants in a meadow.[49] He said nothing about his visions, however, until he was 35, when he felt an impulse to record his impressions in writing. The book which resulted from this impulse, *Aurora*, became the first of a series of works by Boehme dealing with his mystical insights.

Boehme's primary concern in his writings is to describe the essential forces of the cosmos and their operations. His visions are not the symbolic tableaux of Hildegard, but rather depictions of primal elements interacting to generate the forms and conditions of life. The mystic's unorthodox ideas led him to be considered a heretic by certain Lutheran officials. He had enough support in high places, however, to enable him to continue the dissemination of his work until his death in 1624. As a mystic, Boehme would be taken up by future Protestant mystics, such as the eighteenth-century Englishman William Law. As a philosopher, he would have a strong influence on the Romantic and Idealist philosophers, most notably Hegel, who considered Boehme the first modern German philosopher.[50]

With Jacob Boehme we leave the medieval world and enter the world of the late Renaissance. While Boehme's work is much too idiosyncratic to be regarded as a typical product of the time, it nonetheless manifests the influence of several of the intellectual trends of his day. One such trend was a product of the Protestant Reformation. It held that individuals, rather than obediently following their church leaders, should read the Bible for themselves and develop a personal relationship with God. This emphasis on personal piety made it possible for a "simple" shoemaker, such as Boehme, to develop and propound his own interpretation of Scripture. It has, in fact, been said that "the doctrine of Boehme . . . when stripped of its alchemy and theosophy, is good Evangelical Protestant mysticism."[51]

As the above quote suggests, another trend which had a major impact on Boehme's thought was the Renaissance fascination with esoteric symbolism. Boehme was particularly impressed by the concepts of alchemy, which combined theories of symbolic correspondence with a search for the inner essences of nature. Boehme's interest in alchemy helps explain the quasi-chemical flavour of some of his ideas. For our purposes, however, Boehme's most interesting work is the one least influenced by alchemical theories: his first book, *Aurora*. There Boehme describes the cosmic forces not in terms of the alchemical jargon he would later employ, but as the sensory powers which manifested themselves to him as he gazed at a field of flowers or a gleaming pewter dish.

In *Aurora* Boehme states that at the heart of the cosmos are seven spirits: Astringency, Sweetness, Bitterness, Heat, Love, Sound, and Nature. These spirits continually interact with and generate each other. Astringency (sourness) is a force of contraction. Sweetness is a softening force which mollifies astringency. Bitterness is a force of penetration which mobilizes the other two spirits.[52]

Through their interaction these three primary spirits produce the fourth spirit, Heat. When the spirits are kindled by Heat a flash of light occurs. With the creation of light the spirits see each other – giving rise to the sense of sight – and then taste each other – producing the sense of taste. On seeing and tasting each other, the spirits create the fifth spirit, Love. The spirits then smell and feel each other, producing the senses of smell and touch: "So there is nothing else but a hearty, loving and friendly aspect or seeing, a pleasant smell, a good relishing or tasting, and a lovely feeling."[53]

The interaction of the five spirits creates the sixth spirit Sound, along with the sense of hearing. Sound, in turn, gives rise to the seventh spirit, Nature, which Boehme describes as encompassing the other spirits.[54]

Boehme's portrayal of qualities such as sweetness and bitterness as elemental forces had much in common with humoral theories of medicine, which deemed certain "flavors" to operate within the body producing states of health and illness. For Boehme, however, these qualities are not simply physical forces, they are spiritual beings. Thus, while constituting different properties, the seven spirits are complete entities in their own right, each with a full set of senses: "they could all see, feel, taste, smell and hear . . . ."[55]

Together the seven spirits create the universe and everything in it.[56] The particular form and character of any given thing depends on the spirit or spirits which predominate in its make-up. In stones, for example, the contracting astringent quality dominates. Gravel is the result of bitterness breaking up the stones created by astringency. Metals such as copper and iron (which according to Boehme have an auditory dimension due to their resonance when struck)[57] are characterized by a combination of sound and astringency. Gold, silver, and gemstones, in turn, have their source in the flash of light produced by the interaction of the first four spirits.[58]

Boehme provides a vivid description of how the spirits work together to create plants. Sweetness is pursued by bitterness and astringency, which causes a stalk to grow out of the earth. The struggling of the substances creates knots in the stalk, through which sweetness tries to escape, producing stems and leaves. Heat kindles the three flavor-spirits, generating the plant's characteristic colors.

When sweetness is no longer able to flee, it surrenders to astringency and bitterness and brings forth flowers and fruits.[59]

For skeptical readers Boehme offers the practical test of cutting a gash in a tree and tasting its sap. First, he says, you will taste the astringent power, then the bitter, and then the sweet, proving that these three qualities are acting together in the tree.[60]

It is not only tangible objects which are produced by the elemental spirits, however, but also feelings and concepts such as emotions and language. Laughter, Boehme states, is caused by the bitter quality penetrating and rising up in the sweet. Anger, on the other hand, occurs when bitterness overexcites itself.[61] Speech is also fundamentally a gustatory and kinaesthetic process. Words are formed by the contractions produced by the mouth in response to the bitterness or sweetness of a word's meaning.[62]

Boehme's cosmos would seem to be essentially synaesthetic. It is through the interaction of the various sensory properties of the spirits that creation is made possible. This synaesthesia, however, is not a sensory fusion – a merging of colors with odors, flavors with sounds – but a sensory interplay, or, as Boehme puts it, a "loving wrestling."[63] It is this constant "wrestling" of distinct but interdependent forces which ensures the perpetual generation of life.

As regards the ranking of the senses, Boehme places them in their traditional order of importance: sight, hearing, smell, taste, touch. The analogy he uses to explain their operations is the common one of five counselors who bring sensations before their prince, the mind, to be accepted or refused. If accepted, the sensation is conveyed to the heart, which then distributes it through the veins. If refused, the sensation is rejected (as when one spits out a bad taste, for example).[64]

Like Hildegard, Boehme holds that the human body is a replica in miniature of the cosmos, with each body part having its cosmic equivalent. According to this system the senses are associated with the planets.[65] Boehme, in fact, suggests that the bodily senses are created by the influence of the planets. His argument seems to be that, just as the planets create tides in bodies of water, so do they cause "a rising, seeing, feeling, hearing, tasting" in the blood of human beings.[66] Sensory perception is therefore the result of a kind of planetary pull.

Elsewhere in his writings, Boehme associates the seven spirits with the planets: Saturn is astringency, Venus is sweetness, Mars is bitterness, Mercury is sound, and so on. In this scheme of things, each planet is responsible for the production of certain sensory properties on earth. For example:

> If the saturnine property be predominant, and chief in a thing, then it is of a black, greyish colour, hard and spare, sharp, sour, or salt in taste; it gets a long lean body . . . [and] a hard touch.[67]

A combination of planetary influences produces a combination of effects. When Saturn combines with Venus, for instance, there "grows a great, tall slender tree, herb, beast, or man, or whatever it be."[68]

It might seem that there is not much place or need for God in such a sense-based philosophy. For Boehme, however, nothing could be less true: the seven spirits with their sensory properties *are* God. To understand their operations in the world is to recognize the divine will in action:

> You shall find no book wherein the divine wisdom may be more searched into, and found, than when you walk in a flowery fresh springing meadow, there you shall see, smell, and taste the wonderful power and virtue of God.[69]

Boehme acknowledges, nonetheless, that, without the aid of revelation, sensory knowledge is not sufficient to provide us with an understanding of divine reality: "The ploughman doth not understand it; though he seeth, smelleth, tasteth, heareth and feeleth it, yet he but looks on it, and knoweth not how the being thereof is."[70] Sensory knowledge must needs be supplemented by mystical insight.

Boehme's cosmology is, like Hildegard's, a Christian cosmology. The difference is that Boehme interprets virtually all of Christianity in light of the action of his cosmic principles. The concept of the seven spirits comes from Revelation 4:5: "Burning before the throne were seven flaming torches, the seven spirits of God."[71] God, according to Boehme's interpretation, consists of all of these seven spirits together. Jesus is the light produced by the spirits.[72] The Holy Ghost is the "glance or splendour," produced by the light.[73]

The Devil, Boehme states, is the result of a sensory perversion. In his case the seven spirits, by over-exerting themselves, dried up the sweet spirit and made the creation of light impossible.

> Now in all the spirits there was nothing else but a mere hot, fiery, cold and hard corruption, and so one evil quality tasted the others, whereby the whole body grew . . . very fierce and wrathful.[74]

Lucifer's fall from sensory grace introduced corruption to the cosmos and alienated it from God. Due to this alienation, the seven spirits are only able to produce imperfect copies of divine reality, subject to decay and death, in our world:

> Nature laboureth with its utmost diligence upon this corrupted dead earth, that it might generate heavenly forms and species or kinds; but it generateth only dead dark and hard fruits, which are no more than a mere shadow or type of the heavenly.[75]

The human body is likewise a corrupted version of its original ideal form. Before his fall from grace, Adam possessed a heavenly body: he needed no sleep and could see at night; he suffered from neither heat nor cold; he had no bones (he sustained himself by willpower), no "bestial members" of propagation and no entrails, "nor any such hard dark flesh."[76] The absence of digestive organs presented no difficulties to Adam as he ate only pure paradisical fruit. The present human body came into being after Adam and Eve ate the forbidden fruit of the tree of the knowledge of good and evil and thus introduced corruption and death into their bodies.[77]

It is only in heaven that the seven spirits are free to create a world according to their true natures. Boehme understands heaven, therefore, not as a spiritual counterpart to our material earth, but as the divine model of what earth should be. Heaven, he writes, is a garden perpetually in bloom "with fair heavenly colours and smells."[78] The air is soft and pleasant and the water bright and sweet like apple juice. Cold is refreshing without being harsh, and heat is warming without being hot.[79]

The angelic inhabitants of heaven are distinguished by their different colors, "as in the flowers in the meadows."[80] The particular shade of each angel differs according to which spirit is dominant in that angel. Thus: "Some are strongest in the astringent quality and those are of a brownish light . . . . Some are strongest in the bitter quality and they are like a green precious stone . . . . Some are of the quality of heat, and they are the lightest and brightest of all, yellowish and reddish."[81] "There are," says Boehme, "unsearchable varieties of colour and form among the angels."[82]

The angels spend their time singing, each "according to the voice of his quality."[83] This angelic harmony is "wholly soft, pleasant, lovely, pure and thin," – unlike "our [human] gross and beast-like" voices.[84] In the song of the angels, the seven spirits rise up and mingle to create heaven. The sound of the music produces the colors of heaven. From these colors, in turn, celestial plants and fruits spring up, along with all the other forms and figures of heaven; "so that all things grow joyfully, and generate very beautifully."[85]

If on earth sensory life is alienated from the knowledge of the divine, in heaven, the situation is different. There it is not planets which "pull" the senses into being, but God himself. Sense, love, and knowledge become one through the harmonious interaction of the seven spirits. "This harmony of hearing, seeing, feeling, tasting and smelling," writes Boehme, "is the true intellective life."[86]

Charles Fourier

Charles Fourier was not a mystic in any traditional sense, although he believed he had a unique insight into the inner workings of the cosmos. Insofar as his writings offered a blueprint for an ideal society, he was more a literary descendant of utopianists such as More or Campanella than of Christian mystics such as St. Hildegard and Boehme. However, Fourier put forward a vision of the cosmos in his work which rivals the visions of the mystics for its sensory and symbolic power.

Fourier was born in Besançon, France in 1772. His boyhood passions were for music, maps, and flowers; which last he grew directly on the earth-covered floor of his bedroom in color-coded arrangements. At 17 Fourier became a clerk in a bank, beginning a career in commerce which he would follow for most of his life. He devoted his leisure to the study of philosophy and science and to speculation on the nature of society and the cosmos.

At the age of 27 Fourier hit upon what he believed to be God's plan in assigning sensory properties and passions to everything in the universe. He decided that all things, including humans, were linked through bonds of natural attraction. Civilization (a foul word in Fourier's vocabulary) attempted to repress and divert these natural attractions or passions, thus disrupting the social and cosmic order. In the ideal world, however, the carefully orchestrated accommodation of all passions would lead to an harmonious and just world order.

Fourier spent the rest of his life elaborating his utopian blueprint and seeking support for his theories. His extensive writings on the subject ranged from the most minute aspects of life in his ideal society to the history of the universe. While he never attracted enough support to attempt a large-scale trial of his theories, his ideas did inspire several utopian communities in Europe and North America. As a social critique, Fourier's work would be highly regarded by Marx and Engels.

Ironically, while Fourier believed in allowing the passions free rein, his own life was a model of quiet industry. He lived, a bachelor, in rented rooms, devoting himself to his writing, and waiting in vain every day for the philanthropist to appear who would bankroll his utopian vision.[87] He died in Paris in 1837.

Fourier based the organization of his cosmos on the model of music. In heaven, each planet stands for a different musical note. On earth, humans constitute musical notes, with the particular note of each individual determined by his or her dominant character traits. In Fourier's plan for the perfect society, human "notes" are grouped together in work and social units to form "major and minor scales" and "choirs." This plan for harmonizing personality types through social organization gave Fourier's utopia its name, Harmony.

Even the human body was structured by music for Fourier: "Man being the mirror of the universe, his anatomical details must exactly portray all the harmonies of the universe."[88] Thus, for example, the human mouth in the movement of laughing, which is the movement of joy and of harmony, displays to the light the emblems of active harmony, twenty-four [sic] teeth ranged in two octaves, major and minor, in allusion to the twenty-four [social] choirs of active harmony.[89] Likewise, the twelve pairs of ribs are arranged "like the notes of the major key in music."[90] The human frame is therefore a kind of silent, organic, keyboard; music made flesh, or at least bone.

While Fourier's cosmos is ordered by music, it is animated by scent. Fourier states that each planet produces aromas from its north and south poles. The characteristic aroma of Earth is violet, that of Jupiter is jonquil, that of Mercury, rose, and so on.[91] Fourier's association of floral scents with the planets presents an intriguing image of space as a cosmic hothouse. Fourier included under the category of aroma, however, not only odor, but electricity, magnetism, and even light. He seems to have perceived these qualities in a synaesthetic fashion, for he says that "all these aromas have a visible color and a distinct taste."[92] The "aromal" properties of sunlight, he states, are what give fruit their scent and taste.[93]

Aromas are the vital fluids of the universe, according to Fourier, who classified aroma as the fifth element (after earth, water, air, and fire). The planets procreate by intermingling their aromas; either between their own north (male) and south (female) poles or amongst each other. This aromatic intercourse of the spheres is the source of all animal and plant life. Thus cattle, for example, are produced by the aromas of Jupiter, while the narcissus is created through a combination of the aromas of Jupiter and the Sun. If a woman admires Venus shining in the evening sky, Fourier writes:

> she will find it still more charming on learning that she is indebted to this brilliant planet for a cashmere shawl that envelopes and protects her person, and a bouquet of lilac that perfumes her: it is Venus that creates the lilac and the Tibetan goat.[94]

Unfortunately, says Fourier, the rise of civilization on Earth has had the effect of corrupting Earth's aromas and disrupting the cosmic "aromal orchestra."[95] It is only through the establishment of a society dedicated to the expression and development of natural attractions that the polluted atmosphere of Earth can be purified and the full procreative potential of the cosmos realized.

Everything in Fourier's world is linked in chains of correspondence. The planet Earth, for example, corresponds to the musical note do, the scent of violets, the color purple, the metal iron, the gem amethyst and so on. Furthermore, Fourier found in everything – planets, animals, flowers, colors, scents – allegories of the human passions. Take, for example, his analysis of the sensory allegory of the lily. The lily, says Fourier, is the creation of Saturn, the planet which represents honor, and its scent is therefore "the aroma of honor." The firm, straight stem of the lily indicates truth, its orange pollen represents enthusiasm. The fact that those who smell the lily find their faces dusted with pollen signifies that enthusiasm for honor and truth is considered ridiculous in civilization.[96] Fourier looked forward to the day when all the sensory hieroglyphs of nature could be interpreted as readily as we now read writing.

Not surprisingly, given this attention to sensory properties, the cultivation of the senses plays a central role in Fourier's cosmology. Fourier states that, "It is scarcely credible that after 3000 years of studies, men have not yet thought of classifying the senses."[97] His innovation is to turn the traditional ranking of the senses on its head and place the so-called lower senses of taste and touch at the top of the sensory hierarchy.[98] These two senses he characterizes as active, as they produce physical pleasure, whereas sight and hearing are passive, productive only of indirect conceptual pleasure. Smell is a "mixed" sense. While it cannot experience as much pleasure as either taste or touch it still offers more direct satisfaction than sight or hearing.[99] Thus Fourier, considering the example of a woman who prefers an unassuming scented bouquet to a showy odorless one, states: "It is not surprising that the woman prefers the pleasure of an active sense, like smell, over the pleasure of a passive sense, like sight."[100]

Fourier explains his ranking of taste and touch above sight, hearing and smell with a practical illustration:

> The people would by no means perpetuate crime . . . to procure pictures, perfumes or concerts. These three sorts of pleasures would not be able to move the mob, which, on the contrary, is entirely devoted to the impulsions of the two active senses – Taste and Touch. The mob requires to be fed and clothed.[101]

He states his thesis more succinctly by means of an old adage "*Ventre affamé n'a point d'oreilles*" – "A hungry belly has no ears."[102]

Fourier argued that in our present condition all of our senses are impoverished. He divided this impoverishment into what he called internal and external poverties. The internal sensory poverties are the physical limitations of our senses, which oblige us, for instance, to use telescopes to extend our power of sight and dogs to extend our power of smell.

The external poverties consist of the inability of the majority of people to afford or adequately appreciate sensory pleasures, and of the disagreeable sensory impressions which continually assail our senses. As an example of these last Fourier describes the:

> sickening streets in which the French populace dwell; and where the din of the trades, of the hammers, quarrels and beggars, the sight of the hanging rags, of the dirty dwellings and unpalatable labors of the poor, the stifling smell of the drains in which they swarm, so painfully affect the sight, hearing and smell.[103]

So accustomed are we in civilization to sensory ills, says Fourier, that there are some who actually take pleasure in them. He gives as examples those who enjoy looking at "naked and hideous" mountains or listening to dissonant music.[104] ("This defective use of the sense of hearing may be called: Dull earism as to the effect; Dull earish as to the passion; Dull ears as to the individual.")[105]

In Harmony, Fourier states, the elimination of external sensory poverties will eventually lead to the perfection of our sensory faculties. Our sense of smell, he claims, will become so refined that "aromal adepts" will be able to smell out mineral deposits. Even more radical are the changes he foresees to our faculty of sight; for in order to cover a greater field of vision, our eyes will eventually move independently of each other.[106]

Fourier outlines the social changes necessary to accomplish such a sensory revolution. First of all material poverty must be eliminated. Everyone in Harmony will be guaranteed employment suited to their temperament and will have access to a wide range of sensory pleasures. Second, children will have their senses educated from an early age. Such education – as with all education in Harmony – will not be a chore for children because it will develop their own natural interests. The senses of taste and smell will be trained through the study of cuisine, thus taking advantage of children's love of food and turning them from gluttons to gourmets. The senses of sight and hearing will be educated through the presentation of operas, allowing children to indulge in their passion for singing, acting, dressing up, and painting. Touch will be educated through enjoyable manual activities.[107]

Furthermore, where the senses are repulsed and repressed in civilization, they will be attracted and cultivated in Harmony. The sense of hearing will, on the one hand, be flattered by daily concerts, and on the other, no longer be assaulted by noise: carpenters will be confined to isolated quarters and croaking toads will be exterminated. The architecture of Harmony, in turn, will create curved spaces where the voice will resonate, allowing conversations to be carried out at a distance.[108]

Harmony will also be pleasing to the eye. The openness of the architecture will allow the eye to range freely over the city without constantly being obstructed by brick walls. The colors of Harmony will offer both sensuous and spiritual delights to the sight, as every color will be employed in keeping with its symbolic meaning, down to the violet (friendship) reins on the white (unity) horses of the voluntary corps of vestal virgins.[109]

The sense of smell will not be offended in Harmony by such olfactory blights as swamps or putrid hovels. Instead cities will be perfumed with healthful scents, and fragrant flowers will be planted by the roadside to refresh travelers. Such unavoidable malodorous tasks as latrine cleaning will be assigned to bands of children, who display a natural proclivity for filth. These "little hordes" will be rewarded for their labors by an elevated social status.[110]

Fourier is at his most eloquent in describing the pleasures in store for the two cardinal senses of touch and taste in Harmony. As regards the former, Fourier gives such instances of post-civilization advances as vermin-free beds and covered walkways.[111] The pleasures of touch, however, are associated most closely in Harmony with those of love. Fourier lambasts civilization for condemning any form of physical love outside of marriage. He states that this privation of touch "has led to the corruption of the whole system of amorous relations."[112] It is women, above all, who suffer from the bondage of marriage: "Is not a young woman a commodity put up for sale to whoever wishes to negotiate her purchase and exclusive possession?"[113]

In Harmony, however, both men and women will be free to make alliances with whomever they please and for whatever purposes they please, for "amorous fantasies . . . cannot be subject to debate."[114] "Courts of love" will exist for the purpose of matching up suitable partners, so that whatever one's passion – "whether infinitely rare as is heel-scratching, or common as are the sects of flag-ellation"[115] – one will always be assured of a like-minded mate. Through these means touch will lose its current asocial status and become the means for the creation of a network of social bonds.

Taste – "the first and last enjoyment of man"[116] – is the most valued of the senses in Harmony. There the chef, or rather, "gastrosopher," who knows how to match dishes to personality types, will hold the highest place of honor. In order to enjoy all the delicacies available to them, the Harmonians will develop prodigious appetites and will dine five times a day.[117] Sweets will be particularly prevalent on the menu, for Fourier deemed sweetness to be the one flavor capable of pleasing all palates. Even medicine – or hygienic gastrosophy – will be tasteful in Harmony, with cures effected by such treats as candy, grapes, and hot, sugared wine.[118]

Fourier parallels the alliance between touch and love with an alliance between taste and ambition. As matters of taste are, according to Fourier, a natural focus of ambitious desires, the inhabitants of Harmony, instead of arguing over politics or competing for commercial success, will argue over recipes and compete in the cultivation of fruits and vegetables. In this savory new world, wars will be replaced by gastronomic contests, involving armies of competitors. Fourier writes of the conclusion of one such contest:

> On the day of triumph the victors are honored by a salvo . . . . The athletes arm themselves with 300,000 bottles of sparkling wine, whose corks, loosened and held down by the thumb, are ready to pop . . . . The moment [the order is given to fire] all 300,000 corks are released at once.[119]

For those who delight in quibbling over points of dogma, there will be gastronomic councils to replace the theological councils of the past. These councils – during which sects may present heretical theses – will determine the gastronomic policies of Harmony.[120]

Indeed, gastronomy, along with physical love, assumes the status of a religious cult in Harmony. Fourier mocked the asceticism of Christian saints who dedicate themselves "to prayers and austerities which do no one any good."[121] In Harmony sainthood will either be amorous – devoted to the tactile satisfaction of others – or gastronomic – devoted to the gustatory satisfaction of others. Candidates for sainthood in the former field must first pass through the intermediate positions of "angel" and "archangel" by performing a series of charitable amorous tasks.[122] Candidates for sainthood in the latter must be "expert in the . . . functions of Gastroculture and Gastrohygiene."[123] Fourier also thought it possible for exceptional individuals to be amorous saints when young, and gastronomic saints when old.[124]

Fourier found civilized notions of heaven as little to his taste as civilized notions of sainthood. He writes that the pleasures of heaven seem to be confined to two senses, sight and hearing – "moreover, this charm will be reduced by one half for the French, who do not value at all good music or celestial hymns."[125] "Some humorists," he says, "promise children that there will be walls of sugar in paradise, and this is the most receivable statement that has been made about that abode."[126] Fourier's concept of heaven, in fact, was much like his notion of Harmony, a place where all the senses and passions could be gratified, but to an even greater extent than on earth.

In the meantime, with the positive vibrations of Harmonian society resonating throughout the universe, the earth will become an increasingly agreeable place to be. Earth's climate, claims Fourier, will eventually grow temperate around the world and the seas will turn to lemonade.[127] Furthermore, colorful new stars will appear in the sky, enhancing our "celestial decor" both by night and day.[128] In place of the hostile animals of the present world there will be "anti-lions" to pull carriages, and "anti-whales" to guide ships.[129] The human body will also be perfected; among other improvements, people will need only three hours of sleep a day and will have nocturnal vision.[130] Eventually the world will come to an end, Fourier foretold, after some 70,000 years. When this happens however, humans will simply leave their bodies and spiritually migrate to another planet, where they will "resume new bodies, and will return to the delights that harmony will lavish in all its periods."[131]

Patterns and transmutations

As a vision of the world produced in the modern era, Fourier's organic, synaes-thetic cosmos is certainly startling. When considered as a successor (perhaps the last before the triumph of the pictorial and mechanical universe of modern science) to the sensory cosmologies of previous centuries, however, it does not seem so out of place. In some ways, of course, Fourier's hedonistic cosmos is worlds apart from the more austere realms imagined by such earlier cosmologists as St. Hildegard and Jacob Boehme. Yet, certain recurring patterns of sensory and cosmic order can be readily discerned through the transmutations in sacred and social values.

Fourier's cosmos, for example, employs a system of correspondences whereby diverse, and seemingly disparate, elements – planets, metals, flowers, senses, and sensory properties – are interrelated. Such systems of correspondence had been popular from antiquity to the period of the Enlightenment. Of the three cosmologies examined here, Fourier's makes the most extensive use of such chains of associations. However, similar theories can be seen to underlie the cosmic orders of Hildegard and Boehme. Boehme, for example, links flavors, colors, and other sensory properties with different heavenly bodies: Venus is sweet and white; Mars, red and bitter; Saturn, sour and dark; the Sun fragrant and yellow, and so on.[132]

All the elements of the cosmos are deemed to have an allegorical meaning by Hildegard, Boehme, and Fourier. In the words of Boehme: "The whole outward visible world with all its being is a signature, or figure of the inward spiritual world."[133] For Hildegard, a stone could be broken down into moist greenness, tangibility and fire, which stood for the Father, the Son, and the Holy Spirit. Boehme, in turn, found a symbol of the Trinity in the rainbow: the red of the rainbow represented the Father, the yellow the Son, and the blue, the Holy Spirit.[134] In a more secular vein, Fourier proclaimed the orange pollen, straight stem, and sweet scent of the lily to convey the values of enthusiasm, truth, and honor. The claims made by Hildegard, Boehme, and Fourier to be able to decode the sensory signs of the universe constituted the basis of their cosmological authority. It is because each claimed a special knowledge of the nature of the cosmos that she or he could presume to describe and interpret it for the benefit of others.

At the same time as all the sensory signs of the cosmos encode spiritual values in the thought of Hildegard, Boehme, and Fourier, all spiritual values are manifested through sensory signs. Thus, for example, Hildegard and Boehme perceive heaven and its angels as fragrant with odors and gleaming with colors, while Fourier envisions Harmony and its inhabitants adorned with a rainbow of symbolic hues. All three cosmologists create new sensuous worlds for the imagination, as well as mining the perceptible world for its hidden meanings.

The cosmologies presented by Hildegard, Boehme, and Fourier differ from the modern world view in their use of *all* of the senses, not only sight, as models and media for cosmic reality. The visual was highly valued in premodern thought, but it was not considered able to represent the world by itself. The accepted correspondences among senses, elements, planets, and so on made it clear that only one aspect of cosmic reality was allotted to each sense. No matter how exalted one sense might be or how denigrated another, therefore, no sense could ultimately be left out of a complete cosmic paradigm.

Fourier, who lived in an era of rising visualism, can be seen to struggle against the modern hegemony of sight in his writings. For example, in contrast to the modern emphasis on the visual skills of reading and writing, Fourier states that in Harmony education will take place through *all* the senses. Furthermore, while modern technology extends the power of sight over the other senses, through such devices as the telescope, in Harmony *all* the senses will be improved and extended. Fourier's most notable act of rebellion against the tyranny of sight is to topple the traditional sight-dominated sensory order and place taste at the head of the senses. This reversal of the hierarchy of the senses by Fourier was associated with an overturning of gender and class orders which would allow women and the poor to have central positions in Harmony.

Freedom from the conceptual hegemony of any one sense enabled Hildegard, Boehme, and Fourier to explore a variety of sensory models in their cosmologies. One of the most important for all three was that of music. For each, however, music played a somewhat different role. For Fourier it is the structure of music – notes, chords, scales – rather than its aural expression, which provides a framework for the cosmos. Boehme, however, assigns music a creative role: the angels *sing* heaven into being with their divine harmonies. Hildegard, in turn, imagines the cosmos as a song – the lyrics are matter and the music spirit. Like Boehme, Hildegard distinguishes between angelic and planetary harmonies, giving precedence to the former:

> [Angels'] voices have a richer harmony than all the sounds living creatures
> have ever produced, and their voices are brighter than all the splendor of
> the sun, moon, and stars sparkling in the waters. More wonderful is this
> sound than the music of the spheres that arises from the blowing of the
> winds that sustain the four elements . . . [135]

The belief manifested by Hildegard, Boehme, and Fourier in a "music of the
spheres" was an ancient one. Pythagoras and his followers held that the planets
made sounds as they moved, and that the ratio of their orbits corresponded to
musical intervals. In *The Republic* Plato imagined that this celestial harmony was
produced by eight sirens, each sitting on a heavenly sphere of a different color
and singing a different note. This image was later Christianized and the singing
sirens became angelic choirs. The concept of a celestial music came to be
extended to include the microcosm of the human body. For example, in the
sixth century Boethius wrote that just as the cosmos is ordered by a celestial
music, so body and soul are ordered by an interior music.[136] The musical
paradigms of Hildegard, Boehme and Fourier represent variations on this
ancient theme of cosmic and bodily harmony.

The heavens or ideal worlds imagined by Hildegard, Boehme, and Fourier
manifest interesting similarities. All three envision a world made to measure for
human needs – a temperate climate and a domesticated earth. Boehme's apple-
flavored waters of heaven are similar to Fourier's sea of lemonade. Hildegard's
dislike of lofty mountains and treacherous rivers is echoed in Fourier's diatribes
against hideous, bare mountains and pestilential swamps. Fourier's aromatic
planetary system is reminiscent of Hildegard's and Boehme's fragrant heavens.

There are essential distinctions among the three, however. The static quality
of Hildegard's ideal world contrasts with the ceaseless motion which characterizes the world of Boehme, with its wrestling spirits, or that of Fourier, with its
dynamic passions. Fourier, for instance, writes:

> On beholding this Sun . . . whirl about with so great velocity . . . on seeing
> our planet run 600,000 leagues in an ordinary day, how can we think that
> the state of stagnation and of contemplation is a perfect state in the eyes of
> God, who stamps such rapidity on the material movement?[137]

This contrast illustrates the difference between the medieval preoccupation with
eternal archetypes and cosmic stability and the post-Renaissance concern with
the operation of laws of motion, or mechanics.[138] In his *Dialogue Concerning
the Two Chief World Systems* of 1629, for example, Galileo countered the traditional notion of immutability as the "prime perfection and nobility of the . . .
bodies of the universe" with the new idea of incessant movement and change as
"very noble and admirable."[139]

The new emphasis on movement would be taken up by many of Heaven's
scribes. Thus one eighteenth-century Italian account of heavenly life describes
saints whizzing around the cosmos faster than light (due to their anointment

with "quintessential balms" – a throwback to the olfactory dynamics of more traditional cosmologies):

> How often have you been beside yourselves with astonishment at discovering that the sun runs one million, one hundred and forty thousand miles in an hour? . . . And I, in anointing these blessed bodies with quintessential balms . . . enable them to come and go, to circle and walk repeatedly from Earth to Heaven . . . in less time than you need to bat an eyelid.[140]

Boehme and Fourier, hence, were not alone in their efforts to introduce the hectic motion of the new scientific cosmos into their own visionary worlds.

Another of the differing traits of the worlds-to-come in the writings of Hildegard, Boehme, and Fourier concerns the activities of the inhabitants of those worlds. Fourier, for example, would have considered Hildegard's heaven of lyre-playing virgins and martyrs excruciatingly dull. For Hildegard, on the other hand, Fourier's happy, orgiastic, Harmonians would constitute the "adulterers, gluttons, and drunkards" whose destiny it is to be tortured by "stinking dampness" in the hell of sinful taste.

Interestingly, while Fourier's utopia is very far from exemplifying medieval ideals of a heavenly kingdom, it *is* reminiscent of the earthier aspects of medieval life and thought. The amorous pilgrimages which Fourier's Harmonians undertake, for instance, are not that far removed from medieval pilgrimages, which often were little more than pleasure jaunts. According to Huizinga "[medieval] pilgrimages are the occasions of all kinds of debauchery; procuresses are always found there, people come for amorous purposes."[141] The feasts of Harmony, in turn, call to mind the groaning boards of medieval banquets. Ironically Fourier's Harmonians lead the kind of sensuous life that the medieval clergy was often accused of leading. Consider, for example, the following statement by St. Bernard of Clairvaux:

> Ministers of Christ, they serve Antichrist . . . . Hence that *éclat* of the courtesan which you daily see, that theatric garb, that regal state . . . . Hence the splendid tables laden with food and goblets; hence the feastings and drunkenness, the guitars . . . and the jars of perfumes . . . [142]

In Harmony, however, the pursuit of such worldly pleasures is not a sin, but rather a means of achieving secular "sainthood."

One of the most fundamental differences between Fourier's cosmology and the cosmologies of Hildegard and Boehme is that, while the doctrines of Christianity are central to the latter, they appear to be irrelevant to the former. (Fourier's motto is "God helps those who help themselves.") Nevertheless, the notion of a cosmic fall and redemption is as important to the anthropocentric cosmology of Fourier as to the Christian cosmologies of his predecessors. In all three cases this fall and redemption have a sensory dimension: the senses are held to be in a degenerate condition in the present world and to await perfection in a future, paradisiacal, world. While for Hildegard and Boehme these changes come about through divine agency, however, for Fourier they come about through human agency – the power of society to change the course of nature.

Furthermore, while Hildegard and Boehme believe that the senses must be kept in check to be redeemed, Fourier holds that they must be liberated. This point is best illustrated through the different treatments of the senses of taste and touch. For Hildegard and Boehme, the gratification of the sense of taste through the eating of the forbidden fruit occasioned the Fall of humanity.[143] After the Fall the sense of touch became vitiated through the gratification of carnal desire. (Hildegard believed that Adam and Eve procreated in Paradise through a sweet exchange of perspiration.)[144] For Fourier, however, it is precisely such gratification of taste and touch through the gustatory and amatory regimes of Harmony which will redeem humanity.

As regards taste in particular, it is instructive to compare the different roles this sense plays in the three cosmologies examined here. For Hildegard, who values the inner, spiritual senses, over the external, physical ones, taste has as its supreme object the divine sweetness of Christ. She would have said, together with another medieval mystic, Margaret Ebner, "I had the desire to give up all sweet things for the sake of the sweetness I received from God."[145]

In Fourier's case, however, taste ranks first among the senses precisely because of its capacity to experience physical pleasure, to delight in material sweetness. Sugary confections delight Fourier who holds that sugar cane is the "king of vegetables" and that sugar will replace bread as the staff of life in his new world.

Boehme, in turn, is concerned not so much with gustation as with gustatory qualities: sweetness, sourness, and bitterness. These qualities are both spiritual – each one constitutes a divine spirit – and physical; together they create the material world. The novelty of Boehme's work for a modern reader lies largely in this transformation of sensory properties into transcendental, life-giving, principles. Thus sweetness, for example, is not simply a characteristic of fruit, it is the *creator* of fruit. Likewise, sweetness is no longer only a metaphor for God's love, it *is* God's love. Unlike Fourier, however, Boehme made a distinction between pure, paradisiacal sweetness and corrupt worldly sweetness. (As we shall see in the following chapter, Boehme, in fact, associated sugar with the Devil.)

These distinctions bring out the different sensory philosophies held by Hildegard, Boehme, and Fourier. Hildegard expounds a theology of the senses in her work. The senses exist to draw the individual towards divine truth. Boehme combines theology with a chemical philosophy of the senses. Sensory qualities interact in a quasi-chemical fashion to shape both the physical and spiritual realms. Fourier elaborates both a political economy and a sociobiology of the senses. The senses, according to his philosophy, can be culturally and physically shaped by social trends. In turn, society – and by extension the cosmos – is the product of human sensory passions.

For all three cosmologists the universe is organic in nature, a living body made up of living bodies. The cosmos is consequently not only a source of sensations, it is itself a sensing and feeling being. Hildegard envisioned the planets communicating with each other through rays.[146] According to Boehme, the sensory spirits which make up God and the cosmos "could all see, feel, taste, smell and hear" each other.[147] Fourier wrote that "the human passions . . . are also the passions of the stars and of the higher creatures, universes, biniverses, triniverses, &c., up to God."[148]

In asserting the organic, sentient nature of the cosmos Boehme and Fourier were reacting against the growing quantification and mechanization of the universe by contemporary science. Already in the seventeenth century, quantitative analysis had become central to scientific thought, making the following line from the Wisdom of Solomon a favorite quotation among scholars: "You have ordered everything according to measure, number and weight."[149]

If measure, number, and weight were sufficient to arrive at an understanding of the universe, there was evidently no need to take into account such non-quantifiable characteristics as music, scents, or emotions. Susan Bordo writes in *The Flight to Objectivity*:

> For the model of knowledge which results [from the scientific approach], neither bodily response (the sensual or the emotional) nor associational thinking, exploring the various personal and spiritual meanings the object has for us, can tell us anything about the object "itself." *It* can only be grasped, as Gillispie puts it, "by measurement rather than sympathy."[150]

According to the new scientific philosophy, sensory perception was a purely corporeal process with no intrinsic spiritual meaning. For Hildegard, Boehme, Fourier, and other sensory visionaries, however, perception was not simply a physiological act, it was a *moral* act. Even Fourier, with his emphasis on human physicality, understood perception as a God-given means for accomplishing a transformation of society and spirit.

It is this mingling of sense and spirit which makes the cosmologies of Hildegard, Boehme, and Fourier and their like so different from the de-sensualized and de-moralized cosmologies of modern science. The latter leave us with the image of an alien universe in which inanimate planets silently revolve in ultimately meaningless patterns. The former present a universe vibrant with harmonies and aromas, bliss and horror, good and evil; a universe modeled on the familiar form of the human body and set in motion by the transcendent power of the Divine.

2 The breath of God

Sacred histories of scent

In modernity the sense of smell is usually associated with instincts and emotions rather than with reason or spirituality. With few exceptions, smell and smells have been discredited and removed from the arena of intellectual discourse, and, in many cases, from cultural life in general. In this deodorized ambience traditional olfactory concepts such as the "odor of sanctity" appear to be simply quaint relics of a more credulous age and not worthy of serious attention.[1]

Prior to the modern, post-Enlightenment, era, however, smell was taken *very* seriously in the West. Nowhere is this more evident than in the importance assigned to things olfactory by the Church. The concept of the odor of sanctity, which we moderns tend to dismiss as a marginal (and suspect) phenomenon of an outmoded religious life, pre-modern society located at the center of a complex olfactory and spiritual network which encompassed the entire cosmos. As Piero Camporesi has written in *The Anatomy of the Senses*: "Both hell and paradise could be condensed into drops in the boiling still: celestial and infernal distillations opened the senses to an understanding of distant places."[2] To understand the historical significance of odor in Christianity, we must put aside our modern olfactory prejudices and explore the aromatic vapors produced by the fervid stills of earlier imaginations, from the stenches of hell to the sweet scents of heaven.

The odor of sanctity

Belief in an odor of sanctity was based on the notion that Christians who lived in a state of grace would be infused with the divine scent of the Holy Spirit – the breath of God. This divine fragrance served as a means of making the presence of God known to others. St. Paul in his second letter to the Corinthians (2: 14) wrote that God "uses us to spread abroad the fragrance of the knowledge of himself." An odor of sanctity was not the only, or even a necessary, sign of sainthood, but it was popularly regarded as one of the most notable.[3]

Most commonly, an odor of sanctity is said to occur on or after the death of a saint. It was said of the eighth-century St. Hubert of Brittany:

When [St. Hubert] breathed his last, there spread throughout Brittany an odor so sweet, that it seemed as if God had brought together all the flowers of spring to symbolize the heavenly sweetness which Hubert would enjoy in Paradise.[4]

According to report, when the coffin of St. Francis Xavier was opened four months after his death in the sixteenth century, his body was found to be incorrupt and sweet-smelling, although no spices or balm had been used to prepare it for burial.[5]

A supernatural fragrance might also be noted during a saint's lifetime. In a story which indicates how sacred olfactory power might be translated into temporal power, the seventh-century St. Valery is said to have interrupted a lecture given by St. Colomban with his powerful odor of sanctity. Rather than being annoyed, however, St. Colomban declared to the odoriferous Valery: "It is you, not I, who are the veritable head of this monastery."[6] The thirteenth-century Blessed Herman of Steinfeld exhaled an odor of sanctity – "like a garden full of roses, lilies, violets, poppies and all kinds of fragrant flowers" – every time he said grace.[7] In the seventeenth century the nun Giovanna Maria della Croce left a trail of celestial fragrance wherever she went, enabling her fellow nuns to trace her movements around the convent.[8]

While there are hundreds of accounts of instances of the odor of sanctity in the annals of Christian sainthood, certain individuals were particularly renowned for their supernatural scents. Three such are Lydwine of Schiedam (1380–1433), Teresa of Avila (1515–1582), and Benoîte of Notre-Dame du Laus (1647–1718). A description of the various olfactory phenomena which reputedly characterized their lives and deaths will help the reader enter into the more redolent mentality of an earlier time and provide a basis for further exploring the sacred history of scent.

Lydwine of Schiedam

Lydwine was born in Schiedam, Holland in 1380, the daughter of "noble and virtuous, but impoverished" parents. As a young girl Lydwine defied her father's wishes that she marry and announced that she would never take a mortal man for her spouse. At the age of 15 Lydwine broke a rib by falling on the ice. This event and succeeding complications resulted in her spending the next 38 years of her life in bed.[9]

Lydwine became renowned as a model of patience and religiosity, and also as a source of supernatural phenomena, most especially the odor of sanctity:

Both [Lydwine] and her cell were found to be redolent, so that those who entered thought that divers aromatic simples [herbs] had been brought in and scattered there. And this wonderful sweetness was perceived when she was visited or touched by the Saviour or by the angel, or when she returned from Heaven or the regions of Paradise.[10]

The hand by which her guardian angel led Lydwine on frequent heavenly voyages was said to be especially fragrant. Her confessor stated that he could tell by the scent of her hand, which "seemed to have been anointed with the oils of different spices," when she had been visited by an angel. Lydwine's odor on such occasions was described as so powerful that visitors could actually taste it, "as if they had eaten pepper or cinnamon."[11] One visiting priest who experienced the phenomenon found himself moved to confess his sins on smelling Lydwine's fragrant hand.

Visitors to the sickroom were particularly impressed by the sweet scents emitted by Lydwine's many open sores, and even by the worms which were found in the sores when the plasters were taken off to be changed.[12] In 1412 she vomited "little pieces of her lung and liver, with several intestines" and these too were found to be fragrant, leaving a strong scent on the hands of those who touched them.[13]

Lydwine's parents preserved redolent pieces of their daughter's flesh. Discomfited by the attention which these fragments of her body attracted, Lydwine asked that they be buried. However, the fragrant tears of blood which she sometimes wept and which dried on her cheeks overnight were kept in a box. Using the floral symbolism common with her, Lydwine called these tears her roses.

Among Lydwine's remarkable qualities was an apparent ability to live without sleep or food. Lydwine was said to subsist almost exclusively on an occasional swallow of watered-down spiced wine.[14] The public attention which Lydwine attracted led the magistrates of Schiedam to place her under surveillance in order to ascertain the truth of her situation. On September 12, 1421 they testified in a public document that Lydwine did not eat or sleep, and that her body, in spite of her illness, exhaled a sweet odor.[15]

Lydwine was compensated for her bedridden state by the journeys through fragrant paradisiacal meadows and spicy heavenly realms on which she was taken by her guardian angel. During one of her raptures she received from the Virgin Mary an aromatic veil crowned with a garland of flowers. Another time, when Lydwine lost the rod with which she drew back the curtains of her bed, her angel brought her a rod made of the fragrant wood of a tree from Paradise. Numerous people came to see and smell this rod until one day it lost its fragrance after being touched by a libertine.[16]

One Christamas eve Lydwine had a vision of Christ being born with a multitude of virgins in attendance. At the moment of the nativity Lydwine's breasts, along with those of the visionary virgins, swelled with milk. Lydwine was able to feed the woman who attended her with this mystical milk for several days.[17]

Her renown sometimes brought Lydwine unwelcome attentions. The worst of these occurred when she was attacked by a band of soldiers who stripped off her bedclothes, called her a prostitute, accused her of having banquets by night, and pinched her body until it bled. Lydwine had a forewarning of this incident in a vision. Her heavenly Spouse appeared to her and showed her an unfinished crown of flowers, saying that soon it would be complete.[18]

The most difficult time of Lydwine's life apparently came when she fell into a deep depression after the death of a close relative and her guardian angel (whom Lydwine saw as a shining white man with a cross on his forehead) deserted her. Eventually her angel and her ecstasies returned, more powerfully than ever, bringing "such great sweet scent . . . that those who visited her marvelled."[19]

A year before her death Lydwine became concerned about the spiritual welfare of a 12-year-old nephew named Baldwin, whereupon she asked the Lord to afflict the boy with a fever in order to chasten him. Lydwine told her nephew to leave his cup of "light liquor" by her bed overnight. In the morning "he found it by the gift of God filled with a certain strange liquor, as if there were in it a mixture of cinnamon and other simples, sweet-smelling and delicious to the taste." After Baldwin drank from this cup he fell sick with a serious illness for two months. Any liquor poured into the cup for a week afterwards reportedly received "the savour of a most sweet potation."[20]

In one of her visions, an angel had shown Lydwine a rose bush, saying that when all the roses were in bloom her time on earth would be up. In 1433 Lydwine announced that the roses had all opened. She died on April 14 of that year, sweetly redolent from an ecstasy in which the Lord anointed her body with balm.[21]

Lydwine's body, ravaged in life, was reportedly bright and healthy-looking in death. Before her body was interred, a bag of the saint's fragrant tears of blood, her "roses," was placed under her head. The hair belt Lydwine had used to chastise her body was found to be penetrated with fragrance after her death. In the early 1600s the Bishop of Tournai wrote of this belt: "It is still preserved, fragrant with a wondrous odour of sweetness. In fact I have handled it with my own hands, and I know by experience that the demons dread it exceedingly."[22]

Teresa of Avila

Teresa of Avila, also known as Teresa of Jesus, was born in Spain in 1515. As a youth she entered the Carmelite order, which she subsequently undertook to radically reform. Teresa wrote several theological works, including *The Way of Perfection* and *The Interior Castle*, along with her autobiography. These writings and the numerous testimonies of friends and colleagues concerning Teresa's life and death provide a rich fund of information about one of Christianity's most venerated saints. Teresa is probably best known for her mystical raptures, during which she was alternately tormented by the Devil and pierced by the love of God. These raptures were occasionally accompanied by olfactory sensations. Of an unwilling visit to hell, for example, she wrote: "The entrance seemed like a long narrow lane . . . and on the ground there was a filthy mud which reeked of pestilential odours."[23] The most notable olfactory phenomena associated with the saint, however, do not concern her renowned raptures, but the odor of sanctity diffused by her body just prior to, and after, death.[24]

During her last illness, Teresa is said to have emitted a fragrance so powerful that it scented everything she touched. This scent remained on her clothes, on the dishes she used, and even in the water with which the dishes were washed. So persistent was this fragrance that, many days after the saint's death, a nun who noticed a sweet odor in the kitchen traced it to a salt shaker that Teresa had used.[25]

As a treatment for her illness, the saint was prescribed a medicine with a very unpleasant odor. It happened that this medicine was spilt over her bedclothes just as the Duchess of Alba was coming for a visit. Teresa apologized for the foul odor but the Duchess responded: "Don't worry, Mother, for you smell instead as if you had been sprinkled with perfume."[26] On another occasion, a priest, smelling the fragrant breath of the saint, suspected she was freshening her breath with scented candies. When he asked her attendant about this, the woman replied that Teresa was barely able to eat any food because the odor made her nauseous (a chronic affliction of the saint). Much less, therefore, could she have tolerated a strongly flavored candy.[27]

After Teresa's death, in 1582, her body retained its fragrance. So overpowering was this scent, indeed, that it was necessary to keep the window of the room open during the saint's wake. The priest in attendance declared it a marvel "that a dead body . . . which causes more disgust than anything else in this life because of the unbearable stench it usually gives off . . . could produce such a fragrant scent."[28]

When St. Teresa was interred, odors were noted coming from the sepulcher, particularly on the feast days of those saints for whom she had had a special devotion. These odors were said to sometimes smell like lilies, and sometimes like jasmine or violet. Intrigued by the sweet scents, the nuns decided to have the saint's coffin opened to see if her body were incorrupt. When the coffin was taken out it was found to be rotten. Dirt and mold had entered through the rotted wood and covered the body of the saint. Nonetheless, while the saint's clothes were decayed and moldy-smelling, the body itself was whole and fragrant. The nuns removed the soiled clothes and washed the body, an act which filled the whole nunnery with fragrance for several days. Impressed by such signs of sanctity, the priest who had overseen the disinterment cut off the left hand from the corpse and presented it as an important relic to the Carmelite nunnery in Lisbon. The body was then reinterred.[29]

The fragrance of St. Teresa's corpse was not only wondrous in itself, it also performed wonders. One of its reported powers was to cure people who suffered from anosmia – the lack of a sense of smell. During the saint's wake, for example, a nun who had lost her sense of smell regretted not being able to smell the fragrance emanating from the body. On kissing the saint's foot, however, she recovered her lost sense and was able to experience the same fragrance as her sisters. In the Lisbon nunnery where St. Teresa's hand had been taken, there was a novice born without a sense of smell. On bringing the hand close to her nose the novice felt a warm vapor penetrating her nostrils followed by a sensation of odor. To test whether she had actually recovered her sense of smell the nuns brought different scents to the novice and she was able to distinguish those which were fragrant from those which were foul. In Alba, where the saint was buried, a man who had lost his sense of smell for almost two years due to a severe cold recovered it after putting a cloth which had touched the saint's arm on his head. After four days he was able to smell herbal scents, following which he regained his sense of smell in its entirety.[30]

St. Teresa's odor of sanctity accomplished other wonders as well. One case involved a letter that the saint had written to a nun. When the nun took the letter out, some time after St. Teresa's death, she was surprised to discover it had a strong scent, although the place where she had kept it was free from odor. As she re-read the letter she came across certain things which she preferred should be kept secret, and started to erase part of the writing. At that point, the letter became odorless. Later, when a Franciscan priest was talking to the nun about St. Teresa, he remarked to her, "You must have some relic of Mother Teresa, for I can smell the odor that all her things give off." The nun then realized that, although she was no longer able to smell the saint's letter herself, others could still perceive the odor.[31]

Curiosity about the nature of the fragrance emitted by St. Teresa's body led to a number of experiments being performed. One was conducted in the presence of the Lisbon Inquisitor. At that time a portion of civet was found to lose its scent after being brought in contact with St. Teresa's hand. This was considered noteworthy indeed in those days when it was generally believed that "there is nothing which can take away the good odour from civet or musk."[32]

The skeptical prioress of the Lisbon convent inquired privately of a physician whether it might not be the general rule that things lose their odor when coming into contact with a dead body. The physician replied, however, that far from this being the case, persons sometimes placed strong-smelling ointments for a time in malodorous graves to help augment their scent. The doctor then conducted an experiment of his own. He placed the saint's hand inside a perfumed glove and found that the glove was promptly left without any scent. Shortly afterwards the miraculous hand was permanently encased in a silver model, making further olfactory experiments impossible.[33]

As Teresa's reputation for sanctity grew, so did the demand for relics. So incorruptible was her flesh, that it was said that to have a piece of it was as good as having bones of other saints. Desirous to return the saint's body to its birthplace, a group of Carmelite priests had it secretly disinterred from the convent of Alba, in 1585, and taken to Avila. The nuns of Alba were alerted to their loss by a strong fragrance which penetrated the choir where they were reciting matins. They tracked the scent to the main door of the convent, but by that time the body had already been removed. As a consolation, the fathers had left St. Teresa's left arm (less the hand which had previously been removed) for the nuns of Alba.[34]

In Avila St. Teresa's body was examined by physicians, who declared it miraculous that a corpse which had never been embalmed nor treated in any way could be so well preserved and so sweet-smelling. In Alba the arm which had been left behind was discovered to produce a fragrant oil which impregnated the cloths in which it was kept wrapped. Each time this happened the scented material would be given away as a relic and the arm wrapped in a fresh cloth.[35]

The inhabitants of Alba, however, were not content to remain with only an arm of St. Teresa after having possessed the whole body. After much negotiation, the Pope finally ordered that the holy corpse be returned to Alba. On its trip back, in 1586, the body reportedly exhaled such an irresistible odor that, as it was carried by a cornfield, the workers were enticed to drop their flails and follow it. From then on St. Teresa's body remained in Alba.[36]

Benoîte of Notre-Dame du Laus

Benoîte Rencurrel was born in the village of St. Etienne in the French Alps in 1647. The information about her life comes primarily from a biography written in 1711 by Pierre Gaillard, the archdeacon of Gap, who collected reports from persons who knew her.[37]

Benoîte had a particularly hard childhood: her family was poor, her father died when she was 7, and at 8 she went to work as a shepherdess to earn her living. At the age of 16 Benoîte began to have visions of the Virgin Mary as she pastured her sheep in the mountains. During one of these visions, the Virgin told Benoîte that her next visitation would take place in the chapel of Laus, and that the shepherdess would recognize the chapel by the fragrance emanating from the door.[38] The chapel of Laus was a small, rustic edifice on the site of a dried-up lake (*laus* in the local dialect) nearby. It was unknown to Benoîte and "she sniffed at the doors of all the houses she passed searching for the sweet-smelling chapel."[39] Finally, attracted by a perfumed odor, Benoîte discovered the chapel and inside, the Virgin Mary. Mary announced to Benoîte that a church would be built on the site with money from the poor.[40]

When the people of the surrounding towns learned that the Virgin was appearing in Laus, they began to frequent the chapel in large numbers. Various miraculous cures and conversions were reported to have occurred in the building, augmenting its reputation. The chapel was particularly known for its celestial fragrance. On a visit to the chapel, a local judge, for example, noted "a delicious odor . . . unlike anything I had ever smelled before, that gave me such great satisfaction that I felt beside myself."[41] Under the direction of Benoîte, the townspeople contributed money, materials and labor towards the construction of a church on the site. This church was completed in 1669 and named Notre-Dame du Laus.[42]

After midnight mass on December 25, 1669, Benoîte was alone in the new church, praying, when she saw a group of angels come to celebrate the inauguration of the church. The angels were dressed in red or white and carried a standard strewn with flowers and torches. They circled the inside of the church three times, singing and filling the building with perfume. Those people who were in the vicinity of the church marveled to perceive its windows shining with light while sweet scents emanated from its closed doors.[43]

The church of Notre-Dame du Laus was soon well-known for its supernatural odors, which were associated with the Virgin Mary. These perfumes were at times so intense that they diffused from the church throughout the whole valley. Gaillard expressed himself on the subject as follows:

> The odors of Mary are so fragrant, so delightful, and they give such great consolation, that whoever smells them enjoys a foretaste of heaven.[44]

Benoîte herself was said to be impregnated with these divine odors: they issued from her mouth when she spoke, scented everything she touched, and even perfumed the air where she walked. After one of Benoîte's encounters with the Virgin, her clothes would remain fragrant for days. The heavenly odor became particularly powerful whenever Benoîte was in a visionary ecstasy. At such times it was said to intoxicate all those around her with its scent. At one time another local shepherdess also claimed to have visions of Mary, but Benoîte, after being present at one of these visions, declared that she felt none of the usual signs of the Virgin's presence: "neither awe, nor joy, nor scent."[45]

During one of her ecstasies Benoîte was given tangible evidence of her supernatural encounters. The Virgin Mary filled her apron with fresh roses in the winter. These roses were distributed by Benoîte around the village where they amazed everyone by their unseasonal appearance and by their "extraordinary, delicious, sweet scent."[46]

On the feast of the Assumption, 1698, Benoîte went on a mystical voyage to paradise, where "she floated on waves of light, music, and perfume."[47] In paradise Benoîte saw blessed souls, all of them radiant and fair-haired, and a golden tree hung with apples, which the Virgin informed her was the Tree of Life. At the end of the night's journey she was taken back down to earth by an angelic escort. After this visit Benoîte was reportedly so filled with grace that she was able to go without food for fifteen days.[48]

From her personal observations, Benoîte stated that God showers perfumes over all the inhabitants of heaven. Each angel, she said, has its own particular scent. The angelic fragrances, however, are surpassed by the sweetness of the odor of the Queen of Angels, Mary, while the loveliest scent of all is that exhaled by Jesus Christ.[49]

Due to her heavenly voyages, Benoîte was said to be as close to angels as if they were her brothers and sisters. She often perceived her celestial companions as perfumed songbirds, changing color from day to day, or as babies. If Benoîte's angels were birds and babies, her demons were cats, monkeys, and toads, and, on one occasion, an ugly black man with red eyes, a long mustache, and talons. These demons would spirit Benoîte away to precipices and rooftops where they would call her names – "slut," "whore" – and taunt her with impure propositions. Such demoniacal encounters also entailed olfactory assaults whereby Benoîte would be tormented with "such unbearable stench that she would have died had God not sustained her."[50] Then her guardian angel would appear and counter the ill odor with celestial scents. This incessant battle between good and evil, fragrance and stench, would leave Benoîte ill and subject to fits of vomiting.[51]

The illness and injuries Benoîte suffered from her frequent encounters with demons were supplemented by the harm she inflicted on her body through extreme practices of mortification. For example, Benoîte often went for long periods without eating, or eating only bitter herbs. She also made vigorous use of penitential instruments; so much so that several became lodged in her back, causing her considerable pain.[52]

Weakened by ill-health, Benoîte died in 1718. Her tombstone in Laus reads simply: "tomb of Sister Benoîte who died in the odor of sanctity, 1718." The scents of Benoîte, the angels, Mary, and Jesus together make up what local tradition has named the "perfume of Laus," a scent which many pilgrims still claim to perceive in the region.[53]

Heavenly scents

The olfactory phenomena which pervade the histories of Lydwine, Teresa, and Benoîte were understood within the context of age-old beliefs concerning the natural and supernatural qualities of smell. The Christian concept of the odor of sanctity had its roots in the aromatic myths and rituals of the ancient world. The gods of Greece and Rome were believed to exhale the sweet scent of ambrosia, a mythical liquid which served both as food and perfume to the deities. In classical mythology, a supernatural fragrance is one of the characteristic signs of the presence of a deity.[54]

The gods of antiquity not only emitted good odors, they also delighted in receiving them. Fragrant floral garlands, incense, and burnt offerings were all rendered as olfactory tributes to the deities by their followers. In return, it was believed that the gods would occasionally grant the gift of immortality, or at least of corporeal incorruptibility, to a favored mortal by anointing him or her with ambrosia. Thus humans and deities were united in an olfactory cycle, whereby sweet scents traveled up from earth to the gods and down from the gods to earth.

The early Christians made ample use of olfactory imagery drawn from ancient traditions in their writings. The actual employment of perfumes and incense, however, tended to be associated with debauchery and idolatry within Christianity. Prayers, it was held, were the "incense" of Christians, and righteousness, the "perfume." The Church father Origen wrote that Christians "regard the spirit of every good man as an altar, from which ascends incense truly and intelligibly sweet-smelling – the prayers from a pure conscience."[55] God, it was argued, "needs neither blood nor the savour of sacrifices, nor the fragrance of flowers and incense, himself being perfect fragrance."[56]

The ancient custom of offering sweet scents to the gods was too deep-rooted, however, for the early Christians to eradicate. Although the personal use of perfume continued to be discouraged by the Church, incense soon came to be an accepted part of Christian ritual, and fragrant flowers a customary decoration for churches and shrines.[57] Even prayer – the symbolic incense *par excellence* – would eventually be literally sweetened by persons employing rosaries of perfumed beads.[58]

Christians, furthermore, like most peoples of the ancient world, deemed it appropriate that spiritual qualities should be made manifest by perceptible signs, such as odor.[59] Recorded experiences of a perceptible "odor of sanctity" can be found as early as the second century. St. Polycarp is said to have given off "a fragrant odor as of the fumes of frankincense" when burnt at the stake in 155 (an ordeal he managed to survive). Later that century a group of persecuted Christians are reported to have met their martyrdom "perfumed with the glad odor of Christ, so that some thought that they had been anointed with worldly ointment."[60]

In Christian tradition fragrance was closely associated with spiritual integrity and malodor with moral corruption.[61] Baptism, it was believed, made it possible to start one's spiritual life free of the stench of sin. The sweet odor assigned to the baptized soul was considered to be due to the soul being infused with the fragrant Holy Spirit. St. John of the Cross writes in his *Spiritual Canticle*:

> So profuse are these odours at times that the soul seems to be enveloped in delight and bathed in inestimable glory. Not only is it conscious itself of them, but they even overflow it, so that those who know how to discern these things can perceive them. The soul in this state seems to them as a delectable garden.[62]

There was a further notion that the soul was scented by the perfumed ointment – chrism – used in the baptismal rite. Medieval legend held that chrism came directly from the scented exudations of the Tree of Life in the Garden of Eden and therefore partook of its vivifying power.[63] This power was referred to in the Book of Enoch (25: 9–10) where it was said of persons chosen by God that "the sweet odor [of the Tree of Life] shall enter into their bones; and they shall live a long life." The chrism employed in baptism, with its legendary association with the Tree of Life, was thought to confer on those who received it spiritual immortality by imbuing them with the essence of life.[64]

By overcoming sin, saints were believed to overcome, to a certain extent, the physical corruption thought to have entered the world with the original sin of Adam and Eve. This was the explanation for why, when saints were ill, they sometimes smelled sweet rather than foul, and why their bodies on occasion remained fragrant and incorrupt after death. Scriptural support for this phenomenon came from Psalm 16: 10 which says of God: "Thou wilt not suffer thy Holy one to see corruption."

The customary appearance of an odor of sanctity on the death of a saint had to do with the belief that the saint's sweet-scented soul left the body at that time, thus making its odor manifest. In fact, it would seem to have been a commonplace that the departure of the soul at death created a perceptible odor.

Jacob Boehme wrote in the seventeenth century that "when [the common man] sees a blue vapour go forth out of the mouth of a dying man (which makes a strong smell all over the chamber) then he supposes that is the soul."[65]

As the odor of sanctity indicated the triumph of spiritual virtue over physical corruption, it was often considered able to heal physical ills. Numerous stories in saint lore refer to the healing power of the fragrance associated with a saint.[66] (St. Lydwine is unusual in her employment of supernatural odors to *cause* an illness.) In many cases the healing scents are said to arise from the saint's corpse. The fact that corpses at this time were usually held to spread disease by their odor, made the curative power of the scents produced by the saint's corpse another example of how the natural order of bodily decay was reversed in the case of the saint through supernatural grace.

Aside from healing, a variety of wonders are associated with odors of sanctity. The seventeenth-century Dutch nun Mary Margaret of the Angels, deliciously fragrant during life, is said to have prayed that after her death her body might provide oil for the sanctuary lamp.[67] When Mary Margaret died her corpse was left on its bier in the convent chapel. After a few months the body began to produce an aromatic oil, which reportedly provided ample fragrant fuel for a sanctuary lamp (along with curing many invalids).[68] St. Martin of Tours, in turn, reportedly once calmed a storm with his scent (a legend in keeping with the common notion that evil spirits and odors caused storms). The tempest was threatening to sink a ship at sea when the saint was invoked by the sailors on board. A fragrant odor immediately filled the ship, and the sea was promptly stilled by this pouring of scent on troubled waters.[69]

Along with their physical powers, odors of sanctity have the reputed ability to induce repentance and offer spiritual consolation. Lydwine's odor of sanctity convinced a guilty priest to unburden himself of his sins. Teresa's odor was said to soften peoples' hearts and fill them with praises for God.[70] Her contemporary, St. Philip Neri, infused people with good cheer and piety by his scent.[71] Benoîte's odors were similarly deemed to console and inspire: it was said that her fragrance "elevated the soul . . . and filled the heart with joy."[72] In premodern Europe scents were commonly thought to have a potent effect on the spirit, in part because of a perceived similarity in nature between the airiness of odors and the airiness of spirits, and in part because odors were believed to rise through the nose to the brain, the imagined seat of the soul.[73] Odors of sanctity could hence provide the soul with a direct infusion of divine joy and grace.

The divinely sweet scent of the odor of sanctity was deemed to constitute, as was noted in the case of Benoîte, a foretaste of heaven. According to popular belief heaven, and everything associated with it, was pervaded by fragrance.[74] A seventh-century English account of a "near-death" experience brings out this celestial redolence. In this account, the soul of a man presumed dead journeys through the divine realms. He first visits hell with its malodors. He then journeys to:

> a very broad and pleasant plain, full of such a fragrance of growing flowers

that the marvellous sweetness of the scent quickly dispelled the foul stench of the gloomy furnace which had hung around me.[75]

This, he is told by his spirit guide, is the "waiting room" for heaven. The presence of heaven itself is communicated to the soul by a fragrance so wonderful "that the scent which I had thought superlative before, when I savoured it, now seemed to me a very ordinary fragrance."[76] Not being ready yet to enter the celestial kingdom, however, the man must content himself with a whiff of divine delights and return to earth and life.[77]

Angels shared the perfumed nature of heaven. Lydwine's hand was left penetrated with fragrance after having held the hand of an angel. Benoîte experienced angels as birds scenting the air with fragrance. The Blessed Herman of Steinfeld was said to see angels censing his fellow monks during choir, with the amount of incense indicating the monk's degree of sanctity.[78]

Indeed, everything which came from, or came into contact with, the heavenly realms might exhale a celestial scent. In Lydwine's hagiography even the little things of daily life – a rod for drawing back curtains, a cup of beer – are invested with supernatural fragrance thanks to the saint's heavenly intercourse. The touch of an unworthy person, however, might cause an odor of sanctity to disappear – as happened in the cases of Lydwine's rod and Teresa's letter.

Not all accounts of the odor of sanctity were taken seriously by the Church or the public. Skeptics suspected that the aromatics with which bodies were sometimes buried could give rise to false reports of odors of sanctity. In order to dispel such suspicions, accounts of the odor of sanctity frequently emphasize that the saint's body was buried without the use of any spices or herbs, and that the incorruption of the body was verified by physicians.

In fact, reports of encounters with divine beings, ecstasies, and other supernatural phenomena, were disbelieved more often than not by Church officials, particularly after the wonder-working Middle Ages. There were political, as well as religious, reasons for such official disbelief, as the Church wished to retain control over the power of popular devotion.

The most frequent advice given to those who experienced visions and ecstasies was to reject or ignore them as a trick of the Devil or of an overactive imagination. St. Philip Neri, for example, was well known for giving little credence to supposed encounters with the divine, in spite of his own experiences. He reputedly dismissed many presumed cases of demonic possession as imaginary or, in fact, instances of insanity.[79] When one of his penitents wished to tell him of a dream he had had of a fiery hell and a flowery heaven with cherubs throwing down blossoms from treetops, Philip responded brusquely: "He who wishes to go to paradise must be an honest man and a good Christian, and not a believer in dreams."[80]

Hellish scents

The converse of the sweet scents of heaven was the stench of hell. In the twelfth-century St. Hildegard of Bingen (who herself exhaled the odor of sanctity) described hell as "a long and wide marsh filled with filth and vermin of many types and emitting the worst stink," or as a "ditch . . . filled with a fierce fire that gave forth a tremendous stink."[81] Later writers produced more detailed commentaries on the olfactory and other torments of hell. Thus one seventeenth-century Jesuit warned of "the stench of sulfur, the stink of gangrene, the breath of . . . foul-smelling bodies in a completely enclosed sewer" that awaited sinners in hell.[82] According to another account the malodor of hell was so powerful that "the smells of this world . . . would not altogether be as strong smelling as a mere drop of [hell's] burning stench."[83]

As the ruler of hell and the ultimate sinner, the Devil was likewise portrayed as foul-smelling; reeking of sulfur or excrement. Many holy persons faced olfactory assaults from the Devil as part of their struggle for sanctity. The trials of Benoîte of Notre-Dame du Laus in this regard are not unique. In the fifteenth century St. Francesca Romana was similarly tormented by diabolic ill odors until she thought "the whole house [would] perish of suffocation from such a stench."[84] The malodor of the Devil was deemed to have the didactic purpose of communicating the repulsive nature of sin. St. Hildegard stated: "The stink surrounding the uncleanness of the devil is so that the people who had been seduced by him will smell the stink and turn away from their own mistakes."[85] (Hildegard also believed that the Devil induced Eve to sin by infecting her with his poisonous breath.)[86]

As in the case of the Devil, a corrupt odor was thought to arise from sinful humans. Philip Neri is related to have had the following experience of this unholy stench:

> One morning when [Philip] laid his hand on the head of a possessed person, such a pestilential smell was left upon his hand, that though he washed it with soap and different sweet-scented things, the stench lasted for three days, during which he gave his hand to several persons to smell, in order that they might take occasion from it to avoid sin more carefully.[87]

Catherine of Siena, when presented by God with a sniff of human sin was "in such a state that [she] could stand it no more."[88] Christina *Mirabilis*, a twelfth-century Dutch mystic who reputedly died and came back to life, found the sinful smell of humans unendurable after her experience of the divine fragrance. In order to escape their contaminating odors, Christina would hide out in the woods and other solitary places. It was only after being re-baptized that Christina was able to bear the corrupt scent of humans and once more live among them.[89]

The ability to smell human sin is found in a number of hagiographies. The early Christian saint Hilarion was said to have been able "to know from the odor of the body, the clothing, and the things that anyone had touched, what devil or what vice had predominance over him."[90] In the Middle Ages Saint Bernardino stated that "When I enter a city . . . all the good and evil that is done in it comes into my head . . . everything that smells sweet or that stinks."[91] Philip Neri was renowned for his ability to sniff out the sins, particularly the carnal sins, of his fellows. One young man recalled after the saint's death:

> He once told me that I stank, when I had committed a sin of the flesh; and on another occasion he said to me jokingly: "Do you imagine that I do not know your sins? I know them by my nose."[92]

Mary Margaret of the Angels, similarly, was supposedly adroit at "scenting out and discerning hidden sins as a hunting dog puts up game."[93] Another bloodhound of sin, Joseph of Copertino, could reputedly even discover "charms and spells from a distance merely by his sense of smell."[94]

In their sleuthing of sin, these saints were following the model of the Messiah given in the Book of Isaiah (11: 3) which suggests that the Messiah, when he comes, will judge people by his sense of smell, rather than by sight or hearing.[95] Similarly, Benoîte disbelieved a fellow shepherdess's vision of the Virgin, not because she herself did not *see* the Virgin appearing to the shepherdess, but because she did not *smell* her. Smell could thus be presented as the paradigmatic sense for the divination of sin or sanctity.

The stench of sin was particularly associated with non-Christians, who lacked the deodorizing and perfuming sacrament of baptism. In the fifteenth-century *Le Morte d'Arthur*, for example, the corpse of the heathen Sir Corsabrin reeks so abominably that none can abide the stench (while that of the most Christian Sir Lancelot exhales the sweetest savor that his fellows had ever smelled). On the death of Sir Corsabrin, another heathen warrior standing by is told:

> Here have ye seen this day what savour there was when the soul of Sir Corsabrin departed from his body; therefore, we require you to take the holy baptism upon you, that when you die, ye may die in the odour of sanctity.[96]

Certain holy persons with hypersensitive noses found not only sin, but many worldly substances associated with sin, unbearably malodorous. This was particularly the case with food, which seemed to some ascetics to reek of corruption. As noted above, Teresa of Avila had great difficulties overcoming the nausea she felt at the taste and smell of food. The thirteenth-century Mary of Oignes likewise had periods in which "she could not in any way endure even the smell of meat, or of anything cooked, nor of wine."[97]

Worldly perfumes might also seem foul in comparison to the scents of heaven. In the seventeenth century the nun Giovanna Maria della Croce of Roveredo would faint at the smell of perfumes such as musk and amber. Novices who came to the Order wearing scented necklaces (as were common in those redolent times) were obliged to leave them at the convent gate to save Giovanna Maria from an olfactory indisposition. The only perfume the holy nun could tolerate was her own sweet scent of sanctity.[98]

Some saints courted foul earthly odors in order to mortify their sense of smell and be better able to carry out works of charity among the poor and ill. St. Catherine of Genoa, for example, cured herself of the repugnance she felt at the stench emanating from the sores of the ill by rubbing her nose with pus.[99] The Jesuit priest Peter Claver, working among African slaves living and dying in crowded, unsanitary conditions, had to cope with odors so foul they "completely numbed the senses."[100] "Yet such sordid, smelly, fetid and intolerable dwellings were a garden of delights for this evangelical worker," his biographer writes.[101] When Peter Claver himself died, his body exuded a sweet odor "so exuberant that it could be smelt from far away."[102]

While the association of holiness with fragrance and sinfulness with stench is the general rule in Christian hagiography, there are exceptions. Aspiring saints were sometimes warned against sweet scents of diabolic origins:

> [At times] the deceiver maketh a sweet smell to come, as if it were from heaven . . . in order that ye may think that God, on account of your holy life, sends you his grace and his comfort, and so think well of yourselves, and become proud.

(The antidotes for such fiendish fragrance were a sprinkle of holy water and the sign of the cross.)[103]

Furthermore, there are instances of saints being notoriously bad-smelling. In the fifth century the saintly ascetic Simeon Stylites (who gained renown for making his home on top of a pillar) repelled his fellow monks by the stench emanating from his self-inflicted wounds.[104] In the twelfth century the young Alpais of Cudot stank so horribly from illness that her mother refused to feed her. (The Heavenly Mother, however, cured Alpais of her illness, her stench, and also of the need to ever eat again.)[105]

Various rationales were offered for the presence of foul odors in a holy person. In the case of stench arising from illness or wounds, the reason given might be that the person's faith was being tried by God or by Satan. Stench arising from a lack of hygiene was usually interpreted as an instance of the meritorious rejection of sensual luxuries – such as baths and perfumes – on the part of the holy person. In such cases of "holy stench," foul odor served as a potent reminder of the importance of transcending worldly values and prejudices in the pursuit of the divine.[106] Nonetheless, if the saint's body sometimes stank, the saint's *soul* was invariably characterized as fragrant. Indeed, when Simeon Stylites was found dead on top of his pillar, his "true" odor manifested itself: "a scented perfume which, from its sweet smell, made one's heart merry."[107]

Holy virgins and aromatic pain

While in modernity fragrance is often considered a superficial, rather frivolous aspect of existence, in earlier eras it was frequently associated with the most intense of life's experiences. The phenomenon of the odor of sanctity, for example, was coupled both with glorious visions of the Divine and with racking experiences of physical and spiritual pain. As regards the latter, the three holy women profiled above all experienced periods of great suffering throughout their adult lives. St. Teresa, for instance, wrote that she had endured "unbearable pains" which, "according to the physicians, were the worst one can have [in this life]."[108]

The suffering of the saints began with an ascetic way of life. Two of the basic practices of asceticism, celibacy, and fasting, had important olfactory associations. Sexual activity, for example, was considered by many physicians to be a source of malodor.[109] St. Philip Neri, hence, had the support of contemporary medical science when he covered his nose on passing a "woman of bad character," declaring that moral impurity gave off the worst smell in the world.[110] Virginity, by contrast, uncontaminated by the corrupt fluids of coitus, was held to be sweet-scented. Thus, after having experienced the remarkable fragrance of Philip Neri, a penitent did not hesitate to assign its cause to the father's virginal purity.[111] Likewise, it was said of St. Teresa that her virginity helped keep her body from decaying after death: "As Our Lord preserved her from all unchastity during her life, in a perfect state of virginity, so he kept her from all corruption after death."[112]

In a similar way, fasting supposedly decreased bodily corruption and odor by reducing the amount of organic material "decaying" within the body. Saints often found they were compensated for their fasting by receiving divine savors which left them satiated and filled with fragrance.[113] For example, Catherine of Siena, one of the most stringent of fasters, was able to savor the fragrant body and blood of Christ for several days after communion.[114] Of Philip Neri, it was said that:

> In receiving the Lord's Body he had an extraordinary sensible sweetness, making all the gestures which people do who taste something very sweet; for this reason he used to select the largest hosts he could find, that the holy species might remain in him a longer time, and that he might taste the longer that delicious food.[115]

The name itself of Christ was sometimes said to produce a sensible sweetness. The fourteenth-century mystic, Margaret Ebner insisted that when she pressed her heart, where "the sweet name *Jesus Christus* has a special place," she could literally feel a sweet scent and taste rising up into her mouth.[116]

Holy persons might otherwise be fed with celestial odors.[117] Benoîte, for example, found her experience of heavenly perfume so sustaining that it took away her desire for earthly food. Another fasting nun, the fourteenth-century Lukardis of Oberweimar, was said to have been fed by the breath of God. As a result "she was infused with . . . sweetness" and could not eat for three days.[118]

In their celibacy and fasting, and in their consumption of supernatural sweets, saints recreated in their own bodies the incorrupt bodies of Adam and Eve before the Fall. Adam and Eve were sometimes supposed to have been created without organs of generation or of digestion and to have lived on the spiritual fruit and vivifying odors of paradise. (They were also supposed to need little or no sleep, another attribute which some saints, such as Lydwine, replicated.)

Saints, however, were unlike the prelapsarian Adam and Eve in the suffering they experienced within a sinful world. Aside from the aesceticism of their daily lives, holy persons regularly felt the torments of illness and wounds, whether inflicted by God, the Devil, or directly by themselves. Religiously endured, such torments might add to the good odor of a saint. Thus, although Lydwine "from below even to the stomach [was] utterly and wholly putrefied" and needed to be bandaged so that "her holy bowels might not altogether fall out," she still smelled sweet.[119] Pain and illness, moreover, helped preserve the precious fragrance of virginity. One of Lydwine's hagiographers noted of the bedridden woman that: "lest the vanities of the world or the delights of the flesh should violate the seal of virginity, Christ hedged it round with thorns and most grievous pains, that it might not be fit for any nuptial bed."[120]

As a special sign of holy suffering, saints sometimes manifested stigmata, marks on the body resembling the wounds of the crucified Christ. These stigmata (which were occasionally invisible, as happened in the case of Lydwine[121]) were often notable for their fragrance. For example the wounds which St. Veronica of Giuliani (d. 1727) intermittently displayed on her hands, feet, and side "emitted so delicious a fragrance throughout the whole of the convent that this alone was sufficient to inform the nuns whenever the stigmata had been renewed."[122]

While odors of sanctity are recorded of both men and women, they seem to be more frequent and more prominent in the lives, or *Lives*, of women.[123] This is also the case with penitential practices such as severe fasting, saintly illnesses, and stigmata.[124] (One peculiarly feminine phenomenon was the manifestation of a ring-shaped stigma around the ring finger in token of a mystical marriage with Christ. As with other stigmata, such marks of espousal were often fragrant.)[125]

Why this gender difference in expressions of sanctity? Men, it has been argued, who could serve as preachers, missionaries, or Church officials, had the whole world as a field in which to manifest or acquire holiness. Although holy women might engage with the world through such deeds as acts of charity or the foundation and direction of nunneries, they were considerably more limited in their opportunities for religious expression. The body and soul, rather than the world, were a woman's primary field of action.[126] Odors of sanctity (along with other supernatural signs such as stigmata) drew attention to the sacred importance of the work undertaken by women within their restricted sphere.[127]

Popular ideology, furthermore, deemed women to be especially marked for suffering, first of all through childbirth, and second through their supposed closer association with the body and the emotions. Female saints, it was believed, could play a special role in the redemption of the world through undertaking the "womanly" role of suffering and serving as sacrificial victims. Drawing on this theme the nineteenth-century author J.-K. Huysmans wrote in his biography of Lydwine:

God appears to have reserved specially for [women] this vocation of sacrifice. The men who were Saints had a more expansive and more rousing
part to play; they traversed the world, created or reformed orders,
converted idolaters, were active in the eloquence of the pulpit; whilst the
woman, who is not endowed with the sacerdotal character, suffers in silence
on a bed.[128]

For the holy woman herself, however, undergoing this torment was not simply
a matter of "suffering silently on a bed" but of being an actor in a vital cosmic
drama in which she could identify with the crucified Christ and assist in the
expiation of sin and the saving of souls. The odor of sanctity arising from the
tortured body of the saint marked such cosmic suffering as no ordinary pain,
but a sweet sacrifice to God.

Olfactory theology

Odors of sanctity were the subject of considerable theological elaboration in
pre-modernity, as well as being the stuff of legend. The Bible, with its
numerous references to olfaction, provided the primary basis for such elaboration.[129] Indeed, even minor biblical references to odor could inspire an
extended commentary on the theology of smell. John Wycliffe, for example,
made use of the possible etymology of the biblical Jericho as "place of
fragrance" to produce the following statement:

> Jericho is the . . . smelling that men should have, for each man in this life
> should smell Christ and follow him . . . . For this smell is Christ . . . and his
> way is [the] smelling of a full field that God has blessed [Gen 27: 27], and
> this smell had Jacob and other fathers who believed in Christ.[130]

The Song of Songs, with its dialogue between an aromatic bride and a
scented bridegroom, provided a particularly rich source of olfactory imagery for
theological expositions. Using the Song of Songs as his inspiration, John of the
Cross, for instance, wrote an extensive commentary on the olfactory dialogue
between the soul and Christ. The virtues of the soul, said St. John, "are like the
budding flowers of a garden . . . opening under the inspirations of the Holy
Ghost – and [diffusing] most marvellous perfumes in great variety."[131] Christ,
in turn, is a flower exhaling "divine odours, fragrance, grace, and beauty."[132]
The soul and Christ attract each other until they unite, on a symbolic bed of
flowers, in a spiritual marriage.

By making smell a primary model for the interaction between the soul and
God, St. John conveyed the notion of an attraction based on intangible and
invisible virtues, and a pursuit of the divine grounded in faith rather than
knowledge. In saint lore, as we have seen, this olfactory pursuit of the divine
was sometimes presented as quite literal. Farmworkers, attracted by the odor of
sanctity, drop their tools to follow Teresa of Avila's corpse on its journey back

to Alba. Benoîte of Notre-Dame du Laus literally sniffs out the location of her future church.

Similar olfactory expositions can be found in the writings of many mystics and theologians from the Middle Ages to the Enlightenment. One of the most nose-minded was the twelfth-century Bernard of Clairvaux. In one analogy St. Bernard compares the major figures of the Bible to perfumes. Joseph, he writes, "[drew] all the Egyptians to run after him to the odor of his ointments."[133] Samuel's reputation "was diffused abroad like a perfume."[134] Of Job Bernard says:

> What a sweet perfume that man must have radiated throughout the earth . . . . Every action bore its own aroma. Even his own conscience was filled with accumulating perfumes, so that pleasant odors from within tempered the stench of his rotting flesh.[135]

Paul, in turn, is "truly a vessel of myrrh and frankincense and every perfume the merchant knows."[136]

In another analogy, St. Bernard calls the words of the prophets "fragrant belches":

> Moses belched for my profit and there is a goodly fragrance from his belching about the power of creation . . . . Isaiah . . . gave forth the sweet fragrance of mercy and redemption, when he belched . . . . David . . . said "My heart has belched a goodly theme." Do you ask for Jeremiah's belch? I have not forgotten; I was building up to it.[137]

The belch, says Bernard, is an apt metaphor for prophecy because it "burst[s] forth from within, without your will or knowledge," and gives off an odor signifying its nature.[138] The fragrance of the belch of prophecy indicates its spiritual value: "Breathe it in; the sweetness it exudes is . . . sweeter than balsam."[139] "I thank you, Lord Jesus," says Bernard, "who have deigned to allow me at least to sense that odor."[140]

Bernard of Clairvaux does not hesitate to apply olfactory terms to scriptural passages with no ostensible olfactory content. For example, with regard to a reference in Proverbs 5: 16 to streams of water, he assures us that "there is nothing to prevent us seeing them [as] perfume."[141] Bernard also used the language of smell to dismiss criticism of his methods of meditation: "I compared such talk to the scriptural mention of dead flies that spoil the perfumed oil."[142] The saint looked forward to acquiring complete olfactory knowledge of the Bible when he met the authors of Scripture personally in the kingdom to come: "for I shall sense the fragrance of every Psalm . . . every verse, every belch, more fragrant than any perfume."[143]

These examples show how readily and naturally pre-modern theologians were able to incorporate olfactory symbolism into their thoughts. Aside from the writings of particular theologians, however, popular theology linked many of the olfactory references in Scripture and in Christian legend to create an aromatic history of Christianity. This history begins in the fragrant Garden of Eden with its two trees: the Tree of Life and the Tree of the Knowledge of Good and Evil. The Tree of Life was held to be "ineffable for the goodness of its sweet scent" (Apocalypse 8: 3). The Tree of the Knowledge of Good and Evil, by contrast, contained within itself the seeds of corruption, for it was by eating its fruit that Adam and Eve lost their immortality and made themselves prey to the stench and decay of death.

Drawing on ancient imagery,[144] Jacob Boehme wrote a detailed account of the olfactory fall of man. Adam and Eve, said Boehme, lived in a world of perfect fragrance. The Devil, however, tempted the pair with the corrupt forbidden fruit, referred to ironically by Boehme as "sugar." The first humans' consumption of this worldly product brought dung into being, and introduced stench to the Garden of Eden. This unacceptable antithesis of human stench and divine fragrance made it necessary for Adam and Eve to be expelled from Paradise.[145] The Devil's punishment for his misdeed was to eternally dwell in the excremental filth of the world he has corrupted:

> God has prepared such a dwelling-house for him, as Adam lets forth (from the earthly sugar) at the nethermost exit; and that shall be left for him at the corruption of the earth . . . and then that pleasant smell of the stink of sin and abominations . . . shall remain for him, and that sugar he shall eat eternally.[146]

With the birth of Christ a new aromatic history begins. The gifts of myrrh and frankincense offered to Jesus on his birth by the Magi forecast the Son of God's future – the bitterness of myrrh represents death, and the fragrance of frankincense, divine life. The perfume poured over Jesus by Mary Magdalene signifies the homage of humanity to Christ's divinity. Jesus's resurrection of Lazarus from the stench of death indicates that humanity is to be saved from physical and moral corruption. At Jesus's death aromatics once again come to the fore in scripture: his body is buried with spices – aromatic omens of divine immortality.[147]

Popular tradition similarly went beyond Scripture in its olfactory interpretations of the birth, death, and resurrection of Christ. One sixth-century manuscript, the *Transitus Mariae*, for example, indicated that Jesus was conceived through smell. In the account presented there the Holy Spirit penetrates Mary as a sweet odor. Her response to this olfactory grace is to offer up incense to God, thus replying to fragrance with fragrance.[148]

According to medieval legend, the cross on which Jesus was crucified was made from the Tree of the Knowledge of Good and Evil. Christ thus became the new "fruit" of the tree, and one which would bring life, in place of death, to humanity. The cross likewise acquired a pleasant fragrance in keeping with its redeemed status. For this reason supposed relics of the cross were said to exude a scented oil.[149]

The foot of the cross, legend relates, was the burial place of Adam. Christ's perfumed blood fell onto Adam's skull like chrism and baptized him. This cleansed Adam of his sin and enabled him and his descendants to enter, with Christ, into aromatic eternity.[150] Through his crucifixion, therefore, Jesus became a holy perfume "poured out upon men . . . who rotted like animals in their own dung."[151] While for the Devil there is no escape from the dung of sin, humans may once again live in the perfect fragrance of Paradise due to the redemptive odors of Christ.

The olfactory cycle of sacred space and time is hence complete. Scents travel between earth and heaven, and earth and hell, and from the creation of the world to its redemption and back again to its creation.

Spirit and essence

Concepts of sanctity, and of heaven and hell, underwent significant changes from the first centuries of Christianity to the Enlightenment. For example, in early and medieval Christianity, sainthood was closely associated with the performance of miracles and marvels. By the sixteenth century ecstasies had become a more prominent trait of saints.[152] Notions of heaven and hell, in turn, became more elaborate through the centuries, growing from simple visions of paradisiacal gardens and infernal marshes or fires to complex landscapes.[153] Throughout these changes, however, the association of odor with the supernatural remained constant.

Beginning in the Renaissance, theological and folk models of the world were increasingly challenged and influenced by scientific models. Accounts of the odor of sanctity from this period often show an interesting co-opting of scientific methods to examine and support the mystical phenomenon. Physicians, present at the exhumation of a saint, confirmed the fragrant and incorrupt condition of the saint's body, and its defiance of the laws of nature, with all the authority of their status as trained, objective, scientists. Even persons without scientific training were often sufficiently "rational" in their outlook to try and assure that a perceived odor of sanctity could not have arisen from any natural cause. Witness, for example the following declaration by a nun testifying during the canonization process of Francis of Sales in 1627.

> About twenty-five nuns in this monastery, myself included, have at different times since the death of the Blessed [Francis of Sales] had experience of a very sweet and unusual scent in various parts of the monastery. We do not think it could have a natural origin, and we made sure of this by investigating at once whether any sweet-smelling wood or other substance was being burnt in our house; but there was no trace of anything, and so we took it that the Blessed had come to pay us a visit.[154]

The case of St. Teresa provides another example of a scientific approach to the phenomenon of the odor of sanctity and of how this approach could help to enhance the reputation of such phenomena. When the prioress of the convent where St. Teresa's hand is kept suspects that the hand's ability to nullify other scents might be a natural phenomenon, she turns to a physician for the answer. This apparent skepticism is not denounced as a lack of faith, however, but lauded as a sign of a "keen intelligence."[155] The physician to whom the appeal is made declares the phenomenon to be supernatural only after conducting his own olfactory experiment with the hand.

Despite such examples of how belief in the odor of sanctity was able to move with the times, such belief could not ultimately withstand the forces of the new age. The first major blow was the Protestant Reformation. Protestants in general denied the existence of supernatural phenomena such as the odor of sanctity on the grounds that miracles were confined to the biblical era. Apparent cases of the odor of sanctity were consequently denounced as fraudulent.[156]

The concept of the odor of sanctity was further discredited by the scientific rationalism which dominated the critical thought of the eighteenth and nineteenth centuries. This modern rationalism – unlike that of the Renaissance – demanded that there be a natural explanation for every supposedly supernatural occurrence. It was evident from accounts of the odor of sanctity that many people genuinely believed in the phenomenon, and were not simply perpetrating a fraud. The conclusion therefore was that persons who thought they were smelling an odor of sanctity were, in fact, mistakenly attributing a divine origin to a naturally sweet odor of disease or death, or else hallucinating.

St. Teresa of Avila, as the best-known exemplar of the odor of sanctity, provided a favorite example for the rationalist debunkers. Her fragrance was said by physicians who had "made a careful investigation of the subject" to simply be the "peculiar sweet smell" of diabetes.[157] Indeed, according to the reigning ideology of medical materialism, the various aromas reputedly exhaled by saints were nothing more than the olfactory emanations of different pathological conditions. It was said, for example that saints "who [had] long suffered from suppurative conditions emitted an aromatic odor somewhat like strawberries . . . [while] in cases where turpentine had been administered [as a treatment], they diffused an odor of violets."[158]

The implications for the institution of sainthood were even more serious when the experience of an odor of sanctity was held to be an hallucination. Psychologists, in articles such as "Olfactory Hallucinations in the Insane" and "The Pathological Nasal Reflex," linked "olfactory hallucinations" with sexual and mental disorders. There was little doubt in their minds that "smell and taste hallucinations appear to be specially frequent in forms of religious insanity" – such as were supposedly manifested by the saints and their disciples.[159] Through such discourse, the meaning of the odor of sanctity was inverted. It was no longer a sign of physical and spiritual grace, but of physical and spiritual illness, indeed, disgrace.

This reversal of attitude was particularly damaging to the perception and reputation of many holy women, including some of the most prominent female saints, who went from being spiritual superwomen to being diseased hysterics.

Teresa of Avila, for example, was declared to manifest "an instance of organic hysteria as characteristic as possible."[160] Henri Legrand du Saulle wrote in his treatise on hysteria in 1891:

> As far as the hysteric is concerned, finally stripped of her borrowed halo, she has lost her rights to the stake or to canonization. She has the honor today of being a sick person, and depends directly on the [male] doctor.[161]

Such attitudes arose first in Protestant countries, but by the late nineteenth century had influenced Catholic strongholds as well. This is not to say that cases of the odor of sanctity did not and do not still occur.[162] The odor of sanctity, however, is no longer an important phenomenon or concept in mainstream Christian culture. Consequently, the late-twentieth-century biographer of the redolent Benoîte of Notre-Dame du Laus critiques an earlier biographer for his undue attention to smell: "Gaillard goes on at length about the famous perfumes of Laus in his history, making them the basis for a whole olfactory theology of dubious taste."[163]

The decline of belief in the odor of sanctity was due not only to the Enlightenment de-mythologizing of the world, but to a decline in the importance of smell in general. The philosophers of the Enlightenment had concluded that smell was an insignificant, "animal" sense, incapable of serving as a medium for the intellect or the spirit. Condillac thought smell to be the sense that "contribute[s] the least to the operations of the human mind."[164] Kant dismissed smell as the most dispensable of the senses, one which did not even merit aesthetic cultivation.[165]

One theory which has been proposed to account for the decline in importance of smell in modernity is that smell promotes a sense of "merging" with one's environment and fellow beings, whereas in modernity the integrity (and isolation) of the individual is stressed. Thus Horkheimer and Adorno write in *Dialectic of Enlightenment*: "When we see we remain what we are; but when we smell we are taken over by otherness. Hence the sense of smell is considered a disgrace in civilization, the sign of lower social strata, lesser races and base animals."[166]

Whatever the reasons, this deodorizing trend continued (although not without opposition) through the nineteenth and twentieth centuries. On a physical plane, the environment for most people during this time became less redolent as new practices of sanitation and hygiene diminished the presence of both foul and fragrant odors. No more did streets steam with putrid waste. No more were homes strewn with aromatic herbs.[167] As a result, odor slowly evaporated from our modern consciousness. Hell retained its flames and heaven its flowers, but somehow, the scent was no longer there.

If smell has lost much of its traditional meaning for us in the modern West, why was it so important for our forebears? The evident answer to this comes from the ancient association of smell with the spirit. When in the Jewish-Hellenic Book of the Secrets of Enoch (30: 8–9) the various senses are linked with different body parts, smell is assigned to the soul. This association was based on the identification of the sense of smell with the breath, and hence with the life force.

The verse in Isaiah in which the Messiah is said to judge by smell rather than sight or hearing was interpreted by both Christians and Jewish theologians as indicating the high spiritual value of the sense of smell. In the twelfth century Ibn Ezra commented on this passage:

> The ear is sometimes deceived in hearing sounds, which are only imaginary; the eye, too, sees things in motion, which in reality are at rest; the sense of smell alone is not deceived.[168]

Centuries later John Calvin made a similar interpretation:

> We ought to attend, first of all, to the metaphor in the verb *smell*, which means that Christ will be so shrewd that he will not need to learn from what he hears, or from what he sees; for by *smelling* alone he will perceive what would otherwise be unknown.[169]

Therefore, while smell was customarily ranked third in importance of the senses, after sight and hearing, when it came to religion olfaction was sometimes given a certain priority over the other senses.

Smell also had a traditional association with the mind. Odors were thought to have a direct connection with thought by virtue of their traveling up the nose to the brain. The Latin word *sagax* (sagacious), meant both a keen sense of smell and a shrewd mind. The seventh-century theologian, Isidore of Seville, wrote that to smell is to know.[170] According to the twelfth-century Hildegard of Bingen:

> By our *nose* God displays the wisdom that lies like a fragrant sense of order in all works of art, just as we ought to know through our ability to smell whatever wisdom has to arrange.[171]

In the sixteenth century, Girolamo Cardano wrote that a good sense of smell was a sign of a good mind, because both the brain and the sense of smell function according to similar principles.[172] His contemporary Francis of Sales compared the acts of meditation and contemplation to the act of smelling:

> Meditation is like smelling first a carnation, then a rose, then rosemary, thyme, jasmine, orange-flower, each one separately; contemplation is equivalent to smelling the scented liquid distilled from all those flowers put together.[173]

In the seventeenth century the "mystical odorist" Lorenzo Magalotti wrote of the importance of immersing the imagination in a continual bath of perfumes:

from which the imagination, impregnated and satiated, will rise . . . imbuing the soul with vapours purified of every vestige of matter, which when they reach the mind act as a pure spiritual suffumigation, inundating it with so unique a harmony that all plurality is banished.[174]

These examples are sufficient to show that in pre-modern Europe there existed an understanding of olfaction that was fundamentally different from that which reigns today. Yet it is not difficult to see why smell was accorded the status that it had, for the nature of odor renders smell an apt vehicle for expressing concepts about knowledge and divinity. Odor, emanating from the interior of objects, can readily be understood as conveying inner truth and intrinsic worth. The common association of odor with the breath and with the life-force makes smell a source of elemental power, and therefore an appropriate symbol and medium for divine life and power. Odors can strongly attract or repel, rendering them forceful metaphors for moral good and evil. Odors are also ethereal, they cannot be grasped or retained; in their elusiveness they convey a sense of both the mysterious presence and the mysterious absence of God. Finally, odors are ineffable, they transcend our ability to define them through language, as religious experience itself is said to do.

Placed in this context, the traditional belief in the odor of sanctity becomes intelligible as more than mere superstition. The concept of the odor of sanctity is, in fact, the essence of a whole way of life and thought; a rich and rare fragrance, scented with holy pain and mystical rapture, impossible to distill from the secularized values of modernity.

Part II
Gender

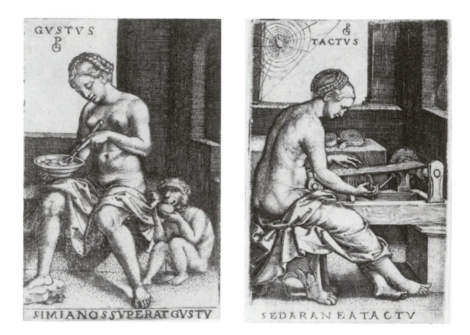

Figure 2 George Pencz, *Tactus* and *Gustus*

Source: From the collection of Den Kongelige Kobberstikssamling, Statens Museum for Kunst, Copenhagen, Denmark.

3 The scented womb and the seminal eye

Embodying gender codes through the senses

The notion that the senses are inflected with gender values has become widespread in cultural studies. The sense of sight, for example, is often considered to be associated with masculinity, and the sense of touch with femininity.[1] One of the foremost exponents of this notion has been the feminist theorist Luce Irigaray. According to Irigaray, men tend to prioritize sight among the senses and employ it as a force of domination (particularly over women).[2] Women, in contrast, are more likely to emphasize the "interactive" and "responsive" sense of touch.[3]

The association between vision and masculinity has proved a particularly productive topic of investigation for scholars, who have examined its implications within such diverse fields as psychoanalysis, art, cinema, and science.[4] While the concept of perception as gendered is a recurrent theme in contemporary thought, however, its roots in Western culture have never been adequately explored. Is theorizing the senses as gendered a strictly modern phenomenon, or does this construction have a social history? How might the senses have been coded by gender in the pre-modern West? Was such earlier gender coding limited to sight and touch – the focus of contemporary scholars – or were other senses also involved? What influence did the gendering of perception have on the lives of women and men?

Exploring the ways in which the senses were gendered in pre-modernity reveals that modern gender paradigms of perception have their origins in a comprehensive symbolic system which invested every aspect of sensory perception – from temperature to taste – with gender values. Much of this system of sensory symbolism was apparently discarded following the rise of the scientific world view in the eighteenth century, when the senses came to be imagined as gender-neutral, objective, data-gathering instruments. Yet traditional gender and sensory codes have continued to influence modern formulations – and critiques – of the relations between the sexes and the senses, from Freud to Irigaray.

The pages that follow examine some of the diverse ways in which gender codes and hierarchies were embodied through the senses in pre-modernity. Traditional gender oppositions within each sensory field are considered, along with those between the senses, such as the classic dualism of sight and touch. This examination uncovers the range of such gender-coding of the senses and brings out some of its social consequences – most dramatically, the role of such "sensotyping" in the witch-hunts. The chapter concludes with one Renaissance woman's "feminist" reworking of the sensory values traditionally assigned to women. Ending on this note underscores that, while pervasive, the gendered sensory order of pre-modernity was not accepted without protest.

Cold women/hot men

According to the traditions and theories of pre-modern Europe, women and men were associated with contrasting sensory qualities, which in turn embodied contrasting cultural values. Within the visual domain, for example, men were generally identified with the "rational" qualities of light and form while women were associated with the "irrational" quality of darkness and the "sensual" quality of color.[5]

The symbolic alliance of masculinity with light and form seemed to fit men for the tasks of enlightening and imposing order on society. The assumed association of femininity with color, in turn, made women suited to play a decorative or seductive social role, while the "darker" side of women made them a potentially disruptive element within society.[6]

One of the most prominent of the sensory differences associated with the sexes in pre-modernity was based on temperature, and contrasted the "coldness" of women with the "heat" of men. Females, in fact, were often deemed to be "half-baked" males, the imperfect result of an insufficient amount of heat during the process of conception and gestation. These ideas about sex differences in temperature were drawn from Aristotle, Galen, and other ancient authorities, and supported by contemporary scholarship and folklore.[7]

The "innate coldness" of women was considered by physicians and philosophers to be the cause of many of the particular characteristics of the female body. Whereas "hot" men quickly burnt up the food they ate, "cold" women, it was thought, stored food as fat, menstrual blood, and milk, enabling them to carry and nourish children. Due to a lack of heat rising up to their heads, women had bodies which were broad at the bottom and narrow at the top. Hot-headed men, by contrast, had narrow hips and broad shoulders. Bald male pates were seen as a sign that men tended to burn up the hair on their heads. Furthermore, whereas heat caused men's organs of generation to be external, insufficient heat, it was reasoned, obliged women's organs of generation to remain within the body.[8]

A variety of sensory qualities were linked with women's essential coldness. For example, women's half-baked status meant that their bodies were "doughy": whiter, softer, and moister than men's. The cold moistness of women was held to predispose them to putridity, making them sources of bodily corruption and foul odors. Coldness also reputedly made women relatively inactive.[9]

All of the different physiological traits which distinguished male and female bodies were deemed to have a corresponding effect on male and female characters. While heat supposedly made men intelligent, courageous, and forthright, cold made women unintelligent, timid, and deceitful. While dryness made men steadfast, moisture was said to make women fickle. Softness, in turn, made women both soft-hearted – compassionate – and soft-minded – incapable of forceful thinking. This supposed softness of women, along with their broad hips and narrow shoulders, were taken as evidence that women were meant to stay at home, leaving hardened, broad-shouldered men to brave the rigors of the world outside.[10]

Women's and men's bodies were thus imagined to present a lexicon of sensory signs, which could be read in accordance with the prevailing gender ideology. Apocryphal stories warned of the sorry fate of women who defied the feminine nature of their bodies. Women who engaged in vigorous physical activity, for example, were said to run the risk of burning up their fat and menstrual blood and becoming masculine in nature. *The Sick Womans Private Looking-Glasse* of 1636 hence warned that "Viragoes and virill women, who through their heat and strength of nature digest and consume all their last nourishment" would end up with changed voices and beards.[11]

It was even thought that such overheating might impel women's internal organs of generation to emerge from the body, and thus be transformed into male genitals. As it was believed that Nature always strives towards (male) perfection, however, there was not thought to be an equivalent danger of men being transformed into women.[12]

The presumed sensory signs of male and femaleness – hot/cold, dry/wet, hard/soft, and so on – were so intimately bound up with gender identity that they were deemed to define both the social and biological roles of men and women. How could women argue for a more independent role in society, when their very bodies spoke against them of their dependent status? As we shall see presently, women who took a feminist position had to redefine the biology of the female body in order to advance an alternative conceptualization of women as intellectual and social beings.[13]

Sensory hierarchies

Along with being assigned different sensory qualities, men and women were associated with different sensory domains. At the most fundamental level, men were associated with the mind and soul and women with the body and senses. "Woman is a symbol of sense, and man, of mind," Philo wrote in the first century.[14] There was no doubt as to which of the sexes had the better part. "Most profitless is it that Mind should listen to Sense-perception, and not Sense-perception to Mind," Philo claimed, "for it is always right that the superior should rule and the inferior be ruled."[15]

While the senses were feminine when opposed to male rationality, however, *within* the domain of the senses, gender distinctions applied as well. In the case of each sense, men would typically be associated with what were thought to be the nobler qualities of that sense, and women with the more ignoble. As regards sight, for example, men were ideally imagined to employ this sense for intellectual activities such as studying, while women made use of it for the sensual ends of acquiring gaudy clothes and admiring themselves in the mirror. Similarly, men were imagined to use the sense of hearing to listen to weighty discourses, while women employed their hearing to attend to frivolous gossip and love talk.

While each sense was considered to have superior and inferior uses, the senses of sight and hearing were held to be more closely associated with the "higher" functions of the mind, and the other senses with the "lower" functions of the body. As regards sight, for example, Philo stated that this sense "first cut and made the road to philosophy," while the fifteenth-century humanist Pico della Mirandola declared that "intellects are eyes, the intelligible truth is light."[16] In accordance with the association of man with mind and woman with body, men tended to be linked with the "rational" senses of sight and hearing, and women with the "corporeal" senses of smell, taste, and touch.

The social consequences of this gendering of the senses were multifold. The fact that the "male" senses of sight and hearing were classified as "distance" senses and the "female" senses of smell, taste, and touch were characterized as "proximity" senses, was interpreted to mean that men were suited for "distance activities," such as traveling and governing, while women were made to stay at home. Furthermore, the customary association of sight and hearing with mental functions, and of smell, taste, and touch with bodily functions, made intellectual endeavors such as the arts and sciences the prerogative of men, while women were in charge of caring for the bodily needs of their families.[17] Witness the list of skills deemed necessary for the "complete woman" in the seventeenth-century *English Housewife*:

> skill in physic, cookery, banqueting-stuff, distillation, perfumes, wool, hemp, flax, dairies, brewing, baking, and all other things belonging to a household.[18]

A "complete" woman evidently had no need to read or write, or to be knowledgeable about anything outside of the day-to-day operations of her home. Her ideal sensory and mental realm was imagined to be that of the taste and smell of dinner, the touch of her husband and children, the scent of the flowers in the garden, the feel of cloth and needle, and the warmth of the hearth.[19]

Gender, class, and race

As was the case with gender ideologies, ideologies of class and race were expressed through a range of sensory metaphors in pre-modernity. The working classes and non-Europeans, for example, were often typed as foul-smelling in relation to the presumed fragrance or odorlessness of middle- and upper-class Europeans.[20] The most important sensory locus for the expression of perceived racial difference was skin color.[21] The "black" skin of the African was frequently put forward as evidence of the African's supposedly "black" nature – deceitful, dirty, and demonic – while the "white" skin of the European was taken as a sign of the qualities of goodness, purity, and grace associated with whiteness.[22] Such symbolism employed potent sensory imagery to give an ostensibly perceptible form to social hierarchies and oppositions.

The sensory symbolisms of gender, class, and race often paralleled each other.[23] The negative values associated with the "darkness" of the foreigner, for example, were similar to those associated with the oft-expressed metaphorical darkness of women and of the lower class. At times, however, sensory symbols were employed in contrasting ways in different social contexts. An example of this can be seen in the shifting usage of temperature symbolism in Western culture. As discussed above, in pre-modernity heat was generally ascribed positive masculine values while cold was ascribed negative feminine values. Beginning in the Renaissance, this system of gender classification by temperature was gradually discarded and an alternative thermal scheme promoted whereby non-Europeans were negatively typed as hot and Europeans positively typed as temperate or cold.[24] The rise of this alternative scheme was influenced by the increasing contact of Europeans with the inhabitants of the "hot" foreign lands of Africa, South America, and India. Within this symbolic system the "heat" of foreign lands and peoples represented (feminine) sensuality, indolence, and anarchy, while the "cold" of Europe and its inhabitants stood for (masculine) rationality, industry, and order.[25]

Such an example indicates that the symbolic classification of social groups relied not just on a static set of ideal values, but developed in response to contemporary concerns. Nonetheless, certain basic symbolic and social oppositions remained fairly constant over long periods of Western history. For example, with minor variations, the working classes and non-Europeans – along with women – were allied with the body and the senses in mainstream Western culture from the Middle Ages to modernity, while upper-class, male Europeans were allied with the mind and reason.

Within the domain of the five senses, the "lower" classes and the "lower" races, like the "lower" sex, were usually associated with the "lower" senses of taste, touch, and smell.[26] As regards the lower class, this association was supported by the manual nature of the labor typical of this class, as well as by the presumed preoccupation of working people with their bellies. Non-Europeans were likewise thought to be more interested in the "animal" satisfactions provided by smell, touch, and taste than in the cultivation of the "spiritual" pleasures of sight and hearing.[27] An eighteenth-century English "authority" on African slaves, for example, stated that Africans' "faculties of smell are truly bestial, nor less their commerce with the other sexes; in these acts they are as libidinous and shameless as monkeys."[28] In the early nineteenth century the natural historian Lorenz Oken imagined a sensory hierarchy of racial types, with the European "eye-man" at the top, followed by the Asian "ear-man," the Native American "nose-man," the Melanesian "tongue-man," and the African "skin-man."[29]

In traditional European culture, gender and class (or estate) constituted the major social divisions. The interrelations of the various categories of these divisions inflected the ascription of standard social hierarchies of perception. An upper-class woman, although linked with the "lower" senses with respect to men of her own class, might in some ways represent the "higher" senses in relation to a working-class man.[30] A lady, for instance, would likely possess the visual skills of reading and writing denied the male laborer on her estate.[31] A craftsman, in turn, might take up a vocation with links to the female sensory and social domain, such as that of weaver, and still assert his masculinity through the public (and hence visual) nature of his work.[32]

While the vocations open to lower-class men differed significantly from those deemed appropriate for upper-class men, women of all classes were expected to busy themselves with domestic duties.[33] A lady *might* read a book while her illiterate maids did the cooking and sewing, but it was considered more suitable for her to spend her time in handiwork, such as spinning or embroidery. Juan Luís Vives wrote in his popular *Formation of the Christian Woman* of 1523 that even princesses and queens should not "be ignorant of those arts which employ the hands."[34] Variations in social roles due to class position could produce considerable variations within the symbolic sensory realm of men – from the "tactility" of the manual laborer to the "visuality" of the scholar – but were not imagined to greatly alter the scope of the feminine sensory domain.

The astrology of gender

According to the astrological lore which pervaded pre-modern thought, gender and sensory categories were not simply biological and social constructions, but were set in the stars, part of the immutable order of the universe. Of the seven heavenly bodies classified as planets, two – the Moon and Venus – were deemed to be female, and four – the Sun, Saturn, Jupiter, and Mars – were deemed male. Mercury was nominally male but was considered able to change genders, making it a hermaphrodite planet.[35] The four male planets customarily occupied the upper rank of the planetary hierarchy, while Mercury, the Moon, and Venus were situated in the lower rank. As the first-century astrologer Manilius put it: "Saturn, Jupiter, Mars, and the Sun, and beneath them Mercury performing its flight between Venus and the Moon."[36] Each planet was also linked with one of the traditional "ages of man." The Moon, Mercury, and Venus were associated with the periods of childhood and youth, while the Sun, Mars, Jupiter, and Saturn governed the ages of maturity.[37]

In keeping with their female gender, the Moon and Venus were generally considered to be cold and moist. They were associated with the sea, with menstruation and reproduction, and, in the case of the Moon, with lunacy. Hermaphrodite Mercury was also imagined to be predominantly moist in nature, although able to vary in wetness and temperature. It was linked with clouds and vapor, and with the fluidity of language. The most typically masculine of the planets, the Sun and Mars, were, by contrast, hot and dry, the quintessential male qualities.[38] In his work *The Planets*, the sixteenth-century philosopher Marsilio Ficino contrasted, as planetary and gender opposites, the "moist sensuality" of the female Venus with the "dry consciousness" of the male Sun.[39]

As regards the sensory faculties of the planets, the Sun was unfailingly associated with sight. Hearing, in turn, was usually linked with Mars. To Mercury fell the pseudo-sense of speech. The female planets, the Moon and Venus, were customarily associated with taste and smell. Touch, as a medium of seduction, might be linked with either the Moon or Venus, or, as a medium of domination, with Mars or Jupiter. In the second century Ptolemy associated the Sun with sight, Mars with the left ear, Saturn with the right ear, Jupiter with touch, Mercury with speech, the Moon with taste, and Venus with smell.[40] In the sixteenth century Agrippa von Nettesheim linked the Sun with sight, Mars with hearing, Mercury with taste, the Moon with touch, and Venus with smell. He dealt with the two planets left over, Jupiter and Saturn, by assigning common sense to the former and imagination to the latter.[41]

While there was some variation in the matching of senses with planets, the overall effect was to reinforce sensory and gender hierarchies. The masculine planets were generally accorded the higher senses of sight and hearing, the senses of the bright, sonorous external world and of rationality. The feminine planets were usually accorded the lower senses of touch, smell, and taste, the senses of the mysterious, corporeal world within: the obscure tremors of love, the whiff of secret perfumes, the dark juices of flavor.[42]

The scented womb

Taste, as a female sense, was customarily traced back to Eve, who brought sin into Paradise by tasting the forbidden fruit. When in a medieval French play, *Jeu d'Adam*, the serpent tells Eve that the forbidden fruit contains "all knowledge," the first woman asks in response: "What does it taste like?"[43] The intellectual and spiritual consequences of consuming the fruit escape Eve. In keeping with her sensual nature, she is only interested in a good feed.

If the femininity of taste was rooted in biblical lore, the association of women with smell had more pagan origins. One source of this association was the suggestion found in classical philosophy that the uterus is a kind of animal, endowed with powers of movement and its own sense of smell.[44] While this notion was rejected by many physicians, it continued to have a strong influence on popular concepts of the nature of women's bodies. For example, in the sixteenth century François Rabelais (who was a physician as well as a satirist) was still describing the womb as sensitive to odors.[45]

The reputed olfactory powers of the womb played a role in making incense a common treatment for gynecological ailments.[46] In the case of a womb deemed to be displacing itself upwards and thereby causing hysteria and fainting, foul scents would be administered to the woman's nose and sweet scents to the vagina. This treatment was meant to encourage the keen-scented womb to travel away from the foul odors and towards the fragrance, back down to its accustomed site. A reverse treatment would be employed for a descended womb.[47] Fumigation with incense could also be used by women to facilitate conception by attracting the womb downwards. One fifteenth-century physician warned, however, that "these women should afterwards breathe in spices through the nose so that once the sperm has been taken in, the womb rise again."[48]

Women were not only associated with smell because of their possession of an extra, internal, nose, so to speak, but also because they were held to be especially productive of odors. As mentioned above, women's cold moistness was thought to predispose the female body to putridity.[49] The center of this putridity was the womb, which, according to prevailing medical theories, produced not only the odorous fluids of menstruation and childbirth, but also pathogenic vapors within the body.[50]

The association of women with malodor was a commonplace both of medical science and of popular culture. Allusions to this association can be found in the works of writers from the fourteenth-century Boccaccio, who stated that women were more foul than pigs, to the eighteenth-century Swift, who declared women to be "gaudy tulips rais'd from Dung."[51] For Swift, even the traditionally ambrosiacal Venus was malodorous. Referring to the goddess's birth from the sea, the satirist pondered over whether malodor was cause enough for the rejection of love: "Should I the Queen of Love refus/Because she rose from stinking Ooze?"[52]

Nonetheless, not all was foul with women. Virginal maidens tended to be associated with pristine fragrance – what the Middle Ages would call a "precious balsam in a fragile glass" and the nineteenth century, "that wondrous aroma of precious delicacy, which is the greatest treasure of womanhood."[53] In their role as exemplars of beauty, women were also deemed seductively sweet by popular culture. In this guise women became the "perfumed sex," enchanted gardens captivating men with their bewitching scents.[54] This symbolism is exemplified by Robert Herrick in his poem, "Upon Julia's Sweat":

> Wo'd ye oyle of Blossomes get?
> Take it from my Julia's Sweat:
> Oyl of Lillies, and of Spike,
> From her moysture take the like:
> Let her breath, or let her blow,
> All rich spices thence will flow.[55]

Through the alchemy of male desire female moisture could be transformed into perfume.

Ultimately, however, olfactory redemption for womankind could come only from God. In the case of the Virgin Mary, the womb became a vessel of divine sweetness through bearing the heavenly fruit of the Son of God. While unable to match the unique bodily purity of the Virgin, holy women might successfully empty their bodies of ill odor and infuse them with sacred fragrance. Through practices of severe fasting, menstruation (and even excretion) could be suppressed.

The piety of the holy faster might, in turn, be signaled by the emission of super-natural odors of sanctity. The fasting nun Lutgard (d. 1246), for example, was said to have started exuding aromatic fluids after she stopped menstruating.[56] In such cases female moisture was imagined to have been literally changed into perfume by the metamorphosis of the corrupt female body into the pristine body of the saint.

Menstruation might otherwise seemingly be superseded in holy women by the periodic bleeding of stigmata, embodied marks of the wounds of Christ. In such occurrences (which are virtually unique to women in saint lore)[57] the stigmata impressed on the saintly female body would open up and bleed on certain holy days, for example, every Friday. This "blood of Christ" was frequently fragrant. "It is worthy of remark," writes the biographer of the seventeenth-century stigmatic St. Veronica Giuliani, "that when the above-mentioned wounds were open, they emitted so delicious a fragrance throughout the whole of the convent that this alone was sufficient to inform the nuns whenever the stigmata had been renewed."[58] In such cases women were able to replace or counteract their "foul" female bleeding with fragrant bleeding based on the holiest of male models: Jesus Christ.

The seminal eye

The association of men with sight, like that of women with smell, was grounded in cosmology, medicine, and popular culture. We have seen how sight was linked with the "male" sun in cosmology. A direct relationship was also posited between sight and the male organs of generation: both were held to have a "seminal nature," making use of similar fluids in their operations. Aristotle, for example, wrote in *Generation of Animals* that "of all the regions in the head the eyes are the most seminal."[59] The notion of the eye as seminal was reinforced by the widespread belief that the eyes did not passively receive visual images, but actively emitted rays which came into contact with the perceived object.[60]

Due to the sharing of seminal fluid between the eyes and the sexual organs, castration, which reduced the amount of fluid in circulation, was presumed to lead to poor sight.[61] Similarly, excessive coitus was believed to harm the sight by depleting the body of seminal fluid. As semen was often considered to be cerebral in origin, the brain was thought to be adversely affected by excessive coitus as well. Albertus Magnus relates an account of a monk who died after satisfying his lust "seventy times before matins." A subsequent autopsy found that the monk's brain had shrunk and his eyes were destroyed. This was taken as proof that semen was shared with both the brain and eyes.[62]

Women, who were symbolically castrated or incomplete men, could be imag-ined as exhibiting the weak sight and intelligence attributed to eunuchs. The hidden, interior position of the female organs of generation did, indeed, seem to suggest to physicians and philosophers that women, like their characteristic organs, were in an inherent state of darkness. In one revealing passage, Galen compared the female reproductive organs to the blind, underdeveloped eyes of moles.[63] Following this simile, the male genitals, external and exposed to the light, would be like fully developed, sighted eyes.

A number of cultural practices supported the association of women with sightlessness. For example, women were expected to keep their eyes downcast and refrain from looking others in the face.[64] Their customary enclosure within the family home[65] further restricted women's visual field. In "A Rule for Women to Brynge Up Their Daughters" (1566) mothers were advised to forcibly prevent their daughters from transgressing the bounds of their physical and visual confinement:

> If they wyll go or gad abrode,
> Their legges let broken bee:
> Put out their eyes if they wyll looke
> Or gase undecentyle.[66]

Moreover, women, like persons who were blind, were believed to need guidance and to be unfit for guiding others. John Knox made use of this popular analogy in *The First Blast of the Trumpet Against the Monstrous Regiment of Women* of 1558:

> For who can deny but it repugneth nature that the blind shall be appointed to lead and conduct such as do see . . . . And such be all women compared unto man in bearing of authority. For their sight in civil regiment is but blindness.[67]

Not only were women perceived as lacking in vision, however, they were also considered to threaten the visual power of men. The case of the lustful monk above is a striking example of a man literally having his eyes destroyed (along with his brain and his life) by succumbing to a woman. According to Aristotle "those who overfrequently indulge in [coitus] have sunken eyes."[68] Such notions suggested that the eyes withdrew into the body to match the corporeal envelopment of the sexual organs during intercourse (at the same time becoming like the internal, "underdeveloped," reproductive organs of women). Even simply desiring a woman was thought sufficient to weaken a man's vision and turn a clear-sighted leader into a blind, brainless follower. Thus, in the thirteenth century Richard de Fournival wrote: "Love seizes the man in those first encounters [with a woman] through his eyes, and through his eyes man loses his brain."[69]

The biblical story of Samson and Delilah provided another example of how a woman's seductiveness might result in a man's blindness. In this story Delilah seduces Samson into revealing the secret of his great strength – his hair. While Samson is asleep in her lap, Delilah disempowers him by having his head shaved, and then delivers him into the hands of the Philistines, who blind him. The blind Samson is put to work as a slave, but takes revenge on the Philistines by knocking over the pillars of the building in which they have gathered, bringing the roof down over their heads (Judges 13–16).

In Milton's version of the story, *Samson Agonistes*, "Dalila" is an archetypal seductress; both heavily perfumed and keen-scented.[70] Samson is first seduced by Dalila's "fair fallacious looks," and then disarmed by the seductress's touch, which robs him of his virile power and allows him to be blinded:

> . . . into the snare I fell
> Of fair fallacious looks, venereal trains,
> Softened with pleasure and voluptuous life;
> At length to lay my head and hallowed pledge
> Of all my strength in the lascivious lap
> Of a deceitful concubine . . .[71]

After the betrayal has taken place and Samson has been blinded, Dalila visits her husband in his cell and offers to have him removed to her home. She tells Samson:

> . . . though sight be lost,
> Life yet hath many solaces, enjoyed
> Where other senses want not their delights,
> At home, in leisure and domestic ease,
> Exempt from many a care and chance, to which
> Eyesight exposes daily men abroad.[72]

Dalila is offering the "effeminately vanquished" Samson the option of living like a woman, visually restricted, but able to enjoy the lesser senses within the confines of the home. Samson, however, refuses, indicating that although he has lost his physical sight through his love for Dalila, he has regained the "sight of reason" and will no longer place himself in her power. Instead of metaphorically burying himself in the life of the lower senses, Samson chooses to avenge his male honor and his lost sight by literally burying the Philistines – and himself – under the rubble of the toppled Philistine edifice.

Male visuality was thus understood to be symbolically, and even physiologically (since it was thought sight could be harmed by sexual relations), opposed to female sensuality – epitomized by the sense of touch. This opposition between sight and sensuality was at times conceptualized in such extreme terms that sight seemed to be placed outside of the realm of the senses altogether, becoming a mental faculty. (Philo, for example, stated that [feminine] sense-perception is blind, being irrational, and that true sight is conferred by the [masculine] mind.)[73]

If sight was in some ways considered separate from sensuality, it was nonetheless highly vulnerable to it. This was thought to be particularly true when the visual power of a man came up against the sensual power of a woman. As the story of Samson and Delilah made clear, unless kept in a position of subjection, women, with their sensory wiles, had the ability to dethrone men, and male visuality, from their position at the top of the gender and sensory hierarchy.

Speech: the hermaphrodite sense

Speech, which (as a seemingly natural faculty) was occasionally classed among the senses, was ambivalent in its gender associations. Properly, speech was the prerogative of men, while women remained silent.[74] In practice, however, it was a commonplace that women were much more given to talking than men.[75] Milton, for example, in a typical description of woman's verbosity, portrays Dalila as using an onslaught of words to wear down Samson's resistance:

> With blandished parleys, feminine assaults,
> Tongue batteries, she surceased not day nor night.[76]

In *The Art of Courtly Love* André le Chapelain advised men that all women are "loud-mouthed" and will "keep up a clamor all day like a barking dog."[77]

As regards its position in the cosmic sensorium, according to which each planet governed a sense, speech was usually assigned to Mercury, the planet-god of communication. This was in keeping with the ambivalent gender status of speech, for, as noted above, Mercury was believed able to change sex from male to female.

The attribution of talkativeness to women was supported by the association made between speech and the feminine quality of fluidity. Speech was imagined to flow like water, and, in the case of women, like an unending stream. Women gushed with words the way they gushed with body fluids. In fact, feminine volubility was held by some to arise from a disorder of that fountain of female fluidity, the uterus. Uterine vapors, it was said, rose up to the brain where they stimulated women into an unnatural loquacity.[78] Thus in one medieval French farce, a man considers administering an enema to his garrulous wife in order to relieve the pressure caused by interior "smoke" on her brain, and thus stem her excessive speech.[79]

In relation to men, women were linked with two kinds of speech: seductive speech and nagging. The first was held to have its prototype in Eve's tempting of Adam with the forbidden fruit. The biblical prohibition on women preaching or teaching (1 Tim 2: 11–12) was said to be a response to this sinful speech by Eve.[80] The second association, nagging, was given a number of fanciful origins. One story stated that Eve had been created out of the tail of a dog, which explained why women "bark" at their husbands.[81]

The nag did not wheedle and flatter, as the seductress did; she complained, demanded, and harangued. So fierce was the nag's tongue that even the (male) Devil was said to stand in awe of it. In one German play Satan tells a scold that "Your poisonous, evil tongue makes my hair stand on end."[82] In a sixteenth-century English play, *The Devil and his Dame*, the Devil is able to make a dumb woman speak, but unable to make her silent again: "The Devil cannot tye a woman's tongue."[83]

By aggressively appropriating the male medium of speech, the nag was imagined to become unpleasantly masculinized in her traits. Instead of being soft and mild, in keeping with her feminine nature, the nag was "as sharp as a thystyll/as rugh as a brere [briar]."[84] Instead of being sweet, the nag was "fulle sowre" with "a galon of gall."[85] A woman's transformation from a seductress to a nag was often satirically stated to be virtually inevitable following marriage. "Soft, modest, meek, demure/Once joined the contrary she proves, a thorn," writes Milton of women in *Samson*.[86] The title character of *Epicoene or The Silent Woman* (1609) by Ben Jonson is a quiet-spoken woman who turns into a mannish loudmouth after marriage, whereupon she is revealed to actually be a man in disguise.[87]

Perhaps the most telling account of male attitudes to women's speech can be found in the English play *Lingua* of 1607. In this allegory of the senses, the female Lingua – Speech – decides that she wants to be counted as a sense. The male Auditus – Hearing – huffily responds that:

> We were never accounted more than five.
> Yet you, forsooth, an idle prating dame,
> Would fain increase the number, and upstart
> To our high seats, decking your babbling self
> With usurp'd titles of our dignity.[88]

For her presumption Lingua is accused of being a witch and a whore, of criticizing men in authority, and of lending wives "weapons to fight against their husbands."[89]

In the end Common Sense, who is judging the dispute, rules that Speech is not a sense, except in the case of women:

> all women for your sake shall have six senses – that is seeing, hearing, tasting, smelling, touching, and the last and feminine sense, the sense of speaking.[90]

This classification of speech as a sense peculiar to women emphasizes the association made between verbosity and femininity. Yet, as is made clear throughout the play and in similar treatments of women's speech, while women may be full of talk, they have nothing worthwhile to say. Their speech is either meaningless babble, deceitful lies, or vindictive criticism. In almost all cases it would be better left unsaid.[91] In women, therefore, the feminine sense of speech is but a travesty of rational male discourse and a transgression of the truly womanly condition of silence.

The sensory bestiary

In *Lingua* each sense is depicted as having an army of animals at its command.

Sight has an army of eagles and other sharp-sighted birds; Hearing has an army of bulls and stags; Smell, of dogs and vultures; Touch, of tortoises, spiders, and hedgehogs; and Taste, of apes.[92] This fanciful scenario drew on a long-standing tradition in which each sense was represented by certain animals deemed to have exceptional acuity in that sense. Thus eagles stood for sight because of their supposed sharp vision, while vultures represented smell because of their presumed keen sense of smell. While there was some variation in the animals held to represent the different senses, the ones listed in *Lingua* were standard.[93]

Although seemingly chosen solely for their acuity in a particular sense, the zoological emblems of the senses were invested with powerful symbolic values, which inevitably expressed and shaped the way in which the various senses were conceptualized. As different senses and animals also had distinct gender connotations, the sensory bestiary was at the same time a menagerie of gender stereotypes.[94]

Several animals were occasionally used to represent one particular sense, with the values associated with that sense shifting according to the animal employed. Hearing, for example, was sometimes symbolized by a mole, an animal presumed to have an enhanced sense of hearing because of its blindness and associated with femininity.[95] When employed as an emblem of hearing the mole signified the opposition between the worlds of sight and sound. In this case hearing took on feminine connotations of sightlessness and darkness. The more customary zoological symbols of hearing, however, were the stag and the bull (as in *Lingua*), animals which emphasized the powerful, masculine, nature of audition.[96]

Animals associated with masculinity, such as the eagle, the bull, and the stag, were typically used to symbolize the two higher senses of sight and hearing.[97] These allegorical animals often carried positive connotations of superiority and morality. The eagle and the stag stood for heavenly aspiration. The bull was a symbol both of sexual potency and sexual temperance (the latter due to the belief that the bull never had relations with a pregnant cow).[98]

The lower senses of smell, touch, and taste, on the other hand, were usually represented by animals with feminine associations, such as vultures, spiders, and apes. These animals often carried negative connotations of inferiority and immorality. Smell, for instance, was represented by the dog and the vulture, animals thought to have a keen sense of smell and associated with the foul odors of carrion. The ideal dog, like the ideal woman, was the guardian of the home, servile and unconditionally devoted to its master.[99] Less ideally, dogs were promiscuous, deceitful, and scavengers, characteristics which were extended to "wanton" women.[100] This motif of woman as dog was exemplified by the legend which claimed the first woman was created from the tail of a dog who had run off with Adam's rib.[101] Hence, while dogs might be characterized as either male or female in bestiary lore, they were understood to have a particular association with femininity.

The vulture, in turn, was conceptualized as a kind of harpy: female, filthy, rapacious, and amoral. The vulture stood in opposition to the eagle, the emblem of sight, in zoological symbolism.[102] From antiquity, the eagle was associated with the (masculine) upper world, light, heat, dryness, and bodily renewal. In old age the eagle was said to fly up to the sun to renew its sense of sight. As a carrion-eater, however, the vulture was associated with the (feminine) underworld, darkness, coldness, wetness, and bodily corruption. While the eagle was flying up to heaven on a visionary quest, the vulture was sniffing out its decaying prey below. The vulture, furthermore, was noted for picking out the eyes of its prey, a trait suggestive of its anti-visual nature.[103] The opposition between these two birds paralleled that between the keen-sighted, hot, dry male and the strong-scented, cold, wet female in gender ideology.

The sense of touch was commonly represented by the tortoise and the spider.[104] The tortoise was thought to have an acute sense of touch because of its tendency to retreat into its shell at the least contact. Forever bound to its shell, the tortoise suggested the quintessential homebody, the woman who never escapes the walls of her house. Using a similar analogy based on the snail, Martin Luther wrote:

> Just as the snail carries its house with it, so the wife should stay at home and look after the affairs of the household, as one who has been deprived of the ability of administering those affairs that are outside and that concern the state.[105]

The tortoise further symbolized wet sensuality and was linked to the goddess of love, Venus.

Like the tortoise, the spider reputedly had great tactile sensitivity:

> For as a subtle spider, closely sitting
> In centre of her web that spreadeth round,
> If the least fly but touch the smallest thread,
> She feels it instantly . . . [106]

The spider represented woman in her traditional role of spinner and homemaker. At the same time, the spider was portrayed as an evil predator, trapping and sucking out the lifeblood of its prey. In this guise the spider served as a symbol of the seductress, who was considered to behave in a similar fashion towards men.

Taste, in, turn, was represented by the ape, due to the supposed craving of that animal for tasty foods. Apes were often typed as feminine. H.W. Janson notes in *Apes and Ape Lore* that: "the Middle Ages associated the ape almost exclusively with female qualities."[107] The ape was understood to signify a degenerate human, manifesting all of the worst human vices, from gluttony and lechery, to pride, sloth, and folly. This image of the ape as a degenerate human echoed the classical notion of woman as an imperfect man.[108] As a symbol of the sense through which Eve was induced to commit the original sin, the ape was also linked with the first woman.[109]

As we have seen, the majority of the standard zoological emblems of the higher senses were associated with predominantly positive "masculine" values, while the majority of those of the lower senses were linked to predominantly negative "feminine" values.[110] The eagle with its heavenly gaze and the stag with its ears pricked to hear the divine word stand in opposition to the vulture with its scent for death and the ape with its sinful pursuit of taste. The sexual temperance of the bull contrasts with the deadly seduction of the spider. The free-ranging flight of the eagle (and of sight) is matched against the slow, cumbersome gait of the tortoise (and of touch).

Aside from the animals customarily employed to represent the five senses, a great many creatures were linked with sensory and gender characteristics in the bestiaries and in folklore. The magpie, for example, could be a symbol of chattering feminine speech, the siren a symbol of seductive feminine speech. The mole, as we have seen, could represent feminine "blindness."

The basilisk, a mythical combination of bird and snake believed to kill with its glance, was employed to signify the dangerous nature of feminine visuality.[111] Corrupt women, wrote Vives in *The Formation of the Christian Woman* "are basilisks . . . who . . . exude poison through their sharp eyes and kill with their sight alone."[112] Interestingly, as implied in this quote and elaborated elsewhere, the fatal ingredient in the basilisk's gaze was thought to be a venomous odor which the animal emitted through its eyes.[113] In a similar fashion, menstruating women were believed to emit a harmful odor through their eyes.[114] This merging of the visual and the olfactory suggests that female sight, like that of the basilisk, had as much to do with smell as with "true" sight.[115]

The eclectic nature of the folklore and symbolism concerning animals in the pre-modern West makes it impossible to fit all of this material into any one scheme of gender, sensory, and moral oppositions. An animal presented as female in one account may be presented as male in another. A "low" animal may be associated with a "high" sense. A "bad" trait may be assigned to a "good" animal. To some extent this expresses the ambivalence surrounding sensory and gender categories: no sense or sex was unequivocally "good" or "bad." To some extent it reflects the fact that zoological lore was a hodge-podge of pseudo-biological observations, classical traditions, popular tropes, and Christian didacticism, rather than a uniform system of classification.

If any interpretation of the gender and sensory symbolism of the bestiaries ends up being somewhat blurred by variations in the material, however, most of the oppositions of sense and sex given above were frequently expressed and widely disseminated from the Middle Ages to the Enlightenment.[116] By presenting animals – symbolic counterparts of humans – as emblematic of sensory and gender traits, the bestiaries made explicit and implicit statements about the nature of human sensory and gender roles in a picturesque and memorable fashion.

Witch-hunts of the senses

The witch-hunters of the fifteenth, sixteenth, and seventeenth centuries took the traditional negative stereotypes of woman's sensory traits and practices and made of them a diabolic female sensorium in which each of the senses was dedicated to evil. The classic witch-hunting manual, the fifteenth-century *Malleus Malleficarum*, supported such demonization of the senses with a quote from St. Augustine:

> [The devil] places himself in figures, he adapts himself to colours, he attaches himself to sounds, he lurks in angry and wrongful conversation, he abides in smells, he impregnates with flavours and fills with certain exhalations all the channels of the understanding.[117]

While men could be accused of witchcraft as well as women, the figure of the witch was nonetheless typically female, as were the people brought to trial as witches.[118]

The diabolic sensorium of the witch began with taste. Eve first rendered this sense a medium of sin by craving the forbidden fruit. With Eve providing the model, women were often typed as gluttons in popular culture. André Le Chapelain wrote in the late twelfth century:

> Woman is . . . such a slave to her belly that there is nothing she would be ashamed to assent to if she were assured of a fine meal, and no matter how much she has she never has any hope that she can satisfy her appetite when she is hungry . . . . We can detect all these qualities in Eve, the first woman, who . . . was not afraid to eat the forbidden fruit.[119]

In order to atone for the feminine failing of sinful taste, virtuous women were expected to lead lives of gustatory restraint. Holy women were renowned for their rigorous fasts, and even ordinary women were expected to discipline their tastes and appetites.[120]

Witches compounded the sin of Eve by indulging their sense of taste, even going so far as to eat the "forbidden fruit" of human flesh. While holy women had visions in which they spurned devils offering them food,[121] witches accepted the devil and took the food. One woman accused of witchcraft in 1432, for example, confessed that she had "begged [the Devil] for food, when he spread a quantity of food on the grass . . . she ate some . . . ."[122]

Eve's gustatory offense consisted not only in having a taste for forbidden fruit herself, but also of passing the fruit along to Adam. This act was the prototype of the venomous practices of the witch, who perverted her feminine role of nourisher by poisoning under the guise of feeding.[123] As a woman, the witch furthermore had control over the potent art of cookery. Cooking was regarded as a quasi-alchemical process, by means of which it was possible to effect transformations in the world outside. In medieval Switzerland, for instance, peasant women were said to cause storms by boiling foul herbs in a pot and then exposing the pot to the sun.[124] Skilled in manipulating the transformational powers of cooking, the witch literally brewed up storms and mischief in her kitchen pots.[125]

Allied to taste through its orality, speech exhibited similar vices when employed by the witch. Instead of holding her tongue and "fasting" from speech, as was thought fitting for a woman, the witch gave free expression to her thoughts and emotions.[126] The witch's speech was an incitement to sin, captivating but deadly. Referring to the witch in her role as seductress, the authors of the *Malleus* wrote:

> Let us consider another property of [the witch], the voice. For as she is a liar by nature, so in her speech she stings while she delights us. Wherefore her voice is like the song of the Sirens, who with their sweet melody entice the passers-by and kill them.[127]

With her seductive words and lies, incantations and curses, the witch stirred up trouble through her speech, just as she did with the evil ingredients of her cauldron.[128]

As with her other senses, the witch's hearing was said to be uncontrolled and deviant. Women in general were deemed to require severe restrictions on their hearing, for the world abounded in discourse which was unsuited for feminine ears, but which women were driven by curiosity to hear. Women's hearing was imagined to be especially vulnerable to the speech of demons. The Church father Tertullian wrote that "evil angels were ever lurking about ready to assail even married women, much more virgins, through their ears."[129] The witch, defying the auditory rules for her sex, kept her ears open to all manner of human and demonic discourse, and was deaf only to the admonishments of her betters, and to the word of God.

With regard to smell, witches were imagined to have a keen olfactory sense. Witches dabbled in odors as their stock in trade, from the scents of aromatic herbs to the smoke of burning spices to the vapors of stewing body parts. Witches themselves – insofar as they were not appearing as beautiful, fragrant maidens in order to seduce men – were imagined to emit foul, poisonous odors:[130]

> [Witches] exhale a stench from the mouth, the whole body, which is communicated to their garments and fills their houses and the vicinity and infects those who approach.[131]

The foul odor of the witch was an intensified form of the reek of "corrupt" womanhood. "Women are . . . monthly filled full of superfluous humours," the sixteenth-century *Discoverie of Witchcraft* stated, "whereof spring vapours, and are carried up, and conveyed through the nostrils and mouth, etc., to the bewitching of whatsoever it meet."[132]

The touch of the witch was thought to inflame men with sinful desire. "All witchcraft comes from carnal lust," declared the *Malleus Maleficarum*, adding that the "mouth of the womb" is insatiable.[133] Touch could also be used by witches as a means of inflicting suffering and death. In the sixteenth century Nicholas Rémy wrote in *Demonolatry* that "[the] touch of a witch is noxious and fatal."[134] Witches were infamous for creating wax models of their victims, which they then burnt or pierced so that the persons represented might feel similar pains in their bodies. When witches themselves were tortured or burnt however, the devil was believed to render them impervious to pain. In fact, one identifying mark of a witch was supposed to be a spot on her body where she felt no pain when pricked with a pin.

The remaining sense in the witch's sensorium is sight. While sight was traditionally located at the top of the sensory hierarchy and associated with reason, the demonic and feminine form of vision employed by the witch was perceived as being more akin to the lower senses and the emotions. In Ireland certain witches were known as "eyebiters" for their imagined ability to injure people through their sight.[135] More generally, witches' sight was conceptualized as a form of venom transmitted through the eyes, and was hence associated with the supposedly turbid sight of the menstruous woman. The fact that it was usually women past the age of child-bearing who were accused of possessing an "evil eye" was not thought to disprove this theory. It was rather explained that, as older women no longer had the natural outlet of menstruation for their corrupt internal fluids, the amount of venom issuing from their eyes was even greater than in young women.[136]

The threat posed by the witch's sensory powers was taken very seriously by the witch-hunters. For example, it was suggested in Germany that accused witches be conveyed to prison blindfolded, gagged, and wheeled in a barrow, in order to limit their sensory sorcery.[137] The *Malleus Maleficarum* warned that judges "must not allow themselves to be touched physically by the witch."[138]

> But let it not be thought that physical contact . . . is the only thing to be guarded against; for sometimes . . . they are able with the help of the devil to bewitch the judge by the mere sound of the words which they utter . . . . And we know from some experience that some witches . . . have importunately begged their gaolers . . . that they should be allowed to look at the Judge before he looks at them; and by so getting the first sight of the Judge they have been able so to alter the minds of the Judge or his assessors that they have lost all their anger against them.[139]

George Sinclair similarly wrote in 1685 in *Satan's Invisible World Discovered*: "Men and Women have been wronged by the touch of a Witches hand, by the breath and kiss of their mouth . . . . By their looks . . . as when a Witch sendeth forth from her heart thorow her eyes venomous and poysonful Spirits as Rayes."[140] The witch's gaze put the final touch, so to speak, on the sensory sequence of her sorcery. Scot writes: "[The witch's] fascination . . . though it begin by touching or breathing, is alwaies accomplished and finished by the eie."[141]

While popular belief about witches cut across gender lines and many of those who accused women of being witches were women themselves, those who pronounced and legislated on witchcraft, who started up (and ultimately stopped) the witch-hunting machinery, were men. The writings of such men reveal a profound fear of women's sensory appetites and abilities, and of women's appetite for social power. On the one hand the witch was a woman out of place, an undomesticated woman existing on the margins of society. Older women, particularly widows, who were seen as no longer having any useful social role, were particularly apt to be stigmatized in this way. On the other hand, the witch was a woman *in* place, a woman in the home who made use of the very basis of her domesticity – her cooking, her cleaning, her child-rearing, her healing – to defy the social and cosmic order. It was manifestly not enough to confine women to their homes and to domestic tasks when they could brew up a storm in a cauldron, suckle demons at their breast, or fly out at night on their brooms.

The witch-hunts were, at least in part, designed to put the fear of God and of the executioner into women, and to clamp down on attempts by women either to aspire to male forms of power, or to empower themselves through traditional women's work. In terms of the senses, just as women were not to strive for mastery through the masculine domain of sight, they were not to seek dominion through traditional feminine pursuits associated with taste, smell, or touch (such as cooking or healing). That the powerful images of witches and witchery presented by the ideologues of the witch-hunts contrast sharply with the often rather pathetic accounts of witchcraft wrung from accused women is an indication of the discontinuity between the monstrous figure of the witch and the real women caught in the witch-hunting machinery.

As a feminine stereotype, the witch was the sensory inverse of the female saint. The saint restricted her senses of taste and touch by fasting and celibacy, limited her speech and sight through rules of silence and enclosure, listened to the word of God, and exhaled the odor of sanctity. The witch, in contrast, reveled in orgies of food and sex, spoke whenever and whatever she pleased, dominated others through her gaze, heeded only the subversive Devil, and emitted venomous odors.

Both saintliness and witchcraft were similar, however, in that they repre-sented means by which women could achieve positions of prominence in the social and cosmic order. While the saint limited her senses on a worldly level, she could lay claim to mystical visions and divine disclosures, thereby acquiring an extraordinary social, and even political, influence. With the rise of Protestantism and the consequent dissolution of religious orders in many Protestant regions however, "sainthood" was abolished as a vocation in much of Northern Europe (the site of the most ferocious witch-hunts).[142] This would seem to have had the effect of focusing social attention on witchcraft as the presumably one remaining avenue through which women could attain social and supernatural power. By extension, *all* ostensible displays of female power, whether through oratory, healing, visions, seduction, or other means, ran the risk of being stigmatized as witchcraft. In this context the burning of witches represented a purging of women's minds and senses by hot, dry male fire; a massive bonfire of transgressive femininity which helped clear the way for a masculine Age of Reason.

Sensory re-visions

While negative characterizations of womanhood were commonplace in Western tradition, they were not universally supported. During the Renaissance, for example, a number of tracts were written by men which exalted the "goodness" of women.[143] What, however, did the women of the Middle Ages and the Renaissance themselves have to say about the portrayal of their sex? How might they have refashioned the prevailing gender and sensory models to suit their own images of themselves? Most of what women had to say was communicated orally and is thus largely lost to us today. A few exceptional women of the Middle Ages and Renaissance, nonetheless, did commit their views on the matter to writing.

In the twelfth century St. Hildegard of Bingen developed a theology of gender in which femininity was a source of sin, but also of salvation; for it was through specifically female flesh that God was incarnated. In a song to the Virgin Hildegard writes:

> O what a great miracle it is
> that into a submissive feminine form
> entered the king . . . .
> And O what great felicity is
> in this form,
> for malice,
> which flowed from woman -
> woman thereafter rubbed out,
> and built
> all the sweetest fragrance of the virtues,
> and embellished heaven
> more than she formerly troubled earth.[144]

In the fifteenth century the Frenchwoman Christine de Pizan dedicated herself to refuting many of the defamations of women circulated by male authors. In *The Book of the City of Ladies* Christine de Pizan writes that she feels oppressed by the number of "famous men . . . so clear-sighted in all things, as it seemed" who had characterized women as evil: "I could hardly find a book on morals where . . . I did not find several chapters or certain sections attacking women."[145] The author describes herself as sitting with her head bowed in shame, when a ray of light falls on her lap. This light, she discovers, comes not from the (male) sun, but from "Lady Reason" who (along with "Lady Rectitude" and "Lady Justice") proceeds to reveal the virtues of womanhood through the brilliance of her light and the wisdom of her discourse.[146]

To the contention that "women are naturally lecherous and gluttonous," Lady Reason responds that women are naturally sober and restrained. Reason counters the asseveration of women's excessive speech with examples of women's wise speech. The notion that women's bodies are imperfect she calls the product of "irrational blindness." The greater physical weakness of women, she argues, is compensated for by their "freer and sharper" minds, which are hampered only by the restrictions of housework.[147]

In certain repects *The City of Ladies* offered a secular, feminine counterpart to religious images of enlightenment. The ray of light which strikes the protagonist's lap is reminiscent of the divine conception of Jesus, often depicted as a ray of light descending on Mary.[148] In this case, however, the ray of light does not come from a male God but from female Reason. Just as her divine "enlightenment" enabled Mary to transcend her condition as a "lowly" woman, the enlightenment Christine receives from Reason enables her to leave behind her self-image as a despised and despicable female and construct a new identity of feminine worth. The product of this enlightenment is not the Messiah of the bible who offers a heavenly city to his followers, but a female "messiah" (the author) who will conduct virtuous women to a symbolic "city of ladies."

Approximately two centuries after Christine de Pizan, the Italian Humanist Lucrezia Marinelli revised some of the most common stereotypes of gender to express her own ideas on feminine nature. We shall conclude with an examination of Marinelli's provocative re-vision of gender and sensory ideology.

In 1600 Lucrezia Marinelli responded to the defamation of woman's character by male writers by publishing an essay on the "excellence" of woman: *La nobilità et l'eccellenza delle donne*. In this work Marinelli took some of the sensory qualities traditionally associated with women that were imbued with negative values and reassigned them positive values.[149]

With regard to temperature, Marinelli argued that the coolness of temperament characteristic of women was more conducive to rational judgment than heat, which over-excited the mind and body and resulted in rash and irrational acts.[150] Far from endowing men with a superior intellect, therefore, heat hindered masculine rationality. The reason why men grow wiser as they age, Marinelli claimed, is because they cool down and become more like women in temperament: "In middle-aged man the intensity of the warmth becomes more tepid than in youth, and coming closer to the feminine nature, he acts more wisely and maturely."[151]

Wetness of temperament, according to Marinelli, had similar advantages to coolness, damping down excessive passion. Due to their cooler temperature and their humidity, she says, "[women's] senses are ruled by reason."[152] This depiction of women rationally controlling their sensory impulses contradicted the standard image of women as creatures of irrational sensuality.

As regards the attribution of softness to women, male philosophers had customarily stated that women's soft bodies were a sign of their weak minds. For Marinelli, however, bodily softness indicated a readiness to receive and respond to ideas: "a soft and delicate flesh reveals that the intellect of such a person understands more quickly than that of someone who has tough and hard flesh."[153] The implication is that while wise minds go with the soft bodies of women, dense and unperceptive minds go with the hard bodies of men.

Marinelli contests the customary attribution of two other sensory traits –

foulness of odor and sharpness of speech – to women by claiming that these characteristics more properly belong to men. On foulness she writes that women are naturally clean and "hate messiness which renders their pretty bodies ugly, and all those things that emanate stinky odor."[154] Men, on the other hand "being rougher creatures, are much more frequently untidy and dirty." In some cases "such a stench comes forth from their body that women who stand by them are obliged to plug their nose."[155] On sharpness of speech Marinelli claims that men who slander women with their falsehoods prove themselves to posess the sharp tongues they attribute to women.[156]

Lucrezia Marinelli refuted the negative sensory and social stereotypes of women common to her time, and symbolically reordered the female body, investing it with new meanings and identities. Women were still cold, wet, and soft, in Marinelli's scheme, but these traits made women the intellectual superiors of men, rather than their inferiors. As regards the customary attribution of a foul odor and a sharp tongue to women, Marinelli declared that in this case men blamed women for faults that belonged more properly to their own sex.

Marinelli's challenge to the contemporary sensory and gender order, like the "feminist" writings of Christine de Pizan and others, demonstrates that the women of pre-modernity were not always accepting of the prevalent characterizations of their physical and moral natures – supported by eminent authorities as these characterizations might be. At the same time Marinelli's work reveals an extraordinary awareness of the fact that the sensory paradigms of women and men embody gender ideologies (rather than simply being statements of biological and moral realities), and as such are not necessarily "set in the stars," but are susceptible to human manipulation.

With the advent of the Enlightenment, the number and scope of inquiries into the gendered order of society by women would greatly increase. Although women were often typed and dismissed as "irrational" beings by Enlightenment thinkers, the new philosophies of the Age of Reason would ultimately provide many women with the stimulus and conceptual framework to "rationally" challenge the conventions defining the nature and role of their sex.

4 Pens and needles

Writing, women's work, and feminine sensibilities

The social construction of women's and men's spheres of activity in pre-modern Europe was informed by the symbolic construction of the five senses. Sight and hearing, as "rational," "distance" senses, were linked with the "intellectual" labors undertaken by men outside the home. Smell, taste, and touch, as "corporeal," "proximity" senses, were associated with the "manual" labors undertaken by women within the home. In actual fact, as many husbands and wives worked together on farms or in cottage industries, the divide between male and female labor was not always so clear, but the symbolic structure was nevertheless there.

While this basic division of male and female spheres of labor and perception would retain considerable social and ideological force right up until the late twentieth century, it would also undergo a number of alterations from the Middle Ages to modernity. A major factor influencing these alterations was the displacement of the traditional religious and organic world view by the modern scientific and mechanical view of the universe. This displacement involved a shift in the gender model of the cosmos, as the former world view had had significant female connotations, while the latter was decidedly male. Thus, the proto-scientists of the sixteenth and seventeenth centuries spoke explicitly of the need to develop an active "masculine philosophy" which would be capable of dominating the "feminine" forces of nature and rendering them subservient.[1]

The natural world had long been understood to be a formidable reservoir of female power. As such, it often seemed a more suitable field of action for wise women or witches than for sober male philosophers.[2] In 1595 the demonologist Nicholas Rémy described witches as having "laboratories stuffed full of animals, plants and metals."[3] For the scientist to take full charge of the laboratory of nature, it was necessary for the witch – the specter of supernatural female agency – to be expelled. The witch-hunts facilitated this transformation by helping to exorcize the image of the witch and of feminine power from the natural world.

During the crucial period of transition in the seventeenth century, dedication to the new experimental philosophy often coexisted with a belief in witchcraft.[4] A story told of the prominent English physician William Harvey (1578–1657), however, indicates the ultimate incompatibility of witchcraft with science. It was reported that while Harvey was physician to King Charles I he went to see a woman who was reputed to be a witch. Harvey sent the woman out of the house on a pretext and then proceeded to dissect her pet toad, which she called her familiar. By examining the toad's entrails Harvey convinced himself that this "witch's" toad was just like any other toad, and that the "witch" was therefore just a deluded woman. On returning home and finding her familiar being pickled, the woman was furious with Harvey: She "flew like a Tigris at his face . . . and twas well his eyes were out of reach, well guarded with prominent bones, otherways it had gone ill with him."[5] Only after threatening to expose the woman as a witch to the authorities was the "Good Doctor" able to take his leave.[6]

For Harvey, discovering that a presumed witch's familiar in the form of a toad was identical in its inner workings to all the other toads he had dissected was proof enough of the non-existence of witchcraft. This discovery was important to Harvey because, for science to offer an encompassing model of the world, it was necessary to have a world which was regular and consistent in nature. The results of experiments would not be reliable if supernatural forces – in the form of witches' familiars, for example – might intervene at any time.

Within the new mechanical model of the universe, nature remained nominally female, but she was a submissive female, ready to give up her secrets to the probing masculine intellect, or, to put it in sensory terms, ready to reveal her hidden forms to the masculine gaze.[7] Thus Thomas Sprat wrote in his *History of the Royal Society* (1667) that through the application of the new experimental philosophy "the Beautiful Bosom of Nature will be Expos'd to our view."[8] Along similar lines J.T. Desaguliers would say of Newton in his allegorical poem of 1729:

> Nature compell'd his piercing Mind obeys
> And gladly shows him all her secret Ways;
> 'Gainst Mathematics she has no Defence,
> And yields t'experimental Consequence.[9]

Women's work and women's senses

This change in world views had direct consequences for traditional women's work. For one, as it was no longer considered infused with the magical forces of nature, much of women's work, from child-rearing to cooking, lost its mythical dimensions and began to be portrayed as banal, simply a matter of good (or bad) housekeeping. For another, just as the traditionally feminine natural world increasingly became a sphere for masculine investigation, so did certain traditionally feminine areas of labor. This was most notably the case with healing, which changed from a largely female concern to an overwhelmingly male one. The transferal of healing from the domain of women's work to that of men's work involved removing healing from its symbolic site among the "lower" senses and relocating it in the domain of vision.[10]

The invention of new technologies of production and the growing industrialization of Europe, in turn, meant that many goods which were traditionally produced by women at home, from textiles to candles, were now commercially produced by male-dominated industries. For example, when the knitting-frame was introduced in the sixteenth century, the knitting of stockings became a masculine trade in some parts of Europe, the argument being that the new technology was too complicated for women to understand.[11] In Margaret Cavendish's seventeenth-century work *Sociable Letters*, a lady decides to occupy herself in a feminine fashion by making preserves and sewing silk flowers only to be told by her housekeeper that much better products than she could make at home are available in the stores.[12] The commercialization of traditionally home-made goods lessened the economic and social importance of woman's work within the home.[13]

The increased availability of commercial products for the home also had the effect of reducing the amount of labor women (with the means to purchase such products) needed to dedicate to maintaining the household. In the fanciful account presented by Cavendish the possibility of buying household goods meant that the lady could spend much of her time reading and writing.[14]

Due in part to the erosion of traditional feminine domains of work and achievement, and in part to the stimulus of new social, scientific, and religious philosophies, from the Renaissance on women of means became increasingly interested and educated in a number of traditionally masculine domains, notably literature and science (or natural philosophy). In terms of the gendered sensory order, this interest on the part of women in books and microscopes constituted a feminine invasion of masculine visual territory. The masculine response was often to refer women back to their traditional perceptual and occupational domain, by stating, for example, that women were more suited to hold a needle than a pen, or to work in a kitchen than a laboratory. Women who took up the pen or the microscope countered by asserting their right to operate in ostensibly masculine territory, or by attempting to reinscribe their new activities within the traditional symbolism of women's work and women's senses.

The present chapter examines historical instances of gender crossings in the traditional sensory and occupational domains of women and men. The primary focus is on the practice of writing by women, and how this practice was construed by women and men as opposed to or allied with the symbolic sphere of feminine activities and sensibilities. The chapter ends with an examination of the work of the seventeenth-century writer, Margaret Cavendish, a self-styled "spinster" of texts. As a woman interested in the male fields of both writing and science, Cavendish continually struggled with gender and sensory stereotypes in her work, trying to negotiate between the domains of men's work and women's work in order to fashion an acceptable identity for herself. Cavendish, like many other female writers of the time, found herself on "pins and needles," or rather, "pens and needles": continually undertaking the delicate task of justifying her "unfeminine" work with the pen in relation to her neglect of "feminine" needlework – "the most unquestioned housewifely art."[15]

From the healing touch to the medical gaze

While male physicians were the élite of medical practitioners, healing was customarily a feminine concern in pre-modernity. As was the case with other traditional female practices, the art of healing was closely associated with the "lower," "feminine," senses of touch, smell, and taste. Sick bodies were cleaned, warmed, cooled, massaged, poulticed, bandaged, and kissed to soothe the pain. Special, easily digested meals were prepared for invalids. Medicines were brewed in the kitchen from aromatic herbs.[16] Women undertook to heal as part of their domestic duties: to nurse a sick family member back to health fell as much within a woman's domain as to prepare the foods which kept her family healthy in the first place. It was only in severe cases of illness or injury, and only by those who could afford it, that a male physician would be called in.

Certain women with a reputation for healing abilities functioned as healers not only within their own homes, but within their communities. These were the "wise women" who often dispensed charms, love-potions, cosmetic preparations, and advice, along with remedies for illnesses. (Men could also serve as folk healers, but the role was considered primarily feminine.) An informative, if contemptuous, portrait of such a wise woman can be found in Fernando de Rojas' turn-of-the-sixteenth century play, *Celestina*:

> She professed herself a kind of physician, and feigned that she had good skill in the curing of little children .... At home in her own house she made perfumes, false and counterfeit storax, benjamin .... She had a trick to supple and refine the skin with the juice of lemons, with turpentines, with the marrow of deer .... For the mending of lost maidenheads, some she holp [helped] with little bladders, and other some she stitched up with the needle .... In another partition she had her knacks for to help those that were love-sick ... [17]

A wide range of abilities and treatments, certainly, but not ones which lay outside the scope of customary "women's work" and "women's senses."

If the wise woman was sometimes the target of scorn, healing skills were generally considered a point in women's favor. Medieval romances, for example, contain many admiring references to women's skill in attending to the injuries of fallen knights. In *Erec und Enide*, Guivret's sisters carefully cut away the dead flesh from Erec's wound before covering it with a plaster. In *Aucassin et Nicolette*, Nicolette sets Aucassin's dislocated shoulder, applies a poultice of flowers and leaves, and then bandages the shoulder with the hem of her chemise.[18]

With the increasing professionalization of medicine from the late Middle Ages on, however, the "unofficial" healing practiced by women became ever more suspect in the eyes of male physicians. According to the medical academy, it was not herbal lore or healing experience – the basis of women's medical knowledge – which qualified one to practice medicine, but the formal study of medicine at universities. As women were not permitted to attend university in most countries, this effectively excluded women from the practice of medicine.

One important concern to physicians was the competition for paying patients which folk healers presented. Ideally, women were not supposed to make their healing skills into a source of income, but rather were supposed to sacrifice their time and money for the well-being of others. In the medieval romance *Eger and Grime*, for example, a knight praises the noblewoman who doctored him for spending £20 on his treatments.[19] In actual fact, many wise women, midwives and folk healers *did* charge for their services. Usually they earned minimal amounts, but occasionally they were able to accumulate substantial wealth. An eighteenth-century verse about a popular bone-setter, Sally Map, warned male physicians of the threat to their income and status posed by such female folk healers:

> Dame Nature has giv'n her a Doctor's Degree,
> She gets all the Patients and pockets the Fee;
> So if you don't instantly prove her a Cheat,
> She'll loll in her Chariot while you walk the street.[20]

Male physicians and the male medical academy, this verse makes clear, must not allow female healers to receive "Doctors' Degrees" from the equally female "Dame Nature."

Both out of self-interest and alleged concern for public health, the medical academy was indeed anxious to suppress professional folk-healers, particularly in those areas where physicians were plentiful. In a well-known case of 1322, a wise woman – Jacoba Félicie de Almania – was brought to court in Paris on the charge of illegally practicing medicine. Former patients testified in her defense that she had succeeded in curing them when licensed physicians had failed. The physicians countered, however, that Jacoba's claim was "frivolous, since it is certain that a man aproved in [medicine] could cure the sick people better than such a woman."[21] The wise woman, forbidden to challenge the authority of the schooled male physician, lost her case.

The pressure on folk healers – both female and male – to stop practicing grew ever stronger from the Renaissance on, as the medical profession became more established and physicians more numerous. This pressure was likewise applied to housewives who customarily took charge of their families' health care needs. In *The Queen-like Closet*, a collection of culinary and medicinal recipes of 1670, Hannah Woolley exhorted women to be their "own Chirugiens and Physicians, unless the case be desperate."[22] Woolley wrote that her own "Mother and Elder Sisters were very skilled in Physick and Chirurgery, from whom I learnt a little."[23] However, this female mastery of healing was becoming a thing of the past, as women were increasingly cautioned to undertake only the most basic medical care within their homes and not to presume to venture into the territory of the trained doctor. Thus Gervase Markham, the author of another seventeenth-century guide for housewives, decisively states:

> [the] most excellent art of physic is far beyond the capacity of the most skilful woman . . . lodging only in the breast of the learned professors; yet

that our housewife may from them receive some ordinary rules and medicines which may avail for the benefit of her family, is in our common experience no derogation at all to that worthy art.[24]

These few words say a great deal about women's presumed subordination to male physicians in medical matters. The possession of healing ability is no longer an acknowledged part of the feminine role, but rather something to be conceded to women in a very limited way by the male medical profession. Receiving medical guidelines and prescriptions from physicians, instead of from her female relatives and her own experience, the housewife becomes a kind of very junior assistant to the physician rather than a capable healer in her own right.

As healing moved more and more out of the domain of women into that of men, it also moved out of the domain of the "lower" senses into that of the "higher." Prior to the Renaissance, both female healers and male physicians employed similar methods and treatments in their medical practice. The unschooled Jacoba took patients' pulses, examined their urine and treated them with aromatic potions and herbal baths, just as did schooled physicians.[25] (Jacoba lost her case not because her methods were deemed unsound, but because she lacked the academic and gender authority to practice them professionally.) Professional medicine's association with a privileged masculine sphere – and with the higher senses – at this point was largely based on its transmission through medical texts and university lectures, and on its interrelationship with other learned disciplines of the day, such as astronomy and dialectics.[26]

By the late eighteenth century, however, professional medicine had grown significantly different from folk medicine in its methods and practices. Traditional medical knowledge and techniques were challenged by new ideas drawn from the increasingly sophisticated practices of anatomical dissection, surgery, and clinical observation. These and other developments allowed medicine to detach itself symbolically, and, to some extent, actually, from the clinging lower senses and become a *visual* science.[27] The modern physician could acquire knowledge of the body by peering into its exposed interior or by "reading" the symptoms of patients lined up in hospital beds like words in the pages of a book. While herbal remedies and bone-setting fell within the domain of the wise woman, anatomical dissection and clinical observation did not.

In the conflict between folk healing and official medicine, it was sometimes stated in defense of the former that folk healers had the practical knowledge which bookish physicians lacked. Agrippa von Nettesheim, for example, declared that while physicians acquired their knowledge from incorrect books, "old wives" learned the colors, forms, tastes, and scents of plants, and their healing virtues, through direct experience.[28] By the late eighteenth century, however, a physician could lay claim to having an *experiential*, and not just theoretical, knowledge of health and illness, through his work in the clinic. The wise woman, with her folk methods of diagnosis and her scented herbs, appeared archaic and inefficient when compared with the professional physician examining patients in the clinic and prescribing modern medicines.

The preparation, as well as the practice, of medicine, in fact, was reformulated as an exclusively professional, masculine concern in modernity. By the late eighteenth century the preparation of medicine had moved from the traditional field of medicinal cookery to the new scientific field of pharmacy.[29] No longer was it the role of women to cook up remedies in their kitchen; they now bought their pills and potions ready-made from the apothecary. Thus, in her cookbook of 1769, Elizabeth Raffald assured her readers that she, unlike many of her predecessors, offered no medical prescriptions among her recipes: "I [have not] meddled with physical receipts, leaving them to the physicians of superior judgement, whose proper province they are."[30] Even if women wanted to continue preparing their own remedies, the ingredients of many modern medicines were unknown and unavailable to them. In his attack on "Lady Doctors," the eighteenth-century physician James M. Adair announced: "it is time for the ladies to retire."[31]

The one area of healing left to women by the modern medical profession was that of nursing. To physically care for sick patients – feed them, bathe them, change their bandages – was beneath the attention of a male physician. Such work required a woman's touch.

Sense and sensibility

The changes which occurred within the sphere of woman's work from the seventeenth to the nineteenth centuries were accompanied by changes in the popular imagery of women. By the late eighteenth century, for example, the coarser images of women – the loud-mouthed nag, the malodorous slattern, the lusty wench – had receded (without disappearing) in favor of the more etherealized feminine paradigm of soft (and few) words, sweet (barely perceptible) smells, and delicate, shrinking touch. Women still signified sensation, as opposed to masculine reason; however, the bold sensuality formerly attributed to the female sex was softened and refined to become a tremulous sensibility. As Hester Mulso Chapone put it in the eighteenth century, while men have "strength of intellect," women have "exquisite perceptions."[32] According to this new paradigm, the converse of masculine intellectual vision was feminine "taste" and tact.[33]

This modern attitude towards womanhood appeared to be more positive than that prevalent in previous centuries – women became fountains of virtue rather than cesspools of vice, "angels" instead of "witches." At the same time, however, it could be more confining. While the former stereotypes of women were often highly negative, they did at least present an image of women as occasionally assertive. In modernity, the passive nature of women was emphasized.

The assumed necessity of keeping feminine "purity" from being sullied by worldly activities was often employed as a rationale by those who sought to exclude women from professional fields, even those fields in which they were formerly active, such as medicine. While in medieval romances women could cut open flesh and bind wounds without losing any of their femininity, but rather enhancing it, such was no longer the case. For instance, according to the critical reviewer of a book advocating professional education for women, no man would want to see his beloved, knife in hand, "burrowing into the bowels of a cadaver at an anatomical theater."[34] (The reviewer chose to ignore that women were expected to carry out similar deeds daily in their kitchens.)

During the seventeenth and eighteenth centuries, the "feminine" senses of smell, taste, and touch declined somewhat in symbolic importance, largely due to what Susan Bordo has called "the disintegration of the organic, female cosmos of the Middle Ages and Renaissance."[35] Concurrently, the Enlightenment emphasis on light and sight as a medium and metaphor for knowledge heightened the role of the "masculine" sense of sight during this period. The "lower" senses belonged to the old, "feminine" world of myth and intuition; sight – and to a lesser extent hearing – belonged to the new "masculine" age of science and reason.[36]

The women of this period, however, were not always content to remain within the confines of their supposed social and sensory domain, and sometimes ventured into masculine cultural territory. Such adventuring involved, in part, taking a more prominent role as spectators (of goods and entertainments) in the developing consumer society.[37] For some women it also involved engaging in scientific inquiry, studying philosophy and literature, and even writing books. Given the strong antagonism to female scholarship, much of the rhetoric occasioned by the subject reasserted the traditional opposition of male and female social domains, and, by implication, of male and female sensory domains. Thus in Molière's satire of scholarly women, *Les Femmes savantes*, a husband complains that his wife has deserted the kitchen for the observatory:

> No science is too profound for [women] . . . . They know about the movements of the moon, the North Star, Venus, Saturn, and Mars . . . but they don't know how my dinner, which I need, is coming along.[38]

The point being made is that if women direct their sight to the stars, it will be at the cost of their tasteful labors in the kitchen.

Other authors attempted to demonstrate the absurdity entailed in the notion of a female scientist or scholar by contrasting her with the figure of a male housekeeper. The 1726 play *The Humours of Oxford*, for example, states that "a Woman makes as ridiculous a Figure, poring over Globes, or thro' a Telescope, as a Man would . . . mending Lace."[39]

It is not supposed by such authors that this female appropriation of male science and male senses could have any useful end. All women can do is to bring science and sight down to the level of their own petty concerns. In *The Humours of Oxford*, "Lady Science" confesses: "I am justly made a Fool of for aiming to . . . move into a Sphere that did not belong to me . . . I will destroy all my Globes, Quadrants, Spheres, Prisms, Microscopes . . . "[40]

Pens and needles

The supposed dichotomy between scholarship as a male domain and housewifery as a female domain, was commonly framed in terms of an opposition between pens and needles. As the debate concerning the degree of education and literary activity suitable for women increased from the Renaissance on, so did the number of references contrasting (masculine) pens with (feminine) needles. In the sixteenth century, for example, the author of *The Necessarie, Fit, and Convenient Education of a Young Gentlewoman* declared:

> Let the small profit got by learning, be compared with the great hurt that may happen to them [women], and they shall be shewed . . . how much more convenient the needle, the wheele, the distaffe, and the spindle . . . then the book and pen.[41]

In the eighteenth century an article in the *Tatler* derisively referred to a "Scheme of a College for young Damsels; where, instead of Scissors, Needles, and Samplers; Pens, Compasses, Quadrants, Books, Manuscripts, Greek, Latin, and Hebrew, are to take up their whole time."[42] While a basic education was generally conceded to be suitable for middle- and upper-class women, it was not supposed to have the effect of turning them away from their "feminine" pursuits. The ultimate purpose of women's education was thought to be to better prepare women to be good wives and mothers.[43]

Women who took up books to read and pens to write often found themselves ridiculed or chastised for leaving behind the needle and the duties of their female sex. In the seventeenth century James I of England reportedly asked when a woman was praised to him for her knowledge of Greek and Latin: "But can she spin?"[44] In the same century the poet Anne Bradstreet wrote of the censure she faced as a female poet:

> I am obnoxious to each carping tongue
> Who says my hand a needle better fits
> A poet's pen all scorn I should thus wrong,
> For such despite they cast on female wits:
> If what I do prove well, it won't advance,
> They'll say it's stol'n, or else it was by chance.[45]

Just as the contrast between star-gazing and cooking evoked by Molière implied a sensory as well as gender opposition, so did the contrast between pens and needles. While writing and needlework both made use of the senses of sight and touch, the former was more closely associated with sight and the latter with touch. Needlework was perceived primarily as an art of the hand, as was indicated by the customary designation of the web-making spider and the spinster as symbols for the sense of touch. This association was no doubt reinforced by the tactile uses to which needlework was usually put, as in clothes and blankets. Writing, by contrast, was considered to be directed primarily to the eye. Even the act of writing itself, while making use of the hand, was thought of as essentially a mental activity, and hence associated with the "rationality" of sight.[46]

Another important sensory and social distinction between writing and needlework was that the former was designed to be disseminated abroad, while the latter was usually destined for use in the home. Writing, like men and like sight, went out into the world. Needlework, like women and like touch, stayed home.

The traditional use of a feather quill for writing suggested a further association between writing and vision, as birds in general were symbolically linked with the sense of sight. This association is brought out by Anne Bradstreet in a poem which refers to male writers as "high flown quills that soar the skies," scarcely deigning to cast their eyes on the "lowly lines" written by women.[47] Over two centuries later in 1878 the French author Jules Barbey D'Aurevilly would publish the following comment on a woman's writing: "That wasn't written with an eagle's quill, but with a magpie's quill, and a sightless magpie at that!"[48] Here the eagle's quill represents the elevated, masculine nature of both sight and writing, while the sightless magpie's quill represents women's writing as blind, frivolous chatter: anti-writing.

The pen and the needle, indeed, could serve not only as symbols of sight and touch, but also as symbols of speech and silence. Writing was conceptualized as a form of public speech, and hence masculine in nature.[49] Needlework, by contrast was perceived as a silent alternative to speech, and hence feminine.[50] The popular image in this regard was that of a woman sitting quietly at home, occupied with her sewing, hardly daring to raise her eyes or speak a word in mixed company. This understanding of needlework as opposed to speech was expressed in 1624 by John Taylor in his poem entitled "In Praise of the Needle":

> And for my countries quiet, I should like,
> That woman-kinde should use no other Pike,
> It will increase their peace, enlarge their store,
> To use their tonges less, and their needles more.
> The Needles sharpness, profit yields, and pleasure
> But sharpness of the tongue, bites out of measure.[51]

The assumption was clearly that women could not "speak" or criticize the social order through needlework, and therefore could not disrupt the status quo.[52]

A woman's pen

> Though some morose Gentleman wou'd perhaps remit me to the Distaff or the Kitchin . . . the proper Employments as they fancy of a Womans Life; yet expecting better things from the more Equitable and ingenious Mr. Norris . . . I presume to beg his Attention a little to the Impertinencies of a Womans Pen.[53]
>
> Mary Astell (1666–1731)

> Alas! A woman that attempts the pen,
> Such an intruder on the rights of men.[54]
>
> Anne Finch (1661–1720)

Women who wrote were well aware that they were considered to be deserting their proper feminine sphere and intruding on masculine ground. Indeed, that writing and scholarship were out of bounds for women was usually impressed on women at an early age. In the sixteenth century Madeleine Fredonnoit des Roches wrote of how girls were conditioned to forsake books in favor of needlework.

> Our parents have the laudable custom
> In order to deprive us of the use of our wits
> Of keeping us locked up at home
> And of handing us the spindle instead of the pen.[55]

Madeleine des Roches lamented that, due to the social pressures placed on her to conform to a model of domestic femininity, "Before I could fly, my [quill] was broken."[56] It was often the case, indeed, that girls were not only restricted in their reading and writing, but prevented from learning how to read and write in the first place. The eighteenth-century author Frances Sheridan, for example, was obliged to learn her letters secretly as her father was strongly opposed to female literacy.[57]

Given the supposed audacity of the act, it was scarcely possible for a woman to take up writing without offering some form of justification, to herself and to others. The works of early female writers, consequently, often contain an explanation of why it is that a woman is holding a pen, rather than a needle. Many female authors agreed that there existed an opposition between the pen and the needle, with the former being an instrument of mental activity and the latter of manual labor. Where they disagreed with convention was in claiming that women had a right to cultivate a mental life and even to neglect their needlework in favor of reading and writing. In the seventeenth century Louise Labé urged women to "raise their minds a little above their distaffs and spindles" and educate themselves; "and if anyone reaches the stage at which she is able to put her ideas into writing, she should do it with much thought and should not scorn the glory."[58] The Spanish writer, Maria de Zayas y Sotomayor, in turn, proclaimed that "the moment I see a book, new or old, I drop my sewing and can't rest until I've read it."[59] Similarly, Madeleine des Roches declared "I'd rather write than spin."[60] In her essay on the "excellency of women" Lucrezia Marinelli cited such female authors as Hildegard of Bingen and Catherine of Siena as examples of "what a little girl can learn if she sets aside needle and cloth."[61]

Many female writers, however, were too timid, or too prudent, to be openly defiant of the gender conventions which assigned women to the needle. Such authors often conceded that writing lay outside of a woman's sphere, but felt that in their case the act was mitigated by special circumstances. For instance, women commonly excused their writing by stating that it was undertaken as a private hobby and by no means intended for the eyes of the public. Thus Katherine Fowler ("Orinda") decried the unauthorized publication of her poems which "seemed to put her in the position of a woman bold and masculine enough to send her writings into the world."[62] Fowler declared that she "never writ any line in my life with any intention to have it printed."[63]

When women *did* seek publication of their work, the reason often given was that this was done solely out of monetary need – to support an aged parent, for example, or a young family.[64] The responsibility for authorship was likewise lessened by publishing books under a pseudonym, or anonymously. Anne Finch said of Lady Pakington, who was reported to have published works anonymously, that she enjoyed the best gift of each sex, from men "the skill to write," and from women "the modesty to hide."[65]

Another rationale put forward by female writers to justify their literary activity was that – while some misguided women might exchange the needle for the pen – in *their* case authorship by no means detracted from the quality of their domestic work. Thus, in the sixteenth century, Catherine des Roches, Madeleine des Roches' daughter, expressed a wistful hope that she might be allowed the occasional use of a pen if she did not neglect her spindle:

> But spindle, my dearest, I do not believe
> That, much as I love you, I will come to grief
> If I do not quite let that good practice dwindle
> Of writing sometimes, if I give you fair share,
> If I write of your merit, my friend and my care,
> And hold in my hand both my pen and my spindle.[66]

A woman could be a writer, Catherine des Roches and others like her held, and still be a housewife. Taking this view to its extreme, a humorous article of 1713 declared that the domestic, sedentary life of women was more suitable for the pursuit of scholarship than the worldly, active life led by men. The author spoke of a family of women who knew how to combine reading with needlework and astronomy with cooking:

> It was very entertaining to me to see them dividing their speculations between jellies and stars, and making a sudden transition from the sun to an apricot, or from the Copernican system to the figure of a cheesecake.[67]

These different approaches to feminine scholarship and authorship all challenged the established sensory order. For women to aspire to an education was to refute their association with the world of sensation, and claim a right to the "masculine" realm of reason. That such a transformation would be beneficial for women was argued from a variety of standpoints. Margaret More Roper claimed that, since women *have* minds, it is better for them to be occupied with learning than with idle fancies.

Reading and studying of books so occupieth the mind that it can have no leisure to muse or delight in other fantasies, when in all handiworks that men say be more meet for a woman the body may be busy in one place and the mind walking in another: and while they sit sewing and spinning with their fingers, may cast and compass many peevish fantasies in their minds.[68]

Louise Labé, in turn, was anxious to convince women that "literature and the sciences" have delights unknown to the senses. While "the pleasures of the senses are immediately lost and never return," she states, "study rewards us with a pleasure all its own which remains with us longer."[69] In the eighteenth century Mary Wollstonecraft made the symbolic division of women and men into "sense" and "mind" a key issue in her *Vindication of the Rights of Woman*. She declared that so long as the view persists that "man was made to reason, woman to feel," women will be unable to achieve intellectual equality with men, for "intellect dwells not [in sensation]."[70]

By claiming for themselves the right to enter the "masculine" realm of reason, women were also claiming the right to employ the "masculine" power of sight, associated with reason and learning.[71] The seventeenth-century scholar of philosophy Damaris Masham asserted that "Men have made no Laws, or put out any Edicts whereby Women are prohibited to open their Eyes; to Read, to Remember what they Read and to make use thereof in their Conversation, or in composing of Works."[72] Yet Masham admitted that, even without actual laws, social pressure was often enough to prevent women from "opening their eyes" and educating themselves.[73]

According to the most conservative view on the matter, no matter how much women studied or wrote, they could never acquire true "sight," for such lay outside the scope of their natures. An oft-repeated saying likened a learned woman to a willful blind horse – both of them bound for a fall.[74] In other words, without intellectual vision, women's will to study could only result in misfortune.[75]

Spinster of texts

The seventeenth-century writer Margaret Cavendish seemed to her contemporaries to provide a perfect example of a "learned lady" who was a "blind horse," rambling through ideas with little direction or prudence. Cavendish was a prolific writer, producing fanciful and erratic plays, stories, poems, and essays on natural philosophy. While Cavendish's literary efforts were met with considerable scorn, the fact that she lived before the rise of the cult of feminine sensibility probably enabled her to put forward her ideas in a more forceful fashion than a woman writing in the more decorous late eighteenth or nineteenth centuries.[76] Cavendish's writing and publishing career was facilitated by the enthusiastic support of her husband, the Duke of Newcastle.[77]

Margaret Cavendish used a variety of metaphors to describe her writing, including those of painting, playing music, and preparing food ("I am like a plain, cleanly English Cook-maid.")[78] Her favorite metaphor, however, was that of spinning. Thus in one of her poems she describes her fingers as a loom, weaving meaning through the writing of words.[79] The traditional images of spinning as a feminine tactile practice and writing as a male visual practice merge when Cavendish (participating in a long tradition of associations between texts and textiles) speaks of herself "spinning writing." It is no longer a case of pens and needles being antagonistic or even complementary, but of the pen taking over some of the functions of the needle, or of the spindle.[80]

Cavendish's interest in the symbolism of spinning is evidenced in her various references to silkworms and spiders. In "The Tale of a Man and a Spider," for example, a man accuses a spider of spinning webs to trap flies. The spider responds that the web is her house, which she must protect from the flies which attack it.[81] For Cavendish, rather than being a deadly seductress, the spider was primarily a positive symbol of feminine creativity and assertiveness.

The image of a spider spinning webs from its own being had been used disparagingly by Francis Bacon to refer to philosophers who attempt to understand the world solely through mental exertion, rather than through active experimentation.[82] Nonetheless, it was precisely this image of the spider, or the silkworm, as an inventive and self-sufficient (feminine) being, which Cavendish found appealing. In her autobiography, for example, she commented that her thoughts "work of themselves, like silk-worms that spins [sic] out of their own bowels."[83]

According to Cavendish, for spinning to be of lasting value, it must necessarily take the form of the spinning out of words on a page. She manifests a profound anxiety not to be forgotten, "buried," by posterity, which she sees as the grim fate of all other spinners, and of women in general. "The Silk-worm," she writes, "digs her Grave as she doth spin/ And makes her Winding-sheet to lap her in."[84] Similarly: "As [Housewives] Draw Threads of Flax, so Time Draws their Thread of Life, as their Web makes them Smocks, so Times Web makes them Deaths Shirts."[85] Cavendish is not prepared to reconcile herself to such a fate. "Shall only men live by Fame, and women dy in Oblivion?" a character protests in one of her plays.[86] Cavendish determines that she, at least, will "spin a Garment of Memory," with her writings, rather than the burial shrouds made by other spinsters.[87] "I cannot say the Web is strong, fine, or evenly Spun, for it is a Course peice; yet I had rather my Name should go meanly clad, then dye with cold."[88]

Cavendish recognized that the spinning of cloths was considered a more appropriate undertaking for women than the spinning of texts, and she therefore provided a number of reasons for her devotion to the latter. In *Poems and Fancies*, for instance, she implied that she turned to writing to compensate for her lack of skill at sewing:

> True it is, Spinning with the Fingers is more proper to our Sexe, then Studying or writing Poetry, which is the Spinning with the braine: but I having no skill in the Art of the first . . . made me delight in the latter.[89]

Similarly, to those men who told her to "Work, Lady, Work, let writing Books alone/For surely wiser Women nere wrote one,"[90] she could reply:

> I cannot Work, I mean such Works as Ladies use to pass their Time . . . Needle-works, Spinning-works, Preserving-works, as also Baking, and Cooking-works . . . I am Ignorant in these Imployments.[91]

Margaret Cavendish further indicated that, even had she been so minded, she had no domestic duties to perform. She was childless and her husband had lost his estate during the English Civil War, leaving her with "nothing for huswifery . . . to employ myself in."[92] Under the circumstances, she insisted, one could hardly blame her for turning to writing to occupy her time.

Cavendish undoubtedly came closer to the truth of the matter, however, when she stated in her autobiography that she was "addicted from my child-hood to . . . write with the pen [rather] than to work with the needle."[93] Writing was not a second-best substitute for Cavendish, it was an irrepressible passion: "I cannot for my Life be so good a Huswife, as to quit Writing."[94]

Her awareness that writing was considered a masculine activity led Cavendish to try to create a feminine, or at least gender-neutral, space for her works. To accomplish this she attempted to present the pen as a quasi-feminine imple-ment in contrast to the masculinity of the sword. Men should be bred to handle the sword more than the pen, she declared, imputing an effeminate quality to writing.[95] For Cavendish the sword is the ultimate, and perhaps the only, external sign of masculinity. "A Gallant Man will never strive for the Breeches with his Wife," she wrote, "but present her with the whole suit, as Doublet, Breeches, and Cloak and all the Appurtenances thereunto and leave himself onely his Sword to protect her."[96]

Cavendish held up her husband, the Duke of Newcastle, as an example of virile (and highly visible) swordsmanship, in contrast to which her own penwomanship seemed "ladylike" (and almost invisible). In an open letter to the Duke she wrote: "[your actions] have been of war and fighting, mine of contemplating and writing: yours were performed publicly in the field, mine privately in my closet: yours had many thousand eye-witnesses, mine none but my waiting-maids."[97]

Cavendish's ruse did not work, for both writing and fighting were consid-ered pre-eminently masculine domains. Cavendish makes her understanding of this fact clear in her preface to *Poems and Fancies* when she states that "Men will cast a smile of scorne upon my Book, because they think thereby, Women incroach too much upon their Prerogatives; for they hold Books as their Crowne, and the Sword as their Sceptr, by which they rule, and governe."[98] For all his heroic swordplay, therefore, it was not surprising that the Duke of Newcastle was thought to have been emasculated by his wife's pen, as the following lines from an anonymous poem attest.

Newcastle and's Horse for entrance next strives,
Well Stuff'd was his Cloakbag, and so was his Breeches
And unbutt'ning the place where Nature's Posset-maker lives,
Pull'd out his Wife's Poems, Plays, Essays and Speeches.[99]

Margaret Cavendish believed she should be able to bend the rules of gender to suit her inclinations. In an introduction to a collection of her plays she wrote:

> I know that there are many Scolastical and Pedantical persons that will condemn my writings, because I do not keep strictly to the Masculine and Feminine Genders, as they call them: as for example . . . Love is the Masculine Gender, Hate the Feminine Gender, and the Furies are Shees, and the Graces are Shees, the Virtues are Shees, and the Seven deadly Sins are Shees, which I am sorry for, but I know no reason but that I may as well make them Hees for my use, as others did Shees, or Shees as others did Hees.[100]

Such reversals of gender conventions could not be so simply accomplished, however, in the world outside Cavendish's texts, where "shees" and "hees" had definite and often mutually exclusive roles. The unresponsiveness of the real world to her ideas no doubt contributed to Cavendish's desire to "spin out" another, more tractable, world in her writing. "My ambition," she proclaimed, "is not only to be Empress, but Authoress of a whole world."[101]

New blazing world: writing the senses

Margaret Cavendish represented the senses and sensory perception in a variety of different fashions and contexts in her writings. She was interested in perception from the standpoint of natural philosophy and her works in this field discuss such topics as the relationship between the mind and the senses, the modes of transmission of the different senses, and the nature of color. While she considered sensation inferior to reason, she nonetheless disagreed with the opinion that "all knowledg is in the Mind and none in the Senses."[102] Cavendish argued that each part of the body and each sense has its own knowledge: "the Eye is as knowing as the Ear, and the Ear as knowing as the Nose, and the Nose as Knowing as the Tongue."[103] She similarly stated in favor of a bodily intelligence that, "The Heads Braines cannot ingross all knowledge to themselves."[104] Given that men's association with the mind and women's with the senses and the body was a commonplace, Cavendish's attribution of knowledge to the body and senses served to draw attention to the intellectual abilities of women (along with implying that writing could arise from bodily knowledge, as well as from the mind.)[105]

In order to describe how the different parts of the body functioned together as a society, Cavendish used the trope of a Parliament or a Commonwealth.[106] In the Commonwealth of the body the senses were given their traditional role of judges, accepting or rejecting the various sensations which came before them.[107] In another metaphor, Cavendish pictured the senses as forming a cabinet, the drawers of which were unlocked by the "keys" of sensation.[108]

The life of the senses was a recurrent motif in Margaret Cavendish's fictional writing, as well as in her philosophical speculations. She was particularly concerned with the subject of sensory fulfillment.[109] Cavendish's image of heaven, for instance, was of a place where all the senses would be gratified.[110] She brought heaven to earth in her play, "The Convent of Pleasure," in which a community of women dedicate themselves to pleasing each of the senses:

> Wee'l Cloth our selves with softest Silk,
> And Linnen fine as white as milk.
> Wee'l please our Sight with Pictures rare;
> Our Nostrils with perfumed Air.
> Our Ears with sweet melodious Sound,
> Whose Substance can be no where found;
> Our Tast with sweet delicious Meat,
> And savory Sauces we will eat:
> Variety each Sense shall feed,
> And Change in them new Appetites breed.[111]

One of the "new appetites" bred is for love, and the founder of the convent, a young heiress, falls in love with a Princess who has joined her community. Fortunately for conventional morality, though unfortunately for the ideal of a self-sufficient society of women, the Princess turns out to be a man in disguise.

The portrayal of a group of women banding together to satisfy their sensory appetites presents a strong contrast with the traditional ideal of the suppression of appetites by women. Nonetheless, Margaret Cavendish also expressed many conventional views about the nature of women and men in her writing. For example, she could not bring herself to refute directly the ancient classification of men as hot, dry, and superior, and women as cold, wet, and inferior. Thus in *Poems and Fancies* she writes:

> It hath seemed hitherto, as if Nature had compounded Mens Braines with more of the Sharp Atomes, which make the hot, and dry Element, and Womens with more of the round Atomes, which figure makes the cold, and moist Element: And though Water is a useful Element, yet Fire is the Nobler.[112]

In *The World's Olio* Cavendish presented this gender opposition in cosmological terms, comparing men to the sun and women to the moon:

> The Sun is more Dry, Hot, Active, and Powerfull every way than the Moon . . . for we find she is Pale and Wan, Cold, Moist, and Slow in all her Operations; and if it be as Philosophers hold, that the Moon hath no Light but what it borrows from the Sun, so Women have no strength nor light of Understanding, but what is given them from Men.[113]

This lack of intellectual light is said by Cavendish to be the reason why women are not "Mathematicians, Logicians, Geometricians, Cosmographers, and the like"; or, indeed, original thinkers in any field. "Whatever did [women] do", she laments, "but like Apes, by Imitation?"[114]

Elsewhere in her work Cavendish refers to other commonplaces about the nature of women.[115] In *Poems and Fancies*, for example, she describes how the male "judges" of sight and hearing are bewitched by the female "witches" of voice and looks:

> Tis true, there is a Law against them, which belongs to the Judges care, as Hearing and Sight; but when they come before them to be examin'd, and to be condemned . . . those bonds that should bind them, they bind them-selves with, and so become voluntary slaves to those Witches.[116]

Although Cavendish employed gender and sensory stereotypes in her work, it is clear that she was also interested in subverting them. This is most notably the case in the story she published in 1666 titled *The Description of A New World Called The Blazing World*. *Blazing World* begins with a lady being kidnapped by a traveling merchant and taken away on his vessel. The boat is driven by the wind towards the North Pole where the merchant and the crew freeze to death, but the kidnapped lady survives. The boat then passes beyond the pole into a new world and the bodies of the dead men thaw and putrefy, emitting a "nauseous smell."[117]

Through this initial sequence of events, Cavendish indicates that there will be a dissolution of traditional gender roles in the story. The improbability of a woman traveling on her own to a new world is solved by having the woman kidnapped and forced to travel against her will. While the narrative begins with an example of male aggression towards women, however, the aggressors are quickly and literally frozen out of the picture by Cavendish. That a reversal of gender traits is taking place is suggested by the fact that it is the men (who would supposedly be hotter in nature) who are killed by the cold, while the woman, preserved by the "heat of her youth," survives. Unable to maintain their hot, dry male integrity, the men are transmuted into the customarily femi-nine qualities of coldness, wetness, and putridity.

Leaving the corpses of the male crew – and the specter of male oppression – behind, the female protagonist steps into the new world. This world turns out to be inhabited by anthropomorphic animals: bear-men, fox-men, bird-men, ape-men, and so on. The lady, who is proclaimed Empress of the new world, divides the populace into various learned societies. The bear-men, for example, are to be experimental philosophers, the bird-men astronomers, and the ape-men chemists. (These last two groupings hint at the symbolism of the bestiary and the association of birds with sight and apes with taste.)

Cavendish, who often found herself excluded from male scientific circles despite her deep interest in natural philosophy, used *Blazing World* to fantasize about a woman who has the power to command a whole kingdom of male scientists. She also employed the story to present a critique of science itself, and, particularly, of scientific visualism.[118]

In the observations on experimental philosophy which accompany *Blazing World*, Cavendish suggests that she regards experimental science as a more suitable field for housewives than for philosophers:

> Our Female-sex ... would prove good experimental Philosophers, and inform the world how to make Artificial Snow, by their Creams, or Possets beaten in froth; and Ice, by their clear, candied, or crusted Quiddities or Conserves of fruits; and Frost, by their candied herbs and flowers ... [119]

Nature was, after all, a housewife herself, according to Cavendish, employing her time "in Brewing, Baking, Churning, Spinning, Sowing."[120]

Similarly, in an introduction he wrote to Cavendish's *Philosophical and Physical Opinions*, the author's husband responded to the question of how Cavendish, as an untrained woman, could speak of medical matters, by saying that any "good Farmer's wife in the Country" would have access to such knowledge.[121] Such homey portrayals of science served to diminish the masculine majesty of the field and bring it within the domestic realm of women.

Cavendish's strongest criticism was directed at the scientific reliance on "Optick Glasses." In *Blazing World* the bear-men scientists try to understand nature by examining it through telescopes and microscopes. It soon becomes evident, however, that such magnifying lenses have a series of deficiencies which lead them to present a grossly distorted image of the world. For example, lenses can produce a magnified image of a louse, but not of a whale, they can operate in light but not in darkness, they can enhance one sense but are no use to any of the others.[122] "Your glasses are false informers, and instead of discovering the truth, delude your senses," the Empress proclaims. "Wherefore I command you to break them."[123] The bear-men find this command unbearable: "[they] kneeled down, and in the humblest manner petitioned that they might not be broken; for, said they, we take more delight in artificial delusions than in natural truths."[124] The Empress relents and allows the experimenters to keep their lenses with the condition that they not cause any public disturbance. As a final jab at the delusions of scientists who imagine that all mysteries can be comprehended through extending the power of sight, Cavendish leaves her experimental philosophers trying to invent a magnifying glass by means of which "they could spy out a vacuum."[125]

One of Cavendish's objections to magnifying lenses was that they revealed only surfaces, and not interiors or "the obscure actions of Nature."[126] In *Blazing World*, for example, the bear-men confess that "their glasses would do them but little service in the bowels of the earth."[127] This gives the animal inhabitants of the inner earth the opportunity to explain that, though they lack light, they are not "blind," but rather employ alternative means of perception. Magnifying glasses are of no use to these beings, unless the scientists can provide "glasses as are proper for their perception."[128]

Cavendish considered one of the guiding objectives of the scientific use of magnifying glasses to be the visual domination of femininity. Nonetheless, Cavendish asserted, the nature of women cannot be discerned through an inspection of visual surfaces, however detailed. "I doubt [scientists] will hardly find out the interior nature of our Sex, by the exterior form of their faces or Countenances."[129]

In Cavendish's story "The Travelling Spirits" a man goes to a witch and asks her to help him travel to the moon. The witch responds that she is unable to do so, as "the Natural Philosophers are the only men for that Journey."[130] ("It was not a Woman that invented Perspective-Glasses to pierce into the Moon."[131]) She is likewise unable to take the man to either heaven or hell. The man then asks the witch to take him to the center of the earth. "That I can do (said she), and so obscurely, that the Natural Philosophers shall never spye us."[132] This is the dark, inner world of sensibility, accessible to the witch, but beyond the searching gaze of the scientist.

In closing, let us consider how Margaret Cavendish, through her writing, challenged the social and sensory norms of her day. Even if Cavendish had never written anything save for what upheld the established order, the mere fact of her writing would have been an affront to the traditional gender division of the senses and of labor. Writing, as an intellectual activity and as a public act, lay outside of the customary bounds of women's work. Similarly, as a "discourse to the eyes" (in Cavendish's words),[133] writing lay outside the bounds of women's symbolic sensory field. As Cavendish noted, the only "discourse to the [male] eyes" that women were expected to present was their own bodies.[134]

Margaret Cavendish's writing was particularly disturbing to readers in its lack of "feminine modesty." Far from recoiling in maidenly horror at the thought of her private "scribblings" being placed before the public view, Cavendish ardently and vociferously desired her works to be seen and disseminated. She speaks of a book she wrote but stored unpublished in a trunk as "buried in a Grave,"[135] the same words she uses to describe the fate of women who are consigned by their manual labor to anonymity. While Cavendish critiqued the hypervisuality of the masculine scientific world view, she was nonetheless anxious to avoid the "obscure" domestic sphere of women and achieve the public visibility largely restricted to men.[136]

Cavendish's play, *Youth's Glory and Death's Banquet*, presents an elaboration of this desire. In this play a young woman, Sanspareile, dedicates herself to studying philosophy. A male philosopher counsels that, in place of her studies, Sanspareile should be instructed "in high huswifry, as milking kyne, as making Cheese . . . and to preserve Confectionary, and to teach her the use of a needle, and to get her a Husband."[137] Sanspareile, however, persists in her scholarly endeavors and eventually wins the respect of all by her intellectual brilliance. One of her male admirers declares: "She deserves a Statue for herself, as well as a Library for her works."[138] This is the visual immortality for which Cavendish, who believed there was a direct link between sight and memory,[139] longed.

It was not only the fact of Margaret Cavendish's writing which challenged contemporary norms, but her style of writing. Cavendish tended to present all opinions and conventions, including her own, as hypotheses which could be accepted, rejected or transformed by the reader. In her "Femal Oration," for example, she had five women discuss a range of possible identities for women, including scholar, sportswoman, housewife, and seductress.[140] The domination of a single, incontrovertible model for behavior is hence broken down by Cavendish into a multiplicity of potential roles and models. Although Cavendish was by no means free of social prejudices herself, her ultimate vision was of a world in which women and men are not obliged to conform to a repressive external standard of behavior but can create their own identities.

> If any should like the world I have made, and be willing to be my subjects, they may imagine themselves such... but if they cannot endure to be subjects, they may create worlds of their own, and govern themselves as they please.[141]

Equally distinctive (and possibly exasperating for many readers) is the form-lessness of Cavendish's work, with its endless prefaces and restatements of ideas, and its frequent contradictions. While Cavendish is interested in recording her thoughts for posterity, she cannot bring herself to present them in any defini-tive, bounded, form. The reader never feels that Cavendish has made a final pronouncement on a subject, that the voice of authority has spoken, for her writing too evidently represents but part of an ever-changing and overflowing stream of ideas. As Janet Todd points out in her study of women's writing, Margaret Cavendish to some extent carried out the strategy which would be advocated by the twentieth-century feminist Hélène Cixous: ``that women break down the majesty and mystery of the closed male text by an endless seam of texts without traditional form or closure.''[142]

Such ``disordering'' of regulative norms, however, is likely to be classified, and hence dismissed, as lunacy, and such was the case with Margaret Cavendish, who came to be known as ``Mad Madge.'' The cult of bashful feminine sensi-bility which developed after Cavendish's death made the ``aberrant'' nature of the writer's brash self-assertiveness even more striking. Virginia Woolf would give picturesque expression to this contrast when she wrote that Margaret Cavendish's work was like a monstrous cucumber running riot over a garden of flowers.[143] Nonetheless, by criss-crossing the symbolic domains of men and women in her writing, Margaret Cavendish was able both to appropriate tradi-tionally masculine prerogatives, and elaborate feminine alternatives to the dominant social and sensory order.

Part III
Aesthetics

Figure 3 Remedios Varo, *Still Life Reviving* (1963)
Source: Courtesy of Walter Gruen.

5   Symbolist harmonies, Futurist colors, Surrealist recipes
Crossing sensory borders in the arts

During the seventeenth and eighteenth centuries the sensual and sacred cosmologies of pre-modernity were largely superseded by a scientific and mechanical view of the world. This view held the primary qualities of the universe to be figure, magnitude, and motion. Sensory qualities such as odors and colors were emptied of their traditional symbolic content and deemed to lack reality outside the minds of their perceivers. As a consequence of this ideological shift, "the world that people had thought themselves living in – a world rich with colour and sound, redolent with fragrance" appeared to many to have become "cold, colourless, silent and dead."[1] As John Keats would put it:

> Philosophy will clip an Angel's wings,
> Conquer all mysteries by rule and line,
> Empty the haunted air and gnomèd mine –
> Unweave a rainbow.[2]

The sensory symbolism suppressed by Enlightenment science, however, would be revived and celebrated as an aesthetic ideal in nineteenth-century art. The role of sensory symbolism was thus transformed from that of providing a mythic framework for understanding the cosmos in pre-modernity to that of inspiring artistic alternatives to mainstream culture in modernity. The ways in which this development affected traditional models of gender will constitute one of the interconnected themes of this chapter.

"Sounds, fragrances and colours correspond"

The revival and reinvention of models of sensory symbolism in the 1800s were due to a convergence of influences. The nineteenth century witnessed a widespread movement by artists directed against what was perceived to be the materialist tendencies of modern culture, principally scientific rationalism, industrial capitalism, and bourgeois worldliness. According to aesthetic philosophers such as Walter Pater, the Enlightenment had produced an artificial split between sense and intellect, body and spirit, which needed to be reconciled through art.[3]

Inspiration for this movement came primarily from the religious and artistic traditions of the pre-modern West, although the aesthetic traditions of other regions of the world, particularly the Orient, had some influence as well. In some instances, the use of consciousness-altering drugs played a role in enhancing, and synaesthetically merging, the sensory perceptions of artists and writers. The Hashish Club of nineteenth-century Paris, for example, included such literary notables as Victor Hugo, Honoré de Balzac, Théophile Gautier, and Charles Baudelaire. This last wrote of his perceptions under hashish: "The senses of smell, sight, hearing and touch alike participate in this development . . . . Sounds are clad in colors and colors contain a certain music."[4]

Science itself, with its investigations into the nature of perception and its speculations concerning the interrelationship of the senses, fanned the interest in sensory aesthetics. For example, there was considerable scientific discussion in the eighteenth and nineteenth centuries concerning possible correspondences between sound and color. In 1704 Isaac Newton proposed that elementary colors matched the notes of the musical scale. In 1725 Bernard Castel, who had undertaken a similar study, suggested that a "colour organ" might be created which would translate musical compositions into colors. In the late 1800s the "Symbolist scientist," Charles Henry, attempted to ground the doctrine of sensory correspondence in a scientific discourse.[5] Although such theories usually ended up being marginalized within science, they nonetheless caught the public imagination and were widely disseminated.

The artistic representation of multisensory phenomena during this period took various related forms. One of these was to attempt to evoke all the senses, including the "lower" senses of smell, taste, and touch, through art.[6] Many nineteenth-century paintings and novels, for example, abound in olfactory imagery, from the Pre-Raphaelites' depictions of swirling incense to the Naturalists' descriptions of body odors. Another form consisted of employing perceptual terms associated with one sense to evoke those of another. An early example of such synaesthesia, or *trans-sensory* aesthetics, occurs in Percy Shelley's poem "The Sensitive Plant":

> And the hyacinth purple, and white, and blue,
> Which flung from its bells a sweet peal anew
> Of music so delicate, soft, and intense,
> It was felt like an odour within the sense.[7]

Finally, certain artists were interested in actually creating art forms for the so-called lower senses, and in combining different sensory stimuli within artistic productions. Already in the late eighteenth century, for example, Horace Walpole had speculated on the possibility of creating a tactile poetry of knotted threads, or else a poetry of odors ("How charming it would be to smell an ode from a nosegay!").[8] Although the notion of extending art to new sensory domains would be more often discussed than practiced, nineteenth-century artists did experiment with theater and concert performances in which colors,

sounds, and perfumes were mingled.⁹ The ultimate goal for many of these synaesthetes was a synthesis of the arts – an omni-art – which would engage all of
the senses and create an aesthetic totality.¹⁰

This multisensory aestheticism influenced a range of nineteenth-century
artistic trends, including Romanticism and Naturalism. The one with which it
was most closely associated, however, was Symbolism, a broad movement based
in France but diffused throughout Europe. The central concern of Symbolism
was to evoke ideas and emotions indirectly through the employment of
symbols. In the Symbolist Manifesto Jean Moréas wrote that "the idea should
not make its appearance deprived of the sumptuous trapping of external analogies, for the essential character of Symbolist art consists in never going straight
to the conception of the idea itself."¹¹ The "sumptuous trappings" employed
by the Symbolists to convey their analogies included the range of sensory
phenomena: from sights and sounds to scents and textures.

The forefather of Symbolism, Charles Baudelaire, played a major role in
promoting a multisensory aesthetics through his poems and essays. The best-
known example of Baudelaire's fascination with the subject occurs in his poem
"Correspondences":

> As far-off echoes from a distance sound
> In unity profound and recondite
> Boundless as night itself and as the light,
> Sounds, fragrances and colours correspond.¹²

"It would be really surprising," Baudelaire reasoned, "if sound could *not* suggest
color, if colors could *not* suggest a melody . . . things being always expressed by a
reciprocal analogy since the day when God presented the world as a complex and
indivisible totality."¹³ Nonetheless, "modern professors of aesthetics," according
to the poet, had "forgotten the color of the sky, the form of plants, the movement and odor of animals," and their "rigid fingers, frozen to their pens" were
unable "to play over the immense keyboard of *correspondences.*"¹⁴

The theory of sensory correspondences espoused by Baudelaire influenced,
to a greater or lesser degree, a multitude of writers and poets, as well as painters
and musicians. The most prominent literary work to evidence this influence was
J.-K. Huysmans' novel *Against Nature* (*A rebours*), in which the protagonist
retires from the world to dedicate himself to a life of sensory refinements and
musings on sensory symbolism.¹⁵

Within the field of poetry, Stéphane Mallarmé, Paul Verlaine, and Arthur
Rimbaud, along with other Symbolist or quasi-Symbolist poets, made considerable use of synaesthetic imagery.¹⁶ The work which for many came to signify
Symbolist synaesthesia was Rimbaud's "Sonnet of Vowels," in which a color is
assigned to each vowel: "A," for example, is described as a "black corset, hairy
with bursting flies," "E" as "white kings, shivering Queen Anne's lace," and
"I" as "crimson, bloody spit."¹⁷

In the visual arts, Gustave Moreau, whose paintings became Symbolist icons, evoked textures, sounds, and scents through the representation of intricately patterned surfaces, musical instruments, and exuberant flowers. In Moreau's *Salome Dancing Before Herod* a surfeit of tactile and visual sensations are suggested through jeweled clothing, engraved walls, and ornate statues, as well as through the dancing body of Salome.[18] In front of Salome a panther – a traditional symbol of seductive scent – lies amidst overblown roses.[19] In the background a woman plays a lute and an ornate censer exhales incense.[20]

The Dutch Symbolist painter Jan Toorop, in turn, aspired to create a style of art which would not only suggest sounds and scents, but would actually transpose them on to a visual plane. In Toorop's works bells ring out swirling sound lines (which transform into angels' hair), voices visibly issue from mouths, and scents rise up like smoke from flowers.[21]

In the field of music, Richard Wagner was praised by Symbolists for achieving a fusion of sound and light in his "music dramas."[22] Claude Debussy, who perhaps came closest to incorporating Symbolist ideals into music, envisioned a lyrical music which would recreate and invest with dream-like significance the sounds, rhythms, and colors of nature.[23]

Alexander Scriabin, although not directly involved in the Symbolist movement,[24] provides what is probably the most pronounced example of a multisensory composer at the turn of the century. Scriabin believed in the necessity of "raising" the senses of touch, taste, and smell to the level of art and thereby transforming "the entire human body into a sounding board" of aesthetic impressions.[25] In his most ambitious project, *Mysterium*, he planned to combine an orchestral performance with dance, colored lights, projected pictures, pillars of incense, and sensations of touch and taste.[26]

The aesthetic philosophies of Symbolism continued to influence many artists who participated in the modernist movements of the early twentieth century, from Wassily Kandinsky in painting to Arnold Schoenberg in music to James Joyce in literature.[27] At the end of this chapter this influence will be explored in relation to two twentieth-century art movements, Futurism and Surrealism. While a number of modernist artists were interested in sensory interplay, however, their work, through its radical disruption of traditional structures of representation, tended to be perceived more in terms of a fragmentation of aesthetic experience, than as an expression of a classic harmony of the senses.

In fact, the theory of a unity of the senses had lost much of its artistic and public favor by the end of the First World War. It was generally taken to be no more than a quaint holdover from *la belle époque*, hardly relevant to the changing social and intellectual climate of the new century. The fact that scientific studies had demonstrated that there was no agreement among synaesthetes as to which color corresponded to which musical note, and so on, seemed to emphasize the idiosyncratic, illusory nature of sensory correspondences.[28] The spread of new technologies in sensory transmission and reproduction, such as the telephone, the phonograph, the radio and the movie camera, called attention to the divisibility of sensory reality, not to its unity. The ideal of sensory interplay, if not entirely forgotten, was nonetheless deemed to be out of date.

The multisensory aesthetics of the late nineteenth century, consequently, provides us with a compelling last glimpse at a shared vision of a world in which "sounds, fragrances and colours correspond."

The Master of Sweet Odours

When art becomes a matter for any and all of the senses, the distinction between art and life blurs. This, indeed, was the ideal of many Symbolist thinkers, who agreed with Walter Pater that for the artist "to treat life in the spirit of art, is to make life a thing in which means and ends are identified."[29] This ideal was taken up by the aesthetes or dandies of the late 1800s, who attempted to live life, or at least to appear to be living life, as a work of art.

In England Oscar Wilde was considered the embodiment of the dandy, arbiter of fashion and creator (in his own words) of "beautiful coloured musical things such as *Salomé* and the *Florentine Tragedy* and *La Sainte Courtisane*."[30] In France the quintessential aesthete was Count Robert de Montesquiou (1855–1921), whose life seemed a fulfillment of Pater's exhortation "to grasp at any exquisite passion or any stirring of the senses, strange dyes, strange colours and curious odours, or the work of the artist's hands, or the face of one's friend."[31]

Robert de Montesquiou wrote poetry in the Symbolist style, taking as his subject matter flowers, colors, scents, exotic settings, and vague, yearning emotions. "Venice/Flavour of aniseed," reads one of his poems, "A bluish-white reflection/Is tinted/With absinthe/Dies of softness."[32] Montesquiou was known among his friends as *Le Chef des odeurs suaves* – "The Master of Sweet Odours" – after the title of one of his collections of poetry (itself taken from a character in Flaubert's novel *Salammbô*).[33]

Montesquiou extolled a Baudelairean blending of sensation in his poetry: bells are "flowers of sound"; perfumes are "more veiled than the voice of violas"; "the senses are fused and the five become one."[34] Montesquiou, indeed, believed the mingling of aesthetically pleasing sensations to be essential to the enjoyment of life. He claimed that when roses filled the streets and music the balconies, "when rare fruits and delicacies resuscitated from ancient menus competed in color with antique ceramic dishes . . . then I felt a ravishing pleasure, a pleasure which finds its exact definition in that subtle Baudelairean verse: 'Fragrances, colors and sounds correspond'."[35] The popular notion of Montesquiou's synaesthetic tendencies was reflected in a cartoon published in *La Vie parisienne* which portrayed the poet playing a harp with a paintbrush.[36]

As befitted an aesthete, Montesquiou owed his reputation for creative flair as much to the artistry of his lifestyle as to his poetry. The poet's imaginatively decorated apartment was a noted attraction in this regard.[37] One room of this apartment had walls lined with different materials in various shades of grey – "mouse-grey" velvet, silvery-blue leather, and transparent gauze painted with fish. Montesquiou was said to comb Paris to find grey flowers to adorn this grey room, which he called "the veritable sanctuary of my aesthetic offices."

Elsewhere in the apartment, tapestries of forest scenes, a mossy carpet, earthen-ware animals, and antique musical instruments combined to turn a passageway into a symbolically melodious forest path. A room furnished with a choir stall, an ecclesiastical chair, sculpted angels, and a bell "with a religious ring" expressed Montesquiou's mystical aspirations. Behind this room lay the bath-room with turquoise tiles and basins and a water-spouting ceramic elephant.[38]

One of the most innovative aspects of the "Master of Sweet Odours" interior design was the employment of perfume as a decorative element. A contempo-rary journalist wrote approvingly of this olfactory furnishing:

> [Montesquiou] has the fantasy, which can be qualified as genial, of intro-ducing, for the very first time, *perfume* into the art of decorating. The visitor who crosses the threshold of his *home* has his olfactory nerve titil-lated by subtle odors, each one having a symbolic meaning. A perfume burner was placed in the room where one eats; another, in the room where one smokes; another in the bedroom; another in the room where one chats. And I really believe that, according to the nature of the conversation, the scents differ, and that the one which encourages flirtation is not the one which encourages political discussion.[39]

Montesquiou's social gatherings were as self-consciously artistic and idiosyn-cratic as the poet's home. Dinner with the poet sometimes consisted of foods all of one color. For an autumnal gathering, female guests were asked to come dressed as autumn leaves. Montesquiou himself enjoyed dressing up as different historical figures, Louis XIV, Ludwig II, or even Plato. "Let's not forget," he wrote, "that I gave parties for egotistical reasons, less to satisfy my guests than to please myself."[40]

Montesquiou's influence on contemporary aesthetics was extensive. For Marcel Proust, Montesquiou was the "Professor of Beauty," and an inspiration for the character of Charlus in *Remembrance of Things Past*. "Monsieur," wrote Gustave Moreau to Montesquiou, "I have often heard you talked about; I knew your delicate and exquisite taste for artistic and spiritual things."[41] In a poem dedicated to Montesquiou, Paul Verlaine enthused "I admire the subtle thinker and the austere aesthete . . . but I love the refined enchanter with the flowery spells."[42] Impressed by a visit to Montesquiou's apartment, Stéphane Mallarmé described the interior of that "Ali-Baba's cave" in glowing terms to Huysmans. The exquisitely tasteful Count Montesquiou thus became the model for Huysmans' aristocratic and hyper-sensitive Des Esseintes in *Against Nature*.[43]

The painted dinner

According to certain Symbolist tendencies, the merging of sense and intellect, life and art, represented an attempt to overcome artificial divisions and discover the correspondences between body and spirit, nature and the imagination. According to others, however, the ideal aesthetic life was a life of artifice, a life opposed to nature. This ideal was embodied by the fictional hero of *Against Nature*, Des Esseintes, who defiantly stated that "Nature . . . has had her day; she has finally and utterly exhausted the patience of sensitive observers by the revolting uniformity of her landscapes and skyscapes."[44]

Most of Des Esseintes' aesthetic experiments in *Against Nature* are dedicated to improving on nature through art. At a dinner party he serves a completely black meal – black puddings, black olives, caviar and mulberries on a black tablecloth – transforming the "natural" function of eating into a contrived expression of aesthetic sensibility. For his home, he prefers colors which will look strong in artificial, rather than natural light. He fills an aquarium with mechanical fish and tints the water different shades to simulate the effects of sun and shade on the sea. He gilds and bejewels the shell of a live tortoise to enjoy the reflections it creates as it moves across his carpet. He creates the illusion of a flowering meadow by spraying a room with floral perfumes – artificial, of course. When, in the most famous passage of the book, Des Esseintes plays "internal symphonies" with his "mouth organ" – a selection of liqueurs said to correspond to different musical sounds – the reader has the impression that he is delighting in the artificiality of the transposition, not in the natural correspondence between sensory modalities.[45]

This nineteenth-century craving for "perverse pleasures" had antecedents in the period of Roman decadence, for which reason Huysmans and Symbolists of similar tendencies were sometimes known as "Decadents."[46] The character of Des Esseintes, indeed, was partly inspired by the legendary third-century Roman emperor Elagabulus.[47] Life, for Elagabulus, was said to be "nothing but a search after pleasures",[48] and nothing was pleasurable to him but what appeared to exceed or violate nature. He reputedly enjoyed reversing the customary activities of day and night, dressing in women's clothing, and wearing jewels on his shoes. Elagabulus had his swimming pools filled with rosewater, except when he was far from the coast, in which case they were filled with sea water. Likewise, the emperor never ate fish when by the sea, only when in the interior. In order to increase the element of artifice, the fish would be cooked in a blue sauce to make them appear to be swimming in water.

At his banquets Elagabulus served "peas with gold pieces, lentils with onyx, beans with amber, and rice with pearls."[49] "Also he gave summer-banquets in different colours, one day a green banquet, another day an iridescent one, and next in order a blue one, varying them continually every day of the summer."[50] (Another decadent Roman, Antoninus Geta, liked to give "alphabet dinners," with foods all beginning with the same letter.)[51] Playing with notions of simulacra, Elagabulus would sometimes taunt his dinner guests with replicas of food, while he was served real food:

> At times he would send to their table only embroidered napkins with pictures of the viands that were set before himself, as many in number as the courses which he was to have, so that they were served only with representations made by the needle or the loom. Sometimes, however, paintings too were

displayed to them, so that they were served with the whole dinner, as it were, but were all the while tormented by hunger.[52]

The emperor's most notorious act was to suffocate guests under a floral shower which descended on them from the false ceiling of his banqueting room.[53]

In these examples, dear to Huysmans and the nineteenth-century Decadents, the notion of sensory correspondence is transformed from one of harmony to one of contrived alliance and even discord: one cannot *eat* a painted dinner. The message seemed to be that, when life is made into art, it ceases to be livable. Yet this itself appealed to the Decadents, who tended to find illness and death much more aesthetic conditions than healthy vitality.[54]

As he concludes his experiments, Des Esseintes, like Elagabulus's flower-buried guests, falls "fainting, almost dying" under the oppressive potency of exotic perfumes.[55] The aesthete decides to go on a journey to England. He gets as far as an English pub in Paris, and then, satisfied with the simulation of English life he finds there, returns to his house, "feeling all the physical weariness and moral fatigue of a man who has come home after a long and perilous journey."[56]

Where the singing flower grows

At the end of *Against Nature* Des Esseintes, exhausted by his unnatural existence yet terrified at the prospect of being engulfed by "human mediocrity," pleads with God for salvation. This longing for divine transcendence was experienced by Huysmans himself, along with many other Symbolists, who turned to the supernatural as the ultimate antidote for world-weariness.

The Symbolist fascination with the sacred represented not only a rejection of bourgeois "banality," but also a revolt against scientific materialism – which threatened to make the whole universe as banal as the bourgeoisie. The writer Villiers de L'Isle Adam, for instance, satirized the false sense of visual dominion offered by photography by representing the inventor Thomas Edison as longing to have been around with a camera in biblical times.

> It would have been delightful to possess good photographic prints (taken on the spot) of *Joshua Bidding the Sun Stand Still* . . . . Or why not several views of *The Earthly Paradise*, taken from the *Gateway of the Flaming Swords*; the *Tree of Knowledge*; the *Serpent*; and so forth?[57]

The painter Edvard Munch, responding to the same issue, declared that "the camera will never be able to rival painting as long as it is impossible to use it in Heaven and Hell."[58] Gustave Moreau, another ardent critic of scientific materialism, stated: "I believe only in that which I do not see and uniquely in that which I sense."[59]

The closed eyes of the figures in many Symbolist paintings exemplify this desire on the part of artists to turn away from external phenomena in search of an ethereal inner vision.[60] At the same time, however, the Symbolists were manifestly interested in external sensory phenomena. These two seemingly opposed tendencies were partially reconciled through the use of sensory imagery to express spiritual ideals, in a fashion reminiscent of that of many mystics.[61] The olfactory evocations frequent in Symbolism heightened the quasi-identification of this movement with religious mysticism, also commonly associated with olfactory imagery. Thus the following commentary on Baudelaire's scent-laden poetry – "one thinks of a contemplation where the mind is not like an eye but like a sensitive and discriminating nostril"[62] – could also be made regarding certain writings by St. Bernard of Clairvaux or St. John of the Cross.

The religious cosmologies popular among the Symbolists typically possessed an elaborate system of sensory symbolism grounded in a transcendent theology. This combination of the aesthetic and the cosmological had a strong appeal for artists who wished to go beyond the mere "flower arranging" of sensation and situate their aesthetic ideals within a celestial framework. The cosmologists discussed in the first chapter of this book, St. Hildegard, Boehme, and Fourier, with their rich sensory analogies and their mystical or utopian ideologies, all attracted the attention of one or another forerunner or follower of Symbolism. Fourier was taken up by Baudelaire and Hildegard was consulted by Huysmans.[63] Boehme influenced the English Symbolists, either directly or mediated through writers, such as Coleridge and Blake, who had found inspiration in his work.[64]

Huysmans' interest in mysticism (which intensified after his conversion to Catholicism) culminated in the novel *The Cathedral*, a book which, in many ways, constitutes a sacred version of *Against Nature*. Whereas the materialist Des Esseintes is only able to toy with colors, gems, and perfumes on a worldly level, the protagonist of *The Cathedral* comprehends them within their cosmological context; he penetrates the divine significance of the fragrances of sanctity and sin, of the "green and sparkling fire" of the emerald, of the "angelic" sky-blues and rose-pinks of medieval art, and of the "perfumed flower beds" of the stained-glass windows of Chartres.[65] Huysmans believed such sacred correspondences to constitute the true "science of symbolism":

> The [medieval] symbolists not only considered the analogies and resemblances they discovered between the form, scent, and colour of a flower and the being with whom they compared it; they also studied the Bible, especially the passages wherein a tree or flower was named, and then ascribed to it such qualities as were mentioned or could be inferred from the text. They did the same with regard to animals, colours, gems, everything to which they could attribute a meaning.[66]

Huysmans' religious leanings prompted him to write a "Symbolist" life of the medieval mystic Lydwine of Schiedam replete with descriptions of miraculous aromas and synaesthetic visions. "The hagiographies," Huysmans commented with approval, "do not contain any biographies which are more perfumed than Lydwine's."[67]

An eighteenth-century mystic with a large following among the Symbolists was the Swedish visionary Emmanuel Swedenborg, who expounded a theory of universal correspondences in his writings. Baudelaire wrote that Swedenborg had demonstrated "that everything, form, movement, quantity, color, odor, both in the spiritual world and in nature, is significant, reciprocal, converse, correspondent."[68] Balzac promulgated the doctrines of Swedenborg in his novel *Seraphita*, in which the heroine proclaims: "I know where the singing flower grows, and the talking light descends, and fragrant colors shine!"[69] Balzac's version of Swedenborgian mysticism became standard reading among Symbolists from Robert de Montesquiou to the English Decadent writer Arthur Symons.[70]

In terms of contemporary movements, Theosophy, with its blend of Eastern and Western mysticism, was popular among artists of the day, as were various forms of occultism.[71] The most notable instance of the latter, as regards Symbolism, was the *Ordre de la Rose + Croix*. This order was founded by the novelist, art critic, and aesthete Joséphin Péladan (a.k.a. Le Sâr Mérodack) with the purpose of fostering a "rebirth of mysticism decisively victorious over Science, materialism, and the Revolution of modern times."[72] The *Ordre de la Rose + Croix* sponsored a number of prominent Symbolist art salons in order to further this ideal.

Satanism, or the idea of Satanism, was also fashionable among Symbolists, who tended to be more interested in vice than virtue. From an aesthetic perspective at least, Satanism enabled artists such as Baudelaire, Moreau, Huysmans, Félicien Rops, and Scriabin, to deal with transgressive aspects of sensuality while retaining a mystical aura. Thus the Decadent writer Arthur Symons described Baudelaire as bringing "every complication of taste, the exasperation of perfumes, the irritant of cruelty, the very odours and colours of corruption, to the creation and adornment of a sort of religion . . . ."[73] In his *Poèmes saturniens* Verlaine told of "beautiful demons, youthful Satans" who "dedicate their five senses to the Seven Sins."[74]

This line by Verlaine reminds us that, unlike the Christian mystics, the Symbolists were usually aesthetes rather than ascetics, interested in cultivating the sensory delights of this world, instead of rejecting them.[75] The Symbolists, in fact, never lost sight of aesthetic values in their search for transcendence: they were artists first and mystics second.[76] Of Huysmans it was said: "It is art and art alone that has converted him. He has been converted to the Christian art of the Middle Ages, not to Christianity."[77] The salons of the *Ordre de la Rose + Croix* were "dedicated to the Art-God with masterpieces for dogma."[78] Scriabin's motto was "From our present life to another life through art."[79] For the artists of the Symbolist era, mysticism provided the ultimate aesthetic experience.

Mal du siècle

While the Symbolist movement attracted widespread interest, it was also the subject of widespread ridicule and condemnation. Symbolism was said to stand in the way of science and progress, to corrupt the arts, and to encourage moral perversion and social disorder. One of the most virulent attacks was presented in 1893 in a book called *Degeneration*, written by the physician and journalist Max Nordau. Nordau, who had studied medicine under the "grand priest of hysteria," Jean Martin Charcot, attempted to prove in this book that the artistic productions of the Symbolists and related groups were the direct result of physical and mental illness.[80]

As has been noted, the Symbolists, and particularly the Decadents, were intrigued by the condition of sickness. From their perspective, illness – world-weariness – was the appropriate response to bustling, materialist modern life, and perhaps a necessary precursor to spiritual enlightenment. From Nordau's perspective, however, sickness led the Symbolists to create doctrines and works which were vitiated and of interest only as examples of a pathological condition.

> The physician, especially if he have devoted himself to the special study of nervous and mental maladies, recognises at a glance . . . in the tendencies of contemporary art and poetry, in the life and conduct of the men who write mystic, symbolic, and 'decadent' works, and the attitude taken by their admirers in the tastes and aesthetic instincts of fashionable society, the confluence of two well-defined conditions of disease . . . degeneration (degeneracy) and hysteria.[81]

According to Nordau, the pathological mental conditions of contemporary artists and writers manifested themselves in actual physical traits. Thus Flaubert's degeneracy was attested to by his reportedly "faun-like" ears, while the vibrating colors employed by the Impressionists were due to "trembling eyes" caused by hysteria.[82]

Nordau considered the artistic critique of science as materialistic to be a further sign of psychological abnormality. "True, science tells us nothing about life after death, of harp-concerts in Paradise, and of the transformation of stupid youths and hysterical geese into white-clad angels with rainbow-colored wings."[83] However, "what saintly legend is as beautiful as the life of an inquirer, who spends his existence bending over a microscope, almost without bodily wants . . . without any other ambition than that perhaps one little new fact may be firmly established?"[84]

The intense visualism of the scientist at his microscope, "almost without bodily wants," provides a contrast to the artistic celebration of multisensory experience. In fact, the most telling evidence of the pathological condition of the Symbolists, according to Nordau, is their confusion of the senses. Attempts to create a "language of the senses," he declared, simply result in "senseless twaddle."[85] Writing, in turn, disintegrates as a medium of intellectual communication when paper and ink are colored and the pages of books perfumed.[86] Sensory mysticism is likewise suspect: "it is an old clinical observation that mental decay is accompanied by color mysticism."[87]

Expressions of synaesthesia in general, according to Nordau, demonstrate "diseased and debilitated brain-activity"; for what healthy mind would want to relinquish "the advantages of the differentiated perceptions of phenomena" and regress to the confused sensory world of "the mollusc"?[88] (The supporters of a multisensory aesthetic responded that Nordau confused "the *sensory chaos* which precedes the development of the perceptual faculties" with the current "*synthetic tendency*" involving a conscious and complex elaboration of sensory relations.[89])

The most apparently anti-intellectual proclamation of the Symbolists in this regard was that it might be possible to develop an art and language of smell and taste: "We await the symbolism of tastes and smells," declared Félix Fénéon in "Une esthétique scientifique."[90] For Nordau and other upholders of the traditional sensory hierarchy, of course, nothing could be *more* abnormal. To raise the "animal" senses of taste and smell to the level of art defied the "evolutionary primacy" of sight and hearing and challenged the whole Enlightenment rationalist and visualist project. Thus, while actual attempts to develop an olfactory art were few,[91] reaction to the idea by Nordau and others was pronounced.

Just as a deficient sense of sight was a symptom of "effeminate" hysteria, in Nordau's opinion, so an "excessive" interest in smell and taste was a sign of "bestial" degeneracy.[92] Such interest must needs be animal in nature since, according to Nordau, it is impossible for humans to conceptualize through smell.

> In order to inspire a man with . . . abstract concepts by scents alone; to make him conceive the phenomenon of the world, its changes and causes of motion, by a succession of perfumes, his frontal lobe must be depressed and the olfactory lobe of a dog substituted for it.[93]

Fortunately, Nordau affirms, the sensory "degenerates" of the late nineteenth century cannot ultimately compete with "men who rise early, and are not weary before sunset, who have clear heads, solid stomachs and hard muscles."[94] By the end of the next, twentieth, century, society would have need of men with nerves of steel and clearly differentiated and hierarchized perceptions:

> a generation to whom it will not be injurious . . . to be constantly called to the telephone, to be thinking simultaneously of the five continents, to live half their time in a railway carriage or in a flying machine, and to satisfy the demands of a circle of ten thousand acquaintances.[95]

Nordau, did not, however, hold out much hope for the arts in this future world of rapid transportation and mass communication. The art of tommorrow, he stated, will continue to distinguish itself by the "spasmodic seeking for new forms" the sole result of which hitherto has been "childish declamation, with colored lights and changing perfumes as accompaniments."[96] Nonetheless, this failure of art to evolve in a meaningful fashion will not prove a problem, according to Nordau, for it is the destiny of art to be ever more marginalized by science, as humanity moves "from instinct to knowledge, from emotion to judgement."[97] Eventually, Nordau concluded, art "will no longer be cultivated except by the most emotional portion of humanity – by women, by the young, perhaps even by children."[98]

Feminine idols

Given the traditional gender divisions of the senses – the association of the "lower" senses with women and the "higher" senses with men – the Symbolist move to unite the senses can be interpreted as representing an attempt to integrate femininity with masculinity. To cross sensory lines, as the Symbolists claimed to do, was to cross gender lines. For many Symbolists, indeed, androgyny, and particularly the feminized male, was an artistic and social ideal. Symbolist paintings often portrayed androgynous beings.[99] The novelist Joséphin Péladan, wrote that "the androgyn is the artistic sex *par excellence.*"[100] The literary magazine *Le Décadent* declared in 1886 that, through the new aesthetics, "Man becomes more delicate, feminine and divine."[101] Montesquiou proclaimed in one of his poems: "The effeminate fights, the effeminate avenges itself, the effeminate conquers."[102]

By concerning themselves with perfumes and savors, with clothing and interior decoration, nineteenth-century aesthetes were certainly delving into traditionally feminine sensory and social fields. While Montesquiou was called the "Master of Sweet Odours," two of his male friends were nicknamed the "Minister of Taste" and the "Floral Chancellor."[103] Such apparent effeminacy on the part of aesthetes and Symbolists inevitably called forth critical comment. In the case of Montesquiou, "people thought that it was rather absurd for a man to busy himself with making such dainty bouquets."[104] Moreau's intricate paintings, in turn, were described by Odilon Redon as "wonderful embroidery" wrought by an "old lady."[105]

Although highly valued in certain Symbolist circles, aesthetic taste would continue to be subordinated or opposed to artistic vision. When a character in a turn-of-the-century story by Sara Jeanette Duncan is told that a painter she admires has taste, she responds explosively: "Taste! . . . He sees things."[106] Edgar Degas dismissed the work of the *fin de siècle* aesthetes by declaring: "Art is killed by taste."[107] The problems in credibility faced by certain "tasteful" exponents of Symbolism had aspects in common with those traditionally faced by artistic women, who were assumed to be guided by (good or bad) "taste," rather than "vision."[108] The artistic endeavors judged suitable for ladies during this period, such as making pictures out of sand or seaweed, or decorations out of hair, often emphasized the lower senses, and were considered to be "crafts," rather than "art."[109]

If women did paint or write, they were expected to do so on a small (tactile) scale and to take as their subject matter homey, sentimental subjects such as flowers or family life. Works of "sweeping vision" were not considered to fall within the feminine domain. Jean Jacques Rousseau, for example, stated in 1762 of the proper bounds of women's artistic endeavors:

Dressmaking, embroidery, lacemaking come by themselves . . . . This spontaneous development extends easily to drawing, because the latter art is not
difficult – simply a matter of taste; but at no cost would I want them to
learn landscape, even less the human figure.[110]

The Symbolist interest in certain traditionally feminine domains of experience suggests that this movement could have created an empowering context
for women who wished to bridge the cultural distance between feminine "handicraft" and art. The participation of women in the Symbolist movement might
have been further aided by the fact that to be an aesthete one did not have to
be a *flâneur* or a man of the world, roaming the streets and mingling with the
crowds (although this lifestyle was often held up as an ideal for the [male]
artist).[111] All of one's aesthetic aspirations could be realized within the feminine
territory of the home, as evidenced by the example of Montesquiou or of his
fictional counterpart, Des Esseintes.

While in the Symbolist ethos male artists might evince a "feminine" interest
in taste and smell, however, female artists were generally not encouraged to
break with tradition and strive after "masculine" visual power in their art.[112]
The Symbolists' "empowering" of women, in fact, consisted primarily in rein-
vesting the image of woman with the potent and contrasting values of the
goddess and the beast, the saint and the sorceress. Thus Baudelaire wrote that
woman "is a divinity, a star . . . a kind of idol" and also that "woman is natural,
which is to say abominable."[113] Huysmans praised Moreau for his depiction of
women as "goddesses" and "feminine idols," and at the same time lauded
Degas for overthrowing the feminine idol and depicting women as "froggish
and ape-like."[114] In another passage Huysmans resurrected the pre-modern
specter of the witch when he wrote of the necessity of defying the prevalent
scientific perception of women as "hysterics eaten up by their ovaries or
nymphomaniacs with brains in the region of their bellies" and portraying them
instead as "essential and beyond all time, the nude and poisonous Beast, the
Mercenary of Darkness and the absolute Handmaiden of the Devil."[115]

The Symbolist emphasis on women and women's senses, consequently,
represented more of a masculine attempt to appropriate and harness traditionally feminine powers than an empowering of women. Despite their aesthetic
excursions into feminine domains and despite the existence of exceptional
female artists and writers in their midst, the Symbolists had little more capacity
to imagine women in the role of aesthetes or artists than most of their contemporaries.[116] "Woman," declared Baudelaire "is the opposite of the dandy."[117]
The rules of the *Ordre de la Rose + Croix* decreed that "following Magical law,
no work by a woman will ever be exhibited or executed by the Order."[118] Thus,
the Symbolists played with myths and domains of femininity in their work while
allowing little agency to actual women.

Monsieur Venus

While not actively encouraged to participate in the Symbolist movement, many women were nonetheless inspired by Symbolist styles of art and notions of multisensory aesthetics. Among them was the Scottish painter and craftswoman Margaret Macdonald (1864–1933). Macdonald's paintings, such as *The Sleeper*, *The Flowery Path*, *La Mort Parfumée*, and *The Three Perfumes* reveal her to be one of the most olfactory of visual artists of her time. In her works Macdonald typically portrays women with closed eyes and long noses immersed in worlds of floral scents. *The Sleeper*, for example, depicts a sleeping woman surrounded by roses, in one of which the woman's dream-self buries her nose (Figure 4). *The Flowery Path* shows two women with closed eyes walking arm-in-arm up a flowery path, seemingly guided by scent, as vapors rise up from the path to their noses. In both of these paintings the indication is that the women themselves are the original sources of the scents they inhale so dreamily. The rose smelled by the dream figure in *The Sleeper* grows out of the pod-like body of the sleeping woman. The vapors which rise up from the path in *The Flowery Path* appear to originate in the women's trailing skirts. Macdonald's paintings seem to suggest that smell offers women a "path" for accessing their essential beings.[119]

One of the most notable women to be influenced by the Symbolist movement was the French novelist Rachilde (Marguerite Eymery). Rachilde's novels employed intense synaesthetic imagery in a style similar to that of Huysmans.[120] In her story *Le Mortis*, for example, Rachilde indulges in an orgy of sensory metaphors to describe how roses have taken over a city emptied of human life by the plague. In one passage the roses are "flames of flesh . . . licking against the incorruptibility of the marble surfaces . . . [producing] torrents of inebriating

Figure 4 Margaret Macdonald, *The Sleeper* (c. 1901)
Source: © Hunterian Art Gallery, University of Glasgow.

odors, violent and exasperated like screams." In another, roses simulate a rich banquet of fruit – oranges, pomegranates, melons – "and if Asti wine did not run . . . one could breathe its suave and sparkling foam in the delicate aroma of the very smallest white roses, whose buds cracked like nuts beneath one's teeth."[121]

Rachilde's luxurious symbolism, together with her recurrent themes of perversion, decay, and death, placed her within the literary tradition of Decadence.[122] The writer also exemplified Decadent ideals in her personal life, for she dressed as a man and called herself an *homme de lettres*. By symbolically presenting herself as male, Rachilde tried to attain the literary freedom accorded to male authors and reconcile her own equivocal feelings about her gender.[123]

The transgression of gender codes was a subject which found frequent expression in Rachilde's fiction.[124] The author's best-known novel, *Monsieur Venus*, created a scandal when it was published in 1884 due to its "pathological" reversal of male and female roles.[125] Rachilde's unorthodox manipulation of symbols of sex and sensuality in this novel makes *Monsieur Venus* a valuable example of a critique of the gender and sensory order by a nineteenth-century woman.

The title of *Monsieur Venus* informs the reader that the novel will deal with an inversion of gender codes, and indeed of the cosmic order, for a man is assuming the role of Venus, goddess and planet of women. By employing this theme, Rachilde recalled the "perversions" of the Decadent emperor Elagabulus, who reportedly enjoyed playing the role of Venus in mythological enactments and once dressed as a bride in a marriage ceremony.

The novel begins with the female protagonist, Raoule de Vénérande, visiting a florist's shop to arrange for a decoration for a ball gown. While the name plate on the shop door says Marie Silvert, inside there is a man making a floral garland. Raoule inquires for Marie Silvert and the man answers, "For the time being, I'm Marie Silvert."[126] He explains that, as his sister, Marie, is ill, he has taken over her job.

The first thing Raoule notices when she enters the room is a powerful smell of cooking apples. She then sees the florist's brother, Jacques Silvert, surrounded by flowers, carefully stitching a chain of satin roses.

> Around his torso, over his flowing blouse, a garland of roses ran down in a spiral; strong, large roses, of flesh-colored satin edged with crimson, which passed between his legs, climbed up to his shoulders and curled around his neck.[127]

The apples and roses, classic symbols of women and of Venus, combine to identify Jacques as a male Venus. The floral setting, the cooking apples, the delicate stringing together of roses, also bring out Jacques' association with the feminine senses of smell, taste, and touch. At first Raoule finds the smell of the apples nauseating – "no smell disgusted her more than that of apples"[128]. However, as she becomes entranced by the beautiful Jacques, her disgust fades, until she ends up imagining that she "could perhaps eat one of those apples without too much revulsion."[129] Jacques here is given the role of Eve, offering the apple of sin to Raoule's Adam.

The reversal of gender roles between Raoule and Jacques is signaled through a variety of means. The "mannish" name of Raoule contrasts with Jacques' feminine "other name" of Marie. Raoule's surname, Vénérande, evokes the word *vénerie*, signifying both the art of hunting and the art of love. Jacques' last name, Silvert, is reminiscent in turn of *sylvestre*, "related to the forest." Raoule, hence, is a hunter of love and Jacques is the wild prey.

Raoule is described as hard and knowing, with a dark, masculine appearance. Jacques, on the other hand, is a soft, pink and white, virginal blonde. Raoule dominates Jacques through her sight, he keeps his eyes submissively downcast. While Jacques busies himself with floral decorations, Raoule studies fencing.

The one common interest between Raoule and Jacques is painting. Whereas Jacques is only a "feminine" amateur, however, Raoule presents herself as a master: "I can paint a work of academy standards in the time it takes you to twist up a peony."[130] This position of superiority invests Raoule with the authority to give a "virulent critique" of Jacques' paintings.[131] Despite her poor opinion of his artistic talents, however, Raoule offers to be Jacques' patron, and sets him up with his sister in a house.

Jacques imagines that he and Raoule will work together as "comrades in art." With Raoule playing the role of Master of Art, however, the only position left for Jacques is that of "mistress." Assuming a male voyeur pose common in Western art, Raoule spies on Jacques bathing, and finds him as beautiful as Venus.[132] She says to herself that this is the essence of masculinity; not the wisdom of a Socrates or the dedication of a Christ, or the "radiant genius" of a Raphael, just naked male flesh.[133] Through this declaration Raoule strips men of their traditional association with intellect and aligns them instead with the body.

As the relationship progresses, Raoule's domination of Jacques grows more forceful. When Jacques tries to compliment her, Raoule asks him to keep quiet: "I don't come here to listen to you."[134] Raoule orders Jacques not to go out of the house, not to smoke, and not to speak to men without her permission. When Jacques involuntarily breaks this last rule, Raoule punishes him violently, tearing his flesh and inscribing her will on his body. By her attempts to exercise a "masculine" control over the power of love, Raoule has become, in her own way, a "Monsieur Venus."

Raoule decides that she can best control Jacques by marrying him. He, habituated to his role, responds that "a man doesn't marry his mistress."[135] She replies, "You will be my dear wife just as you have been my adored mistress! . . . It will be so sweet to be your husband, to secretly call you Madame de Vénérande – because I'll give you my name!"[136] After they are "married", however, Jacques cannot hide his disappointment that Raoule is not a "real" man. Dressed as a woman he tries to seduce Raoule's former suitor and ends up being forced to fight a duel with the man. The irony of the situation is that

Raoule, who has studied fencing, is much more fitted to fight a duel than the helpless Jacques. Fatally stabbed by a sword thrust, Jacques symbolically loses his virginity and dies at the same time.[137] Raoule, the "hunter of love," is left with her dead prey.

Monsieur Venus ends with Raoule entering a room in which a life-size wax doll reclines on a shell-shaped bed, watched over by a marble statue of Eros. "The red hair, the blond eyelashes, the golden down on the chest are natural, the teeth in the mouth, the nails on the hands and feet, have been torn from a cadaver . . . a spring in the side of the body animates the mouth."[138] With this perfect simulacrum of her lover's body, Raoule has created a counterpart to the mechanical woman of the future imagined in Villiers de l'Isle-Adam's novel *L'Eve future*, and to the so-called anatomical Venuses, life-like wax models of women's bodies commonly used in the study of medicine.[139] To be dominated and evoked at will, Venus must be made into a lifeless statue.[140] The fact that the one part of the artificial body that remains animate is the mouth, and this only for the purpose of kissing, not for speaking, signifies that this idealized object of love can offer only a purely tactile response to the ardent gaze of its idolater.

In *Monsieur Venus* Rachilde (who was herself nicknamed "Mademoiselle Baudelaire") inspires the reader with repugnance for both the traditionally domineering role of men in gender relations, and the traditionally passive role of women. By reversing the standard positions of the male and the female artist, she also exposes and critiques the gender ideologies of contemporary art. The feminine Jacques' desire to be a painter is pitted against the masculine Raoule's desire to fashion and possess Jacques *as* art. Through the replacement of Jacques with a mannequin, Raoule, the "male" artist, at last accomplishes her aim of making Jacques/Venus into a work of art, and of transforming the feminine principle into an artistic ideal.

Futurist colors

In 1921, a few months before his death, the Symbolist aesthete *par excellence*, Robert de Montesquiou, wrote in his memoirs:

> An impression more singular in nature than painful, is that which consists of realizing all at once, without warning, that one's life is over. One is still there, more or less physically dilapidated, or still resistant, one's faculties apparently intact, but ill-adapted to the taste of the day, one feels disaffected, a stranger to contemporary civilization . . . . In a word, a watertight partition separates you from the artistic conceptions of Picasso, from Czechoslovakian aesthetics or Negro art, and it is not a good way to feel in fashion.[141]

While the Symbolist movement lasted well into the 1900s, the new century had its own artistic fashions: Expressionism, Cubism, Non-Objective Art . . . .

In contrast to the dreamy interweaving of multisensory images and emotions practiced by the Symbolists, the new movements, whatever their theoretical bases, seemed to emphasize a bold, fragmented visualism of line and color.

While many modernist paintings brought a new sensuality into art by highlighting the dynamic nature of color, they nonetheless continued to support a visually-dominated world view. The early twentieth-century painter of "simultaneous colors" Robert Delaunay declared in 1912: "*The Eye* is our highest sense, the one that communicates most closely with our *brain, our consciousness*.... Our comprehension is correlative with our *perception. Let us try to see.*"[142] Critics proclaimed this emphasis on "pure" sight, stripped of the conventions of traditional representation, to be one of the defining characteristics of modern art.[143]

Despite appearances, however, elements of the multisensoriality favored by the Symbolists *did* play a role in early twentieth-century art movements. A prominent example of this is presented by Futurism, an Italian-based art movement founded in 1909.

Although they shared certain interests in common,[144] the Futurists presented themselves as the antithesis of the Symbolists: "Today we hate our glorious intellectual forefathers ... the great Symbolist geniuses."[145] Where the Symbolists drew inspiration from a mystical and languorous past, the Futurists grounded themselves in the machine-driven, fast-paced life of modernity. In the first Futurist Manifesto of 1909 the poet and chief Futurist ideologue F.T. Marinetti proclaimed that the roar of automobiles had put the angels to flight: "Mythology and the Mystic Ideal are defeated at last!"[146]

Similarly, whereas the Symbolists spurned the worlds of commerce and science, the Futurists (sounding at times like Max Nordau) embraced them. Commerce appealed to the Futurists as "the muscle of modern life"[147] and they declared a shop window to be more aesthetically pleasing than a museum exhibit.[148] Science, in turn, was considered "the vivifying current" of modern art, with the molecules observed under the microscope corresponding to the teeming, impersonal life of the city.[149]

While Symbolism catered to a privileged élite and (as would also be the case with Surrealism) emphasized the imaginative life of the individual, Futurism appealed to the working classes and emphasized collective experience. It was not the sensibilities of the aesthete in his fashionable retreat, which interested the Futurists, but those of the passengers on a street car, or of the workers in a factory.[150]

As regards sensory orientation, the Futurists placed a high value on color and light, particularly the vibrant luminosity of sunshine and electric light, which they contrasted with the "sickly" darkness of the Symbolists, the "last lovers of the moon."[151] At the same time, however, the Futurists were interested in the aesthetic potential of a wide range of sensory properties. In *The Painting of Sounds, Noises and Smells*, the painter Carlos Carrà stated that works of art modeled on sounds and smells were "much more suggestive than those created by our visual and tactile senses."[152] "If we are shut up in a dark room," he wrote, "with flowers, petrol or other things with a strong smell, our plastic [i.e. artistic] spirit will gradually eliminate the memory sensation [of sight] and construct a very special plastic whole which corresponds perfectly, in its quality of weight and movement with the smells found in the room."[153] Futurist paintings which attempt to convey non-visual sensations include *Jolts of a Cab* by Carrà, *The Noises of the Street Invade the House* by Umberto Boccioni, and *Perfume* by Luigi Russolo.

Russolo, a painter and a musician, is best known for his essay on "The Art of Noises" in which he stated that if we "cross a great modern capital with our ears more alert than our eyes" we will appreciate a diversity of sounds – "the howl of mechanical saws, the jolting of a tram on its rails, the cracking of whips, the flapping of curtains and flags" – all of which could be imaginatively combined into a new form of art.[154]

In literature Marinetti proposed the creation of "words-in-freedom" which would allow the literary imagination free rein in its choice of syntax and imagery and thereby "plunge the essential word into the water of sensibility."[155] Their sensory imaginations unleashed, writers should, among other things, be able "to render the landscape of smells that a dog perceives."[156] The resulting work was to be printed in "*three or four colors of ink*, or even twenty different typefaces if necessary."[157]

It must be noted that the multisensory ideals of the Futurists often ended up being translated into visual terms. While Carrà's image of an artist in a dark room seeking inspiration through smell appears to offer an olfactory alternative to Delaunay's fixation on the characteristics of light, the paintings of both artists are actually somewhat alike, with their abstract juxtapositions of bright colors. The painting of noises and smells, according to Carrà, required "rrrrrrreds that shouuuuuuut" and "greeeeeeeeeeeens that screeeeeeam."[158] "Any continued series of sounds, noises and smells," he wrote, "imprints on the mind an arabesque of form and color."[159] In "The Plastic Analogies of Dynamism" of 1913 Carrà's colleague Gino Severini declared: "All sensations, when they take artistic form, become immersed in the sensation *light*, and therefore can only be expressed with all the colors of the prism."[160]

While giving sensory priority to sight, the Futurists nonetheless challenged traditional, static models of visuality. They held that visual art should portray objects in motion, integrated into a dynamic environment.[161] Futurists criticized the Cubists (with whom they were often grouped) for allegedly using painting to immobilize, "kill," and "dissect" the images they portrayed.[162] Boccioni claimed that the Cubists took Cezanne's exhortation to artists to "make the museum in the presence of nature" literally, and, in fact, "forgot nature and made the museum."[163]

As part of their project to shatter the "museum of sight," the Futurists tried to give a dynamic role to the spectator of art.[164] Futurist paintings, collages, and sculptures aimed to represent the "inner forces," rather than external appearance of things, and sometimes included movable parts for the observer to manipulate.[165] With regard to theater, the conventional role of the audience as a "stupid voyeur" was denounced.[166] Instead the Futurists advocated "throwing nets of sensation between stage and audience" so that the latter could actively participate in the performance.[167]

At the same time as they challenged visual models, the Futurists challenged scientific models (despite their averred enthusiasm for science).[168] Marinetti used compelling sensory imagery to disrupt the visual precision and purity associated with science. In the first Futurist manifesto Marinetti (who portrays himself and his friends as racing through dark streets in their cars) states that the "sick lamplight through window glass taught us to distrust the deceitful mathematics of our perishing eyes."[169] In his poetry Marinetti combined mathematical signs with potent sensory evocations, as in the line "faecal odour of dysentry + the honeyed stench of plague sweats + smell of ammonia" in "Train Full of Sick Soldiers."[170]

The Futurists, in fact, were concerned with the *sensations* of modernity – the speed of the car, the noise of the factory – rather than with the scientific rationality that made modern technology possible. Indeed, in the manifesto *Futurist Science* of 1916 the Futurists expressed their disillusionment with the rigid rationalism of science and called for "an audaciously exploratory Futurist science, sensitive, vibrant, influenced by far-off intuitions, fragmentary, contradictory . . . ."[171]

The Futurists' interest in the rough and ready sensations of modernity distinguished them from the Symbolists, with their cult of the rare and beautiful. The Futurists furthermore chose to convey these sensations in a breathless, spontaneous style, rather than in the exquisite, refined fashion of the Symbolist aesthete.[172] "In order to achieve . . . *total painting*, which requires the active cooperation of all the senses," Carrà stated, "you must paint, as drunkards sing and vomit, sounds, noises and smells!"[173]

While both Symbolists and Futurists advocated an integration of the senses and the arts, in the case of the former this union was to be harmonious, and in the latter it was rife with oppositions and disorder. The difference lay between a transcendent ideal of sensory harmony (whether "natural," as in the case of Baudelaire's "Correspondences" or contrived, as in Huysmans' *Against Nature*) and the urban experience of sensory confusion.[174] The desire for intense, dynamic and chaotic sensations within a modern technological context would lead the Futurists to glorify warfare as the supreme aesthetic experience of modernity.

As in Symbolism, women had an ambivalent position in Futurism. The Futurists tended to associate women with the despised ideals of their Symbolist predecessors – moonlight, reverie, perfume – which were to be "blinded" and vanquished by the bright, virile sun of Futurism. At the same time, however, they promoted the "semi-equality of man and woman and a lessening of the disproportion in their social rights."[175] The "semi-equality" the Futurists considered according to women in society had similarities with the semi-equality they accorded to the "lower" senses in art.

While the ideal of smell, taste, and touch as sweet and soft and languorous was rejected, the Futurists praised the value of pungent, rough, dynamic sensations. The odors Carlos Carrà wished to represent through art, for example, were those of "brothels, railway stations, ports, garages."[176] Marinetti drew inspiration from the turbulent sensations of war: the harsh odors of the battleship and the searing heat of the machine gun.[177] This "masculinization" of "feminine" sensibilities was part of the Futurist campaign to free culture from the spell of romantic sentimentality. At the same time, given that the "lower" senses were commonly associated with the "lower" classes, as well as with women, by incorporating these senses into works of art the Futurists attempted to fulfill their ideal of creating an art for the people.

The most prominent woman in the early Futurist movement was the writer Valentine de Saint-Point, who wrote a "Manifesto of the Futurist Woman" in 1912. Influenced by her mentor Marinetti (and probably also by Rachilde), Saint-Point preferred the image of woman as "battle-axe," to that of woman as "angel." She stated that "Women are the Furies, the Amazons . . . the women warriors who fight more ferociously than men."[178] As a substitute for the "tenderness" which makes woman into a "nurse," Saint-Point proposed the ideal of lust, "which destroys the weak and excites the strong."[179] The author disagreed with projects to increase women's civil rights for she believed that these would result in the imposition of rational order on the instinctual power of women. In the end, however, Saint-Point deemed woman's most important role to be that of inspiring and producing male heroes.[180]

The Futurists contended that war was the ultimate means of liberating society from the murky, clinging feminine past. In Nietzschean manifestos, such as "Let's Murder the Moonshine," Marinetti stated that "our nerves demand war and scorn women."[181] To some extent the Futurists were proven right in their contention. The First World War did effectively vanquish many sentimental, "feminine," nineteenth-century ideals and clear the way for a more prosaic "masculine" age of business and technology. However, the Futurists did not realize that in this desired new society their own model of multisensoriality, far from being the norm, would be almost completely marginalized by the dominant visualist discourse.

After the First World War (which took the lives of several prominent Futurists) the tenor of Futurism in Italy was somewhat altered. While the movement continued its interest in warfare and nationalism, participating in Fascist politics, a spiritual dimension was introduced into Futurist ideology. The machine was now said to serve as a symbol of the mysterious force of the infinite. A manifesto on "Sacred Futurist Art" published in 1931 lauded the "mystical" experience of airplane flight and put forward suggestions for a Futurist cathedral.[182] During this period the movement made further strides towards elaborating a multisensory aesthetic. Marinetti proposed inventing art forms for all the senses, and along those lines developed a tactile art and, together with L.C. Fillìa, a Futurist cuisine.

During the 1920s and 1930s more women became involved with the Futurist movement. Benedetta Cappa, who married Marinetti in 1923, painted and wrote Futurist novels, as well as experimenting with the new field of tactile art. Leandra Angelucci Cominazzini specialized in tapestries and ceramics. Regina Prassade Cassolo worked in aluminum, producing sculptures and tactile-visual pictures, such as *Aerosensibility* and *The Country of the Blind*.[183]

While Futurism had a global influence on modern art, the movement as a whole, particularly in its later period, has received relatively little attention.[184] This critical neglect is due to several factors. The fact that the movement was based in Italy distanced it from the established centers of art, while its post-First World War involvement with Fascism isolated it politically. The Futurists' populism went against the tendency of modern art to confine itself to an intellectual élite. The working classes were not *supposed* to relate to Picasso. The Futurists' championing of modern technology seemed naively ignorant of the forces behind, and the consequences of, the technological revolution. Their glorification of war appeared jingoistic and callous.[185]

The Futurists' radical proposals for developing art forms for all of the senses, in turn, were largely rejected by the art world and by the public, as no more than a farcical play for attention. The new Surrealist movement, it seemed, although in some ways more conventional than Futurism, had captured the market for "bizarre" art. A few decades earlier, when such notions as perfume concerts were all the rage, the Futurists' plans for an art of touch or for painting odors might have aroused more interest. The cultural climate had changed since the era of the Symbolists, however, and by the 1920s the concept of a multisensory aesthetics now seemed more passé than "futurist," more "surreal" than practicable.

Surrealist recipes

The Surrealist movement, founded in Paris in 1924 by André Breton, was the most notable twentieth-century heir to the Symbolist aesthetic. While placing a special emphasis on the role of the unconscious in the production of art, the Surrealists took as aesthetic guides many of the figures associated with Symbolism – Baudelaire, Moreau, Huysmans – and found inspiration in many of the subjects – mystical cosmologies, esotericism, decadence – which had fueled the Symbolist imagination. To put it in Futurist terms, the Surrealists, like the Symbolists, were "lovers of the moon."

The Surrealist movement would be much more successful than Futurism in attracting long-lasting interest. Much of the popular appeal of Surrealist art, however, lay in its presumed ability to offer an enjoyably "safe" form of irrationality in an (apparently) increasingly prosaic world. The fact that Surrealist works evoked the realm of dreams and fantasies seemed to limit their ability to threaten the daylight world of common sense.

Although the Surrealists would not go as far as the Symbolists or the Futurists in developing a multisensory aesthetic, they were nonetheless interested in exploring alternative sensory orders.[186] In opposition to the scientific construction of sight as rational, for example, the Surrealists invested vision with the disruptive power of magic.[187] The juxtaposition and interplay of different sensory modalities also played a role in Surrealism. For example, in a Surrealist exhibition of 1938, vegetables formed part of the art work, roasting coffee filled the gallery with the "perfumes of Brazil," and a loudspeaker played a German march.[188]

Such Surrealist evocations of multisensoriality were often based less on Baudelaire's theory of correspondences than on Rimbaud's notion of a "derangement of the senses."[189] A literary example of the rupture in customary chains of perceptual associations which the Surrealists hoped to produce through unusual sensory conjunctions is found in the following line from a poem by the Surrealist Jean Arp: "the stones have ears to eat the exact time."[190] The idea of a universal system of sensory symbolism, nonetheless, did appeal to the Surrealists, and in his "Ode to Charles Fourier," Breton praised the visionary who "set about looking for analogies in the vegetable garden."[191]

Like their Symbolist predecessors, the Surrealists were fascinated with the domains and mythologies of the feminine. André Breton linked the exposure of the unconscious (male) mind deemed essential to artistic creativity by the Surrealists, with the (masculine) exposure of feminine consciousness:

> It rests with the artist to make visible everything that is part of the feminine, as opposed to the masculine, system of the world. It is the artist who must rely exclusively on the woman's powers to exalt, or better still, to jealously appropriate to himself everything that distinguishes woman from man with respect to their styles of appreciation and volition.[192]

Women's psychic and sensory powers, and their effect on men, constitute a major theme in Surrealism, as they had in Symbolism. Surrealist art and literature are replete with imagery evoking both the masculine domination of women through sight, and the masculine fear/desire of being blinded by the sight of women. Well-known works employing such imagery include Georges Bataille's *Story of the Eye*, René Magritte's painting *The Rape*, and Man Ray's *Object of Destruction* (consisting of a photograph of a woman's eye attached to the arm of a metronome).[193] The classic Surrealist film, *Un Chien Andalou*, opened with an image of a man slicing through a woman's eye (actually a cow's eye) with a razor-blade.[194]

Despite the stereotypical images of women promoted by male Surrealists, the Surrealist movement offered women considerable room for participation and self-expression, compared to previous artistic movements. Furthermore, the development of the women's movement in the twentieth century provided a more encouraging atmosphere for women to explore their sensibilities through art than had existed at the turn of the century. With Surrealism, therefore, we have the opportunity to examine sensory cosmologies elaborated by female artists.

A number of women associated with the Surrealists combined an interest in women's creative powers with a fascination for esoteric traditions of mysticism and alchemy to invent new images of femininity and female artistry. These artists' works often contain powerful evocations of the non-visual senses and of the interplay of the senses within the context of traditional feminine domains – the home, the natural world, and the supernatural world of the witch.

The artists who are perhaps most interesting in this regard are Remedios Varo (1908–63)[195] and Leonora Carrington (1917–), both of whom came under the influence of the Surrealist movement in the 1930s and developed their own ideas of surrealist art during subsequent decades. Varo and Carrington shared a deep interest in esoteric doctrines and in the aesthetic and cosmological dimensions of everyday domestic practices such as cooking, sewing, and gardening.[196]

Many of Remedios Varo's paintings show women or androgynous beings carefully blending and transmuting sensory modalities in wistful acts of creation and nourishment. In *Solar Music*, a woman draped in a mossy cloak plays on rays of light with a bow, causing flowers to spring up from the forest bed. In *Celestial Pablum* a woman grinds up starlight which she spoon-feeds to a caged baby moon. In *The Creation of the Birds* an owl-woman blends starlight, color, and music to "paint" birds into life.

Varo's painting *Embroidering Earth's Mantle* (Figure 5) depicts women sitting in a mysterious tower embroidering the surface of the earth, with its towns, forests, and seas, on an immense, billowing cloth. The thread for this labor emerges from the vapor of an alchemical vessel in the center of the tower, making the cloth – the surface of the earth – the textile manifestation of an aromatic emanation. The whole operation, however, is controlled by a standing male figure who stirs the vessel while reading a book (infusing the broth with his literary speculations?). A similar, androgynous, figure plays a flute in the background.

Rich in sensory allusions, *Embroidering Earth's Mantle* hints at a division between sight as a dominant masculine sense (the standing male book-reader) and touch as a subordinate feminine sense (the seated female embroiderers). One of the embroiderers in Varo's picture, however, rebels against this apparent hierarchy by secretly embroidering a scarcely perceptible image of herself embracing a lover into the cloth – a reassertion of the primacy of touch.[197]

Remedios Varo delighted in challenging the desensualized, empiricist universe of the scientist in her paintings. In her painting *The Unsubmissive Plant*, a scientist grows plants which bloom into mathematical formulae, except for one, "unsubmissive" plant which has unexpectedly produced a rose. In *The Revelation or the Watchmaker*, a watchmaker is surprised by a luminescent sphere floating in the window, its presence heralded or perhaps attracted by the incense wafting from a burner on the floor. This surprising apparition breaks open the closed mechanical cosmos of the watchmaker, causing the gearwheels of watches to roll off the table and plants to burst through the floor.[198]

Varo's last completed work before her death, *Still Life Reviving* (Figure 3) shows fruit swirling in starry rings above a set table. As the fruit collide and explode, their seeds fall to the ground, creating new plants.[199] In Varo's

Figure 5 Remedios Varo, *Embroidering Earth's Mantle* (1961)
Source: Courtesy of Walter Gruen.

Spanish title "still life" is *naturaleza muerta*, "dead nature." The painting, hence, can be interpreted as a depiction of (feminine) nature, previously "killed" by artists, magically coming back to life and creative potency. An important distinguishing feature between the work of Surrealist women such as Varo and Carrington and that of their male counterparts, in fact, is that the former generally emphasizes the need for a reconciliation with the natural world, while the latter often expresses motifs of violence against Nature, in the style of the Decadents.[200]

As in the case of Remedios Varo, Leonora Carrington's work is rich in multi-sensory evocations.[201] This is particularly evident in Carrington's stories, which abound with descriptions of colors, textures, smells, and tastes. One of the central themes of Carrington's novel of 1946, *The Stone Door* is, indeed, the recovery of the senses through entry into the worlds of femininity, nature, and myth. Early in the novel a character describes achieving sensory potency by means of a dream encounter with a wild animal:

> Last night in a dream it returned. A creature wearing a shaggy skin and smelling of dust and cinnamon. Screaming I entered the fur, wool, or hair, crying tears that were dark and sticky like blood . . . . Then I was in entire possession of the five sensorial powers and their long roots were as visible as the sun.[202]

Later on in the story a magical egg gives birth to a star which, like the stars in medieval cosmology, radiates sensory energies: "The Star stretched and broke the oval contour; each one of the five prongs became a sense and each sense shot out five bright rays, which bit into the earth and up into the air like long sharp teeth."[203]

Zacharias, the male protagonist of the *The Stone Door* must recover his senses and his sense of the feminine in order to pass the "stone door" and escape from the land of death into that of life. Along the way Zacharias is required to perform the feminine tasks of cooking and sewing. These tasks, however, are to be carried out with the embalmed body of the "Wise King" (who resembles Zacharias). The King's skin serves Zacharias as the cloth with which to sew a pair of trousers, and the embalmed flesh is transformed into a soup: "With a sudden loud pop the Wise King burst: a cascade of spiced juices poured into the boiling pot. The whole cavern stank of musk, cinnamon and other spices . . . . 'Delicious! Fit for a King!' "[204]

Using a witch's broom to paddle his boat, Zacharias enters the subterranean waterways of the earth in the last stage of his journey. "We shall knit a ladder of Black hair and climb into the center of the Earth to our roots" his feminine guide has told him, "and when these long strands join again we will Hear, Taste, See, Smell, and Touch."[205] Arriving at the stone door, the sensorially-whole Zacharias is finally able to leave the country of the dead behind and pass through.[206]

While attentive to all the senses, Carrington's work shows an exceptional interest in sensations of touch, smell, and taste. The sense of touch is emphasized by Carrington as a means of nonverbal communication. In her book *Down Below*, which describes a bout of "madness" Carrington experienced in the 1940s, the artist writes: "I heard the vibrations of beings, as clear as voices, I understood with each particular vibration the attitude of each towards life."[207] During this period Carrington also felt herself able to communicate with animals through a "tactile" language.

> I proposed to myself an agreement with the animals: horses, goats, birds. This was accomplished through the skin, by means of a sort of "touch" language, which I find it difficult to describe now that my senses have lost the acuity of perception they possessed at that time.[208]

The importance of such inter-species contact is brought out in the human–animal embraces depicted by Carrington in her stories, and in paintings such as *Crookhey Hall, Pastoral, Nine, nine, nine,* and *Transference.* (Through her novel combinations of zoological and sensory symbols, Carrington can be said to be creating an anarchic bestiary of sensory interchange, in contrast to the hierarchical "sensory bestiaries" of pre-modernity.)

The sense of smell, in turn, is employed by Leonora Carrington to invent a feminist olfactory mythology in which the sanctimonious scent of an oppressive patriarchal religious order is dispelled. In *The Stone Door*, the Wise King's embalmed corpse is dissolved into a spicy broth. In the story, "As They Rode Along the Edge," the woodswoman Virginia Fur, confronts and overcomes the odor of sanctity emanating from the pretentious St. Alexander, with her own wild smell "of spices and game, the stables, fur and grasses."[209] In Carrington's novel, *The Hearing Trumpet*, an abbess-sorceress recovers the perfumed ointment of Mary Magdalene – "a high initiate of the mysteries of the Goddess [who] had been executed for the sacrilege of selling certain secrets of her cult to Jesus of Nazareth" – and employs it to perform magic.[210]

As regards the sense of taste, one of Carrington's fictional characters comments: "Taste . . . has a system of ecstasy and philosophy all its own which is in no way inferior to the gifts of the other four senses."[211] Together with Varo, Carrington was known for creating "surrealist recipes," dishes composed of unusual combinations of foods which confused the boundary between "art" and "cuisine."[212] Many of Carrington's paintings – *The Meal of Lord Candlestick*, *Edwardian Hunt Breakfast*, and *Grandmother Moorhead's Aromatic Kitchen*, among others – depict meals or the preparation of meals in an atmosphere charged with cosmological significance.[213] Carrington's stories likewise often describe cooking and eating as processes of cosmic transformation. At the end of Carrington's novel *The Hearing Trumpet*, the female protagonists renew themselves by stepping into a boiling cauldron and then supping the broth made from their old bodies.[214] Taste for Carrington is definitely not a matter of "tastefulness," but rather a source of vitality and occult wisdom.[215]

For Carrington, as for Varo, there are "no hierarchical differences between the cooking pot and the alchemist's alembic, between the knitting of a jumper and the weaving of the soul from 'cosmic wool'."[216] In the late nineteenth century the Symbolist author Barbey D'Aurevilly had condemned female authors for attempting in vain to rise above the domestic concerns natural to their sex. Erudition in the case of such women, he wrote, was reduced to a matter of "picking up pins in between making pots of jam."[217] Although Carrington and Varo only touched on the possibilities of developing art forms for the "lower" senses, they disdained distinctions between "high" culture and traditional women's work.[218] "Painting," Carrington stated, "is like making strawberry jam – really carefully and well."[219]

Varo's and Carrington's artistic work incorporates many sensory concepts characteristic of pre-modern cosmologies, from the odor of sanctity and the music of the spheres to the interplay of the senses. Such concepts are re-imagined within a new sensory and symbolic world in which traditionally feminine domains of knowledge play a valued role, and in which all fields of perception and endeavor are open to both sexes. Surrealist techniques are used by these artists to disrupt conventional models and divisions of the senses and to suggest new perceptual paradigms in which the senses not only correspond, as in the Symbolist aesthetic, but are the media for radical social and cosmic transformation.

While conceived within a framework weighted with masculine stereotypes of women, Surrealism nonetheless helped women to imagine alternative gender and sensory orders. If the surreal was acceptable and laudatory, why not the surreal possibility of a feminist alternative to patriarchy? Whitney Chadwick writes of Remedio Varo's feminine imagery: "the women in Varo's paintings . . . are alchemists, magicians, scientists and engineers who travel through forests, along rivers, and above the clouds in jerry-built conveyances that run on star-dust, music, and sunlight."[220] Whereas Symbolism evoked feminine sensibilities from an almost exclusively masculine perspective, the Surrealist project would enable women to set out on their own voyage of discovery into the feminine aesthetic and sensory imagination.

6 A feel for the world

Lessons in aesthetics from the blind

Despite the flowering (or fragmenting) of art into a multitude of styles and forms in the twentieth century, Western aesthetics remains overwhelmingly visual.[1] Picasso's multi-perspectival figures, Pollock's paint-splattered canvases, Rauschenberg's all-white paintings, Warhol's pop art, among other prototypical manifestations of modern art, have greatly expanded our notions of art and representation, but only within the sensory field of sight. The aesthetic role of vision has, if anything, increased in the twentieth century due to such technological developments as color photography, the cinema, television, and computer graphics.

Not even dance and music are free from the visualizing tendencies of modernity. For most people in the contemporary West, dance exists more as a visual spectacle than as a tactile and kinaesthetic experience. The colonization of music by sight, in turn, is evidenced by the proliferation and cinematic refinement of music videos. The absence of visual allure, it would seem, is a leading factor in the current decline of popular support for symphony orchestras. To quote a spokesperson for a major American orchestra: "What can you say about an art form in which the star of the show (i.e. the conductor) turns his back to the audience?"[2]

There are, it is true, a number of works by contemporary artists which engage both visual and non-visual senses, particularly in the areas of performance and installation art. Such works, however, have thus far failed to generate widespread interest in a multisensory aesthetics, either among the public or among scholars of art, who each year produce ever more articles and books on the relationship between aesthetics and sight, art and the eye. Where then, as we prepare to enter the twenty-first century, can we look for a model of aesthetics which is not dominated by sight?

One answer is: in the experiences of the blind.[3] This response might at first appear to involve a leap from culture to biology, from a social sensory order to one imposed by physiology. Nonetheless, given the current sensory climate of hypervisuality, it may be the case that only the physiological absence of sight can provide a context for allowing the non-visual senses to participate fully in cultural life.[4]

While there has long been a fascination with blindness in Western art and culture, this fascination has centered on the *absence* of vision, rather than on the *presence* of non-visual experience.[5] By going beyond representations of blindness to attend to the experiences of the blind themselves, we who are sighted can begin to learn what it might be like to apprehend the world as a sound- and smellscape, or to appreciate the contours and textures of our environment through touch. Exploring the sensory lives of the blind can help uncover a hidden world of non-visual sensations and representations, as well as inspire the creation of aesthetic forms based on senses other than sight. At the same time, such an exploration brings home to those of us who live in the visual panoply of modern, or postmodern, Western society that, while the blind may lack the sense of sight, the sighted are often out of touch with their other senses.

Beauty and the blind

The Western privileging of sight as *the* aesthetic sense has led philosophers and psychologists to question whether persons who lack sight can have any aesthetic experiences. The usual conclusion has been that they cannot. For example, the Enlightenment encyclopedist Denis Diderot, while in many ways sympathetic to the experiences of the blind, stated that, "when [a blind man] says 'that is beautiful', he is not making an aesthetic judgement, he is simply repeating the judgement of one who can see . . . . Beauty is only a word for the blind."[6]

This view, with exception sometimes made for the ability of the blind to appreciate music and poetry, continued to be widely held by art theorists into the twentieth century. In the 1930s, the psychologist Géza Révész undertook a major study of aesthetic abilities among the blind, entitled *Psychology and Art of the Blind*. In this study Révész attempts to systematically disprove any suggestion that the blind can either appreciate or create art by touch. As regards appreciation, Révész provides various examples of how blind persons were unable to accurately identify or judge the aesthetic value of sculpted busts. The fact that one blind man mistook a "beautiful head of the young Nero" for a representation of an ugly, old man, or that another judged a bust of a stern-looking Roman official to represent a handsome youth, and so on, is taken as indisputable proof by Révész of his assertion that "we have to deny absolutely the ability of the blind to enjoy plastic works aesthetically."[7]

As regards the creation of sculptures by the blind, Révész is equally severe. In the case of children creating clay models, he states that: "Even the worst representations of human figures by untrained sighted children are in every respect on a much higher level than the best work achieved by trained blind children."[8] Révész grudgingly acknowledges that an "exceptionally gifted" blind sculptor may create a technically correct and seemingly aesthetic representation of a model, but holds that this will always, on close inspection, be seen to lack "genuine artistic worth":

> The blind artist will never be able to reach the same heights as the seeing one; all his energy and talent will not help him to attain the highest spheres . . . . He will never create new forms . . . or exert any marked influence on artistic trends. For that, seeing, *artistic seeing*, is indispensable.[9]

A number of biases can be seen to inform Révész's aesthetic judgments. With respect to the failure of the blind to accurately identify the subjects of busts, Révész does not consider that the blind do not have the same experience in recognizing sculptures of different eras and styles as the sighted, who see sculptures not only during trips to museums, but in churches, parks, pictures, and many other places. Given the variety and number of things which can be taken in with just one glance, the sighted have a more extensive knowledge of forms and figures in general than the blind, who only know the forms of those things they personally touch. When one takes this into account, it is hardly surprising to find that a sighted person can identify the subject of a sculpture more readily than one who is blind. It is apparently a matter of experience more than of sensory or aesthetic capacity.

More importantly there is no recognition on the part of Révész that the works of art he is using for the purpose of judging the aesthetic capabilities of the blind were created primarily for the sense of vision, not for that of touch. Nor does it occur to him that the correct identification of the subject matter of specific sculpted representations might not be essential to a general appreciation of aesthetics. Révész believes that there is one universal code of aesthetics – his own. If a blind man calls a sculpted head ugly which Révész himself takes to be beautiful, it is not because the man might have a different idea of beauty, or because he is not familiar with the canons of Western art, but because he lacks an aesthetic sense. It is, in fact, apparent that Révész is not at all interested in the aesthetic judgments made by his subjects in their own right; his only concern is to prove that, according to his criteria, they are "getting it wrong."

Révész's one-sided understanding of art appreciation by the blind extends to art production by the blind. As Révész holds that the visual is the one valid aesthetic medium, he has no qualms about judging sculptures created by touch strictly according to their visual appearance. Insofar as sculptures by the blind appear to reflect tactile, rather than visual, experience, they are considered by him to be distorted. Examples which he provides of this are a clay figure with outstretched arms in which the arms and hands are disproportionately large, and a sculpture of a kiss which focuses on the mouth and omits the back of the head.[10] According to our everyday haptic experience, when one stretches out one's arms, they *do*, in fact, seem larger, and when one kisses, one's attention *is* focused on one's mouth, rather than the back of one's head. When one *looks* at someone with outstretched arms, however, the proportions of the body remain stable, and when one looks at someone kissing, the back of the head is there as well as the mouth. It is this visual experience which provides Révész with his artistic norm.

There is no possibility, according to Révész's model of artistic worth, of the blind being able to elaborate an aesthetics of touch. Nor is Révész impressed by the fact that the blind can experience pleasure in creating and feeling works of art.

> The pleasure which . . . the blind derive from works of art is a sensual plea-
> sure, a joy created by the clearness of the structure and the architectural

arrangement, but not a blissful appreciation of artistic values. The blind remain in the psychological sphere, in the sphere of slightly differentiated sensations of pleasure and displeasure, and are unable to force their way into the realm of Aesthetics.[11]

The aesthetic doctrines of Révész and others like him are based on cultural prejudices, assumptions about the identity of the aesthetic with the visual which have long been entrenched in Western culture. Even the blind themselves have often held these assumptions. In the early twentieth century Pierre Villey, a blind professor of literature, stated that the visual arts were beyond the scope of the blind to appreciate and that "there can be no question of constituting an art specially suitable to the touch."[12]

For many contemporary artists and scholars of art, the notion of a non-visual art is still unthinkable, or simply not worthy of thought. For example, one recent study of the role of vision in artistic creation claimed that the only imaginable scenario in which an artist could dispense with sight would be "when a great artist, after years of experience, goes blind and has no eyes left to help him."[13] The artist in this case, it is stated, must rely on his visual memory and picture his work in his mind. The possibility that a truly creative artist, on becoming blind, would explore how senses other than sight might serve as the media or locus for the elaboration of aesthetic concepts is simply not in the picture. Aesthetics lies in the (culturally mediated) encounter between a spectator and a spectacle. If the "spectator" is blind, or if the spectacle is missing, is there anything left to experience?

Seeing and nothingness

In *Being and Nothingness,* Sartre describes the situation of a man standing in an empty park. Seeing but unseen, the man dominates the layout of the park – the lawn, the benches, the walk – with his gaze. When someone else enters the park, however, his visual hegemony over his surroundings is disturbed. The watcher finds himself watched, displaced from his position of authority and transformed into an object in another's field of vision.[14] As Norman Bryson puts it, "the intruder becomes a kind of drain which sucks in all of the former plenitude, a black hole pulling the scene away from the watcher self into an engulfing void."[15]

Consider, now, the case of a blind man standing in a park.[16] Imagining the park to be empty, as Sartre does, and not particularly aromatic, as parks often are not, what would his experience be? Of nothing in particular, or rather, of nothing in particular outside his customary consciousness of his own being. It is precisely when someone else enters the park – when the tread of footsteps is felt, the sound of a voice heard – that the world comes out of nothingness into being.

Take, for example, the following description by the blind writer, John Hull, of his experience of sitting on a park bench:

Where nothing was happening there was silence. That little part of the world then died, disappeared. The ducks were silent. Had they gone, or was something holding their rapt attention? . . . Nobody was walking past me just now. This meant that the footpath itself had disappeared. . . . There is a sudden cry from the lake, "Hello Daddy!"; my children are there in their paddleboat. Previously, a moment ago, they were not there.[17]

For the blind, "intruders" do not so much "take the park away" as they create it. Without such intrusions there *is* no park. As Hull remarks:

Mine is not a world of being; it is a world of becoming . . . . The rockery, the pavilion, the skyline of high-rise flats, the flagpoles over the cricket ground, none of this is really there. The world of happenings, of movement and conflict, that is there.[18]

The world thus exists for the listener not as a stable scene, but as a dynamic sequence of sounds.[19] It is too changeable, too transient, to be dominated – as one dominates a landscape through sight – it can only be attended to and engaged with.

To return to Sartre, despite his fascination with the gaze, he was highly distrustful of the hegemony of sight. In work after work, the philosopher denounced the objectifying character of vision and sought an escape in the transcendent realm of the imagination.[20] Nonetheless, Sartre was ultimately unable to imagine a satisfactory alternative to visualism. For Sartre sight furnished the perceptual model for all the senses,[21] and the imagination itself thrived on visual experience. "I think with my eyes," he admitted.[22] When, in his old age, Sartre became blind, he described himself as a "living corpse," unable to interact with the world.[23] Despite his critique of the tyranny of sight, it would seem in the end that for Sartre the only alternative to seeing was "nothingness."

A world of one sense

It is sometimes the case that a person is so fixated with one particular passion or perspective that the whole world seems to be understood solely in relation to it. The utopianist Charles Fourier named such single-minded persons "monogynes" in his writings. From his personal experience he gave the example of an obsessive wine fancier, a "monogyne with the dominant of taste, the tonic of drinking":

This fellow saw everything in wine; instead of reckoning time by hours and half-hours, he reckoned it by the number of bottles drunk . . . . One of the two coaches on the road . . . passed us going down a hill, but he called out to it in a bantering tone, "Bah, bah, we shall drink before you" (that is to say, we shall arrive before you, for why do you arrive at all if not to drink?) . . . . A lady experienced sickness from the movement of the coach . . . the monogyne [said], "You had better drink a little wine, Ma'am!" (for what is the remedy for every sickness, if it be not wine?) . . . [24]

"He was not a sottish drunkard," Fourier notes, "but a man gifted with a marvellous instinct for referring all the circumstances of life to wine."[25]

In the twentieth century, the Western world in general, and the academic world in particular, can be said to have a fixation with the sense of sight. This unisensoriality is somewhat obscured by the fact that the concept of sight, like an object reflected in a room of mirrors, has assumed so many different guises in our culture that it can provide us with the illusion of a complete sensorium. Paintings, photographs, and films, for example, are said by some critics to represent and evoke non-visual sensations so well, that the non-visual senses can scarcely be said to be absent from these media.[26] In many contemporary academic works sight is so endlessly analyzed, and the other senses so consistently ignored, that the five senses would seem to consist of the colonial/patriarchal gaze, the scientific gaze, the erotic gaze, the capitalist gaze, and the subversive glance.[27]

Whether scholars are interested in celebrating, condemning, or rehabilitating sight, their focus remains visual, and other sensory domains remain unexplored. In keeping with the current trend to seek visual alternatives to visualism,[28] Martin Jay, for example, has suggested that the hegemony of vision in modernity might be displaced by an ocular multiplicity: "the multiplication of a thousand eyes" (or views).[29] In postmodernity sight still reigns supreme, but it is the vision of the kaleidoscope, rather than the telescope. (It is perhaps ominous in this regard to note that the inventor of the kaleidoscope, David Brewster, went blind by staring at the sun.)[30]

The examples of unisensoriality given above are based on culture rather than physiology. What, however, if a person were *actually* possessed of only one sense? How would the world seem to such a person? This is the question the Enlightenment philosopher Etienne de Condillac tried to answer in *Treatise on the Sensations*, when he considered the situation of a statue which comes to life possessing just one sense.[31] There is a world of difference, of course, between a statue with one sense imagined for the sake of a philosophical inquiry and a human being with one, living within society. The former is a thought-provoking intellectual exercise, the latter seems unthinkable.

Nevertheless, physiological unisensoriality can exist. Let us consider here the case of Laura Bridgman, a nineteenth-century American who had her sight, hearing, and much of her smell and taste destroyed by scarlet fever in her infancy, leaving her with touch as her one fully functioning sense.[32] Although Laura's senses were ravaged by disease, her mental faculties apparently remained unimpaired. She was educated at the Perkins Institute for the Blind in Massachusetts where she learned to communicate through tactile hand language and writing. The notable success of Laura Bridgman's education demonstrated that one can learn to think and communicate with only one sense – at least in the case of that one sense being touch.

Laura kept up a constant manual exploration of her surroundings. A report on her tactile abilities as a child states that:

> Like the feelers of some insects which are continually agitated . . . so Laura's arms and hands are continually in play; and when she is walking with a person she not only recognizes everything she passes within touching distance, but by continually touching her companion's hands she ascertains what he is doing.[33]

The absence of the distance senses of sight and hearing would seem to have heightened Laura's consciousness of bodily sensations. She was very attentive, for example, to the movement of blood in the body, which, due to her under-standing of sound as vibration, she characterized as sound. One of her teachers states:

> In talking of the circulation of the blood she insisted that it made a noise, and put my hand on her neck to feel the pulsations, saying, "Sit very still and see if you do not hear it."[34]

With no memories of sounds or sights, even Laura's dreams were exclusively tactile. Witness, for example, her description of a nightmare:

> My heart ached, I was very much frightened last night. I do not know what made my blood make a noise . . . . I think dream was very hard and heavy and thick; it made me grow quick, my blood ran very hard.[35]

As might be expected, Laura was exceptionally adept at reading "body language." One of Laura's teachers remarked "Laura not only observes the *tones of the finger language*, she finds meaning in every posture of the body and in every movement of limb." Given her tactile acuity, the persons around Laura found it very difficult to conceal feelings from her. Changes of mood were quickly noticed by her sensitive fingers, giving the sensorially deprived girl a reputation for having an extra, compensatory sense of mind reading.[36]

Although Laura's sense of aesthetics was never cultivated, the pleasure she took in a number of things indicates what areas might have proved fertile for such a cultivation. For example, despite her somewhat Puritanical upbringing, Laura took great delight in fine and silky clothing and in jewelry, both on herself and on others. Laura also enjoyed handling figurines and other hand-sized ornaments, and kept a shelf full of such ornaments in her room.[37]

Interestingly, Laura's greatest treasure was a music box. Although she was unable to hear music, she could *feel* it, for sounds are communicated through vibrations. Laura could thus take pleasure in the reverberations of her music box, just as she could enjoy the rhythm of a drumbeat or distinguish differences in pitch.[38] While such "tactile music" has traditionally been excluded from the realm of aesthetics in the West, there is no reason, aside from custom, why a

musical form specifically directed to the sense of touch should not be elaborated.

In her enjoyment of poetry, which she both read and wrote, Laura came
closest to participating in the standard Western notion of aesthetics. Nonetheless,
even poetry was deemed to be only partly accessible to Laura due to her
inability to understand visual imagery and sound-based cadences and rhymes.

> Even when [art] speaks directly to the heart and mind by poetry, sight and
> hearing remain the essential instruments of aesthetic enjoyment, so much
> are rhythm, the music of words, the images evoked, the integrant elements
> of this.[39]

If there can be a poetry of sounds, however, why should there not be a poetry of
shapes, of tactile rhythms and tactile rhymes? Why should Laura not have been
able to feel a poem as deeply in her fingers, as the hearing can with their ears?

The case of Laura Bridgman indicates that, although touch is placed at the
bottom of the traditional Western sensory hierarchy, it has the potential to serve
as a medium for a full range of ideas and emotions. However, this was not
usually the conclusion reached by Laura's contemporaries. In keeping with the
visual emphasis of Western culture, the tendency was to downplay the role of
touch in Laura's development and to imagine that her abilities were due to a
hidden, inner sight. This was the view expressed, for example, in a nineteenth-
century poem about the girl:

> The lonely lamp in Greenland cell,
> Deep 'neath a world of snow,
> Doth cheer the loving household group
> Though none beside may know.
>
> And sweet one, doth our Father's hand
> Place in thy casket dim
> A radiant and peculiar lamp
> To guide thy steps to him?[40]

Laura herself, in turn, rather than serving as an example of how the sense of
touch might be developed, became a tourist spectacle, one of the "must-sees"
of Boston. Visitors came by the thousands to see Laura put on display at the
weekly exhibitions held by the Perkins Institute, and she was obliged to sign as
many autographs as a twentieth-century movie star.[41] Later on, this role of
sensory showpiece would be taken over by the renowned blind-deaf writer
Helen Keller, who was said to constitute one of the two wonders of America,
the other being Niagara Falls.

The sensory lives of Laura Bridgman and other blind-deaf persons bring the
perceptual biases of the Western world view into sharp relief. Perhaps the most
striking example of this contrast between tactile and visual worlds can be seen in

a photograph taken of a Canadian blind-deaf girl, Ludivine Lachance, at the turn of the century (Figure 6).[42] In this photograph Ludivine is shown seated in a room, surrounded by nuns and physicians, fingering what seems to be a mounted fish. She is the subject of the gaze of everyone around her, the subject of the gaze of the photographer, and, finally, the subject of the gaze of all who look at the photograph. Everyone is trying to capture, to penetrate, the mystery of this blind-deaf girl through sight, and yet Ludivine herself remains remote, inaccessible, perceiving the world through touch.

Tactile museums

> My world is built of touch-sensations, devoid of physical color and sound; but without color and sound it breathes and throbs with life. Every object is associated in my mind with tactile qualities which, combined in countless ways, give me a sense of power, of beauty, or of incongruity.[43]
>
> Helen Keller, *The World I Live In*

As a marginal group within society, the blind, and the blind-deaf, have long had their experience of the world slighted or ignored by the sighted majority. Nonetheless, particularly in the last twenty-five years, a number of significant projects have been undertaken in the fields of psychology and art dedicated to understanding and catering to the tactile abilities of the blind. These include attempts to translate pictures into tactile images for educational purposes and the creation of museums of "tactile arts."

Figure 6 "The Blind-Deaf Ludivine Lachance"

Source: From Corinne Rochelau, *Hors de sa prison*, Montréal, Arbour and Dupont, 1927.

Art Education for the Blind, a New York-based organization founded in 1987, is involved in transposing key works of Western art from the realm of sight to that of touch. One of the works which has undergone this transposition is Marcel Duchamp's famous Cubist painting *Nude Descending a Staircase*. Duchamp's painting presents a series of overlapping images of a machine-like figure descending a staircase. Its tactile representation consists of a series of merged angular wooden statuettes – heads, arms, legs, and bodies combined into one mass – descending a staircase. As an auditory accompaniment to this sculpture, a tape is played of staccato footsteps going downstairs. At the end of the tape the footsteps blend into mechanical sounds. The sculpture and tape are intended to illustrate the predominant features of Cubism – the presentation of several perspectives or successive events simultaneously and the depiction of bodies as sums of geometrical forms – in such a manner that the sightless can have a direct sensory appreciation of this style of art.[44]

The customary restriction of the blind to three-dimensional forms of art is based on the seemingly obvious consideration that the blind have no direct way of knowing pictures. Research now indicates, however, that the blind *can* identify and even draw pictures, insofar as these are available to the touch by means of raised lines. Those who are blind from birth are at a disadvantage in identifying the subjects of drawings because they have no previous experience of pictures. Nevertheless, even blind persons with no knowledge of the conventions of pictorial representation have been found to be able to recognize common images such as a human body or a table when presented to them as simple, raised line drawings. (This ability is not universal, however, and may depend on a person's level of tactile discrimination.) Interestingly, the fact that a full-length human body is presented as only a few inches high on a page or that a three-dimensional and multi-textured form can be represented by a few simple lines does not seem to pose a problem for the blind. The tactile pictures, when they are recognized, make sense.[45]

This discovery makes it possible for books for the blind to contain tactile illustrations and for visual pictures to be translated into tactile images. In Great Britain, for example, the Living Paintings Trust produces albums of simple relief reproductions of the paintings of old and modern masters. Each album has ten reproductions and is accompanied by detailed information about the works and their creators.

Depictions of the outlines of objects can be understood both through sight and through touch. Many of the common elements of Western pictorial representation, such as color, shading, and perspective, however, only work within a visual context. In order to portray such sensations as texture, three-dimensionality and distance, tactile artists would have to develop their own set of pictorial conventions. For example, to depict the roundness of a jar in visual drawings, the sides may be shaded with darker lines. As regards the *tactile* drawing of a jar, however, its roundness may be indicated by placing more prominent raised lines on the front of the jar – the part nearest to the touch – and less prominent lines on the sides.[46] With respect to the depiction of distance, perhaps the visual technique of representing things as smaller the further away they are might work metaphorically for touch as well, or perhaps objects in the background of a picture could be depicted with dotted lines to indicate that they are out of touching distance.

When Diderot learned of a blind man who could recognize the portrait of a friend from a drawing made on his hand, he suggested that, "The blind could thus have their own kind of painting, in which their skin would serve as their canvas."[47] The examples of tactile art we have been considering above all involve a manipulation of external objects and images. It is also possible, however, for tactile images to be impressed directly on the skin. This can be most readily accomplished through the use of electronic devices which convert visual images into a tactile display of vibrating points.

In one experiment a television camera transmitted images of objects or photographs to an array of 400 tiny vibrators mounted in the back of a chair. Subjects who were seated in the chair, their backs bare, could feel the images as patterns of vibration on their skin. Almost all subjects were able to recognize simple geometrical shapes and patterns quickly, but the identification of more complex images, such as faces, required a period of training. When subjects were able to pan the television camera over the object they were trying to iden-tify (the way that eyes move over a scene), the consequent changes in the pattern of vibration assisted them in making identifications.[48]

Such technology has the effect of turning the skin into a tactile eye. For example, to blind subjects who had previously had no direct experience of the visual phenomenon of perspective, it came as a revelation when the tactile shapes communicated to them through the vibrators grew larger or smaller as an object was moved closer or further away from the camera. Insofar as the vibrators are positioned at one's back, however, there is a strange reversal of the customary perceptual process: one perceives from behind objects which lie in front. Apparently, however, subjects readily adjusted to this unusual state of affairs and mentally located objects in front of them which they tactilely perceived at their backs.[49]

Thus far we have been looking at ways in which touch can simulate vision. Touch, however, has a rich sensory dynamic and aesthetic potential of its own which is well worth exploring. The primary critique of touch as an aesthetic modality is that it is a sensory snail, perceiving objects piecemeal rather than all at once. Rudolf Arnheim writes of this aspect of touch in *Visual Thinking*:

> Dependent upon immediate contact, it must explore shapes inch by inch; it must laboriously build up some notion of that total three-dimensional space which the eye comprehends in one sweep.[50]

The assumption is that tactile exploration is a tedious, time-consuming activity compared to the ease and speed of visual scanning. Yet if touch is slower than sight, it can afford a greater pleasure of discovery, of making sense of something not all at once, but in stages. It is this delight of anticipation and gradual revelation which leads us, for example, to wrap presents in paper, perhaps concealing a smaller box inside a larger one, rather than displaying them as they are, to be immediately apprehended by sight.

Furthermore, there is no reason why a tactile work of art could not be made small enough to obviate the need for an extensive process of manual investigation.[51] Just as the form of a statue can be grasped at once by the eye, the form of a figurine can be grasped at once by the hand. This is not to say that one would not want to explore the different parts of the figurine further with one's fingers, just as one's eyes might linger on various details of the statue. Works of visual art, moreover, are not necessarily "eye-size." Paintings, such as murals, can be too large to grasp in one glance, and no one can see both the back and front of a sculpture at once, or the inside and outside of an architectural work. As with the tactile apprehension of large objects, visual images also often need to be compiled piece by piece.

This leads us to a fundamental difference between sight and touch. To see something properly one must distance oneself from it. Even if the object is very small, it is necessary to keep it at least a few inches away from one's eyes in order to focus on it. To be able to experience something by touch, however, one has to do exactly the opposite and unite oneself with it. This makes the tactile experience of art a much more intimate process than the visual experience of art. When touch is involved a physical bond is created between a work of art and the person perceiving it. The detached air of contemplation which is supposed to characterize the aesthetic attitude in the West becomes impossible as art work and art connoisseur are joined.

If the primary argument against touch as an aesthetic sense is based on its inability to achieve a "unified and spontaneous apprehension of form," the secondary argument lies in its ignorance of color and the play of light and shadow. The assumption is that, without color and light, all touch can offer is form. Yet touch, in its splendid diversity, offers much more to engage the mind than the mere sensation of form. For example, a sphere, besides being round, can be hard or soft, warm or cool, slippery or sticky, textured or smooth, heavy or light, moving or still. Some of these different qualities of touch are listed by Helen Keller:

> The delicate tremble of a butterfly's wings in my hand, the soft petals of violets curling in the cool folds of their leaves . . . the clear, firm outline of face and limb, the smooth arch of a horse's neck and the velvety touch of his nose . . . .[52]

With a little imagination one can see that there would be an infinity of possibilities for combining these different properties into both representational and abstract works of art. To give a very basic example, a tactile "painting" of the sea could employ a combination of sand and metal to convey the graininess of the shore and the cool swells and curves of the waves. Tactile works of art would tend to wear away through repeated touching, but durability – while enabling artistic creations to be "timeless" museum pieces – has nothing to do with the aesthetic experience per se.

Tactile aesthetics can be extended from sculptures and pictures to include living spaces. In this regard it should be noted that even the experience of visiting an exhibition of visual arts is, in part, a tactile or kinaesthetic one, as one moves through the gallery from exhibit to exhibit.[53] Most buildings, however, are currently designed to have a neutral tactile environment; walls and floors are smooth, the air is still, and the temperature is constant. With respect to this last point, Lisa Heschong remarks in *Thermal Delight in Architecture* that "there is an underlying assumption that the best thermal environment never needs to be noticed and that once an objectively 'comfortable' thermal environment has been provided, all of our thermal needs will have been met."[54] This assumption disallows all the pleasure and stimulation that can be experienced from variations in temperature.

The one consciously designated location for tactile aesthetics in the modern, urban world is the museum designed for the blind. In such museums the rule is the opposite of that of ordinary museums – "Touch!" Various cities of Europe and America offer tactile museums, but perhaps the most innovative is Gallery Tom in Tokyo. In Japan the blind constitute a more powerful social force than in most parts of the world. Thanks to this, Tokyo has such aids for the visually impaired as corrugated tiles indicating safe routes in train and subway stations and at street crossings. Gallery Tom represents a further development of this heightened social awareness of the needs and interests of the blind.[55]

The gallery, designed by Hiroshi Naito, is situated on a street corner to make it easier for blind persons to locate. Inside, changes in floor texture – from cedarwood to *tatami* matting – and temperature help to orient visitors and contribute to their sensory experience. The exhibits present sculptures by Western and Japanese sighted artists together with works by blind artists. Eye masks are available for sighted visitors who wish to turn off the visual world for once and revel in touch. On the ground floor there is a large performance space, which can be used for music, dancing, or as a meeting place. The last word, as one leaves the gallery, is a poem in braille on the stone doorknob of the exit door.

Despite the existence of museums such as Gallery Tom, works of tactile art are still considered more of a novelty, or a second-class aesthetics for those who lack sight, than a genuine art form. Many visitors to museums of tactile art undoubtedly find the experience, after the novelty wears off, somewhat tedious. The different shapes and textures of the works are sensed, but they have no particular meaning, they are not enlivened by any symbolic code. This has nothing to do with any intrinsic aesthetic deficiency of touch but rather with the lack of a cultural tradition of tactile representation.

Rudolf Arnheim, who came to support the development of a haptic aesthetics in his later writings, stated that:

> The blind have to live in a society that suffers from a serious neglect of the
> sense of touch, a society in which, for example, the many hours of televi-

sion viewing transform the world into a distant spectacle. The natural intimacy of handling things by which human beings normally learn remains excluded. The [aesthetic] education of the blind should be viewed, therefore, in the broader context of the need to reeducate an entire sensorially crippled population.[56]

That persons accustomed to perceiving art only through sight are unable immediately to appreciate the aesthetic potential of tactile works of art, does not mean that there can be no tactile works of art. It means, rather, that the art of touch must be fostered and elaborated within a community, whether that of the blind, or that of society at large, for tactile arts to attain their full aesthetic and cultural potential.

Olfactory aesthetics

> I doubt if there is any sensation arising from sight more delightful than the odors which filter through sun-warmed, wind-tossed branches, or the tide of scents which swells, subsides, rises again wave on wave, filling the wide world with sweetness. A whiff of the universe makes us dream of worlds we have never seen, recalls in a flash entire epochs of our dearest experience.[57]
>
> Helen Keller, *The World I Live In*

While the idea of an art of touch has received a certain amount of public attention, the notion of an art based on odors remains fantastical to most people. This continues to be the case even though modern techniques of fragrance engineering have made it possible to reproduce virtually any odor at will, and thus to "paint" scenes with odors, as with colors.

At various times since the 1800s a call has been made for the elaboration of an olfactory aesthetics. In Huysmans' nineteenth-century classic *Against Nature* the protagonist reasoned that "it was no more abnormal to have an art that consisted of picking out odorous fluids than it was to have other arts based on a selection of sound waves or the impact of variously colored rays on the retina of the eye."[58] In 1952 Etienne Souriau, a French professor of aesthetics, offered an exhibition of artistic scents produced by a "smell machine." Souriau stated that "there is no reason why hearing and seeing should be the only centres capable of receiving great art, since a trained nose can detect several thousand perfumes."[59] Such statements in favor of an art of odors, however, have generally been regarded as fleeting novelties rather than as true stimuli to the aesthetic imagination.

Some might argue that perfumery is the "art of odors" and that it is hence unnecessary to call for an olfactory aesthetics. To limit olfactory aesthetics to the productions of the perfume industry, however, would be like limiting the visual arts to the field of fashion design. There is a whole world of vital olfactory imagery and meaning which cannot be, and is not meant to be, encompassed within a perfume bottle.

Odors defy Western conceptions of art in that they are immaterial. An odor cannot be hung on the wall as a visual image can, or placed on the floor like a sculpture. Furthermore, the fact that odors do not confine themselves to discrete areas, but spread and merge, means that the scent of one olfactory work would mingle with that of another. In visual terms it would be as though the colors of one painting were to run across the wall and blend into those of the painting next to it. While from a postmodern perspective this merging of supposedly independent creations might be an admirable quality, from a traditional point of view, artistic integrity would definitely be compromised. Each olfactory exhibit would have to be placed in its own, air-tight, room.

In their invisible, intangible, and transgressive nature, odors seem more like sounds than colors. A model drawn from music might therefore appear more appropriate for the elaboration of an olfactory art than one drawn from the visual arts.

However, in certain key ways, odors are closer to colors than sounds. While many objects in our environment are soundless, nearly all present both olfactory and visual images. Thus a flower, for example, could be realistically represented by odor as well as by color and line, while it could only be represented in a metaphorical way by sound. Perhaps olfactory art would turn out to occupy a middle ground between music and painting, and an olfactory art gallery would be made up of different cubicles which people would enter to be enveloped in an interplay of scent.

Until recently the question might have arisen as to whether "bad" odors can make "good" art. Referring to a painting of the entombment of Christ in which a bystander is depicted holding his nose, Gotthold Lessing argued in *Laocoon* that artists should avoid suggesting loathsome sensations: "For not only the actual smell, but the very idea of it is nauseous."[60] C.S. Lewis similarly stated that "a bad smell is beyond the reach of art."[61] Nowadays "loathsome" sensations are so commonly the subject of art, that bad odors would certainly not be ruled out as unaesthetic on the grounds of their repugnant nature. Smells, however, *would* tend to be more physically intrusive than visual presentations. For example the visual nature of certain current "artworks" consisting of the decaying bodies of animals sealed inside glass cases allows for a degree of detachment which would scarcely be possible in olfactory art.

Protests against olfactory art might be made by those who believe in an inodorate sanctity of public space, free of perfume, tobacco smoke, and air freshener. These protests usually stem from concerns about health rather than aesthetics, although the latter undoubtedly plays a role. In order to be responsive to such concerns, perhaps galleries could set aside certain areas of their exhibition space for non-olfactory art, the way restaurants currently reserve sections for non-smokers.

The basic deterrent to the development of an olfactory art, however, is not one of presentation, but one of meaning. Not only do we lack a well-elaborated code of odors in the West, we are often unable to recognize even the most familiar odors when these are separated from their source.[62] That is, we know the smell of a rose when the rose itself is there, but if only an odor of roses is present, a large percentage of people would be unable to identify it.[63]

The blind and deaf Hellen Keller, by contrast, had an acute olfactory consciousness. She could recognize an old country house by its "several layers of odors," discern the work people engaged in by the scent of their clothes, and remember a woman she'd met only once by the scent of her kiss. So important a role did smell play in her life, that when Keller lost her senses of smell and taste for a short period, and was obliged, like Laura Bridgman, to rely wholly on her sense of touch, she felt she finally understood what it must be like for a sighted person to go blind. "It seemed incredible, this utter detachment from odors, to breathe the air in and observe never a single scent."[64]

The heightened olfactory awareness sometimes displayed by persons who are blind is not a special compensatory ability, but the result of intense cultivation of the sense of smell. It was once thought that the ability to identify people solely by their voices was a peculiar talent of the blind. Thanks to the invention of the telephone and the radio, however, almost all of us who make use of these devices have this ability today.

Helen Keller emphasized that "By themselves, odours suggest nothing. I must learn by association to judge from them . . . "[65] That olfactory associations could be painful, as well as enjoyable, is conveyed by her in the following passage.

> The other day I went to walk toward a familiar wood. Suddenly a disturbing odor made me pause in dismay. Then followed a peculiar, measured jar, followed by dull, heavy thunder. I understood the odor and the jar only too well. The trees were being cut down.[66]

Suppose Keller's sensations on that day were to be transformed into a gallery exhibit. One would walk into a room entitled, say, *The Disappearing Forest*. The room would be visually empty but filled with the sharp scent of a cut tree. The vibrations of sawing would reverberate throughout the room, followed by a heavy thud. Would such an exhibit, lacking as it does any visual referents, be any less moving or evocative than a painting or photograph of a tree being felled?

Even given the importance of making the fullest possible use of all their remaining senses, the blind-deaf often feel restrained in their elaboration of smell by the opprobrium attached to this sense in the West. Helen Keller commented that due to "the prejudices of mankind" she found it hard "to give an account of odor-perceptions which shall be at once dignified and truthful." Similarly, in his discussion of the sensory skills of the blind-deaf, John Macy wrote in 1902 that "The sense of smell has fallen into disrepute, and a [blind-deaf] person is reluctant to speak of it."[67]

That this "sensist" conception of smell has not changed much since then can be seen in the stereotypical imagery of Patrick Süskind's popular novel of the 1980s, *Perfume*, which portrays a depraved aromaphile who murders women for their scent.[68] It was just such a fate that high-minded critics worried might await the blind-deaf with their utter reliance on the so-called lower senses. In the words of one nineteenth-century educator: "Destitute of the spiritualizing refining influences exerted by the eye and ear, the blind deaf-mute is tempted to an excessive indulgence of his lower animal nature."[69] The sense of smell was evidently considered much too uncivilized in the modern West to make its education desirable, or even safe.

The last word here should go to Helen Keller:

> We should not condemn a musical on the testimony of an ear which cannot distinguish one chord from another, or judge a picture by the verdict of a color-blind critic. The sensations of smell which cheer, inform, and broaden my life are not less pleasant merely because some critic who treads the wide, bright pathway of the eye has not cultivated his olfactive sense.[70]

Dark continents: blindness, race, gender

The traditional exclusion of the proximity senses from art is linked with the traditional exclusion of certain groups of people from art. These groups include the blind, women, and peoples typed by the West as "primitive." Though each of these social groups contains an immense variety within itself, each has been stereotyped by mainstream Western culture as a "dark continent" of otherness. Many of the aesthetic practices conventionally associated with the blind, such as weaving and basketry, have also been associated with women and/or "primitive" peoples, and classified as handicraft rather than art.[71]

The blind have often been directly linked with "primitive" peoples by Western theorists due to the supposed dependence of both groups upon the proximity senses. In *The World of the Blind* Pierre Villey likened the "tactile music" of the blind-deaf to "the extremely simple music of many uncivilized races."[72] The nineteenth-century physician William B. Carpenter associated the apparent tactile acuity of the blind with the tactile sensitivity of weavers in India. Carpenter added:

> A like improvement is also occasionally noticed in regard to Smell, which may acquire an acuteness rivaling that of the lower animals; and this not only in the blind, but among the races of men whose existence depends upon such discriminative power. Thus we are told by Humboldt that the Peruvian Indians in the darkest night cannot merely perceive through their scent the approach of a stranger whilst yet far distant, but can say whether he is an Indian, European, or Negro.[73]

A number of scholars have considered "primitive" and ancient peoples to express a haptic orientation similar to that of the blind in their art.[74] In his study of the nature of creative activity Viktor Lowenfeld stated that the tactile emphasis found in the art of the blind can also be found in, among other places, "Australian drawings made on the bark of trees," and "Babylonian, Assyrian and Egyptian art."[75] To illustrate his point Lowenfeld juxtaposed a photograph of a

Peruvian sculpted head with a head sculpted by a blind person; both heads, he argued, express muscular sensations rather than visual impressions.[76]

It is indeed the case that many cultures less visualist than the modern West are concerned to express proximity sensations – along with visual impressions – in their aesthetic productions. Hence Navajo sand paintings are meant to be felt as well as seen, Amazonian basketry conveys meanings through textures and odors as well as through visual design. Such productions, which are often functional instead of purely formal, may not fit the standard Western definition of art, but they do conform to indigenous concepts of the aesthetic.[77]

In terms of conventional Western thought, however, the interest shown by "primitive" peoples in the proximity senses renders their artifacts, and indeed their lives, unaesthetic. Friedrich Schiller stated in *On the Aesthetic Education of Man* that "aesthetic freedom" comes only with the elevation of sight above the other senses, and "as long as man is still a savage he enjoys by means of [the] tactile senses."[78]

Although "primitive" peoples may possess the faculty of sight for practical purposes, as regards art they are deemed to be blind. "Suppose I place the *Mona Lisa* of Leonardo da Vinci in front of a Pawnee Indian or a Kaffir tribesman," wondered Thomas Edison as portrayed in a novel by Villiers de l'Isle-Adam, "However powerful the glasses or lenses with which I improve the eyesight of these children of nature, can I ever make them really *see* what they're looking at?"[79]

To an even greater extent than "primitive" peoples, women have shared the symbolic space of the blind in Western culture. In the traditional imaginary, the blind (regardless of sex) are symbolic females: confined to the home, immersed in the world of the body rather than the intellect, and dependent on guidance from their "enlightened" "superiors." As in the case of the blind, it has often been assumed that women (while full of dark intuitions) lack the visionary ability to be great artists.[80]

Like the blind, and like many non-Western peoples, women can challenge the traditional visualism of Western art by drawing on their particular aesthetic experiences to develop a non-visualist, or multisensory aesthetics. While many female artists have concentrated on learning and re-inventing the visual codes of art, some have manifested an interest in employing art to evoke the traditional non-visual elements of women's lives in a context of critical reflection.

The contemporary work of this nature which has probably drawn the most attention is Judy Chicago's *The Dinner Party* (1974–79). In this work, painted ceramic plates on embroidered runners set on a triangular table commemorate notable women from Western history. Using the conventionally feminine media of china and embroidery, *The Dinner Party* combines evocations of taste, touch, and women's work in an artistic exhibit. Judy Chicago wrote of this work:

> I had been trying to establish a respect for women and women's art; to forge a new kind of art expressing women's experience .... It seemed appropriate to relate our history ... through techniques traditionally associated with women – china-painting and needlework.[81]

A work which engages the proximity senses more directly than *The Dinner Party* is the 1978 tacto-visual sculpture *Femme d'espérance* (Woman of Hope) by Azélie-Zee Artand and Jovette Marchessault. This work consists of a 6-foot-tall feminine figure with outstretched arms composed of such odds and ends as yoghurt containers, jam jars, and egg cartons. The sculpture is labeled "Présence vitale" in Braille and "Femme d'espérance" in relief shorthand. Artand and Marchessault say of their work:

> We have animated this refuse into:
> Woman of exploration,
> Woman of dynamism,
> Woman of color,
> Woman of excitement,
> Manifestation of energy![82]

By making their work an object for touch as well as for sight, the artists emphasize the dynamic, forceful nature of the *Femme d'espérance* who reaches out to grasp the future – and the museum-goer.

Since the 1970s a number of women have created works of art which involve the proximity senses, and in particular touch. The Chilean artist, Cecilia Vicuña, for example, has drawn from the traditional aesthetic domains of both women and indigenous Andeans (for whom weaving is of great cultural importance) to develop a haptic aesthetics in her woven installations and performance art. In Vicuña's *12 Hilos en un corral* (12 Threads in a Corral) of 1994, woolen threads criss-crossed a traditional stone corral from wall to wall. This work offered those who entered into it the unique opportunity of situating themselves *within* a weaving and not simply perceiving it from outside.[83]

There is an enormous aesthetic terrain to be explored with regard to the senses of touch, smell, and taste. Many of the existing paths into this terrain come from the experiences and artworks of the blind, from the aesthetic practices of non-Western peoples, and from the traditions of women around the world. This circumstance by no means indicates that an aesthetics of the blind may be identified with a feminine aesthetics or with the aesthetic systems of non-Western societies. It does, however, give women, non-Westerners, and the blind a special potential and motivation for making the "dark continent" of the proximity senses part of the world of (Western) art.

Back to the Futurists

Although most artists and art critics have followed "the wide, bright pathway of the eye" in their work, not all in the history of art is scopic. As we saw in the previous chapter, the concept of a multisensory aesthetic was proposed over a century ago by the Symbolists and subsequently elaborated by the Futurists.

It is in Futurism, indeed, that we find the most extensive and innovative employment of the proximity senses in art to date. In 1924 F.T. Marinetti wrote a manifesto which announced the invention of tactile art: "a launch that will carry the human spirit to unknown shores."[84] In this manifesto Marinetti described how he had cultivated a desire for tactile variety by wearing gloves for several days, and developed his tactile sensitivity by feeling objects in the dark. This training in tactile awareness prepared the poet for the creation of the first tactile artworks, which consisted of tables covered with materials of different textures in accordance with a theme.

Marinetti insisted that tactile art "had nothing in common with painting or sculpture," but required a whole new aesthetic approach. It was unwise, therefore, for tactile art to be undertaken by persons trained in the visual arts, for such persons would "naturally tend to subordinate tactile values to visual values." With this new art, Marinetti suggested, it would be necessary to bypass visual rationality and concentrate on the "force–thought–sentiment" which takes place in the encounter between hand and matter.[85]

The most complete realization of the Futurist ideal to involve all the senses, and particularly the neglected proximity senses, in art occurred in 1932 with the invention of Futurist cuisine. The following description of one course of a Futurist culinary artwork illustrates the multisensory nature of this new art form (as well as the piquant humor of its creators):

> The second course consists of four parts: on a plate are served one quarter of a fennel bulb, an olive, a candied fruit and a tactile device. The diner eats the olive, then the candied fruit, then the fennel. Contemporaneously, he delicately passes the tips of the index and middle fingers of his left hand over the rectangular device, made of a swatch of red damask, a little square of black velvet and a tiny piece of sandpaper. From some carefully hidden melodious source comes the sound of part of a Wagnerian opera, and, simultaneously, the nimblest and most graceful of the waiters sprays the air with perfume.[86]

The Futurists invented terms to describe sensory combinations which might aptly be employed in culinary art. *Disluce*, for instance, referred to "the complementary nature of a given light with the flavour of a given food" and *contattile* to the affinity between particular textures and flavours. An example of the former was "the *disluce* of chocolate ice-cream and a hot orange light," and of the latter, "the *contattile* of banana and velvet".[87]

As testified by the paucity of tactile or culinary works of art today, Futurist multisensoriality never really caught on in the art world. In the 1960s the alternative art movement Fluxus briefly revived Futurist notions of multisensory art, presenting works such as Ay-O's *Tactile Box* and Takako Saito's *Smell Chess*.[88] Among contemporary artists, there are a number who, while not participating in any collective movement to expand the sensory bounds of aesthetics, engage the non-visual senses in their work.[89] As with the sensory innovations of the Futurists, however, such cross-sensory explorations do not seem to be making much of a mark on mainstream art. In fact, while possessing non-visual elements, most of these contemporary artworks are still basically visual exhibits, displayed to be *seen*, first and foremost. Marinetti was undoubtedly correct when he suggested that in the present sensory order the visual will inevitably dominate over the non-visual when the two are united in a work of art.

The Futurists believed that the technological developments and social upheavals of the new, twentieth, century would occasion an overthrow of the traditional sensory order. Vibration, and not vision, was to be the dominant sensory model of a modern age characterized by electricity and speed. Even light was understood by the Futurists more in kinaesthetic terms of vibration than in classical terms of clarity. Marinetti imagined a "Saint Speed" bubbling in his electric lamp and predicted that in the future "eyes and other human organs" would become "true accumulators of electric energy."[90]

The proliferation of electric devices and of ever-faster modes of transportation in the twentieth century has made Marinetti's prediction true in a sense: vibration and speed *are* characteristic sensations of modern life. Yet Marinetti and the Futurists failed to predict the ways in which the new technologies would give rise to potent new realms of visual imagery and visual ideology, making sight, and not kinaesthesia, the dominant sense of the desired new age. Hence we are left with the irony that at the end of the twentieth century the Futurist ideal of art forms for all of the senses remains futurist.

We can learn much about the social life of the senses from the Futurist foray into multisensoriality. Futurism, for example, demonstrates that multisensory aesthetics need not be a matter of other-worldly harmonies (as imagined by the Symbolists and Theosophists), or of pre-cultural synaesthestic fusions (as conceptualized by Merleau-Ponty and other phenomenologists of perception),[91] but can convey the complex dissonances and conflicts of contemporary life.

Futurism also makes it apparent that multisensory aesthetics, like all forms of aesthetics, can be the vehicle for the expression of diverse social ideologies.[92] When the Futurists called for an "upstart" multisensory art, they were at the same time interested in employing aesthetics to empower the "upstart" working classes, whom they considered to be excluded from traditional "visualist" museum culture. (Ironically, one of the reasons why the Futurists initially favored Fascism over Socialism as a workers' movement was that they found the representatives of the latter to be "unfailingly opposed to all revolutionary artistic practices.")[93] Just as Futurist art aimed to liberate the senses from conventional aesthetic hierarchies, it aimed to liberate the classes from conventional social hierarchies.

Nonetheless, while sensory hierarchies are closely interrelated with social hierarchies, to champion a greater equality of the senses is not necessarily to support social equality for all people. In his tactile art work *Sudan–Paris* Marinetti employed "crude, greasy, rough, sharp, burning tactile values" to signify Sudan and "soft, very delicate, warm and cool at once, artificial, civilized" values to signify Paris. While Marinetti was more apt to esteem the rough Sudanese set of tactile values than the soft Parisian one, this division of tactilities indicates how a tactile art might be employed to perpetuate conventional social divisions, such as between First and Third World.

Despite their revolutionary aesthetic ideals, and, in fact, because of their association of those ideals with populism, the Futurists ended up supporting a repressive fascist regime. It cannot be assumed, consequently, that a multisensory aesthetics – with its commitment to overthrowing sensory hierarchies – will be inherently subversive of social hierarchies and productive of a more open, just, or compassionate social order. In order to promote values of openness, justice, and compassion any aesthetic exploration must be explicitly and consistently linked to those values.

Crossroads of the senses

What are the possibilities for the elaboration of a multisensory aesthetics as we enter the twenty-first century? On the one hand, current efforts to open up the traditional boundaries of the visual arts would seem to promise a more welcoming environment than in the past for the development of new, non-visual art forms. Julia Kristeva has commented that the apparently fractured nature of contemporary visual representation might allow "hearing, skin, taste and so on to enter into account."[94] Along similar lines Jacques Derrida has suggested that smell and taste might be employed as the sensorial basis for an alternative model of writing – a notion which Gregory Ullmer, in his commentary on Derrida, has expanded to include art.[95]

On the other hand, as at the turn of the twentieth century, the current collapse of the boundaries of visual representation appears to be leading more to new departures within the visual arts (such as computer-generated images or Sherry Levine's photographs of photographs) than to non-visual art forms. We have, perhaps, more kinds of sights to look at than ever before, but not many more aesthetic elaborations of smell or touch.[96]

In the scopic regime of postmodernity, vision is implicitly presented as the slick, powerful, First-World sense of the future, while the other senses are largely relegated to the background, poor Third-World relations, unsophisticated and underdeveloped. In this cultural climate the concept of multisensory art runs the risk of being dismissed as passé, a nineteenth-century Symbolist fad or a McLuhanesque relic of the 1960s, before it has ever had the opportunity to be adequately developed. Why labor over an aesthetics of touch when one can experiment with state-of-the-art computer graphics?[97]

The New Age movement, with its concern to overcome the "mind–body split" of modernity through such sensuous practices as aromatherapy and reflexology, perhaps offers the closest approach in contemporary society to a multisensory aesthetics. It is often argued that this movement lacks critical consciousness and is no more than a "feel-good" jumble of modern and historical, Western and non-Western, ideas and practices. Nonetheless, the continuing popularity of the New Age movement indicates the existence of a widespread desire for alternative models of perception and interaction – indeed, for a new sensory cosmology.

There can be little doubt that Western culture as a whole, and Western art in particular, is going to continue down the visual highway in the immediate future. The momentum in this direction is too great to allow for any large-scale deviation. In order to even imagine an alternative path it is necessary first to make a conceptual break with visual culture. One means of creating this break is by considering the aesthetic experiences of the blind and the blind-deaf. What better antidote to Western society's hypervisualism than the tactile universe of Laura Bridgeman or Helen Keller's world of touch, smell, and taste?

The value of making such a break is that it can open up new ways of under-standing our cultural histor(y/ies) and new realms to be explored by the aesthetic imagination. This departure, in turn, may suggest novel perspectives and contexts for examining our tyrannical and fascinating visual culture. It is to be hoped, for the enrichment of us all, that a growing number of perceptive wayfarers will be enticed to enter this alternative sensory and intellectual terri-tory, and that the blind, who have a long history of adventuring in the realm of the non-visual senses, can help lead the sighted on this journey.

Notes

Introduction

1 Recent contributions to the discussion of the role of sight in modernity include D. Le Breton, *Anthropologie du corps et modernité*, Paris, Presses Universitaires de France, 1990; D.M. Levin, ed., *Modernity and the Hegemony of Vision*, Berkeley, University of California Press, 1993; M. Jay, *Downcast Eyes: The Denigration of Vision in Twentieth-Century French Thought*, Berkeley, University of California Press, 1994; P. Messaris, *Visual "Literacy": Image, Mind, and Reality*, Boulder, CO, Westview, 1994; K. Robins, *Into the Image: Culture and Politics in the Field of Vision*, London, Routledge, 1996.

2 This multiplicity of sensory meaning can be found across cultures. See further D. Howes, ed., *The Varieties of Sensory Experience: A Sourcebook in the Anthropology of the Senses*, Toronto, University of Toronto Press, 1991; C. Classen, *Worlds of Sense: Exploring the Senses in History and Across Cultures*, London, Routledge, 1993.

3 For example Levin, ed., *Hegemony of Vision* and Jay, *Downcast Eyes.*

4 T. Eagleton, *The Ideology of the Aesthetic*, Oxford, Basil Blackwell, 1990, p. 13.

5 L. Vinge, *The Five Senses: Studies in a Literary Tradition*, Lund, Sweden, Royal Society of Letters at Lund, 1975, p. 17.

6 "The Book of the Secrets of Enoch", in R.H. Charles, ed., *The Apocrypha and Pseudepigrapha of the Old Testament in English*, vol. 2, Oxford, Clarendon, 1919, 30: 8–9. The Gnostic philosopher Simon Magus associated a different sense with each of the first five books of the Bible, linking sight with Genesis, taste with Exodus, smell with Leviticus, hearing with Numbers, and touch with Deuteronomy. Hippolytus, *Philosophumena*, vol. 2, F. Legge, trans., London, Society for Promoting Christian Knowledge, 1921, pp. 10–11.

7 Ignatius of Loyola, *The Spiritual Exercises*, J. Morris, trans, London, Burns and Oates, 1952, pp. 29–30.

8 J. Huizinga, *The Waning of the Middle Ages*, F. Hopman, trans., London, Edward Arnold, 1948, pp. 136–7.

9 Dionysius the Areopagite, *The Mystical Theology and the Celestial Hierarchies*, Surrey, England, The Shrine of Wisdom, 1965, pp. 65–6.

10 Hildegard of Bingen, *Book of Divine Works with Letters and Songs*, M. Fox, ed., Santa Fe, NM, Bear and Company, 1987, 6, pp. 178, 180–1.

11 J. Boehme, *The Aurora*, J. Sparrow, trans., London, John M. Watkins and James Clarke, 1960, 12: 26, p. 272.

12 E. Swedenborg, *Heaven and its Wonders and Hell*, J.C. Ager, trans., New York, Swedenborg Foundation, 1930, xx: 177–82, pp. 130–4.

13 C. Baudelaire, *Les Fleurs du mal*, Paris, Classiques Garnier, 1994, "Orgueil," p. 177.

14 Hildegard, *Divine Works*, 5: 1–7, pp. 152–61.

15 Boehme, *The Aurora*, 13: 157, p. 345.

16 Cited by I. Merkel, "*Aurora*; or The Rising Sun of Allegory: Hermetic Imagery in the Work of Jakob Böhme," in I. Merkel and A.G. Rebus, eds., *Hermeticism and the Renaissance*, Washington, DC, Folger, 1988, p. 305.

17 M.C. Spencer, *Charles Fourier*, New York, Twayne, 1981, p. 154.

18 R. Barthes, *Sade, Fourier, Loyola*, R. Miller, trans., Berkeley, University of California Press, 1989.

19 See, for example, D. Howes, "Controlling Textuality: A Call for a Return to the Senses," *Anthropologica*, 1990, vol. 32, no. 1, pp. 55–73.

20 One particularly influential work on visual imagery in Western religion is M. Miles, *Image as Insight: Visual Understanding in Western Christianity and Secular Culture*, Boston, MA, Beacon Press, 1985. Pioneering works in the study of olfactory symbolism include J.-P. Albert, *Odeurs de sainteté: la mythologie chrétienne des aromates*, Paris, Editions de l'Ecole des Hautes Etudes en Sciences Sociales, 1990, and Susan Harvey's articles on smell in early Christianity: for example, "Olfactory Knowing: Signs of Smell in the *Vitae* of Simeon Stylites," in G.J. Reinink and A.C. Klugkist eds., *Change and Continuity in Syriac Christianity: A Festschrift for H.J.W. Drijvers*, Louvain, Peeters Press, forthcoming.

21 A. N. Whitehead, *Science and the Modern World*, cited by S.R. Bordo, *The Flight to Objectivity: Essays on Cartesianism and Culture*, Albany, NY, State University of New York Press, 1987, p. 99.

22 L. Irigaray, *Speculum of the Other Woman*, G.C. Gill, trans., Ithaca, NY, Cornell University Press, 1985.

23 There is a substantial literature on gender divisions of labor and knowledge. See, for example, E.F. Keller, *Reflections on Gender and Science*, New Haven, CT, Yale University Press, 1985. For accounts of medieval representations of female sensoriality, see C.W. Bynum, *Holy Feast and Holy Fast: The Religious Significance of Food to Medieval Women*, Berkeley, University of California Press, 1987; and H. Solterer, "Seeing, Hearing, Tasting Woman: Medieval Senses of Reading," *Comparative Literature*, 1991, vol. 16, no. 2, pp. 129–45.

24 Books dealing with this subject include C. Brant and D. Purkiss, eds., *Women, Texts and Histories: 1575–1760*, London, Routledge, 1992; J. Todd, *The Sign of Angellica: Women, Writing, and Fiction 1660–1800*, London, Virago, 1989; K.M. Wilson, ed., *Women Writers of the Renaissance and Reformation*, Athens, University of Georgia Press, 1987.

25 J. Barbey D'Aurevilly, *Les Bas-bleus*, Paris, Société Générale de Librairie Catholique, 1878, p. xxiii.

26 B.G. MacCarthy, *The Female Pen: Women Writers and Novelists, 1621–1818*, New York, New York University Press, 1994, p. 25.

27 See, for example, N. Bryson, *Vision and Painting: The Logic of the Gaze*, New Haven, CT, Yale University Press, 1983; H. Foster, ed., *Vision and Visuality*, Seattle, WA, Bay Press, 1988; J. Crary, *Techniques of the Observer: On Vision and Modernity in the Nineteenth Century*, Cambridge, MA, MIT Press, 1994.

28 C. Baudelaire, "L'Art romantique', in C. Baudelaire *Curiosités esthétiques: l'art romantique, et autres oeuvres critiques*, Paris, Editions Garnier Frères, 1962, p. 239.

29 C. Owens, "The Discourse of Others: Feminists and Postmodernism," in H. Foster, ed., *The Anti-Aesthetic: Essays on Postmodern Culture*, Port Townsend, WA, Bay Press, 1983, p. 71. Many excellent studies have been written on the role of "patriarchal" models in the visual arts. See, for example, R. Kendall and G. Pollock, eds., *Dealing with Degas: Representations of Women and the Politics of Vision*, New York, Universe, 1992.

30 M. Nordau, *Degeneration*, New York, D. Appleton, 1900, p. 502.

31 In this spectacle scents and savors (purchasable in convenient packages) serve only as supplements, like popcorn at a movie. On the visualism of the cinema see J.-C. Carrière, *The Secret Language of Film*, J. Leggatt, trans., New York, Pantheon Books, 1994.

32 W.R. Paulson, *Enlightenment, Romanticism and the Blind in France*, Princeton, NJ, Princeton University Press, 1987, p. 52.

33 W. Brodey, "Sound and Space," *New Outlook for the Blind*, 1965, vol. 59, no. 1, pp. 1–4; J.M. Kennedy, *Drawing and the Blind: Pictures to Touch*, New Haven, CT, Yale University Press, 1993; L. Heschong, *Thermal Delight in Architecture*, Cambridge, MA, MIT Press, 1990; J.M. Hull, *Touching the Rock: An Experience of Blindness*, New York, Pantheon, 1990.

34 R. Barthes, *Sade, Fourier, Loyola*, R. Miller, trans., Berkeley, University of California Press, 1989, p. 95.

35 H. Keller, *The World I Live In*, New York, Century, 1909, p. 11.

1 On the color of angels

1 At times these customary elements of Christian ritual would be supplemented by a variety of "special effects." Thus, in certain places during the commemoration of the descent of the Holy Ghost at Pentecost, flowers were showered down from the church rafters, along with wafers of different colors and burning bits of tow. Doves might also be let loose in the church and accompanied by a sound of rushing wind. E. Atchley, *A History of the Use of Incense in Divine Worship*, London, Longmans, Green, and Co., 1909, pp. 300–1.

2 Huizinga wrote of the medieval fascination with natural symbolism in *The Waning of the Middle Ages*: "Nothing is too humble to represent and to glorify the sublime. The walnut signifies Christ; the sweet kernel is His divine nature, the green and pulpy outer peel is His humanity, the wooden shell between is the cross." J. Huizinga, *The Waning of the Middle Ages*, F. Hopman, trans., London, Edward Arnold, 1948, p. 187.

3 D. Nicholl, "St. Bede," in J. Walsh, ed., *Pre-Reformation English Spirituality*, New York, Fordham Press, 1985, p. 6. Nicholl writes of Bede that he "impressed the names and places, numbers, colours and shapes of Scripture so deeply upon his heart that his heart itself became a Holy Land." Ibid.

4 *S. Petri Damiani Opera Omnia*, I (Patrologia Latina 144) Paris 1853, cited by L. Vinge, *The Five Senses: Studies in a Literary Tradition*, Lund, Sweden, Royal Society of Letters at Lund, 1975, p. 65.

5 Philo, *Questions and Answers on Genesis*, R. Marcus, trans., Cambridge, MA, Harvard University Press, 1961, p. 429.

6 Ibid., pp. 47–8.

7 Nor were all mystics convinced of the value of sensory experience, mystical or otherwise. Indeed, what appeared to be a revelation from God, might in fact be an illusion wrought by the devil. The author of the fourteenth-century guide to mysticism, *The Cloud of Unknowing*, for example, warns that:

> [Misguided mystics] strain themselves, as though they could possible see inwardly with their bodily eyes and hear inwardly with their ears; and so with all their senses of smell, of taste and of touch . . . . They so overtax their imagination with this fantastic behaviour and without the least discretion, that finally they turn their brains in their heads. The result is that the devil has power to fabricate false lights or sounds, sweet smells in their nostrils, wonderful tastes in their mouths and many other strange ardours and burnings . . . .
>
> *The Cloud of Unknowing*, J. Walsh, ed., New York, Paulist Press, 1981, p. 220.

8 For a review of medieval ideas about the "spiritual senses" see K. Rahner, "La Doctrine des 'sens spirituels' au moyen-age", *Revue d'ascétique et de mystique, 1933*, Brussels, Culture et Civilisation, 1964, pp. 263–99.

9 On the sensuous nature of medieval mysticism see R.D. Hale, "'Taste and See, for God is Sweet': Sensory Perception and Memory in Medieval Christian Mystical Experience", in A.C. Barlett, ed., *Vox Mystica: Essays on Medieval Mysticism*, Rochester, NY, D.S. Brewer, 1995, pp. 3–14.

10 Hildegard's medical writings are available in Hildegard of Bingen, *Liber simplicis medicinae*, in J.-P. Migne, ed., *Patrologiae cursus completus: series latina*, vol. 197, Paris, Migne, 1864, pp. 1125–1352, and Hildegard of Bingen, *Causae et curae*, P. Kaiser, ed., Leipzig, 1903.

11 It was also once thought that Hildegard painted the illustrations which accompany her work. While there is no evidence to support this claim (and indeed the illustrations in the *Divine Works* manuscript date from after her death) Hildegard may well have been involved in the preparation of at least the miniatures accompanying the text of *Scivias*. S. Flanagan, *Hildegard of Bingen: A Visionary Life*, London, Routledge, 1990, p. 224.

12 Hildegard of Bingen, *Book of Divine Works with Letters and Songs*, M. Fox, ed., Santa Fe, NM, Bear and Company, 1987. Letter to Wilbert of Gembloux, p. 349.

13 Hildegard of Bingen, *Scivias*, B. Hozeski, trans., Santa Fe, NM, Bear and Company, 1986, pp. 2, 4.

14 Ibid., 1: 4, p. 39.

15 Ibid., pp. 45–8. The process of making cheese was apparently a common metaphor for procreation in premodern Europe. B. Newman, *Sister of Wisdom: St. Hildegard's Theology of the Feminine*, Berkeley, University of California Press, 1987, pp. 139–40. See also C. Ginzburg, *The Cheese and the Worms: The Cosmos of a Sixteenth-Century Miller*, J. Tedeschi and A. Tedeschi, trans., Harmondsworth, England, Peguin Books, 1987, p. 53.

16 Hildegard, *Scivias*, 3: 8, pp, 294, 299.

17 Ibid., 1: 2, 3, pp. 398, 399.

18 Ibid., 2: 2, p. 90.

19 Hildegard of Bingen, *Symphonia: A Critical Edition of the Symphonia armonie celestium revelationum*, B. Newman, ed., Ithaca, NY, Cornell University Press, 1988, p. 243.

20 Hildegard, *Divine Works*, Letter to the nuns at Rupertsberg, p. 294.

21 Hildegard, *Scivias*, 1: 4, p. 55.

22 Ibid., p. 51.

23 Ibid., p. 42.

24 Hildegard of Bingen, *The Book of the Rewards of Life*, B. Hozeski, trans., New York, Garland, 1994, 6: 28, p. 278.

25 Hildegard, *Scivias*, 2: 6, p. 138.

26 Hildegard, *Divine Works*, 4: 4, p. 99.

27 Ibid., 2: 5, pp. 152–61.

28 Ibid., p. 156.

29 Ibid.

30 Hildegard, *Divine Works*, 2: 5, p. 156.

31 For example, a medieval English herbal describes certain herbs as being effective "against the white poison, against the purple poison, against the yellow poison, against the green poison . . . " A.L. Meaney, "The Anglo-Saxon View of the Causes of Illness", in S. Campbell, B. Hall, and D. Klausner, eds., *Health, Disease and Healing in Medieval Culture*, New York, St. Martin's Press, 1992, pp. 12–33.

32 Hildegard, *Scivias*, 2: 7, pp. 165–6. Later on, Hildegard describes the yellow poison as being "lukewarm." Ibid., p. 172. Christ's wounds were similarly sometimes associated with the five senses in mystical literature.

33 Assuming that Hildegard's customary ranking of the senses holds true here as well, the green poison would be associated with sight, the white with hearing, the red with smell, the yellow with taste and the black with touch.

34 Hildegard, *Divine Works*, 2: 5, pp. 160–1.

35 Hildegard, *Rewards of Life*, 6: 30, p. 281.

36 Ibid., pp. 282–3.

37 Hildegard, *Divine Works*, 1: 1, p. 10.

38 Ibid., 1: 4, pp. 89–127. Hildegard, in fact, compared the process of sensing to the rays of light emitted and received by planets. Ibid., pp. 91, 109.

39 Ibid., p. 47.

40 Flanagan, *Hildegard of Bingen*, pp. 96–7.

41 Hildegard, *Scivias*, 3: 13, p. 390.

42 Hildegard, *Divine Works*, Letter to the prelates of Mainz, p. 357.

43 Ibid., p. 359.

44 Hildegard, *Scivias*, 3: 13, pp. 375–95; B. Newman, "Introduction," in Hildegard of Bingen, *Symphonia: A Critical Edition of the Symphonia armonie celestium revelationum*, B. Newman, ed., Ithaca, NY, Cornell University Press, 1988, p. 19.

45 Hildegard, *Scivias*, 3: 12, p. 372.

46 On this tradition see M.H. Nicolson, *The Breaking of the Circle: Studies in the Effect of the "New Science" upon Seventeenth-Century Poetry*, rev. edn, New York, Columbia University Press, 1962, p. 114.

47 Hildegard, *Physica*, cited in Flanagan, *Hildegard*, p. 96.

48 Hildegard, *Scivias*, 3: 12, p. 372.

49 One of his admirers, the physician Tobias Kober, reported that Boehme could often divine the properties of a plant from its form and color, and infer the meaning of a foreign word from its sound. The Greek word *Idea*, for example, presented itself to him as a "pure and heavenly maiden." H.L. Martensen, *Jacob Boehme*, T. Rhys Evans, trans., New York, Harper and Brothers, 1949, p. 7.

50 D. Walsh, *The Mysticism of Innerworldly Fulfillment: A Study of Jacob Boehme*, Gainesville, University of Florida Press, 1983, p. 6.

51 A. Warren, "William Law: Ascetic and Mystic," in W. Law, *A Serious Call to a Devout and Holy Life, The Spirit of Love*, P.G. Stanwood, ed., New York, Paulist Press, 1978, p. 26.

52 J. Boehme, *The Aurora*, J. Sparrow, trans., London, John M. Watkins and James Clarke, 1960, 8: 22–48, pp. 151–7.

53 Ibid., 9: 69, p. 202.

54 Ibid., 10: 1, 11: 19, pp. 207, 239.

55 Ibid., 13, p. 321.

56 Ibid., 9: 74–5, p. 203.

57 Ibid., 4: 35, p. 94.

58 Ibid., 18: 12–19, pp. 454–6.

59 Ibid., 9:54 pp. 164–8.

60 Ibid., 8: 82–97, 9: 54, pp. 164–7, 199.

61 Ibid., 8: 45–50, pp. 156–7.

62 Boehme breaks down the word *Erden*, earth, for example, into two syllables, *er* and *den*. *Er*, he says, stands for the kindled astringent and bitter qualities, "before which the tongue is as it were afraid, and croucheth at the nether gums." *Den*, however, is of a more pleasant nature, and therefore, when pronounced, rises up through the nostrils towards the brain. Together *er* and *den* contain the theological meaning of

"earth": that God will reject the corrupt nature of the world while retaining its good spirit. Ibid, 18: 76–80, pp. 469–70.

63 Ibid., 11: 100, p. 256.
64 Ibid., 5: 41–65, pp. 111–16.
65 Ibid., 2: 31–57, pp. 56–61.
66 J. Boehme, *The Three Principles of the Divine Essence*, J. Sparrow, trans., London, John M. Watkins, 1910, 4: 29, p. 44.
67 J. Boehme, *The Signature of All Things*, London, J.M. Dent, 1934, 9: 33, p. 98.
68 Ibid., 9: 34, p. 98.
69 Boehme, *Principles*, 8: 11, p. 110.
70 Boehme, *Aurora*, 18: 24, p. 458.
71 Ibid., 8: 42, p. 155.
72 Ibid., 11: 34–5, p. 242. "The seven spirits are the father of the light, and the light is their son, which they always continually generate thus from eternity to eternity." Ibid., 11: 22, p. 239.
73 Ibid., 11: 37, p. 243.
74 Ibid., 13: 157, p. 345.
75 Ibid., 4: 27, pp. 92–3.
76 Boehme, *Principles*, 10: 7, 18–20, pp. 154, 160–1.
77 Ibid., 17: 91, p. 408. Hildegard also believed that the human body had changed for the worse since the Fall. See Flanagan, *Hildegard*, p. 100.
78 Boehme, *Aurora*, 4: 23, p. 92.
79 Ibid., 8: 15–16, p. 150.
80 Ibid., 12: 12, p. 270.
81 Ibid., 12: 13–16, pp. 270–1.
82 Ibid, 12: 26, p. 272.
83 Ibid., 12: 34, p. 274.
84 J. Boehme, *Mysterium Magnum*, J. Sparrow, trans., London, John M. Watkins, 1965, vol. 1, 5: 10, pp. 21–2.
85 Ibid., 4: 36–8, 12: 35, pp. 94–5, 275.
86 Ibid., 5: 14, p. 21.
87 For a comprehensive biography of Fourier see J. Beecher, *The Visionary and His World*, Berkeley, University of California Press, 1986.
88 C. Fourier, *The Passions of the Human Soul, and Their Influence on Society and Civilization*, H. Doherty, trans., London, Hippolyte Baillière, 1851, vol. 2, p. 273.
89 Ibid., p. 275.
90 Ibid., vol. 1, p. 40.
91 Ibid., vol. 2, p. 279.
92 Ibid., vol. 1, p. 83.
93 Ibid., p. 185.
94 Ibid., vol. 2, p. 264.
95 Ibid., p. 272.
96 Ibid., pp. 253–9.
97 Ibid., vol. 1, p. 29.
98 Such is the force of tradition, however, that when analyzing or grouping the senses, Fourier often employs the customary order of sight, hearing, smell, taste, touch.
99 Ibid., pp. 29–31.
100 C. Fourier, *Oeuvres complètes*, Paris, Editions Anthropos, 1967, vol. 12, p. 100.
101 Fourier, *Passions*, vol. 1, pp. 31–2.
102 Ibid., vol. 2, p. 247.
103 Ibid., vol. 1, p. 47.
104 Ibid., pp. 59–60.
105 Ibid., vol. 2, p. 274.

106 Ibid., vol. 1, pp. 70–1, 165.
107 Fourier, *Oeuvres*, vol. 6, p. 222. Fourier thought the opera one of the few places in civilization to offer visual and auditory pleasure. *Passions*, vol. 1, p. 162.
108 Ibid., pp. 60–1, 164.
109 Fourier, *Oeuvres*, vol. 5, p. 257; vol. 12, pp. 695–708.
110 Ibid., vol. 5, pp. 140–56; *Passions*, vol. 2, p. 329.
111 Ibid., vol. 1, pp. 50–1.
112 Fourier, *Oeuvres*, vol. 7, p. 442.
113 Ibid., vol. 1, p. 130.
114 Ibid., vol. 7, p. 384.
115 Ibid.
116 Fourier, *Passions*, vol. 1, p. 29.
117 Fourier, *Oeuvres*, vol. 7, p. 133.
118 Ibid., vol. 12, p. 111; vol. 6, p. 260; vol. 7, pp. 128–9.
119 Ibid., vol. 5, p. 358.
120 Ibid., vol. 7, pp. 142–4.
121 Ibid., p. 119.
122 Ibid., pp. 119–20.
123 Fourier, *Passions*, vol. 1, p. 33.
124 Fourier, *Oeuvres*, vol. 7, p. 123.
125 Fourier, *Passions*, vol. 1, p. 216.
126 Ibid.
127 Fourier, *Oeuvres*, vol. 1, pp. 44–5.
128 Ibid., vol. 7, p. 495.
129 Ibid., vol. 4, p. 254.
130 Fourier, *Passions*, vol. 1, pp. 78, 148.
131 Ibid., p. 217.
132 Boehme, *Signature of All Things*, pp. 85–6. In the sixteenth century Hieronymus Cardanus, for example, classified Mars with blueness and saltiness, Venus with whiteness and sweetness, and Saturn with blackness and bitterness. For the seventeenth-century Gerónimo Cortés, on the other hand, Mars was red and spicy, Venus was blue and musky, and Saturn was black and acid. L. Schrader, *Sensación y sinestesia*, Madrid, Editorial Gredos, 1975, pp. 325–7.
133 Ibid., p. 91.
134 Boehme, *Mysterium Magnum*, pp. 274–6.
135 Hildegard, *Divine Works*, 6, pp. 181–2.
136 For a description of the role of music in premodern cosmological thought see K. Meyer-Baer, *Music of the Spheres and the Dance of Death: Studies in Musical Iconology*, Princeton, NJ, Princeton University Press, 1970, pp. 7–41.
137 Fourier, *Passions*, vol. 1, pp. 222–3.
138 Thus Thomas Hobbes (1588–1679), for example, considered that all life could be reduced to a mechanical principle of motion. C.J. Friedrich and C. Blitzer, *The Age of Power*, Ithaca, NY, Cornell University Press, 1957, pp. 62–3.
139 Galileo Galilei, *Dialogue Concerning the Two Chief World Systems – Ptolemaic and Copernican*, S. Drake, trans., Berkeley, University of California Press, 1962, p. 58.
140 F. Zuccarone, *Prediche quaresimali*, cited by P. Camporesi, *The Incorruptible Flesh: Bodily Mutilation and Mortification in Religion and Folklore*, T. Croft-Murray and H. Elsom, trans., Cambridge, Cambridge University Press, 1988, p. 28.
141 Huizinga, *Waning of the Middle Ages*, p. 145.
142 St. Bernard of Clairvaux, cited by H.O. Taylor, *The Medieval Mind: A History of the Development of Thought and Emotion in the Middle Ages*, vol. 1, Cambridge, MA, Harvard University Press, 1962, p. 490.

143 Christian tradition often associated the Fall with the sense of taste. As a fifth-century writer states: "It was the pleasure of taste that drove us from Paradise." Abbot Nilus, *Tractatus de octo spiritibus malitae*, cited by C.W. Bynum, *Holy Feast and Holy Fast: The Religious Significance of Food to Medieval Women*, Berkeley, University of California Press, 1987, p. 36.

144 See Newman, *Sister of Wisdom*, p. 111.

145 L. Hindsley, *Margaret Ebner: Major Works*, New York, Paulist Press, 1993, p. 128.

146 Hildegard, *Divine Works*, p. 91.

147 Boehme, *Aurora*, 13, p. 321.

148 Fourier, *Passions*, vol. 2, p. 279.

149 Friedrich and Blitzer, *Age of Power*, p. 39. The medieval passion for symbolism made arithmetic into a moral science in the Middle Ages. According to Alain de la Roche, for example, the ten commandments times the fifteen virtues gives the 150 moral habits. Huizinga, *Middle Ages*, p. 189.

150 S. Bordo, *The Flight to Objectivity: Essays on Cartesianism and Culture*, Albany, NY, State University of New York Press, 1987, p. 99.

2 The breath of God

1 C. Classen, *Worlds of Sense: Exploring the Senses in History and Across Cultures*, London, Routledge, 1993, pp. 15–36; C. Classen, D. Howes, and A. Synnott, *Aroma: The Cultural History of Smell*, London, Routledge, 1994, pp. 78–92. Piero Camporesi writes that in modernity the sense of smell has been "challenged to the core for the supposed precariousness of its perceptions, indeed, attacked as too imprecise and deceptive to be deemed useful by a culture that presumes to know the world solely through an abstract and absolutely intellectual cognitive methodology." P. Camporesi, *The Incorruptible Flesh: Bodily Mutilation and Mortification in Religion and Folklore*, T. Croft-Murray and H. Elsom, trans., Cambridge, Cambridge University Press, 1988, p. 209.

2 P. Camporesi, *The Anatomy of the Senses: Natural Symbols in Medieval and Early Modern Europe*, A. Cameron, trans., Cambridge, Polity Press, 1994, p. 125.

3 André Vauchez writes that "if a servant of God did not exhale an 'odor of sanctity', veneration could stop as quickly as it started":

> The importance of [the odor of sanctity] as a criteria of saintliness was such that clerics sometimes hesitated for a long time before translating the remains of a highly-esteemed person to another site, for fear that a malodorous emanation might arise from the relics.
>
> A. Vauchez, *La Sainteté en Occident aux derniers siècles du Moyen Age*,
> Rome, Ecole Française du Rome, 1981, pp. 500–1.

4 P. Guerin, ed., *Les Petites Bollandistes: Vies des saints*, Paris, Bloud et Barral, 1878, vol. 6, p. 312.

5 E. Cobham Brewer, *A Dictionary of Miracles*, Detroit, Gale Research Company, 1966, p. 512.

6 Ibid.

7 Guerin, ed., *Vies des saints*, vol. 4, p. 275.

8 H. Thurston, *The Physical Phenomena of Mysticism*, J.H. Crehan, ed., London, Burns and Oates, 1952, p. 229. Similarly, the nuns under the Blessed Maria degli Angeli (d. 1717) noted that whenever they wanted their Reverend Mother "we tried to track her by the fragrance she had left behind." Sernin-Marie, *Vie de la B. Marie des Anges*, 1865, cited by Thurston, *Physical Phenomena*, p. 232.

9 Guerin, ed., *Vies des saints*, vol. 4, pp. 402–3. Accounts of Lydwine's life, based on the testimony of persons who knew her, may be read in J. Carnandet, ed., *Acta*

Sanctorum, Paris, Victor Palmé, 1866, vol 11, April 14, pp. 266–365. This material is summarized and discussed by C.W. Bynum, *Holy Feast and Holy Fast: The Religious Significance of Food to Medieval Women*, Berkeley, University of California Press, 1987, pp. 124–9.

10 T. à Kempis, *St. Lydwine of Schiedam*, V. Scully, trans., London, Burns and Oates, 1912, pp. 117–18.

11 Ibid., pp. 118, 190.

12 "When [Lydwine's] plasters were taken off to be changed, there remained on them little grey worms with black heads, giving forth from them no bad odour, but offering a sweet smell to those who beheld them." Ibid., p. 66.

13 Ibid., p. 67.

14 Ibid., p. 64. "Sometimes also she would eat a little spice or sugar or cinnamon or musk or grapes." Ibid. Lydwine's diet, while scanty, appears to have been highly aromatic. This may indicate a concern on her part about the production of body odors.

15 Ibid., pp. 18–19.

16 Ibid., pp. 122–3, 130–1.

17 Ibid., pp. 118–20.

18 Ibid., p. 136; Guerin, ed., *Vies des saints*, vol. 4, p. 405.

19 Kempis, *St. Lydwine*, pp. 145–6.

20 Ibid., p. 186.

21 Ibid., pp. 186, 191; Guerin, ed., *Vies des saints*, vol. 4, p. 405.

22 Kempis, *St. Lydwine*, p. 197.

23 Teresa de Jesús, *Libro de la vida*, in *Obras completas*, E. de la Madre de Dios and O. Steggink, eds., Madrid, Biblioteca de Autores Cristianos, 1972, p. 143.

24 St. Teresa recounts an instance of the odor of sanctity in her *Book of Foundations*, where she tells of a cave-dwelling noblewoman named Catalina de Cardona who scarcely ate, who punished her body severely with chains, and who (before taking on the habit of a nun) dressed as a man in order to avoid attention. After receiving a visit from the saintly Catalina, Teresa's sister nuns in Toledo remarked on her holy fragrance. Teresa writes:

> All [the nuns] tell me that she emitted such a strong fragrance of relics that it made one want to praise the Lord. Even her habit and belt, which she took off and left behind after being given another, had this odor . . . although because of the great heat one would rather have expected them to smell bad.

> Teresa de Jesús, *Libro de las fundaciones*, in *Obras completas*, 28: 32, p. 608.

25 F. de Ribera, *Vida de Santa Teresa de Jesús*, Barcelona, Gustavo Gili, 1908, pp. 339–40. First published in 1590.

26 Ibid., p. 334.

27 Ibid., p. 340.

28 Ibid.

29 Ibid., p. 527–8.

30 Ibid., pp. 340, 546, 558.

31 Ibid., pp. 561–2.

32 Paracelsus, *The Hermetic and Alchemical Writings*, vol. 2, A.E. Waite, ed., London, James Elliot, 1894, p. 61.

33 Ibid., p. 547.

34 Ibid., pp. 529–30, 536.

35 Ibid., pp. 532, 536.

36 Ibid., p. 532. Further pieces of the saint's body, however, continued to be distributed over the years as relics. V. Sackville-West, *The Eagle and the Dove: A Study*

in Contrasts, St. Teresa of Avila, St. Thérèse of Lisieux, London, Sphere, 1988, pp. 104–6.

37 Gaillard's writings on Benoîte are excerpted in the biography by R. de Labriolle, *Benoîte la bergère de Notre-Dame du Laus*, Gap, France, Louis-Jean, 1977.

38 Guerin, ed., *Vies des saints*, vol. 5, pp. 219–20.

39 P. Gaillard, cited by Labriolle, *Benoîte*, p. 55.

40 Guerin, ed., *Vies des saints*, vol. 5, pp. 220–1.

41 F. Grimaud, cited in Labriolle, *Benoîte*, p. 94.

42 Guerin, ed., *Vies des saints*, vol. 5, pp. 222–3.

43 P. Gaillard, cited by Labriolle in *Benoîte*, p. 222; Guerin, ed., *Vies des saints*, vol. 5, p. 224.

44 P. Gaillard, cited in Guerin, ed., *Vies des saints*, vol. 5, p. 224.

45 P. Gaillard, cited by Labriolle, *Benoîte*, p. 114; Guerin, ed., *Vies des saints*, vol. 5, pp. 223–4.

46 Ibid., pp. 225–6; Labriolle, *Benoîte*, p. 103.

47 Guerin, ed., *Vies des saints*, vol. 5, p. 226.

48 P. Galliard, cited by Labriolle, *Benoîte*, pp. 219–21; Guerin, ed., *Vies des saints*, vol. 5, p. 226.

49 Ibid., p. 224, 226.

50 P. Gaillard, cited by Labriolle, *Benoîte*, p. 122.

51 Ibid., pp. 122, 214–19; Guerin, ed., *Vies des saints*, vol. 5, pp. 226–7.

52 Labriolle, *Benoîte*, p. 267.

53 Ibid., pp. 224, 227, 259–96.

54 On the roles of odor in antiquity see further Classen, Howes, and Synnott, *Aroma*, pp. 13–50.

55 Origen, *Contra Celsum*, cited by E. Atchley, *A History of the Use of Incense in Divine Worship*, London, Longmans, Green, and Co., 1909, p. 84.

56 Athenagoras, *Legatio pro Christianis*, cited by Atchley, *Incense in Divine Worship*, p. 81.

57 Atchley, *Incense in Divine Worship*, pp. 117–30.

58 Camporesi provides a seventeenth-century recipe for making perfumed rosaries in *The Incorruptible Flesh*, pp. 185–6.

59 For example, the legend of the fourth-century St. Ambrose describes the saint as "a heavenly honeycomb in his sweet interpretation of the Scriptures," and then goes on to state that when Ambrose was a baby a swarm of bees flew into his mouth, attracted by his sweetness. J. de Voragine, *The Golden Legend*, G. Ryan and H. Ripperger, trans., London, Longmans, Green, and Co., 1941, pp. 24–5. (A similar story was told of Saint Isidore. Guerin, ed., *Vies des saints*, vol. 4, p. 186.)

60 Eusebius, *Ecclesiastical History*, R.J. Deferrari, trans., New York, Fathers of the Church, 1953, pp. 241, 281.

61 The fourteenth-century theologian John Wycliffe draws on this association between smell and virtue when he states that "some men are good smelling and some are stinking to God." T. Arnold, ed., *Select English Works of John Wyclif*, Oxford, Clarendon, 1869, vol. 1, p. 262.

62 John of the Cross, "Spiritual Canticle", in *The Complete Works of Saint John of the Cross*, D. Lewis, trans., London, Longmans, Green, and Co., 1864, vol. 2, stanza xvii, p. 98.

63 J.-P. Albert, *Odeurs de sainteté: la mythologie chrétienne des aromates*, Paris, Editions de l'Ecole des Hautes Etudes en Sciences Sociales, 1990, pp. 83–4.

64 The quality of sweetness itself was believed from antiquity to possess a preservative power. Thus, for example, Paracelsus writes that "we are certainly assured that

bodies may be preserved from corruption by sweetness." *Alchemical Writings*, p. 73.

65 J. Boehme, *The Three Principles of the Divine Essence*, J. Sparrow, trans., London, John M. Watkins, 1910, p. 479. See further R. Onians, *The Origins of European Thought about the Body, the Mind, the Soul, the World, Time and Fate*, Cambridge, Cambridge University Press, 1951, pp. 49–50.

66 A fragrant cure of a sick nun by the Virgin Mary is recorded in the *Life* of the twelfth-century recluse, Christina of Markyate:

> When she sat down before the patient's bed, she took out a small box in which she had brought an electuary of unusual fragrance . . . . [She] gave the lozenge to the sick woman and cured her . . . . You see how easily and appropriately God cured His virgin daughter with heavenly medicine through His virgin Mother . . .

> C.H. Talbot, ed. and trans., *The Life of Christina of Markyate: A Twelfth-Century Recluse*, Oxford, Clarendon Press, 1959, p. 125.

67 This request was not as odd as it might sound to modern ears, for the corpses of many holy persons were reputed to have produced aromatic oils. On this see H. Thurston, *Physical Phenomena*, pp. 268–70.

68 A. Imbert-Gourbeyre, *La Stigmatisation*, J. Bouflet, ed., Grenoble, France, Editions Jérôme Millon, 1996, pp. 303–4.

69 Atchley, *Incense in Divine Worship*, pp. 108–9.

70 Ribera, *Santa Teresa*, p. 546.

71 See, for example, P. Bacci, *The Life of St. Philip Neri*, F. Antrobus, trans., London, Kegan Paul, Trench, Trubner, and Co., 1902, vol. 1, p. 317.

72 Guerin, ed., *Vies des saints*, vol. 5, p. 223.

73 For an outline of pre-modern medical theories of smell see R. Palmer, "In Bad Odour: Smell and Its Significance in Medicine from Antiquity to the Seventeenth Century," in W.F. Bynum and R. Porter, eds., *Medicine and the Five Senses*, Cambridge, Cambridge University Press, 1993, pp. 61–8.

74 On the reputed fragrance of paradise see Camporesi, *Incorruptible Flesh*, pp. 243–57.

75 B. Colgrave and R. Mynors, eds., *Bede's Ecclesiastical History of the English People*, Oxford, Clarendon, 1969, p. 493.

76 Ibid., p. 495.

77 Ibid., pp. 495–6.

78 Guerin, ed., *Vies des saints*, vol. 4, p. 276.

79 Bacci, *St. Philip Neri*, vol. 1, pp. 224–5, 356–60, vol. 2, p. 56–7.

80 Ibid., p. 360.

81 Hildegard of Bingen, *The Book of the Rewards of Life*, B. Hozeski, trans., New York, Garland, 1994, pp. 157, 161.

82 C.G. Rosignoli, *Verità eterne eposte in lettioni*, Milan, C.A. Malatesta, 1688, p. 157, cited by P. Camporesi, *Fear of Hell: Images of Damnation and Salvation in Early Modern Europe*, L. Byatt, trans., Cambridge, Polity Press, 1991, p. 60.

83 B. de la Riya, *Il libro de la scriptura negra*, in *Le opere volgari di Bonvesin da la Riva*, Rome, 1941, cited by Camporesi, *Fear of Hell*, pp. 15–16. See also Camporesi, *Incorruptible Flesh*, pp. 52–3, 109.

84 B.M. Amico di Milano, *Vita di Santa Francesca Romana*, cited by Camporesi, *Incorruptible Flesh*, p. 55.

85 Hildegard of Bingen, *Scivias*, B. Hozeski, trans., Santa Fe, NM, Bear and Company, 1986, p. 362.

86 See B. Newman, *Sister of Wisdom: St. Hildegard's Theology of the Feminine*, Berkeley, University of California Press, 1987, p. 115.

87 Bacci, *Saint Philip Neri*, vol. 1, p. 354.

88 Catherine of Siena, *The Dialogue*, S. Noeffke, trans., New York, Paulist Press, 1980, p. 238.

89 M. King, "The Sacramental Witness of Christina *Mirabilis*: The Mystic Growth of a Fool for Christ's Sake," in L. Thomas Shank and J.A. Nichols, eds., *Medieval Religious Women II: Peaceweavers*, Kalamazoo, MI, Cistercian Publications, 1987, pp. 150–2.

90 St. Jerome, "Life of St. Hilarion," in R.J. Deferrari, ed., *Early Christian Biographies*, Washington, Fathers of the Church, Catholic University of America Press, 1952, p. 266.

91 I. Origo, *The World of San Bernardino*, New York, Harcourt, Brace, and World, 1962, p. 37.

92 L. Ponnelle and L. Bordet, *St. Philip Neri and the Roman Society of his Times*, R. Kerr, trans., London, Sheed and Ward, 1937, p. 147. The saint also declared that his cat had a keen nose for musk – the perfume of lovers – because of her virginity. Ibid.

93 J.-K. Huysmans, *The Cathedral*, C. Bell, trans., London, Kegan Paul, Trench, Trubner, and Co., 1925, p. 90.

94 *Vita di Giuseppe di Copertino*, Florence, 1768, cited by Camporesi, *Incorruptible Flesh*, p. 55.

95 Modern translations of this verse usually do not refer directly to smell, preferring to use a circumlocution instead.

96 T. Malory, *Le Morte d'Arthur*, M. Oskar Sommer, ed., London, D. Nutt, 1889. Along similar lines, a foul odor was popularly accorded to Jews due to their non-Christian status. Certain myths stated that Jews drank the blood of baptized babies so as to rid themselves of their malodor. According to others, Christians who converted to Judaism had to be scrubbed with water and sand in order to remove their scent of baptism. V. Newall, "The Jew as Witch Figure," in V. Newall, ed., *The Witch Figure*, London, Routledge and Kegan Paul, 1973, p. 105.

97 Cited by Thurston, *Physical Phenomena*, p. 342.

98 Thurston, *Physical Phenomena*, pp. 229–30.

99 Catherine of Genoa, "The Spiritual Dialogue," in *Catherine of Genoa*, S. Hughes, trans., New York, Paulist Press, 1979, p. 131.

100 Longaro degli Oddi, *Della vita del Beato Pietro Claver*, Rome, 1852. Cited by Camporesi, *Anatomy of the Senses*, p. 183.

101 Ibid.

102 Ibid., p. 151.

103 J. Morton, *The Ancren Riwle: A Treatise on the Rules and Duties of Monastic Life*, New York, Johnson Reprint Corporation, 1968, pp. 105–7.

104 S.A. Harvey, "Olfactory Knowing: Signs of Smell in the *Vitae* of Simeon Stylites," in G.J. Reinink and A.C. Klugkist, eds., *Change and Continuity in Syriac Christianity: Festschrift for H.J.W. Drivjers*, Louvain, Peeters Press, forthcoming.

105 Alpais's ascetic life is discussed in Bynum, *Holy Feast and Holy Fast*, pp. 73, 134.

106 "They shall smell celestial odors who, in this life, had stench and rank smells of sweat from iron or from hair-cloth which they wore." Morton, *Ancren Riwle*, p. 105.

107 Harvey, "Olfactory Knowing."

108 Teresa, *Libro de la vida*, 32: 2, p. 143.

109 This was deemed to be especially the case with prostitutes, of whom it was thought that "excessive indulgence in coitus provoked a positive overflow of sperm into the woman's humors, putrefied the liquids, and engendered an intolerable stench." A. Corbin, *The Foul and the Fragrant: Odor and the French Social Imagination*, M. Kochan, R. Porter, and C. Prendergast, trans., Cambridge, MA, Harvard University Press, 1986, p. 46.

110 Bacci, *St. Philip Neri*, vol. 1, p. 249.

111 Ibid.

112 Ribera, *Santa Teresa*, p. 528.

113 An association of sweetness with divinity can be found in several biblical passages. Psalm 34: 8 reads, for example: "Oh, taste and see that the Lord is sweet." The Protestant reformer Martin Luther commented on this passage: "He puts tasting before seeing, because this sweetness cannot be known unless one has experienced and felt it for himself." M. Luther, "The Magnificat," in *Luther's Works*, J. Peliken, ed., A. Steinhaeuser, trans., St. Louis, MI, Concordia, 1956, vol. 21, p. 302.

114 Catherine of Siena, *Dialogue*, p. 239. The body of Jesus Christ, consumed in the host during communion, was considered to "[excel] all savoury tastes and [surpass] all sweetnesses." G.B. Sanguire, *Erario della vita cristiana*, Venice, 1711, cited by Camporesi, *Fear of Hell*, p. 148.

115 Bacci, *St. Philip Neri*, vol. 1, p. 147. Interestingly, after his death, portions of the body of St. Philip were reverently consumed by persons seeking miraculous cures (ibid., vol. 2, pp. 202–3). It was not, in fact, unusual to partake of the flesh of a human corpse as a medical remedy in pre-modern Europe. (See P. Camporesi, *Bread of Dreams: Food and Fantasy in Early Modern Europe*, D. Gentilcore, trans., Cambridge, Polity Press, 1989, pp. 46–9). A saint's flesh combined physical and spiritual efficacy as a medicine and made it possible for sinners to temporarily invest their own bodies and souls with the odor of sanctity.

116 L. Hindsley, *Margaret Ebner: Major Works*, New York, Paulist Press, 1993, pp. 155, 158. See also Bacci, *St. Philip Neri*, vol. 1, pp. 147, 151.

117 The notion of the sustaining power of celestial odors is ancient. In the fourth century, for example, St. Ephrem the Syrian wrote that "Instead of bread, it is the very fragrance of Paradise that gives nourishment/instead of liquid, this life-giving breeze does service." S.A. Harvey, "St. Ephrem on the Scent of Salvation," *Journal of Theological Studies*, 1998, vol. 49, no. 1.

118 Bynum, *Holy Feast and Holy Fast*, p. 132. Bynum supplies further examples of holy fasters being sustained by heavenly food, e.g. ibid., pp. 131–4.

119 Kempis, *St. Lydwine*, pp. 19, 66.

120 Ibid., p. 57.

121 In a vision the Lord imprinted Lydwine with his sacred wounds; the saint requested that these stigmata remain invisible to enable her to avoid undue celebrity. Guerin, ed., *Vies des Saints*, vol. 4, p. 404.

122 F.M. Salvatori, *Life of Veronica Giuliani*, cited by Thurston, *Physical Phenomena*, p. 228. Imbert-Gourbeyre, *La Stigmatisation*, p. 388; see also pp. 176, 227, 327, 359, 388.

123 This is at least true from the late Middle Ages on (when new trends in popular religiosity led to an increase in the number of female saints). On the relative proportion of female to male saints in different periods see D. Weinstein and R.M. Bell, *Saints and Society: The Two Worlds of Western Christendom, 1000–1700*, Chicago, University of Chicago Press, 1982, pp. 220–5.

124 Ibid., pp. 228–35; Thurston, *Physical Phenomena*, p. 123.

125 The sixteenth-century St. Catherine of Ricci, for example, manifested a fragrant stigma on her ring finger. One of Catherine's sister nuns went so far as to put this finger in her mouth in order to ascertain its taste. Thurston, *Physical Phenomena*, pp. 138–9.

126 Similarly, whereas both holy men and women were concerned with combating sin, the former tended to imagine sin in terms of external temptations and failings, while the latter typically saw it as an evil internal to themselves (and therefore necessitating bodily mortification). These attitudes were consistent with current

ideologies which, for example, presented men as being tempted to sin by women, and women as inherent temptresses. Weinstein and Bell, *Saints and Society*, p. 236.

127 Ibid., p. 232.

128 J.-K. Huysmans, *Saint Lydwine of Schiedam*, A. Hastings, trans., London, Kegan Paul, Trench, Trubner, and Co., 1923, pp. 207–8. Huysmans suggests that if more women were willing "to inflict voluntary suffering on themselves and endure the chastisement which sin had made inevitable," more people in general might be spared the consequences of God's anger. Ibid., p. 220.

129 For an examination of olfactory references in the Hebrew Bible see P.A.H. de Boer, "Job 39: 25," in P. Ackroyd and B. Lindars, eds., *Words and Meaning: Essays Presented to David Winston Thomas*, Cambridge, Cambridge University Press, 1968.

130 Arnold, *Works of John Wyclif*, vol. 1, pp. 107–8.

131 John of the Cross, "Spiritual Canticle," stanza xxiv, p. 129. "No language," John states, "can describe the fragrance which every one of [the flowers of the soul] diffuses." Ibid., stanza xvii, p. 98. The image of the soul as a fragrant garden was also favored by Teresa of Avila, who wrote: "It was of great delight to me to think of my soul as a garden; and I begged the Lord who visited it to intensify the odor of its virtuous flowers." Teresa de Jesús, *Libro de la vida*, 14: 10, p. 71.

132 John of the Cross, "Spiritual Canticle," stanza xxiv, p. 126.

133 Bernard of Clairvaux, *On the Song of Songs*, K. Walsh, trans., Spencer, MA, Cistercian Publications, 1971, vol. 1, p. 79.

134 Ibid.

135 Ibid.

136 Ibid., p. 78.

137 Ibid., vol. 3, p. 9.

138 Ibid., p. 8.

139 Ibid., p. 9.

140 Ibid.

141 Ibid., vol. 2, p. 17.

142 Ibid., vol. 1, p. 84.

143 Ibid., p. 11.

144 See for example the early Christian account of the malodorous departure of Adam and Eve from the fragrant Garden described in Harvey, "St. Ephrem."

145 Boehme, *Three Principles*, p. 180.

146 Ibid., p. 410.

147 Albert, *Odeurs de sainteté*, pp. 208–30.

148 The olfactory references in this text are discussed by Susan Ashbrook Harvey in "Incense Offerings in the Syriac *Transitus Mariae*: Ritual and Knowledge in Ancient Christianity," in A. Malherbe, F. Norris, and J. Thompson, eds., *The Early Church in its Context: Studies in Honor of Everett Ferguson*, Leiden, E.J. Brill, 1998.

149 Ibid., pp. 146, 166–70. See also Boehme, *Three Principles*, p. 189.

150 Albert, *Odeurs de sainteté*, p. 146.

151 Clairvaux, *Song of Songs*, p. 108.

152 Cobham Brewer, *Dictionary of Miracles*, p. 37. See further Weinstein and Bell, *Saints and Society*, pp. 236, 239–49, 289.

153 On changing concepts of heaven and hell see C. McDannell and B. Lang, *Heaven: A History*, New Haven, CT, Yale University Press, 1988 and Camporesi, *Fear of Hell*.

154 E. Stopp, *St. Francis de Sales: A Testimony by St. Chantal*, London, Faber and Faber, 1967, p. 161.

155 Ribera, *Santa Teresa*, p. 547.

156 Classen, *Worlds of Sense*, p. 28.

157 C. Thompson, *Mystery and Lure of Perfume*, London, John Lane, The Bodley Head, 1927, pp. 131–2.
158 Ibid., p. 131.
159 H. Ellis, *Studies in the Psychology of Sex*, vol. 1, New York, Random House, 1942, part 3, p. 72. Such medical materialist approaches to the odor of sanctity yielded an unusual result in the case of the hygienist Gustav Jaeger (1832–1917), who developed a theory which associated the soul with body odor. Jaeger is best known for his creation of a very popular line of woolen underwear. S. Kern, "Olfactory Ontology and Scented Harmonies: On the History of Smell," *Journal of Popular Culture*, 1974, vol. 7, no. 4, p. 820.
160 G. Hahn, "Les Phénomènes hystériques et les révélations de Sainte Thérèse," *Revue des questions scientifiques*, 1883, cited by J.H. Leuba, *The Psychology of Religious Mysticism*, New York, Harcourt, Brace, and Company, 1925, p. 197.
161 H. Legrand du Saulle, *Les Hystériques: état physique et état mental*, Paris, Ballière, 1891, cited by C. Mazzoni, *Saint Hysteria: Neurosis, Mysticism, and Gender in European Culture*, Ithaca, NY, Cornell University Press, 1996, p. 14.
162 Thurston mentions instances of the odor of sanctity (including one involving a spiritualist medium) from the nineteenth century in *Physical Phenomena*, pp. 225–7, 232. For an example of the continued relevance of this phenomenon in rural Europe see J. de Pina-Cabral, "Cults of Death in Northwestern Portugal," *Journal of the Anthropological Society of Oxford*, 1980, vol. 11, no. 1, pp. 1–14.
163 Labriolle, *Benoîte*, p. 94.
164 E. de Condillac, *Treatise on the Sensations*, G. Carr, trans., London, Favil, 1930, p. xxxi.
165 I. Kant, *Anthropology from a Pragmatic Point of View*, V.L. Dowdell trans., Carbondale and Edwardsville, Southern Illinois University Press, 1978 [1798], 22, p. 46.
166 M. Horkheimer and T.W. Adorno, *Dialectic of Enlightenment*, J. Cumming, trans., New York, Herder and Herder, 1972, p. 184.
167 See Classen, Howes, and Synnott, *Aroma*, pp. 78–84.
168 M. Friedlander, ed., *The Commentary of Ibn Ezra on Isaiah*, vol. 1, New York, Philip Feldheim, 1873, p. 60.
169 J. Calvin, *Commentary on the Book of the Prophet Isaiah*, vol. 1, J. Pringle, trans., Grand Rapids, MI, Baker Book House, 1981, p. 376.
170 Isidoro de Sevilla, *Etymologiae*, XI, 1, 47, cited by L. Schrader, *Sensación y sinestesia*, Madrid, Editorial Gredos, 1975, p. 352.
171 Hildegard of Bingen, *Book of Divine Works with Letters and Songs*, M. Fox, ed., Santa Fe, NM, Bear and Company, 1987, p. 130.
172 Hieronymus Cardanus, cited by Schrader, *Sensación y sinestesia*, pp. 353, 355.
173 Francis de Sales, *The Love of God: A Treatise*, V. Kerns, trans., Westminster, England, The Newman Press, 1962, p. 231.
174 L. Magalotti, *Lettere sopra i buccheri*, cited by Camporesi, *Incorruptible Flesh*, p. 184.

3 The scented womb and the seminal eye

1 See, for example, E.F. Keller and C.R. Grontkowski, "The Mind's Eye," in S. Harding and M.B. Hintikka, eds., *Discovering Reality: Feminist Perspectives on Epistemology, Metaphysics, Methodology and Philosophy of Science*, Dordrecht, Netherlands, D. Reidel, 1983, p. 207.
2 "Investment in sight is not privileged in women as in men. More than any of the other senses, the eye objectifies and masters . . . . In our culture, the predominance of the gaze over smell, taste, touch, and hearing has led to an impoverishment of

corporeal relations." L. Irigaray, "Interview avec Luce Irigaray", in M.-F. Hans and G. Lapouge, eds., *Les Femmes, la pornographie et l'érotisme*, Paris, Editions du Seuil, 1978, p. 50.

3 "Woman takes pleasure more from touching than from looking, and her entry into a dominant scopic economy signifies, again, her consignment to passivity." L. Irigaray, *This Sex Which Is Not One*, C. Porter and C. Burke, trans., Ithaca, NY, Cornell University Press, 1985, p. 26.

4 For example, G. Pollock, *Vision and Difference: Femininity, Feminism, and Histories of Art*, London, Routledge, 1988; L. Mulvey, *Visual and Other Pleasures*, London, Macmillan, 1989; L. Jordanova, *Sexual Visions: Images of Gender in Science and Medicine between the Eighteenth and Twentieth Centuries*, New York, Harvester Wheatsheaf, 1989.

5 As regards physical appearance, a certain degree of darkness was often valued in a man as a sign of strength and seriousness – dark colors usually being considered "stronger" and "more serious" than light colors. Fairness, on the other hand, would be preferred in a woman as a sign of submissiveness and frivolity (light colors being "weak" and "playful.")

   This opposition had its roots in antiquity, with Aristotle considering "fair-skinned women [to be] typically feminine" and dark women to be masculine in appearance. Aristotle, *Generation of Animals*, A.L. Peck, trans., Cambridge, MA, Harvard University Press, 1963, p. 101.

6 An ancient example of this dualism can be found in Plutarch's *De Iside* in which the Egyptian god Osiris is described as wearing clothes of pure light because he embodies pure principle, while the goddess Isis wears vestments of various colors because she rules over the material world. Plutarch, *De Iside et Osiride*, Swansea, University of Wales Press, 1970, p. 241. For a discussion of the gender symbolism of light, darkness, and color during the Enlightenment see R. Salvaggio, *Enlightened Absence: Neoclassical Configurations of the Feminine*, Urbana, IL, University of Illinois Press, 1988.

7 For example, Aristotle, *Generation of Animals*, pp. 103, 385–91; Galen, *On the Usefulness of the Parts of the Body*, M.T. May, trans., Ithaca, NY, Cornell University Press, 1968, pp. 629–32. See also P. Allen, *The Concept of Woman: The Aristotelian Revolution, 750 BC–AD 1250*, Montreal, Eden Press, 1985, pp. 47–8, 95–7, 101–3, 187–9, 364–5, 389–90. On the prevalence of this notion during the Renaissance see I. Maclean, *The Renaissance Notion of Woman: A Study in the Fortunes of Scholasticism and Medical Science in European Intellectual Life*, Cambridge, Cambridge University Press, 1980, pp. 31–5.

8 Ibid. pp. 34–5.

9 Ibid., pp. 39–42. Biblical grounds for the greater softness of women were found in the creation of Eve from "soft" flesh – Adam's rib – as opposed to the creation of Adam from the "hard" ground. Hildegard of Bingen, for example, wrote that "through the vital powers of the earth, Adam was manly . . . Eve, however, remained soft in her marrow." Cited by Allen, *Concept of Woman*, p. 296.

10 Maclean, *Renaissance Notion of Woman*, pp. 41–3. Albertus Magnus wrote that "because of the coldness of the constitution of woman . . . her intellect is weaker," and that "it is according to the nature of woman to have inconstant ideas, because of moisture." Cited in Allen, *Concept of Woman*, pp. 373–4. As regards body shape, Martin Luther stated that "Women ought to stay at home; the way they were created indicates this, for they have broad hips and a wide fundament to sit upon." M. Luther, "Table Talk," *Luther's Works*, vol. 54, T.G. Tappert, trans. and ed., Philadelphia, PA, Fortress Press, 1967, p. 8.

11 J. Sadler, *The Sick Womans Private Looking-Glasse*, Amsterdam, Theatrum Orbis Terrarum, 1977, p. 17.

12 Thomas Laqueur discusses pre-modern concepts concerning the mutability of sex in *Making Sex: Body and Gender from the Greeks to Freud*, Cambridge, MA, Harvard University Press, 1990, pp. 140–2.

13 Such redefinitions of female biology continue to be made by feminists today, such as Luce Irigaray. See Irigaray, *This Sex Which Is Not One*. Elizabeth Grosz considers the social construction of female biology in Western culture in *Volatile Bodies: Towards a Corporeal Feminism*, Bloomington, Indiana University Press, 1994.

14 Philo, *Questions and Answers on Genesis*, R. Marcus, trans., Cambridge, MA, Harvard University Press, 1961, 1: 37, p. 22.

15 Genevieve Lloyd discusses this passage in *The Man of Reason: "Male" and "Female" in Western Philosophy*, London, Methuen, 1984, pp. 22–5. Richard A. Baer writes of Philo's association of perception with femininity that "his depreciation of actual woman and of female sense-perception are frequently so closely intertwined that no clear separation between the two can be made." R.A. Baer, *Philo's Use of the Categories Male and Female*, Leiden, E.J. Brill, 1970, p. 40.

16 Philo, *Genesis*, 2: 34, pp. 112–13. G. Pico della Mirandola, *Heptaplus or Discourse on the Seven Days of Creation*, J.B. McGraw, trans., New York, Philosophical Library, 1977, p. 71. At the turn of the sixteenth century León Hebreo similarly stated:

> True light is that which is intellectual in nature . . . . From this light the light of the sun is derived . . . and in man, ocular sight, so as to enable him to understand all bodies, not just those of the lower world . . . but also those of the divine world.
>
>> L. Hebreo, *Diálogos de Amor*, M. de Burgos Núñez, ed., "El Inca," Garcilaso de la Vega, trans., Seville, Padilla Libros, 1992, p. 141.

17 Discoursing on a theme which would be endlessly repeated and elaborated over the centuries, the anonymous author of the fourteenth-century housekeeping manual *Le Ménagier de Paris* advised women to keep their husbands warm, clothed, fed, and sexually satisfied. *Le Ménagier de Paris*, Geneva, Slatkin Reprints, 1966, pp. 168–9.

18 G. Markham, *The English Housewife*, M.R. Best, ed., Montreal, McGill-Queens University Press, 1986.

19 Although "woman's work" in fact employed *all* the senses, it was symbolically confined to the "lower" senses.

20 On the olfactory symbolism of class and race see chapter 4, "The Odour of the Other", in C. Classen, *Worlds of Sense: Exploring the Senses in History and Across Cultures*, London, Routledge, 1993.

21 "In surveying the different appearances which the human form assumes in the different regions of the earth, the most striking circumstance is that of color." G.L.L. Buffon, *Natural History of Man, the Globe, and of Quadrupeds*, New York, Leavitt and Allen, 1857, p. 33.

22 W.D. Jordan discusses the European mythology of skin color in *White Over Black: American Attitudes Toward the Negro, 1550–1812*, Chapel Hill, University of North Carolina Press, 1968.

23 Parallels among Renaissance and Enlightenment ideologies of gender, race, and class are noted in M. Hendricks and P. Parker, eds., *Women, "Race," and Writing in the Early Modern Period*, London, Routledge, 1994.

24 Such climatological determinations of national temperament had roots in antiquity. However, unlike in the modern period, the ancients usually associated the colder regions of the world with negative qualities. Hippocrates, for example, considered people living in "cold, moist" lands to be lazy and effeminate. Hippocrates, *Airs,*

Waters, Places, W.H.S. Jones, trans., Cambridge, MA, Harvard University Press, 1923, pp. 123–7. Ptolemy thought the inhabitants of cold lands to be "savage in their habits." In another geographical division of character types (which would likewise be later overturned), he declared the peoples of western lands to be "feminine, softer of soul, and secretive . . . for it is always in the west that the moon emerges." Ptolemy, *Tetrabiblos*, F.E. Robbins, ed. and trans., Cambridge, MA, Harvard University Press, 1980, pp. 123, 126–7.

25 Such climatological theories of culture were prevalent from the eighteenth to the early twentieth centuries. See, for example, Buffon, *Natural History of Man*, p. 33, and E. Huntingdon, *The Character of Races*, New York, Scribner, 1925. In the early seventeenth century, the physiognomist Giovan Battista Della Porta was still trying to reconcile the conflict between the ancient concept of heat as a positive quality of temperament and the modern concept of heat as a negative quality of countries. He argued that the inhabitants of cold lands in fact have a greater internal heat (and therefore superior moral qualities) than those of hot lands, who require cool temperaments. J. Schiesari, "The Face of Domestication: Physiognomy, Gender Politics, and Humanism's Others," in M. Hendricks and P. Parker, eds., *Women, "Race" and Writing in the Early Modern Period*, London, Routledge, 1994, pp. 64–5.

26 P. Stallybrass and A. White examine the association of sight with the upper classes and touch and smell with the lower classes within the context of nineteenth-century society in *The Politics and Poetics of Transgression*, Ithaca, NY, Cornell University Press, 1986, pp. 125–48.

27 The native peoples of Africa and the Americas might seem to have a perceptual advantage over Europeans in this mythology of "sensory otherness." While the latter were sometimes imagined to have blunted senses, the former were often attributed keen sensory faculties. However, the alleged acuity of the native's senses served to reinforce the association of non-Europeans with the "pre-cultural" domain of the body and the senses.

28 Edward Long, *History of Jamaica*, 1774, cited in J.N. Pieterse, *White on Black: Images of Africa and Blacks in Western Popular Culture*, New Haven, CT, Yale University Press, 1992, p. 41.

29 S.J. Gould, *The Flamingo's Smile: Reflections in Natural History*, New York, W.W. Norton, 1985, pp. 204–5.

30 Upper-class women, however, did not necessarily exercise greater sensory freedom than the men – or women – who served them. If allowed limited privileges of study and dominion, "gentlewomen" were expected to live up to stricter ideals of feminine probity. As Christine de Pizan wrote in her fifteenth-century guidebook for women: "Sobriety . . . should be evident in all the lady's senses." C. de Pizan, *A Medieval Woman's Mirror of Honor: The Treasury of the City of Ladies*, M.P. Cosman, ed., C.C. Willard, trans., New York, Persea Books, 1989, p. 92. Women were always presumed to be subordinate to their husbands, even if these came from a lower class than themselves.

31 The modern project to extend literacy to all classes of people met with great resistance from those who feared that literate laborers would no longer be content with their humble lot. "No man who can *see* beyond his depressing trade will ply it with patience and courage" (my italics). Sarah Trimmer, *Reflections upon the Education of Children in Charity Schools*, 1792, cited in J. O'Faolain and L. Martines, eds., *Not in God's Image*, San Francisco, Harper and Row, 1973, p. 246.

32 On the culture of professional weaving see P. Burke, *Popular Culture in Early Modern Europe*, London, Temple Smith, 1978, pp. 37–8.

33 "Occupations which filled books especially addressed to gentlemen encompassed government, war, the learned professions, agriculture, and commerce; but for

women only one occupation was recommended – housewifery." R. Kelso, *Doctrine for the Lady of the Renaissance*, Urbana, University of Illinois Press, 1956, pp. 3–4. See also C. Jordan, "Renaissance Women and the Question of Class," in J.G. Turner, ed., *Sexuality and Gender in Early Modern Europe: Institutions, Texts, Images*, Cambridge, Cambridge University Press, 1993, pp. 90–106.

34 J.L. Vives, "Formación de la mujer cristiana," in L. Riber ed., *Obras completas*, vol. 1, Madrid, M. Aguilar, 1947, pp. 992–3.

35 "With good reason the view has been handed down to us that the moon and Venus are feminine . . . and that the sun, Saturn, Jupiter, and Mars are masculine, and Mercury common to both genders." Ptolemy, *Tetrabiblos*, p.41.
    The planets were heavily imbued with the symbolism and mythology of the deities whose names they bore. See, for example, Hebreo, *Diálogos de Amor*, pp. 91–110.

36 Manilius, *Astronomica*, G.P. Goold, trans., London, William Heinemann, 1977, p. 47.

37 Ptolemy, *Tetrabiblos*, pp. 441–7. See also S.J. Tester, *A History of Western Astrology*, Woodbridge, England, Boydell Press, 1987, p. 67.

38 Jupiter was deemed to be hot and moist and Saturn, cold and dry. See, for example, Ptolemy, *Tetrabiblos*, pp. 35–9.

39 T. Moore, *The Planets Within: Marsilio Ficino's Astrological Psychology*, London, Associated University Presses, 1982, p. 144.

40 Ptolemy, *Tetrabiblos*, pp. 319–21. Ptolemy reinforces aspects of this celestial sensory model in the nature of the professions he links with the different planets. For example, he says that Venus (the planet of smell) "makes her subjects persons whose activities lie among the perfumes of flowers or of unguents, in wine, colors, dyes, spices, or adornments." Ibid., p. 385.

41 A. von Nettesheim, *De Occulta Philosophia*, Graz, Austria, Akademische Druck, 1967, p. 137. See also the section on the planets and the senses in L. Schrader, *Sensación y sinestesia*, J. Conde, trans., Madrid, Editorial Gredos, 1975, pp. 324–32.

42 One ostensible exception to this was the association made by certain astrologers of the right eye with the Sun and the left eye with the Moon. As the left eye had a reputation for evil-doing, however, the connection of this eye with the feminine Moon linked the latter more with the maleficent character of the evil eye than with the power and prestige of sight.

43 Cited by E.J. Burns, *Bodytalk: When Women Speak in Old French Literature*, Philadelphia, University of Pennsylvania Press, 1993, p. 81.

44 See, for example, Plato, *Timaeus*, B. Jowett, trans., New York, The Liberal Arts Press, 1949, p. 74. The first-century physician Soranus disputed the notion, stating that "the uterus does not issue forth like a wild animal from its lair, delighted by fragrant odors and fleeing bad odors." Soranus, *Gynecology*, O. Temkin, trans., Baltimore, MD, Johns Hopkins University Press, 1956, p. 153. See also Maclean, *Renaissance Notion of Woman*, p. 40.

45 A.-F. Le Double, *Rabelais: Anatomiste et physiologiste*, Paris, Ernest Leroux, 1899, pp. 239–41. Martin Luther implied an association between the womb and the nose when he chided a cleric for disapproving of women on account of their "stinking, putrid, private parts" by saying: "As if I were to ridicule man's face on account of his nose! For the nose is the latrine of man's head." Luther, "Table Talk," p. 171. A relationship was also sometimes posited between the nose and the penis in folklore. See M. Bakhtin, *Rabelais and His World*, H. Iswolsky, trans., Bloomington, Indiana University Press, 1984, pp. 315–16.

46 On the history of fumigation as a treatment for ailing wombs see I. Veith, *Hysteria: The History of a Disease*, Chicago, University of Chicago Press, 1965.

47 Trotula wrote that "If it happens after childbirth that the womb descends too low, aromatic herbs should be applied to the nostrils." At the same time the woman should be fumigated "from below with strong-smelling things such as burnt linen cloth." Trotula of Salerno, *The Diseases of Women*, E. Mason-Hohl, trans., Los Angeles, Ward Ritchie Press, 1940, p. 12.

48 D. Jacquart and C. Thomasset, *Sexuality and Medicine in the Middle Ages*, Princeton, NJ, Princeton University Press, 1988, p. 131. See also R. Martensen, "The Transformation of Eve: Women's Bodies, Medicine and Culture in Early Modern Europe," in R. Porter and M. Teich, eds., *Sexual Knowledge, Sexual Science: The History of Attitudes to Sexuality*, Cambridge, Cambridge University Press, 1994, p. 107.

49 Similarly, the cold, moist, feminine Moon was thought to be a celestial cause of putridity. See, for example, Ptolemy, *Tetrabiblos*, p. 35.

50 Jacquart and Thomasset, *Sexuality and Medicine*, pp. 73–5, 173–7.

51 G. Boccaccio, *The Corbaccio*, A.K. Cassell, trans. and ed., Urbana, University of Illinois Press, 1975, p. 24; J. Swift, "The Lady's Dressing Room," in H. Davis, ed., *Poetical Works*, London, Oxford University Press, 1967, p. 480.

52 Ibid., p. 478.

53 *The Ancren Riwle*, J. Morton, ed., New York, Johnson Reprint, 1968, p. 166; A. Trollope, *Can You Forgive Her?*, London, Oxford University Press, 1975, p. 474.

54 The idea also existed, however, that women required perfumes to cover up their natural stench. Jewish legend, for example, stated that women needed perfume because Eve was made out of corruptible flesh (Adam's rib). J.A. Phillips, *Eve: The History of an Idea*, San Francisco, Harper and Row, 1984, p. 29.

55 L.C. Martin, ed., *The Poetical Works of Robert Herrick*, Oxford, Clarendon, 1956, p. 244.

56 C.W. Bynum, *Holy Feast and Holy Fast: The Religious Significance of Food to Medieval Women*, Berkeley, University of California Press, 1987, pp. 122–3. A similar story is told of a fifteenth-century faster, Colette of Corbie. Ibid., p. 138.

57 H. Thurston, *The Physical Phenomena of Mysticism*, J.H. Crehan, ed., London, Burns and Oates, 1952, p. 69.

58 F.M. Salvatori, *Life of St. Veronica Giuliani*, cited by Thurston, *Physical Phenomena*, p. 228.

59 Aristotle, *Generation of Animals*, p. 247. Discussed by Jacquart and Thomasset, *Sexuality and Medicine*, p. 56. Pre-modern physiologists (contradicting Aristotle) often asserted that women, as well as men, possessed sperm. Nonetheless, this fluid was generally considered first and foremost a male production. Ibid., pp. 61–70.

60 This notion was put forward by Plato, who wrote:

> The pure fire which is within us [was] made to flow through the eyes in a stream smooth and dense . . . . When the light of day surrounds the stream of vision, then like falls upon like, and they coalesce, and one body is formed by natural affinity in the line of vision, wherever the light that falls from within meets with an external object.

Timaeus, pp. 27–8

61 See, for example, L. Thorndike, *A History of Magic and Experimental Science*, vol. 6, New York, Columbia University Press, 1934, p. 402.

62 Albertus Magnus, "Quaestiones de Animalibus," in *Opera Omnia*, vol. 12. Cited by Jacquart and Thomasset, *Sexuality and Medicine*, pp. 52–6.

63 Galen, *Parts of the Body*, p. 629.

64 Vives, for example, stated that women should "keep their eyes lowered, be bashful, and silent." Vives, "Formación de la mujer cristiana," p. 1001.

65 Vives writes: "It will be necessary for a maiden to leave the house at times, but this should be as infrequently as possible." Ibid., p. 1036. In this regard he refers approvingly to Plutarch's statement that Egyptian women were kept barefoot so that they would be obliged to stay at home. Ibid., p. 1021.

66 S.W. Hull, *Chaste, Silent and Obedient: English Books for Women, 1475–1640*, San Francisco, Huntingdon Library, 1982, p. 76.

67 J. Knox, "The First Blast of the Trumpet Against the Monstrous Regiment of Women", in *The Political Writings of John Knox*, M.A. Breslow, ed., Washington, Folger Books, 1985, pp. 42–3.

68 Aristotle, *Generation of Animals*, p. 249.

69 R. de Fournival, *Master Richard's Bestiary of Love and Response*, J. Beer, trans., Berkeley, University of California Press, 1986, p. 9. Fournival's sensory imagery is analyzed in E. Sears, "Sensory Perception and its Metaphors in the Time of Richard of Fournival," in W.F. Bynum and R. Porter, eds., *Medicine and the Five Senses*, Cambridge, Cambridge University Press, 1993, pp. 17–39.

70 Dalila is described as emitting an "odorous perfume" and as conceiving of the betrayal of Samson through the "scent" of a bribe. J. Hunter, ed., *Milton's Samson Agonistes and Lycidas*, London, Longmans, Green, and Co., 1872, pp. 24, l. 390; 38, l. 720.

71 Ibid., p. 31, lines 534–7.

72 Ibid., p. 45, lines 914–19. See also J. Guillory, "Dalila's House: *Samson Agonistes* and the Sexual Division of Labor," in M.W. Ferguson, M. Quilligan and N.J. Vickers, eds., *Rewriting the Renaissance: The Discourses of Sexual Difference in Early Modern Europe*, Chicago, University of Chicago Press, 1986, pp. 106–22.

73 Baer, *Philo*, p. 43.

74 See, for example, Vives, "Formación de la mujer cristiana," pp. 1042–4.

75 On the medieval topos of woman as "riot" see R.H. Bloch, *Medieval Misogyny and the Invention of Western Romantic Love*, Chicago, University of Chicago Press, 1991, pp. 14–22.

76 Hunter, *Samson*, pp. 25–6, lines 403–4.

77 A. le Chapelain, *The Art of Courtly Love*, J.J. Parry, trans., New York, Frederick Ungar, 1941, p. 207.

78 Maclean, *Renaissance Notion of Woman*, p. 41.

79 "Il luy fault prendre ung bon clystére/Pour luy alleger le cerveau." Burns, *Bodytalk*, pp. 35–6.

80 Maclean, *Renaissance Notion of Woman*, pp. 15, 18.

81 C. Camden, *The Elizabethan Woman*, Mamaroneck, NY, Paul P. Appel, 1975, p. 24.

82 L. de Bruyn, *Woman and the Devil in Sixteenth-Century Literature*, Tisbury, England, Compton Press, 1979, p. 145.

83 Ibid.

84 G. England, ed., "Secunda Pastorum", in *The Towneley Plays*, London, Oxford University Press for Early English Text Society, 1897, p. 119.

85 Ibid.

86 Hunter, *Samson*, p. 50, lines 1036–7.

87 B. Jonson, *Epicoene or The Silent Woman*, L.A. Beaurline, ed., Lincoln, University of Nebraska Press, 1966.

88 "Lingua", in W.C. Hazlitt, ed., *A Select Collection of Old English Plays*, New York, Benjamin Bloom, 1964, p. 339.

89 Ibid., p. 397.

90 Ibid., p. 429.

91 Examples of "good" feminine speech could be found in a number of female saints, notably Catherine of Alexandria, who were renowned for their holy discourse.

92 "Lingua", pp. 379–82.

93 The use of different animals as representatives of the senses in Western art and literature is treated in L. Vinge, *The Five Senses: Studies in a Literary Tradition*, Lund,
Sweden, Royal Society of Letters at Lund, 1975, pp. 47–58, 90–3. The strength of
the association between zoological symbolism and sensory symbolism can be seen
in the *Bestiary of Love*, in which Fournival makes the senses a central theme.

94 The symbolic qualities attributed to animals are described in medieval and
Renaissance bestiaries. See, for example, F. McCulloch, *Medieval Latin and French
Bestiaries*, Chapel Hill, University of North Carolina Press, 1962; D. Hassig,
Medieval Bestiaries: Text, Image, Ideology, Cambridge, Cambridge University Press,
1995. Many medieval bestiaries were a rewriting of a second-century work known
as *The Physiologus*. T.H. White, ed. and trans., *The Bestiary*, New York, G.P.
Putnam's Sons, 1960, pp. 231–2.

95 See, for example, E. Topsell, *The History of Four-Footed Beasts and Serpents and
Insects*, vol. 1, New York, Da Capo, 1967, pp. 389–91.

96 Ibid., p. 48; White, ed., *Bestiary*, p. 38. Beryl Rowland, *Animals with Human
Faces: A Guide to Animal Symbolism*, Knoxville, University of Tennessee Press,
1973, p. 46.

97 Ibid., pp. 105–7; P. de Beauvais, *A Medieval Book of Beasts*, G.R. Mermier, trans.,
Lampeter, Wales, Edwin Mellen Press, 1992, pp. 45–6.

98 White, ed., *Bestiary*, pp. 38, 105–6; Topsell, *History of Four-Footed Animals*, p. 49.

99 On the virtues of house-dogs see White, ed., *Bestiary*, p. 62.

100 Rowland, *Animals with Human Faces*, pp. 59–60.

101 In his entry on the dog Topsell notes that a "wicked discourse or dispraise of
Women affirmeth, that the . . . clamorous, implacable and wanton-rowling-eyed
Women, were derived from Dogs." *History of Four-Footed Beasts*, p. 114.

102 For an account of the opposition between the eagle and the vulture in the
mythology of ancient Greece see M. Detienne, *The Gardens of Adonis: Spices in
Greek Mythology*, J. Lloyd, trans., Atlantic Highlands, NJ, The Humanities Press,
1977, pp. 23–5.

103 McCulloch, *Latin and French Bestiaries*, p. 185. In a similar vein Topsell
commented that "the Crow is enemy to Bulls and Asses, for in her flight she will
strike at their eyes." *History of Four-Footed Beasts*, p. 49. See also Fournival,
Bestiary of Love, pp. 8–9.

104 Occasionally touch would be represented as a bird biting a woman's thumb. This
representation brings out the painful dimensions of touch and also positions woman
in the role of sufferer. See C. Nordenfalk, "The Sense of Touch in Art", in K.-L.
Selig and E. Sears, eds., *The Verbal and The Visual: Essays In Honor of William
Sebastian*, New York, Italica Press, 1990, p. 115.

105 Cited by A.P. Coudert, "The Myth of the Improved Status of Protestant Women:
The Case of the Witchcraze," in J.R. Brink, A.P. Coudert, and M.C. Horowitz,
eds., *The Politics of Gender in Early Modern Europe*, Kirksville, MO, Sixteenth
Century Journal Publishers, 1989, p. 78.

106 "Lingua", p. 427.

107 H.W. Janson, *Apes and Ape Lore in the Middle Ages and the Renaissance*, London,
The Warburg Institute, 1952, p. 109.

108 Ibid., pp. 14–15, 32. In the eighteenth century, however, when modesty began to
be deemed a characteristic feminine trait, female apes were often depicted as
demure rather than wanton. L. Schiebinger, *Nature's Body: Gender in the Making of
Modern Science*, Boston, MA, Beacon Press, 1993, pp. 99–106.

109 In a variation of the dog's tail story, Eve was sometimes said to have been created
from a monkey's tail originally sported by Adam.

110 Bruno Roy writes, with some overstatement: "There are only bad animals in the bestiary of woman." B. Roy, "La Belle e(s)t la bête: aspects du bestiaire féminin au moyen âge", *Etudes françaises*, 1974, vol. 10, no. 3, p. 322.

111 The thirteenth-century cleric, Matheolus, for example, wrote of women: "they slay us with a look, like the basilisk." The fourteenth-century *Mandeville's Travels*, in turn, announced the discovery of an island where the women slay men "with the beholdynge as doth the Basilisk." Cited by Rowland, *Animals with Human Faces*, pp. 30–1. In one medieval illustration of a *mala mulier*, a "bad" woman is shown with an ape on the left and a basilisk on the right, indicating her corrupt sense of taste on the one hand and her venomous sense of sight on the other. Janson, *Apes and Ape Lore*, p. 115.

112 Vives, "Formación de la mujer cristiana", p. 1027.

113   The reason why the basilisk is able to kill a man by its gaze is because when it sees him, owing to its anger a certain terrible poison is set in motion throughout its body, and this it can dart from its eyes, thus infecting the atmosphere with deadly venom. And thus the man breathes in the air which it has infected and is stupefied and dies.

> H. Kramer and J. Sprenger, *The Malleus Maleficarum of Heinrich Kramer and Sprenger*, M. Summers, ed. and trans., Salem, NH, Ayer, 1948, p. 18.

114 Jacquart and Thomasset, *Sexuality and Medicine*, pp. 74–5.

115 Another possible symbol for faulty feminine sight was the snake, often associated with femininity (Phillips, *Eve*, pp. 61–2) and sometimes described as having poor sight (i.e. "all snakes suffer from bad eyesight and they seldom see forward," White, *Bestiary*, p. 189). The snake's enemies were said to be the sharp-eared stag (ibid., p. 37) and the sharp-eyed eagle. In Homer's *Iliad* the appearance of an eagle carrying a snake in its talons during the battle of Troy symbolized "the victory of the [Greek] patriarchal principle over the female one of Troy, whose Asiatic goddess, Aphrodite, had induced Helen to break the bonds of her marriage." Rowland, *Animals with Human Faces*, p. 143.

116 On the immense popularity of bestiary literature see White, *Bestiary*, pp. 232–6, 261–2.

117 Kramer and Sprenger, *Malleus Maleficarum*, p. 32.

118 The sixteenth-century French magistrate Jean Bodin stated that "for every male witch there are fifty female witches." J. Bodin, *De la démonomanie des sorciers*, Paris, Iacques du Puys, 1580, p. 225.

119 Le Chapelain, *Art of Courtly Love*, pp. 203–4.

120 Vives, for example, counsels women to eat little and to remember that "our first mother was thrown out of Paradise for a bite of food, and that many maidens . . . who went out of their homes in search of tasty delicacies lost their chastity." "Formación de la mujer cristiana", p. 1011. Caroline Bynum discusses the suppression of appetite among medieval women in *Holy Feast and Holy Fast*.

121 See, for example, Bynum, *Holy Feast and Holy Fast*, p. 147.

122 H.C. Lea, *Materials Toward a History of Witchcraft*, vol. 1, New York, Thomas Yoseloff, 1957, pp. 232–3. At the same time as witches satisfied their own appetites, they took away food from others. Witches were notorious for harming their neighbors' crops and animals, thus bringing "hunger and barrenness into the countrie." R. Scot, *The Discoverie of Witchcraft*, London, Centaur Press, 1964, p. 49.

123 Women were presumed to have a special vocation for poisoning, just as they had a special vocation for witchcraft. Reginald Scot writes: "As women in all ages have beene counted most apt to conceive witchcraft . . . so also it appeareth, that they

have been the first inventers, and principal practisers of poisoning." Scot, *Discoverie of Witchcraft*, p. 112. See further M. Hallisey, *Venomous Woman: Fear of the Female in Literature*, New York, Greenwood Press, 1987.

124   Lea, *History of Witchcraft*, vol. 1, p. 144.

125   A familiar example of a witch's brew occurs in Shakespeare's *Macbeth*:
> Fillet of a fenny snake,
> In the cauldron boil and bake:
> Eye of newt, and toe of frog,
> Wool of bat, and tongue of dog . . .
> For a charm of powerful trouble
> Like a hell-broth boil and bubble.
>
> (Act IV, Sc. 1)

126   In *Malleus Maleficarum* this volubility of witches is described in terms of their "slippery tongues." Kramer and Sprenger, *Malleus Maleficarum*, p. 44.

127   Ibid., p. 46.

128   The one time when witches were speechless was when they were called on to confess their demonic practices. In the *Malleus Maleficarum* a section is devoted to the different means by which an accused witch may be compelled to confess, for "a prudent Judge will not consider it safe to bind himself down to one invariable rule in his method of dealing with a prisoner who is endowed with a witch's power of taciturnity." Ibid., p. 227.

129   Cited by F.C. Conybeare, *Myth, Magic, and Morals: A Study of Christian Origins*, London, Watts and Co., 1910, p. 233. Conybeare writes that it was in order to safeguard their sense of hearing that nuns kept their ears covered. Ibid.

130   Some of the traditional associations between the witch and odor are discussed by Hélène Cixous and Catherine Clément in *The Newly Born Woman*, B. Wing, trans., Minneapolis, University of Minnesota Press, 1986, pp. 37–9.

131   Johann Joseph Von Görres, *La Mystique divine, naturel et diabolique*. Cited by Lea, *History of Witchcraft*, pp. 1489–1518.

132   Scot, *Discoverie of Witchcraft*, p. 236.

133   Kramer and Sprenger, *Malleus Maleficarum*, p. 47. Not only did witches seduce and debauch men, however, they went so far as to rob them of their manhood. The *Malleus* recounts the story of one young man who, on finding that his organ of generation had disappeared after an encounter with a witch, choked the woman until she promised to return his member to him. Released, the woman touched the ailing spot and the aggrieved lover found his manhood magically restored. Ibid., p. 119.

134   N. Rémy, *Demonolatry*, E.A. Ashwin, trans., London, John Rodker, 1930, p. 244.

135   Scot, *Discoverie of Witchcraft*, p. 73. Scot seems to have extended this "eye-biting" quality to all women, for he writes that women "have such an unbridled force of furie and concupiscence naturallie that . . . upon everie trifling occasion, they (like brute beasts) fix their furious eies upon the partie whom they bewitch." Ibid., p. 236.

136   Jacquart and Thomasset, *Sexuality and Medicine*, p. 75.

137   Lea, *History of Witchcraft*, vol.1, p. 257.

138   Kramer and Sprenger, *Malleus Maleficarum*, p. 228.

139   Ibid. In the bestiaries, the disabling power of "first sight" is associated with a number of animals. See, for example, White, *Bestiary*, p. 58.

140   Cited by Lea, *History of Witchcraft*, vol. 3, p. 1326.

141   Scot, *Discoverie of Witchcraft*, p. 399.

142   See Coudert, "The Myth of the Improved Status of Protestant Women."

143 See, for example, A. von Nettesheim, "Female Pre-eminence," in *The Feminist Controversy of the Renaissance*, Delmar, NY, Scholars' Facsimiles and Reprints, 1980.

144 Hildegard of Bingen, *Symphonia: A Critical Edition of the Symphonia armonie celestium revelationum*, B. Newman, ed., Ithaca, NY, Cornell University Press, 1988, p. 121. See further B. Newman, *Sister of Wisdom: St. Hildegard's Theology of the Feminine*, Berkeley, Uinversity of California Press, 1987.

145 C. de Pizan, *The Book of the City of Ladies*, E.J. Richards, trans., New York, Persea Books, 1982, p. 4.

146 Ibid., pp. 6, 8. "I do not know which one of my senses was more overwhelmed," Christine de Pizan wrote, "my hearing from having listened to such worthy words or my sight from having seen her radiant beauty." Ibid., p. 8.

147 Ibid., pp. 23, 25–6, 29–30.

148 Tertullian, for example, wrote that when Gabriel announced to Mary that she would give birth to the Messiah "a divine ray of light glided down into her and, descending, was made concrete as flesh in her womb." Cited by Conybeare, *Myth, Magic, and Morals*, p. 230.

149 Ginevra Conti Odorisio provides a condensed version of "La nobilità e l'eccellenza delle donne", together with a discussion of the work in *Donna e societa' nel seiciento*, Rome, Bulzoni editore, 1979.

150 P. Allen and F. Salvatore, "Lucrezia Marinelli and Woman's Identity in Late Italian Renaissance," *Renaissance and Reformation*, 1992, vol. 28, no. 4, p. 24.

151 Ibid., p. 22.

152 Ibid., p. 24.

153 Ibid., p. 18.

154 Ibid., p. 28.

155 Ibid.

156 Ibid., p. 21.

4 Pens and needles

1 The secretary of the Royal Society in England wrote in 1664 that the aim of the new experimental philosophy was "to accumulate a good stock of such accurate observations and experiments, as may afford [The Royal Society] ... to raise a masculine philosophy upon." H. Oldenburg, "The Publisher to the Reader," in R. Boyle, *Experiments and Considerations Touching Colours*, in R. Boyle, *The Works*, T. Birch, ed., Hildesheim, Germany, Georg Olms, 1965, p. 667. See further C. Merchant, *The Death of Nature: Women, Ecology and the Scientific Revolution*, New York, Harper and Row, 1980; B. Easlea, *Witch Hunting, Magic and the New Philosophy: An Introduction to Debates of the Scientific Revolution 1450–1750*, Sussex, England, The Harvester Press, 1980, pp. 212–14; S. Bordo, *The Flight to Objectivity: Essays on Cartesianism and Culture*, Albany, NY, State University of New York Press, 1987, pp. 97–118.

2 The symbolic association of nature with female power in pre-modernity is discussed by Merchant in *The Death of Nature*, pp. 1–41.

3 N. Rémy, *Demonolatry*, E.A. Ashwin, trans., London, John Rodker, 1930, p. 5.

4 Such prominent members of the Royal Society as Robert Boyle (1627–91) and Joseph Glanvill (1636–80), for example, believed in the reality of witchcraft. Easlea, *Witch Hunting*, pp. 201–7.

5 Cited by G. Keynes, *The Life of William Harvey*, Oxford, Clarendon Press, 1966, p. 214.

6 Ibid., p. 215.

7 See further L. Jordanova, *Sexual Visions: Images of Gender in Science and Medicine between the Eighteenth and Twentieth Centuries*, New York, Harvester Wheatsheaf, 1989.

8 T. Spratt, *History of the Royal Society*, J.I. Cope and H.W. Jones, eds., St. Louis, MI, Washington University Press, 1966, p. 327.

9 J.T. Desaguliers, *The Newtonian System of the World, the Best Model of Government, An Allegorical Poem*, Westminster, 1729, cited in M.H. Nicolson, *Newton Demands the Muse: Newton's Optiks and the Eighteenth Century Poets*, Princeton, NJ, Princeton University Press, 1966, p. 136.

10 Ludmilla Jordanova writes that "science and medicine have been explicitly concerned with the correct interpretation of visual signs, and skill in those fields was pre-eminently seen as a form of visual acuteness." *Sexual Visions*, p. 91.

11 M.E. Weisner, *Women and Gender in Early Modern Europe*, Cambridge, Cambridge University Press, 1993, p. 85.

12 M. Cavendish, *Sociable Letters*, Menston, England, Scolar Press, 1969, pp. 311–13.

13 See, for example, the chapter on "The Undermining of the Family Economy," in B. Hill, *Women, Work, and Sexual Politics in Eighteenth-Century England*, Montreal, McGill-Queen's University Press, 1994, pp. 47–68. While many women would find employment outside the home in the new industries, such labor did not count as traditional "women's work."

14 Cavendish, *Sociable Letters*, p. 313.

15 R. Kelso, *Doctrine for the Lady of the Renaissance*, Urbana, University of Illinois Press, 1956, p. 46.

16 So allied was medicine with food that literate housewives often jotted down medicinal and culinary recipes together in the same notebook. D. Evenden Nagy, *Popular Medicine in Seventeenth-Century England*, Bowling Green, Ohio, Bowling Green State University Popular Press, 1988, pp. 67–8.

17 F. de Rojas, *Celestina*, D. Sherman Severin, ed., J. Mabbe, trans., Warminster, England, Aris and Phillips, 1987, pp. 56–7.

18 M.J. Hughes, *Women Healers in Medieval Life and Literature*, Freeport, New York, Books for Libraries Press, 1943, pp. 50–60.

19 Cited by Hughes, *Women Healers*, p. 54.

20 G. Williams, *The Age of Agony: The Art of Healing 1700–1800*, London, Constable, 1975, p. 184.

21 W.L. Minowski, "Physician Motives in Banning Medieval Traditional Healers," *Women and Health*, 1994, vol. 21, no. 1, p. 92.

22 H. Woolley, *The Queen-like Closet or Rich Cabinet*, London, R. Chiswel, 5th edn, 1684, p. 8.

23 Ibid.

24 G. Markham, *The English Housewife*, M.R. Best, ed., Montreal, McGill-Queens University Press, 1986, p. 8.

25 Hughes, *Women Healers*, pp. 90–1. Physical examination of the patient, in a modern sense, did not become common in medical practice until the nineteenth century. R. Porter, "The Rise of Physical Examination," in W.F. Bynum and R. Porter, eds., *Medicine and the Five Senses*, Cambridge, Cambridge University Press, 1993, pp. 179–97.

26 In the fourteenth century Guy de Chauliac wrote of the importance of higher education for keeping the practice of medicine out of the hands of the common people: "If the doctors have not learned geometry, astronomy, dialectics, nor any other good discipline, soon the leather workers, carpenters, and furriers will quit their own occupations and become doctors." G. de Chauliac, *La grande chirugie*, cited by V.L. Bullough, *The Development of Medicine as a Profession*, Basel, S. Karger, 1966, p. 95.

27 See M. Foucault, *The Birth of the Clinic: An Archaeology of Medical Perception*, A.M. Sheridan Smith, trans., New York, Random House, 1975; B.M. Stafford, *Body Criticism: Imaging the Unseen in Enlightenment Art and Medicine*, Cambridge, MA, MIT Press, 1991. This is not to say that modern medicine excluded the use of the non-visual senses, but rather that observation was accorded a new primacy. See, for example, S.C. Lawrence, "Educating the Senses: Students, Teachers and Medical Rhetoric in Eighteenth-Century London," in W.F. Bynum and R. Porter, eds., *Medicine and the Five Senses*, Cambridge, Cambridge University Press, 1993, pp. 154–78.

28 W. Pagel, *Paracelsus: An Introduction to Philosophical Medicine in the Era of the Renaissance*, Basel, Karger, 1958, p. 296.

29 On the transition from medical cookery to pharmacy and its effects on women see L. Schiebinger, *The Mind Has No Sex? Women in the Origins of Modern Science*, Cambridge, MA, Harvard University Press, 1989, pp. 112–16.

30 E. Raffald, *The Experienced English Housekeeper*, cited by Schiebinger in *Mind Has No Sex?*, p. 115.

31 Cited in Schiebinger, *Mind Has No Sex?*, p. 116. Women argued in vain that practices such as midwifery were as much a part of the feminine domain as sewing or cooking, and therefore off-limits to men. The eighteenth-century midwife, Elizabeth Nihell, for example, declared that men should not "spin, make beds, pickle and preserve, or officiate as a midwife." E. Nihell, *A Treatise on the Art of Midwifery*, London, A. Morley, 1760. See further Schiebinger, *Mind Has No Sex?*, p. 10 and J. Todd, *The Sign of Angellica: Women, Writing and Fiction 1660–1800*, London, Virago, 1989, pp. 203–4.

32 Cited in Todd, *Angellica*, p. 117.

33 The late eighteenth-century champion of feminine sensibility Hannah More wrote, for example, that "the female . . . is perpetually turned aside [from intellectual pursuits] by her characteristic taste and feelings," and that women "have a certain *tact* which often enables them to feel what is just more instantaneously than they can define it." Cited by G.J. Barker-Benfield, *The Culture of Sensibility: Sex and Society in Eighteenth-Century Britain*, Chicago, University of Chicago Press, 1992, pp. 384–5.

   For an analysis of Kant's association of women with taste see J. Kneller, "Discipline and Silence: Women and Imagination in Kant's Theory of Taste," in H. Hein and C. Korsmeyer, eds., *Aesthetics in Feminist Perspective*, Bloomington, Indiana University Press, 1993, pp. 179–92.

34 Cited in Schiebinger, *Mind Has No Sex?*, p. 236.

35 Bordo, *Flight to Objectivity*, p. 101.

36 For a discussion of this transition as regards the senses of smell and sight, see C. Classen, *Worlds of Sense: Exploring the Senses in History and Across Cultures*, London, Routledge, 1993, pp. 26–30.

37 This role of woman as spectator, and purchaser, of consumer goods would become pronounced in the nineteenth century. See, for example, R. Bowlby, *Just Looking: Consumer Culture in Dreiser, Gissing and Zola*, New York, Methuen, 1985.

38 Molière, *Les Femmes savantes*, Boston, D.C. Heath, 1896, Act 2, Scene 7, p. 36. In a similar statement with regard to women's interest in letters, the same character declares: "I need good soup, not pretty words." Ibid., p. 33.

39 J. Miller, "The Humours of Oxford," in H.W. Wells, ed., *Three Centuries of English and American Plays: England, 1500–1800*, vol. 3, New York, Redex Microprint Corporation, 1963, p. 79.

40 Miller, "Humours of Oxford," p. 79.

41 Giovanni Bruto, cited by S.W. Hull, *Chaste, Silent and Obedient: English Books for Women, 1475–1640*, San Francisco, Huntingdon Library, 1982, p. 155.

42 Cited by Todd, *Angellica*, p. 32.

43 For an account of women's limited literacy and educational opportunities from the sixteenth to the eighteenth centuries see Wiesner, *Women and Gender*, pp. 119–45.

44 C. Camden, *The Elizabethan Woman*, Mamaroneck, NY, Paul P. Appel, 1975, p. 43.

45 A. Bradstreet, "The Prologue," in A. Stanford, ed., *The Women Poets in English*, New York, McGraw-Hill, 1972, p. 46.

46 In contrast to the general opinion of the inferiority of needlework relative to scholarship, François Poullain de la Barre declared in the seventeenth century that embroidery required *more* skill than academic pursuits. F. Poullain de la Barre, *The Equality of the Two Sexes*, D. Frankforter and P.J. Morman, trans., Lampeter, Wales, Edwin Mellen Press, 1989.

47 Ibid., p. 47.

48 J. Barbey D'Aurevilly, *Les Bas-bleus*, Paris, Société Générale de Librairie Catholique, 1878, p. 189.

49 "Rhetoric in all its forms – public discussion, forensic argument, logical fencing, and the like – lies absolutely outside the province of women." Lionardo Bruni, 1405, cited by A.R. Jones, "Surprising Fame: Renaissance Gender Ideologies and Women's Lyric," in N.K. Miller, ed., *The Poetics of Gender*, New York, Colombia University Press, 1986, p. 75.

50 That the needle could not compare to the pen as a medium of self-expression was generally taken for granted. A letter to *The Spectator* in 1714, for example, ridiculed the notion that women might fulfill their authorial ambitions through needlework:

> I cannot forbear wishing, that several Writers of [the female] Sex had chosen to apply themselves rather to Tapestry than Rhime . . . . How memorable would that Matron be, who should have it inscribed upon her monument, "That she wrought out a whole Bible in Tapestry, and died in a good old Age, after having covered three hundred Yards of Wall in the Mansion-House."

> Cited by M. Reynolds, *The Learned Lady in England: 1650–1760*, Gloucester, MA, Peter Smith, 1964, p. 261.

Some women *did* undertake large-scale embroidery projects. See, for example, W. Chadwick, *Women, Art, and Society*, 2nd edn, London, Thames and Hudson, 1996, p. 152.

51 John Taylor, "In Praise of the Needle," in *The Needle's Excellency*, London, 1624. Discussed by R. Parker, *The Subversive Stitch: Embroidery and the Making of the Feminine*, London, The Women's Press, 1984, p. 86. Rozsika Parker explores the history of women through the history of embroidery in this work.

52 For similar reasons, women would often be taught to read, but not to write. Wiesner, *Women and Gender*, p. 123.

53 M. Astell, "Letter to John Norris of Bemerton," in R. Perry, *The Celebrated Mary Astell: An Early English Feminist*, Chicago, University of Chicago Press, 1986, p. 355.

54 Cited by Todd, *Angellica*, p. 37.

55 Cited by T.A. Sankovitch, *French Women Writers and the Book*, Syracuse, NY, Syracuse University Press, 1988, p. 48.

56 Ibid., p. 49.

57 B.G. MacCarthy, *The Female Pen: Women Writers and Novelists, 1621–1818*, New York, New York University Press, 1994, p. 24.

58 L. Labé, "To Mademoiselle Clémence de Bourges of Lyon," in K.M. Wilson, ed., *Women Writers of the Renaissance and Reformation*, Athens, University of Georgia Press, 1987, p. 149.

59 M. de Zayas, *Amorous and Exemplary Novels*, H.P. Boyer, trans., Berkeley, University of California Press, 1990, p. 2. See further, S.M. Zoa, "Maria de Zayas y Sotomayor: Sibyl of Madrid (1590?-1661?)," in J.R. Brink, ed., *Female Scholars: A Tradition of Learned Women Before 1800*, Montreal, Eden Press, 1980, pp. 54–67.

60 Cited by Sankovitch, *French Women Writers*, p. 50.

61 P. Allen and F. Salvatore, "Lucrezia Marinelli and Woman's Identity in Late Italian Renaissance," *Renaissance and Reformation*, 1992, vol. 28, no. 4, p. 37, n.70, also pp. 23–4. M. de Zayas similarly wrote: "When our parents bring us up if, instead of putting cambric on our sewing cushions and patterns in our embroidery frames, they gave us books and teachers, we would be as fit as men for any job or professorship." Zayas, *Amorous and Exemplary Novels*, p. 1.

62 Reynolds, *Learned Lady*, p. 57. "Oh my reader," wrote Maria de Zayas, "no doubt it will amaze you that a woman has the nerve not only to write a book but actually to publish it." Zayas, *Amorous and Exemplary Novels*, p. 1.

63 Cited by Reynolds, *Learned Lady*, p. 58.

64 Todd, *Angellica*, p. 126.

65 Cited by Reynolds, *Learned Lady*, p. 316.

66 Cited by Sankovitch, *French Women Writers*, p. 52. On this poem see also J. Marcus, "Still Practice, A/Wrested Alphabet: Toward a Feminist Aesthetic," in S. Benstock, ed., *Feminist Issues in Literary Scholarship*, Bloomington, Indiana University Press, 1987, pp. 85–6. Elsewhere in her writings, Catherine des Roches described spinning as a cruel labor imposed on women by men jealous of their wives' intelligence. Sankovitch, *French Women Writers*, p. 60.

67 Cited by Reynolds, *Learned Lady*, p. 329.

68 M. More Roper, "A Devout Treatise upon the 'Pater Noster'," in Wilson, ed., *Women Writers*, pp. 465–6.

69 Labé, "Mademoiselle Clémence," in Wilson, ed., *Women Writers*, pp. 149–50.

70 M. Wollstonecraft, *A Vindication of the Rights of Woman*, New York, Source Book Press, 1971, pp. 81–2. See further S.M. Conger, *Mary Wollstonecraft and the Language of Sensibility*, Rutherford, NJ, Farleigh Dickinson University Press, 1994.

71 To many women book study seemed an acceptably feminine appropriation of sight, a way of seeing the world while staying at home. See, for example, C. Jordan, *Renaissance Feminism: Literary Texts and Political Models*, Ithaca, NY, Cornell University Press, 1990, p. 140.

72 D. Masham, *Occasional Thoughts In Reference to a Vertuous or Christian Life*, London, Black-Swan, 1705, p. 204.

73 Ibid. Curiously, John Norris, a writer on religion, mistakenly believed that Damaris Masham had lost her sight through excessive reading. He wrote:

> The chief reason why your Ladyship is so concerned for the loss of your Sight, is because you are thereby deprived of Conversation with your books and consequently retarded in your earnest pursuit after Learning and Knowledge.
>
> J. Norris, *Reflections Upon the Conduct of Human Life*,
> London, Awnsham and John Churchill, 1696, "Dedication."
> Discussed in A. Wallas, *Before the Bluestockings*, London,
> George Allen and Unwin, 1929, p. 78.

74 See, for example, Reynolds, *Learned Lady*, p. 393, and F.A. Nussbaum, *The Brink of All We Hate: English Satires on Women: 1660–1750*, Lexington, University Press of Kentucky, 1984, p. 148.

75 Reference to the once common association between literary women and blindness is made in S.M. Gilbert and S. Gubar, *The Madwoman in the Attic: The Woman Writer and the Nineteenth-Century Literary Imagination*, New Haven, CT, Yale University Press, 1979, p. 50.

76 In the eighteenth century, writing by and for women would come to mean writing with a heightened awareness of feminine "sensibility." "Synonymous with sentiment and sensibility, women must write moral didactic or sentimental works suitable, above all, for the perusal of other women." Todd, *Angellica*, p. 127.

77 For biographies of Cavendish see D. Grant, *Margaret the First*, London, Rupert Hart-Davis, 1957 and S.H. Mendelson, *The Mental World of Three Stuart Women: Three Studies*, Amherst, MA, University of Massachusetts Press, 1987.

78 M. Cavendish, *Playes*, London, John Martyn, James Allestry and Tho. Dicas, 1662, "To the Readers" (epilogue).

79 M. Cavendish, *Nature's Pictures Drawn by Fancies Pencil to the Life*, London, J. Martin and J. Allestrye, 1656, p. 70.

80 The relationship between women's spinning and women's writing has been explored in several recent works. See, for example, Gilbert and Gubar, *Madwoman*, p. 525; N.K. Miller, "Arachnologies: The Woman, The Text, and the Critic," in N.K. Miller, ed., *The Poetics of Gender*, New York, Colombia University Press, 1986, pp. 270–93; R. Salvaggio, *Enlightened Absence: Neoclassical Configurations of the Feminine*, Urbana, University of Illinois Press, 1988, pp. 114–20.

81 Cavendish, *Nature's Pictures*, pp. 170–1. In one of her books Cavendish similarly speaks of her writing as a house she has made. M. Cavendish, *The World's Olio*, London, J. Martin and J. Allestrye, 1655, "Epistle to the Reader."

82 For a discussion of Bacon's imagery of the spider in relation to that of Cavendish see S. Bowerbank, "The Spider's Delight: Margaret Cavendish and the 'Female' Imagination," in K. Farrell, E.H. Hageman, and A.F. Kinney, eds., *Women in the Renaissance: Selections from English Literary Renaissance*, Amherst, University of Massachusetts Press, 1971.

83 M. Cavendish, "A True Relation of my Birth, Breeding and Life," in M. Cavendish, *The Life of William Cavendish*, C.H. Firth, ed., London, George Routledge and Sons, n.d., p. 173.

84 Cavendish, *Nature's Pictures*, p. 84.

85 M. Cavendish, *Sociable Letters*, Menston, England, Scolar Press, 1969, p. 429.

86 Cavendish, "Bell in Campo," *Playes*, p. 609.

87 M. Cavendish, *Poems and Fancies*, Menston, England, Scolar Press, 1972, "Dedication."

88 Ibid.

89 Ibid.

90 Ibid., "To All Noble and Worthy Ladies."

91 Cavendish, *Sociable Letters*, "To His Excellency The Lord Marquis of Newcastle."

92 Cavendish, *Poems and Fancies*, "To the Reader."

93 Cavendish, "A True Relation," p. 172.

94 M. Cavendish, *The Philosophical and Physical Opinions*, London, J. Martin and J. Allestrye, 1655, "Dedication."

95 Cavendish, *Nature's Pictures*, p. 334.

96 Cavendish, *World's Olio*, p. 71. Cavendish occasionally wore masculine articles of dress herself.

97 Cavendish, *William Cavendish*, p. xxxviii. In her book *Nature's Pictures* Cavendish states that she writes because "all heroick Actions, publick Imployments, powerfull Governments, and eloquent Pleadings, are denied our Sex in this age." *Nature's Pictures*, "To the Reader."

98 Cavendish, *Poems and Fancies*, "To All Noble and Worthy Ladies."

99 Cited by Mendelson in *Stuart Women*, p. 60.

100 Cavendish, *Playes*, "To the Reader."

101 M. Cavendish, *The Description of A New World Called The Blazing World*, K. Lilley, ed., London, William Pickering, 1992, p. 224.

102 M. Cavendish, *Observations Upon Experimental Philosophy*, London, A. Maxwell, 1668, p. 185.
103 Ibid., pp. 1–2.
104 Ibid., p. 183.
105 The notion of "writing from the body" has figured prominently in the work of many modern feminists. Hélène Cixous, for example, argues that "Woman must write her body, must make up the unimpeded tongue that bursts partitions, classes, and rhetorics." H. Cixous and C. Clément, *The Newly Born Woman*, B. Wing, trans., Minneapolis, University of Minnesota Press, 1986, p. 94. Ann Rosalind Jones writes that "to the extent that the female body is seen as a direct source of female writing, a powerful alternative discourse seems possible: to write from the body is to recreate the world." A.R. Jones, "Writing the Body: Toward an Understanding of *l'Ecriture féminine*," in E. Showalter, ed., *The New Feminist Criticism: Essays on Women, Literature, and Theory*, New York, Pantheon, 1985, p. 366.
106 See, for example, Cavendish, *Poems and Fancies*, p. 201, and M. Cavendish, *Grounds of Natural Philosophy*, London, A. Maxwell, 1668, p. 51.
107 Cavendish, *Poems and Fancies*, p. 201.
108 Ibid., p. 126.
109 In one of Cavendish's plays, for example, a servant details to his master how each of his senses will suffer as a result of leaving the city for the country:

> Alas Sir, will you change your Organ for a Bag-pipe, your Harpsichord, for a Cymbal; your Viol, for a Country Fiddle . . . ? . . . will you change . . . your most curious Sallads for Onions and Garlick? all your choice fruits for Crabs? and all your Confectionaries for starcht Carrowaies . . . ? . . . Will you change . . . your Spanish perfumes for choaking Juniper? your Jessamin and Orange-Flowers for a Posie of Dock-leaves . . . ? . . . Will you change your fine Damask Linnen for Country Huswives Cloth, to rub off your Worships fine skin . . . ?
>
> M. Cavendish, *Plays, Never Before Printed*, London, A. Maxwell, 1668, "Scenes," pp. 152–4.

110 M. Cavendish, *Orations of Divers Sorts*, London, n.p., 1662, pp. 199–201. Elsewhere she writes: "Why may not we our Senses all delight/Heaven our Senses and our Souls unite," *Nature's Pictures*, p. 50.
111 Cavendish, *Plays, Never Before Printed*, "The Convent of Pleasure," p. 8.
112 Cavendish, *Poems and Fancies*, p. 122.
113 Cavendish, *World's Olio*, "To the Reader."
114 Ibid.
115 For example, in several plays Cavendish has male characters refer to the supposed bad odor of women. See "The Bridals," *Plays, Never Before Printed*, p. 63; "Scenes," *Plays, Never Before Printed*, p. 154.
116 Cavendish, *Poems and Fancies*, p. 213. While Cavendish made use of the stereotype of the witch, she was skeptical about the existence of witches: "I dare say, that many a good, old honest woman hath been condemned innocently, and suffered death wrongfully, by the sentence of some foolish and cruel Judges, meerly upon this suspition of Witchcraft." M. Cavendish, *Philosophical Letters*, London, n.p., 1664, p. 298. See also *Poems and Fancies*, p. 285.
117 Cavendish, *Blazing World*, pp. 125–6.
118 Such satires of contemporary science were common in the seventeenth and eighteenth centuries. See, for example, M.H. Nicolson, *Science and the Imagination*, Ithaca, NY, Great Seal Books, 1963, pp. 135–52.
119 Cavendish, *Observations*, p. 103.
120 Ibid., p. 102.
121 In Cavendish, *The Philosophical and Physical Opinions*, "An Epistle."

122 *Blazing World*, pp. 140–5, 150–1.
123 Ibid., p. 141.
124 Ibid., p. 142.
125 Ibid., p. 145.
126 Cavendish, *Observations*, "Preface."
127 Cavendish, *Blazing World*, p. 150.
128 Ibid., p. 151.
129 Cavendish, *Observations*, p. 268.
130 Cavendish, *Nature's Pictures*, p. 249.
131 Cavendish, *World's Olio*, "To the Reader."
132 Cavendish, *Nature's Pictures*, p. 251. For an exploration of the symbolism of inner space in women's writing see Gilbert and Gubar, "The Parables of the Cave," in *Madwoman*, pp. 93–104.
133 Cavendish, *Playes*, p. 667.
134 Cavendish, *Philosophical and Physical Opinions*, "To the Reader."
135 Cavendish, *World's Olio*, "An Epistle to the Reader."
136 Cavendish apparently agreed with tradition in considering sight to be foremost among the senses. She wrote that sight "is the most Curious, Glorious, and Precious Jewel in Nature's Treasury." *Sociable Letters*, p. 274.
137 *Playes*, p. 134.
138 Ibid., p. 163.
139 Employing traditional associations, Cavendish linked each physical sense with a mental faculty: "Knowledge is as the Sense of Touch; Memory as the Sense of Sight; Reason, as the Sense of Hearing; Understanding, as the Sense of Tast; and Imagination as the Sense of smelling." *World's Olio*, p. 198.
140 Cavendish, *Orations*, p. 226.
141 Cavendish, *Blazing World*, pp. 224–5.
142 Todd, *Angellica*, p. 62. See also Cixous and Clément, *The Newly Born Woman*, pp. 94–100.
143 V. Woolf, *A Room of One's Own*, London, Chatto and Windus, 1984, pp. 57–8.

5 Symbolist harmonies, Futurist colors, Surrealist recipes

1 E.A. Burtt, *The Metaphysical Foundations of Modern Physical Science*, rev. edn, London, Routledge and Kegan Paul, 1950, pp. 238–7.
2 "Lamia" in J. Keats, *The Poems of John Keats*, M. Allott, ed., London, Longman, 1970, p. 646. Goethe similarly proclaimed that the new quantitative cosmology was responsible for "draining the universe of warmth and colour." P. Gay, *The Enlightenment: An Interpretation, The Rise of Modern Paganism*, New York, Alfred Knopf, 1967, p. 400.
3 F.C. McGrath discusses Walter Pater's views on the estrangement of sense from intellect in *The Sensible Spirit: Walter Pater and the Modernist Paradigm*, Tampa, University of South Florida Press, 1986, pp. 164–83.
4 C. Baudelaire, *Artificial Paradise: On Hashish and Wine as Means of Expanding Individuality*, E. Fox, trans., New York, Herder and Herder, 1971, pp. 54–5. Gautier, for his part, described an experience with the drug as follows: "My fingers moved over an absent keyboard; the sounds spurted out blue and red, in electric sparks." T. Gautier, *Le Club des Hachichins*. Cited by R. Etiemble, *Le Sonnet des voyelles*, Paris, Gallimard, 1968, p. 120.
5 J.A. Argüelles, *Charles Henry and the Formation of a Psychophysical Aesthetic*, Chicago, University of Chicago Press, 1972.
6 According to the Symbolist author Saint-Pol-Roux, "the maximum of art in literature" could only be achieved through a "federation of all the senses." Cited in

V. Ségalen, "Les Synesthésies et l'école symboliste," *Mercure de France*, 1902, vol. 4, p. 90.

7 P.B. Shelley, *The Complete Poetical Works of Shelley*, G.E. Woodberry, ed., Boston, MA, Houghton Mifflin, 1901, p. 372.

8 H. Walpole, *Horace Walpole's Correspondence with the Countess of Upper Ossory*, W.D. Wallace, and A.D. Wallace, eds., New Haven, CT, Yale University Press, 1965, vol. 33, pp. 261–3.

9 A. Balakian, *The Symbolist Movement: A Critical Appraisal*, New York, New York University Press, 1977, p. 124.

10 In this regard, Baudelaire praised Wagner for his integration of music with drama: "the art par excellence, the most synthetic and the most perfect." C. Baudelaire, "L'Art romantique", in C. Baudelaire, *Curiosités esthétiques: L'Art romantique, et autres ouevres critiques*, Paris, Editions Garnier Frères, 1962, p. 270.

11 J. Moréas, "The Symbolist Manifesto." Cited by J. Milner, *Symbolists and Decadents*, London, Studio Vista, 1971, p. 51.

12 C. Baudelaire, *Selected Poems*, J. Richardson, trans., Harmondsworth, England, Penguin, 1975, p. 43.

13 C. Baudelaire, "L'Art romantique," in Baudelaire, *Curiosités esthétiques et autres ouevres*, p. 696.

14 C. Baudelaire, "Exposition universelle," in Baudelaire, *Curiosités esthétiques et autres ouevres*, p. 213.

15 J.-K. Huysmans, *Against Nature*, R. Baldick, trans., Harmondsworth, England, Penguin, 1959.

16 According to Symbolist synaesthetics, the visual layout of a poem – or of a music score – could also be considered part of the artwork. D.W. Seaman, *Concrete Poetry in France*, Ann Arbor, MI, UMI Research Press, 1981, pp. 117–50; R. Shattuck, *The Banquet Years: The Origins of the Avant-Garde in France, 1885 to World War I*, Salem, NH, Ayer Company, 1984, pp. 175–7. The interplay between music and poetry in Symbolism is treated in D.M. Herz, *The Tuning of the Word: The Musico-Literary Poetics of the Symbolist Movement*, Carbondale and Edwardsville, Southern Illinois University Press, 1987.

17 Arthur Rimbaud, "Voyelles." Cited by Etiemble, *Le Sonnet des voyelles*, p. 53. The possibility of correspondences between colors and letters of the alphabet occasioned interest long before Rimbaud wrote his sonnet. In 1821, for example, an English author assigned the color white to "A," blue to "E," yellow to "I," red to "O," and black to "U." Etiemble, *Le Sonnet des voyelles*, p. 100.

18 Salome herself has her eyes closed, emphasizing the dream-like nature of her dance. She is guided not by eyesight, but by the magical sight of the "third eye" dangling from a bracelet on her outstretched arm.

19 The English Symbolist poet Charles Swinburne made use of this association in his poem "Laus Veneris":

> As one who hidden in deep sedge and reeds
> Smells the rare scent made where a panther feeds,
> And tracking ever slotwise the warm smell
> Is snapped upon by the sweet mouth and bleeds,
> His head far down the hot sweet throat of her -
> So one tracks love, whose breath is deadlier . . .
>
> A.C. Swinburne, *The Poems of Algernon Charles Swinburne*, vol. 1, London, Chatto and Windus, 1912, p. 20.

20 "Amid the heady odour of these perfumes", Huysmans wrote of this painting in *Against Nature*, "Salome slowly glides forward on the points of her toes . . .

begin[ning] the lascivious dance which is to rouse the aged Herod's dormant senses." Huysmans, *Against Nature*, p. 64.

21 In a commentary on his painting, "The Three Brides," Toorop states that "fluid lines of sound bind the Seraphim to an enormous bell, upheld by the crucified Christ." The flower-enveloped central bride is described by Toorop as "a perfumed, hardly blossomed flower," hiding under her veil "the aroma of tenderness." M. Gibson, *The Symbolists*, New York, Harry N. Abrams, 1988, p. 131; R. Goldwater, *Symbolism*, New York, Harper and Row, 1979, p. 252.

22 Baudelaire wrote that when listening to Wagner he experienced an "intensity of light." Baudelaire, "L'Art romantique," in Baudelaire, *Curiosités esthétiques et autres ouevres*, p. 697. Mallarmé similarly claimed that, with Wagner's music, "we now *hear* undeniable rays of light." S. Mallarmé, "Crisis in Poetry," in *Mallarmé: Selected Prose, Poems, Essays, and Letters*, B. Cook, trans., Baltimore, Johns Hopkins University Press, 1956, p. 39.

23 L. Vallas, *The Theories of Claude Debussy*, M. O'Brien, trans., New York, Dover Publications, 1967, p. 11. Debussy, in fact, believed that music was better able than painting to "bring together all manner of color and light." A.B. Wenk, *Claude Debussy and the Poets*, Berkeley, University of California Press, 1976, p. 207. In the twentieth century the French composer Olivier Messiaen has continued in Debussy's tradition of representing color through sound.

24 Scriabin's relation to Symbolism is discussed in B. de Schloezer, *Scriabin: Artist and Mystic*, N. Slonimsky, trans., Berkeley, University of California Press, 1987, p. 314.

25 Ibid., pp. 84. 255–6.

26 Ibid., pp. 255–8.

> The choreography [of *Mysterium*] would include glances, looks, eye motions, touches of the hands, odors of both pleasant perfumes and acrid smokes, frankincense and myrrh. Pillars of incense would form part of the scenery. Lights, fires, and constantly changing lighting effects would pervade the cast and audience, each to number in the thousands.
>
> F. Bowers, *Scriabin: A Biography of the Russian Composer*, vol. 2, Tokyo, Kodansha, 1969, p. 253.

While this work was never performed, Scriabin's piano concerto *Prometheus* occasioned much discussion for its use of a *clavier à lumières*, a keyboard designed to produce colored lights in response to musical tones.

27 Kandinsky discussed the harmony of colors with other sensations in his landmark essay of 1912, *Concerning the Spiritual in Art*.

> Many colors have been described as rough or prickly, others as smooth and velvety, so that one feels inclined to stroke them . . . . The expression "perfumed colors" is frequently met with. The sound of colors is so definite that it would be hard to find anyone who would express bright yellow with bass notes, or dark lake with treble.
>
> W. Kandinsky, *Concerning the Spiritual in Art and Painting in Particular*, M. Sadleir, trans., New York, George Wittenborn, 1947, p. 45.

28 Two psychological studies of synaesthesia which include some of the phemonenon's cultural history are L.E. Marks, *The Unity of the Senses: Interrelations among the Modalities*, New York, Academic Press, 1978, and R.E. Cytowic, *Synesthesia: A Union of the Senses*, New York, Springer-Verlag, 1989. Cytowic has published a popular version of his study of synaesthesia in *The Man Who Tasted Shapes*, New York, Warner Books, 1993.

29 Cited by W. Isler, *Walter Pater: The Aesthetic Moment*, Cambridge, Cambridge University Press, 1987, p. 81.

30 O. Wilde, *De Profundis*, cited by H.M. Hyde, *Oscar Wilde*, New York, Farrar, Straus and Giroux, 1975, p. 321.

31 Cited by P. Jullian, *Prince of Aesthetes: Count Robert de Montesquiou, 1855–1921*, J. Haylock and F. King, trans., New York, The Viking Press, 1965, p. 85.

32 Jullian, *Prince of Aesthetes*, p. 134.

33 G. Flaubert, *Salammbô*, Paris, Librairie Armand Colin, 1960, p. 143.

34 R. de Montesquiou, *Le Chef des odeurs suaves*, Paris, Georges Richard, 1907, pp. 105, 126, 277.

35 R. de Montesquiou, *Les Pas effacés: Mémoires*, vol. 3, Paris, Emile-Paul Frères, 1923, pp. 62–3.

36 E. Munhall, *Whistler and Montesquiou: The Butterfly and the Bat*, New York and Paris, The Frick Collection, Flammarion, 1995, p. 53. Similarly, in 1888, a cartoon depicted a baby Rimbaud "babbling" his first colored vowels with a paintbrush. Etiemble, *Le Sonnet des voyelles*, p. 12.

37 Montesquiou was inspired in his interior decorating by Baudelaire who proclaimed that "in an apartment decorated with ingenious furniture and caressing colors, one feels one's spirit brighten and one's nerves ready themselves for good fortune." Cited by Montesquiou, *Les Pas effacés: Mémoires*, vol. 2, p. 96.

38 R. de Montesquiou, *Les Pas effacés: Mémoires*, vol. 2, pp. 108–22; Jullian, *Prince of Aesthetes*, pp. 43–7.

39 Cited by Munhall, *Whistler and Montesquiou*, pp. 47–8. Montesquiou's interest in perfumes led him to write a commentary for the perfumery exhibit of *Exposition Universelle* in 1900. R. de Montesquiou, *Pays des aromates*, Saint-Cloud, France, Imprimerie Belin Frères, 1903.

40 Montesquiou, *Les Pas effacés*, vol. 3, p. 66.

41 Ibid., p. 55.

42 Montesquiou, *Le Chef des odeurs suaves*, p. xiii.

43 Montesquiou, *Les Pas effacés*, vol. 2, pp. 123–7.

44 Huysmans, *Against Nature*, p. 36.

45 Ibid., pp. 27, 29, 34, 54, 58–9, 119, 124.

46 The ideals of the Decadent movement are explored in J. Pierrot, *The Decadent Imagination: 1880–1900*, D. Coltman, trans., Chicago, University of Chicago Press, 1981.

47 Huysmans refers to Elagabulus in *Against Nature*, p. 45.

48 D. Magie, trans., *The Scriptores Historiae Augustae*, London, William Heinemann, 1922, vol. 2, p. 145. Some of the stories told of Elagabulus in this account are undoubtedly fanciful.

49 Ibid., p. 147.

50 Ibid., p. 143.

51 Ibid., p. 43.

52 Ibid., p. 161.

53 Ibid., pp. 147–8.

54 In *Against Nature*, for example, Des Esseintes revels in descriptions of the ravages of disease. Huysmans, *Against Nature*, p. 102.

55 Ibid., p. 129.

56 Ibid., p. 143.

57 V. de l'Isle-Adam, *Tomorrow's Eve*, R. Martin Adams, trans., Urbana, University of Illinois Press, 1982, p. 22.

58 P. Jullian, *Dreamers of Decadence: Symbolist Painters of the 1890s*, R. Baldick, trans., New York, Praeger Publishers, 1971, p. 89.

59 J.A. Kaplan, *The Art of Gustave Moreau: Theory, Style, and Content*, Ann Arbor, MI, UMI Research Press, 1982, p. 13.

60 As, for example, in paintings by Gustave Moreau, Jan Toorop, Jean Delville, and Fernand Khnopff.
61 Sainte-Beuve distinguished two forms of sensuality in nineteenth-century literature, one which "concealed . . . sensuality behind a cloud of mysticism," the other which "frankly unmasked it." Cited by I. Babbitt, *The New Laokoon: An Essay on the Confusion of the Arts*, Boston, MA, Houghton Mifflin, 1910, p. 146.
62 A.P. Bertocci, *From Symbolism to Baudelaire*, Carbondale, Southern Illinois University Press, 1964, p. 153.
63 See, for example, Baudelaire, "L'Art romantique," in Baudelaire, *Curiosités esthétiques et autres ouevres*, p. 734 and J.-K. Huysmans, *The Cathedral*, C. Bell, trans., London, Kegan Paul, Trench, Trubner, and Co., 1925, pp. 192–3.
64 M.L. Bailey, *Milton and Jakob Boehme: A Study of German Mysticism in Seventeenth-Century England*, New York, Haskell House, 1964, pp. 170–81.
65 Huysmans, *The Cathedral*, pp. 113, 123, 297–302.
66 Ibid., p. 198. Huysmans conceives of this symbolic system as a tree:

> the trunk was the Symbolism of the Scriptures . . . the branches were the allegorical purport of architecture, of colours, gems, flowers and animals . . . . A small bough represented Liturgical perfumes, and a mere twig, dried up from the first and almost dead, represented dancing.
>
> Ibid., p. 329.

67 J.-K. Huysmans, *Saint Lydwine of Schiedam*, A. Hastings, trans., London, Kegan Paul, Trench, Trubner, and Co., 1923, p. 190.
68 Baudelaire, "L'Art romantique", pp. 734–5. See further E. Swedenborg, *Heaven and its Wonders and Hell*, J.C. Ager, trans., New York, Swedenborg Foundation, 1930, p. 67.
69 H. de Balzac, *Seraphita*, K. Prescott Wormeley, trans., Boston, Roberts Brothers, 1889, p. 118.
70 Jullian, *Prince of Aesthetes*, p. 63.
71 The traditions of medieval mysticism also had an influence on Symbolist painters. Gustave Moreau found the iconography of medieval sacred art highly attractive and made extensive use of it in his paintings. J. Paladilhe and J. Pierre, *Gustave Moreau*, B. Wadia, trans., London, Thames and Hudson, 1972, p. 29. Kaplan, *The Art of Gustave Moreau*, pp. 18–20. Jan Toorop, who dedicated his later work to religious themes, said that he wished to evoke "the great, pure, and mystic periods of the past" in his paintings. Cited by Gibson, *The Symbolists*, p. 131.
72 Cited by J. Milner, *Symbolists and Decadents*, London, Studio Vista, 1971, p. 73.
73 So entranced was Symons by the Decadent lure of Satanism that, in his translations of Baudelaire's poems, he often inserted the name of Satan where it did not occur in the original. J.M. Munro, *Arthur Symons*, New York, Twayne, 1969, p. 121. T.S. Eliot critiqued Symons' interpretation of Baudelaire as markedly 1890s. T.S. Eliot, *Essays: Ancient and Modern*, New York, Harcourt, Brace, and Company, 1936, pp. 60–74.
74 Paul Verlaine, *Poèmes saturniens*. Cited by Jullian, *Dreamers of Decadence*, p. 250.
75 Walter Pater, indeed, considered the medieval sublimation of worldly passions to have produced "a beautiful disease or disorder of the senses," the remedy for which was a return "to the earlier, more ancient life of the senses." Like most Symbolists, Pater was nonetheless fascinated by the luxurious sensory symbolism produced by the "overwrought spiritualities of the middle age." W. Pater, "Poems by William Morris," *Westminster Review*, 1868, vol. 90, pp. 302, 307.
76 Jean Pierrot discusses "aesthetic Roman Catholicism" in *The Decadent Imagination*, pp. 85–9.

77 J. Rivière, *Corréspondance avec Alain-Fournier*, Paris, 1926. Cited by S. Jarocinski, *Debussy: Impressionism and Symbolism*, R. Myers, trans., London, Eulenburg Books, 1976, p. 68. Huysmans wrote of his experience of one early morning service: "we offer God a luxurious cult . . . going across in the darkness for Matins, I was met with a blaze of light and colour from the lamps and copes, and waves of incense." R. Baldick, *The Life of J.-K. Huysmans*, Oxford, Clarendon Press, 1955, p. 281.

78 Milner, *Symbolists and Decadents*, p. 73. The composer Erik Satie broke off from the Rosicrucians to found his own "Metropolitan Church of the Art of Jesus the Conductor." Shattuck, *The Banquet Years*, p. 123.

79 Schloezer, *Scriabin*, p. 100. The Theosophical Scriabin imagined that by engaging all the senses in a transcendent work of art he might "make the world beautiful, endow it with aesthetic value, and transfigure it for all eternity." Ibid., p. 261.

80 Nordau was by no means alone in considering Symbolist art to be pathological in origin. See, for example, the discussion of Theophilus Hyslop in S. Trombley, *"All that Summer She was Mad": Virginia Woolf and Her Doctors*, London, Junction Books, 1981, pp. 209–40.

81 M. Nordau, *Degeneration*, New York, D. Appleton and Company, 1900, p. 15.

82 Ibid., p. 27.

83 Ibid., p. 109.

84 Ibid., p. 110.

85 Ibid., p. 139.

86 Ibid., p. 539.

87 Ibid.

88 Ibid., p. 142. The classic opposition between sense and intellect was expressed in the belief that the expansion of sensory awareness (except in the case of sight, the most "rational" of the senses) entails a diminution of intellectual activity. Thus in his essay on the "confusion of the arts" Irving Babbitt stated that "we can trace with special clearness in the romanticism of nineteenth-century France this tendency toward a hypertrophy of sensation and an atrophy of ideas, toward a constantly expanding sensorium and a diminishing intellect." Babbitt, *The New Laokoon*, p. 145.

89 Ségalen, "Les Synesthésies," p. 85.

90 Cited by Argüelles, *Charles Henry*, p. 83, n. 12.

91 Babbitt writes, for example, that "in 1902 there was given at New York the 'first experimental perfume concert in America,' which included among its attractions 'a trip to Japan in sixteen minutes,' conveyed to the audience by a series of odors." *The New Laokoon*, p. 182.

92 Nordau, *Degeneration*, pp. 27, 501–3.

93 Ibid., p. 503.

94 Ibid., p. 541.

95 Ibid.

96 Ibid., p. 544.

97 Ibid., p. 543.

98 Ibid.

99 As in the works of Gustave Moreau, Pierre Puvis de Chavannes, and Fernand Khnopff.

100 Mario Praz discusses Péladan's fascination with androgyny in *The Romantic Agony*, A. Davidson, trans., London, Oxford University Press, 1970, pp. 330–41.

101 Cited in J. Milner, *Symbolists and Decadents*, p. 20.

102 Cited by Jullian, *Prince of Aesthetes*, p. 108.

103 Jullian, *Prince of Aesthetes*, p. 138.

104 Ibid., p. 132.

105 Jullian, *Dreamers of Decadence*, p. 89.

106 S.J. Duncan, "An Impossible Ideal," in S.J. Duncan, *The Pool in the Desert*, Harmondsworth, England, Penguin, 1984, p. 43.

107 Jullian, *Prince of Aesthetes*, p. 90.

108 See, for example, P. Gerrish Nunn, *Victorian Women Artists*, London, The Women's Press, 1987, p. 76.

109 Ibid., p. 4.

110 J.J. Rousseau, *Emile*, cited by W. Chadwick, *Women, Art, and Society*, rev. edn, London, Thames and Hudson, 1996, p. 148. Music was similarly regarded as only suitable for women in a very limited way as a domestic pastime. R. Leppert, *The Sight of Sound: Music, Representation and the History of the Body*, Berkeley, University of California Press, 1993, pp. 67–70.

111 In *The Painter of Modern Life*, Baudelaire contrasts the dandy with the *flâneur*. C. Baudelaire, *The Painter of Modern Life and Other Essays*, New York, Garland, 1978, p. 9. On art and the gendering of public space in the nineteenth century see G. Pollock, *Vision and Difference: Femininity, Feminism and Histories of Art*, London, Routledge, 1988, pp. 50–90.

112 In accordance with age-old stereotypes, women's eyes were assumed by the Symbolists to exist primarily for the purpose of seducing. An example of this can be found in Baudelaire's poem "Le Voyage" which speaks of male astrologers drowning in the eyes of a tyrannical seductress "with dangerous perfumes." C. Baudelaire, *Les Fleurs du mal*, Paris, Classiques Garnier, 1994, p. 155.

113 Baudelaire, *Painter of Modern Life*, p. 30, and Pierrot, *The Decadent Imagination*, p. 124.

114 J.-K. Huysmans, *Down Stream, and Other Works*, S. Putman, trans. and ed., New York, Howard Fertig, 1975, pp. 272, 278. Anthea Callen considers Huysmans' response to Degas' paintings of women bathing in "Degas' *Bathers*: Hygiene and Dirt – Gaze and Touch," in R. Kendall and G. Pollock, eds., *Dealing with Degas: Representations of Women and the Politics of Vision*, New York, Universe, 1992, pp. 174–6.

115 Huysmans, *Down Stream*, pp. 314–15. See also C. Bernheimer, "Huysmans: Writing Against (Female) Nature," in S.R. Suleiman, ed., *The Female Body in Western Culture*, Cambridge, MA, Harvard University Press, 1986. In the novel *L'Eve future* by Villiers de L'Isle-Adam, a mechanical woman is created which so far surpasses the woman of nature as to appear divine. "*She is an angel*," the machine's inventor declares, "if indeed it's true, as the theologians teach us, *that angels are simply fire and light!* Wasn't it Baron Swedenborg who went so far as to add that they are 'hermaphrodite and sterile'?" Villiers de L'Isle-Adam, *Tomorrow's Eve*, p. 144. For a feminist analysis of this book see N. Schor, *Breaking the Chain: Women, Theory and French Realist Fiction*, New York, Columbia University Press, 1985.

116 The Symbolist author and dandy Barbey D'Aurevilly wrote of female artists: "They remain unfailingly women, even when they are at their most artistic; and the very arts in which they perform best, are the . . . *feminine arts*. In effect, you will search in vain in the field of literature, for a women who is worth a Mlle Tangloni in the field of dance." J. Barbey D'Aurevilly, *Les Bas-bleus*, Paris, Société Générale de Librairie Catholique, 1878, p. xxii.

117 Cited by Pierrot, *Decadent Imagination*, p. 124. See further J.R. Feldman, *Gender on the Divide: The Dandy in Modernist Literature*, Ithaca, NY, Cornell University Press, 1993.

118 Cited by Milner, *Symbolists and Decadents*, p. 73.

119 The artworks of Margaret Macdonald, along with those of her sister Frances, are described in J. Helland, *The Studios of Frances and Margaret Macdonald*, Manchester, Manchester University Press, 1996.

120 C. Dauphiné, *Rachilde*, Paris, *Mercure de France*, 1991, p. 248. Rachilde, interestingly, was one of the few female writers of the period admired by Huysmans, who generally scoffed at literary "amazons." M. Harry, *Trois ombres: J.-K. Huysmans, Jules Lemaitre, Anatole France*, Paris, Ernest Flammarion, 1932, pp. 37–8.

121 Cited and analyzed by R.A. Kingcaid, *Neurosis and Narrative: The Decadent Short Fiction of Proust, Lorrain, and Rachilde*, Carbondale and Edwardsville, University of Illinois Press, 1992, pp. 127–32.

122 For discussions of Rachilde's work within the context of Decadence see J. Waelti-Walters, *Feminist Novelists of the Belle Epoque*, Bloomington, Indiana University Press, 1990, and Kingcaid, *Neurosis and Narrative*.

123 Rachilde was strongly affected by the belief that her parents would have preferred her to have been male. M. Lukacher, *Maternal Fictions: Stendhal, Sand, Rachilde, and Bataille*, Durham, NC, Duke University Press, 1994, pp. 112–14. Dauphiné places the author within the context of her fellow female writers in *Rachilde*, pp. 168–200.

124 Rachilde's novels dealing with a reversal of gender roles include *Madame Adonis*, Paris, J. Ferenczi et Fils, 1929 and *The Marquise de Sade*, L. Heron, trans., Sawtry, England, Dedalus, 1994.

125 Rachilde was accused of having "invented a new vice" with this book, to which Verlaine replied, in true Decadent fashion: "Ah! My dear child, if you've invented an extra vice, you'll be a benefactor of humanity!" Dauphiné, *Rachilde*, p. 56.

126 Rachilde, *Monsieur Venus*, Paris, Ernest Flammarion, 1926, p. 27.

127 Ibid., p. 26.

128 Ibid.

129 Ibid., p. 31.

130 Ibid., p. 55.

131 Ibid.

132 Raoule's appropriation of the power of the male gaze is examined in M.C. Hawthorne, "*Monsieur Venus*: A Critique of Gender Roles," *Nineteenth-Century French Studies*, 1987/88, vol. 16, nos. 1 and 2, pp. 170–4.

133 Rachilde, *Monsieur Venus*, p. 60.

134 Ibid., p. 79.

135 Ibid., p. 185.

136 Ibid., pp. 187–8.

137 Ibid., p. 242.

138 Ibid., pp. 246–7.

139 Rachilde refers to "anatomical Venuses" in her novel *Marquise de Sade*, p. 187. Ludmilla Jordanova discusses the symbolism of these wax models at length in *Sexual Visions: Images of Gender in Science and Medicine between the Eighteenth and Twentieth Centuries*, New York, Harvester Wheatsheaf, 1989, pp. 44–65.

140 On the reification of the female form in Western painting and sculpture see M. Warner, *Monuments and Maidens: The Allegory of the Female Form*, New York, Atheneum, 1985.

141 Montesquiou, *Les Pas effacés*, vol. 3, p. 229.

142 R. Delaunay, "Light," in S.A. Buckberrough, *Robert Delaunay: The Discovery of Simultanaeity*, Ann Arbor, MI, UMI Research Press, 1982, pp. 245–6. Delaunay reputedly spent months observing the spectrum produced by a ray of sunlight entering a dark room, attempting to outdo the Impressionists in his quest to paint the vibrating colors of light. Buckberrough, *Robert Delaunay*, pp. 196–7.

143 G. Vriesen and M. Imdahl, *Robert Delaunay: Light and Color*, New York, Harry N. Abrams, 1967, p. 72; C. Greenberg, "On the Role of Nature in Modernist Painting," in C. Greenberg, *Art and Culture: Critical Essays*, Boston, MA, Beacon Press, 1965, p. 172. Martin Jay reviews arguments for and against the typing of

modern art as ocularcentric in *Downcast Eyes: The Denigration of Vision in Twentieth-Century French Thought*, Berkeley, University of California Press, 1994, pp. 149–209.

144 Key elements of Futurist ideology, such as a fascination with machinery, violence, and the bustle of the modern city, can also be found in the work of certain Symbolists.

145 F.T. Marinetti, "Nous renions nos maîtres les symbolistes, derniers amants de la lune," in F.T. Marinetti, *Le Futurisme,* Lausanne, L'Age D'Homme, 1980, p. 117.

146 F.T. Marinetti, "The Founding and Manifesto of Futurism," in U. Apollonio, ed., *Futurist Manifestos*, London, Thames and Hudson, 1973, p. 20. The "Manifesto of the Futurist Painters" of 1910 elaborated:

> Our forebears drew their inspiration from a religious atmosphere which fed their souls; in the same way we must breathe in the tangible miracles of contemporary life – the iron network of speedy communication which envelops the earth, the transatlantic liners, the dreadnoughts, those marvellous flights which furrow our skies . . .
>
> U. Boccioni, C. Carrà, L. Russolo, G. Balla, G. Severini, "Manifesto of the Futurist Painters," in Apollonio, ed., *Futurist Manifestos*, p. 25.

147 B. Corradini and E. Settimelli, "Weights, Measures and Prices of Artistic Genius," in Apollonio, ed., *Futurist Manifestos*, p. 149.

148 G. Balla, "The Futurist Universe," in Apollonio, ed., *Futurist Manifestos*, p. 219.

149 Boccioni et al., "Futurist Painters," p. 28. Many Futurist notions of artistic representation were grounded in contemporary scientific theories of the nature of perception. See, for example, J. Sharp, "Sounds, Noises, and Smells: Sensory Experience in Futurist Art," in A. Coffin Hanson, ed., *The Futurist Imagination*, New Haven, CT, Yale University Art Gallery, 1983, pp. 19–21.

150 The Futurists made various efforts to communicate their art and ideals to the working classes, such as holding talks at union centers and organizing an exhibition in an abandoned factory. G. Lista, *Futurism*, C.L. Clark, trans., New York, Universe Books, 1986, pp. 14, 24.

151 The Futurist painters claimed that, next to the paintings in the museums, their own pictures would "shine like blinding daylight compared with deepest night." Boccioni et al., "Futurist Painters," p. 29.

152 C. Carrà, "The Painting of Sounds, Noises and Smells" in Apollonio, ed., *Futurist Manifestos*, p. 114.

153 Ibid.

154 L. Russolo, "The Art of Noises," in Apollonio, ed., *Futurist Manifestos*, p. 85. For the purpose of performing such auditory art Russolo invented a series of *intonarumori*, "noise-intoners."

155 F.T. Marinetti, "Destruction of Syntax – Imagination Without Strings – Words-In-Freedom," in Apollonio, ed., *Futurist Manifestos*, p. 100.

156 Ibid., p. 88. Onomatopoeia was particularly favored by Marinetti for its evocative power. He stated, for example, that the onomatopoeia *dum-dum-dum-dum* in his poem "Dunes," expressed "the circling sound of the African sun and the orange weight of the sun." Ibid., p. 158.

157 Ibid., p. 105.

158 Carrà, "Painting of Sounds," p. 112.

159 Ibid., p. 114.

160 G. Severini, "The Plastic Analogies of Dynamism," in Apollonio, ed., *Futurist Manifestos*, p. 124. Enrico Prampolini similarly believed that all auditory sensations could be perceived and represented as color. E. Prampolini, "Chromophony and the Colours of Sounds," in Apollonio, ed., *Futurist Manifestos*, pp. 115–18.

161 Boccioni et al., "Futurist Painters," pp. 27–8.
162 U. Boccioni, "Futurist Painting and Sculpture," in Apollonio, ed., *Futurist Manifestos*, pp. 172–81.
163 Ibid., p. 175. The relationship between Futurism and Cubism is treated in M.W. Martin, *Futurist Art and Theory: 1909–1915*, New York, Hacker Art Books, 1978.
164 Ibid., p. 177.
165 For example, "Dancer with Movable Parts," by Severini.
166 F.T. Marinetti, "The Variety Theatre," in Apollonio, ed., *Futurist Manifestos*, p. 127.
167 F.T. Marinetti, E. Settimelli, and B. Corra, "The Futurist Synthetic Theatre," in Apollonio, ed., *Futurist Manifestos*, p. 196.
168 Boccioni, for example, held that the concept of "dispassionate, scientific measurement" prevalent in modern art "kills the dynamic warmth" of artwork and "turns the artist into an analyst of immobility." Boccioni, "Futurist Painting and Sculpture," p. 173.
169 Marinetti, "The Founding of Futurism," p. 20. "The scent, the scent alone is enough for our beasts [automobiles]," Marinetti declares. Ibid.
170 F.T. Marinetti, "Geometric and Mechanical Splendour and the Numerical Sensibility," in Apollonio, ed., *Futurist Manifestos*, p. 159.
171 Cited in P. Hulten, ed., *Futurism and Futurisms*, New York, Abbeville, 1986, p. 566. In some ways quantum theory may be said to have fulfilled the Futurist model for science.
172 F.T. Marinetti, "Destruction of Syntax," pp. 98, 105.
173 Carrà, "Painting of Sounds," p. 115.
174 Marinetti wrote: "A new beauty is born today from the chaos of the new contradictory sensibilities that we Futurists will substitute for the former beauty." Marinetti, "Geometric and Mechanical Splendour," p. 154.
175 Marinetti, "Destruction of Syntax," p. 97. Although he wavered between considering the femininity he scorned a construct of nature or a construct of culture, Marinetti stated:

> As for the supposed inferiority of woman, we think that if her body and spirit had, for many generations past, been subjected to the same physical and spiritual education as man, it would perhaps be legitimate to speak of the equality of the sexes.
>
> F.T. Marinetti, "Against *Amore* and Parliamentarianism," in R.W. Flint, ed., *Marinetti: Selected Writings*, R.W. Flint and A.A. Coppotelli, trans., New York, Farrar, Straus and Giroux, 1972, p. 73.

176 Carrà, "Painting of Sounds," p. 114.
177 Marinetti, "Geometric and Mechanical Splendour," p. 155 and "Destruction of Syntax," p. 100.
178 V. Saint-Point, "Manifesto of the Futurist Woman," in B. Katz, "The Women of Futurism," *Woman's Art Journal*, 1986/7, vol. 7, p. 12.
179 Ibid. Saint-Point further expressed her ideas on the creative potential of lust in "Futurist Manifesto of Lust," in Katz, "Women of Futurism," p. 13.
180 Saint-Point, "Manifesto of the Futurist Woman," p. 12.
181 F.T. Marinetti, "Let's Murder the Moonshine," in Flint, ed., *Marinetti*, p. 46.
182 R.T. Clough, *Futurism*, New York, Philosophical Library, 1961, pp. 135–7, 141–3.
183 B. Katz, "The Women of Futurism," *Woman's Art Journal*, vol. 7, 1986/7, pp. 3–13.
184 Martin, *Futurist Art and Theory*, pp. xxix–xxxii.

185 For an influential critique of the Futurist fascination with warfare see W. Benjamin, "The Work of Art in the Age of Mechanical Reproduction," in W. Benjamin, *Illuminations*, H. Zohn, trans., New York, Schocken Books, 1968, pp. 241–2.

186 Breton stated that Futurism opened up "the possibility of a purely tactile art which would . . . reject all that might be tyrannical and decadent in the realm of *sight.*" A. Breton, "Genesis and Perspective of Surrealism in the Plastic Arts," in F. Rosemont, ed., *What is Surrealism?*, London, Pluto Press, 1978, p. 220.

187 Breton wrote, for example, "I believe that men will long continue to feel the need of following to its source the magical river flowing from their eyes." A. Breton, *What Is Surrealism?*, D. Gascoyne, trans., London, Faber and Faber, 1936, p. 18.

188 M. Jean, *The History of Surrealist Painting*, S. Watson Taylor, trans., New York, Grove Press, 1960, pp. 281–2. The Symbolist and Surrealist interests in the senses are linked in the turn-of-the-century works of Alfred Jarry, among others. See, for example, A. Jarry, "Les Cinq Sens," in A. Jarry *Les Minutes de sable mémorial*, in *Oeuvres complètes*, vol. 1, Paris, Gallimard, 1972, pp. 206–9.

189 See A. Breton, "Second Manifesto of Surrealism," in A. Breton *Manifestos of Surrealism*, R. Seaver and H.R. Lane, trans., Ann Arbor, University of Michigan Press, 1969, pp. 174–5. Breton wrote: "It seems to me absolutely necessary to point out that the time of Baudelairean 'correspondences', of which certain people have tried to make an odious critical commonplace, is past . . . . Oneiric values have once and for all succeeded the others." *What Is Surrealism?*, p. 25.

190 Cited by Jean, *Surrealist Painting*, p. 193.

191 A. Breton, *Ode to Charles Fourier*, K. White, trans., London, Cape Goliard, 1969. Breton included a selection from Fourier's work in his *Anthologie de l'humour noir*, Montreuil, SIP, 1966.

192 Cited by W. Chadwick, *Women Artists and the Surrealist Movement*, Boston, Little, Brown, 1985, p. 65. As part of their exaltation of the hidden and subversive feminine psyche, Surrealists believed hysteria to be a form of expression rather than a pathology. See A. Balakian, *Literary Origins of Surrealism: A New Mysticism in French Poetry*, New York, New York University Press, 1947, p. 16.

193 These works and others have been examined in relation to Surrealist attitudes to women by a number of authors. See, for example, X. Gauthier, *Surréalisme et sexualité*, Paris, Gallimard, 1971; Chadwick, *Women Artists*; M.A. Caws "Ladies Shot and Painted: Female Embodiment in Surrealist Art," in S. Rubin Suleiman, ed., *The Female Body in Western Culture*, Cambridge, MA, Harvard University Press, 1985; R.E. Kuenzli, "Surrealism and Misogyny," in M.A. Caws, R.E. Kuenzli, and G. Raaberg, eds., *Surrealism and Women*, Cambridge, MA, MIT Press, 1991.

194 Jean, *Surrealist Painting*, p. 206. The ocular preoccupations of the Surrealists are discussed by Martin Jay in *Downcast Eyes*, pp. 216–62.

195 The year of Varo's birth is often mistakenly given as 1913. B. Varo, *Remedios Varo: En el centro del microcosmos*, Mexico, Fondo de Cultura Económico, 1990, pp. 75–6.

196 Varo was an accomplished cook – "I know how to cook in the most succulent and sumptuous manner ever known in the annals of cookery" – and seamstress. Ibid., pp. 19, 218.

197 Varo's works are discussed in J.A. Kaplan, *Unexpected Journeys: The Art and Life of Remedios Varo*, New York, Abbeville Press, 1988.

198 These paintings and others are described by Remedios Varo in Varo, *Remedios Varo*, pp. 235–8.

199 Kaplan, *Art and Life of Remedios Varo*, pp. 182–3.

200 Janice Helland discusses this distinction in relation to Carrington's work in "Daughter of the Minotaur," PhD Dissertation, Victoria, BC, University of

Victoria, 1984, pp. 70–5. See also J. Helland, "Surrealism and Esoteric Feminism in the Paintings of Leonora Carrington," *Canadian Art Review* 16, 1989, pp. 53–61.

201 Interestingly, Carrington began her artistic career influenced by Purism, a twentieth-century movement which called for the development of a rationalist, non-sensual "order of the eye." Helland, "Daughter of the Minotaur," p. 17.

202 L. Carrington, *The Stone Door*, New York, St. Martin's Press, 1976, p. 13.

203 Ibid., p. 26.

204 Ibid., pp. 109–10.

205 Ibid., p. 67.

206 Gloria Feman Orenstein has written several analyses of esoteric imagery in Carrington's work, including "Leonora Carrington's Visionary Art for the New Age," *Chrysalis*, 1978, vol. 3, pp. 65–77 and "Manifestations of the Occult in the Art and Literature of Leonora Carrington," in F. Luanne, ed., *Literature and the Occult: Essays in Comparative Literature*, Arlington, University of Texas Press, 1977.

207 L. Carrington, *Down Below*, Chicago, Black Swan Press, 1983, p. 18.

208 Ibid., p. 11.

209 L. Carringdon, "As They Rode Along the Edge," in L. Carrington, *The Seventh Horse and Other Stories*, K. Talbot and A. Kerrigen, trans., London, Virago, 1989, p. 3.

210 L. Carrington, *The Hearing Trumpet*, New York, St. Martin's Press, 1974, pp. 75, 79.

211 Carrington, *The Stone Door*, p. 46.

212 In *The History of Surrealist Painting*, Marcel Jean fondly describes the surrealist dishes served to guests by Leonora Carrington, before going on to analyze the "optical phenomenon" in the paintings of the male artist Malitte Matta. Jean, *Surrealist Painting*, p. 324.

213 In her representation of "The Temptation of St. Anthony," Carrington portrayed a woman preparing an "unctuous broth" of "(let us say) lobsters, mushrooms, fat turtle, spring chicken, ripe tomatoes, gorgonzola cheese, milk chocolate, onions and tinned peaches." Cited by Jean, *Surrealist Painting*, p. 324.

214 Carrington, *Hearing Trumpet*, p. 138.

215 The associations made by Carrington between eating and mystical knowledge are examined in G. Feman Orenstein, *The Reflowering of the Goddess*, New York, Pergamon Press, 1990, p. 63. In *Down Below* Carrington wrote that she experienced her stomach as the seat of society, "the place where I was united with all the elements of the earth," p. 164.

216 M. Warner, "Introduction," in L. Carrington, *The Seventh Horse and Other Stories*, K. Talbot and A. Kerrigen, trans., London, Virago, 1989.

217 Barbey D'Aurevilly, *Les Bas-bleus*, p. 76.

218 As the products of female artists, however, Carrington's and Varo's work has not escaped being typed in terms of second-class feminine handicrafts. In a review entitled "A Surreal Sampler," for example, Carrington's novel *The Stone Door* was described as "a prettily embroidered sampler . . . controlled by tastefulness." J. Miller, "A Surreal Sampler," *Times Literary Supplement*, 1977. Cited by M. Warner, "Introduction," in Carrington, *The Seventh Horse*.

219 Cited by M. Warner, "Leonora Carrington's Spirit Bestiary; or the Art of Playing Make-Believe," in A. Schlieker, ed., *Leonora Carrington: Paintings, Drawings and Sculptures*, London, Serpentine Gallery, 1991, p. 13.

Along similar lines, Carrington wrote in 1946:

Inspired painting, I find, favours a rather bucolic and opaque frame of mind on a continually replenished stomach – preferably with heavy and indigestible foods such as chocolate, sickly cakes, marzipan in blocks . . . . That's why I painted so beautifully when I was pregnant, I did nothing but eat.

> Cited by A. Schlieker, "Introduction," in A. Schlieker, ed., *Leonora Carrington: Paintings, Drawings and Sculptures*, London, Serpentine Gallery, 1991, p. 9.

220 Chadwick, *Women Artists*, p. 195.

6 A feel for the world

1 On the visual character of Western aesthetics see A. Berleant, "Toward a Phenomenological Aesthetics of Environment," in D. Ihde and H. Silverman, eds., *Descriptions*, Albany, State University of New York Press, 1985, pp. 112–28.

2 A. Kaptainis, "Can the Band Play On?", *The Gazette*, Montreal, February 24, 1996.

3 Although many persons who are legally blind in fact have some vision, the term blind is used here primarily to signify "sightless."

4 One of the most notable examples of how sightlessness can promote alternatives to the dominant cultural sensory order is the invention by a blind man of a tactile language – braille.

5 This artistic and literary preoccupation with the unseeing eye is explored in J. Derrida, *Memoirs of the Blind: The Self-Portrait and Other Ruins*, P.-A. Brault and M. Naas, trans., Chicago, University of Chicago Press, 1993.

6 D. Diderot, "Letter on the Blind," cited in M.J. Morgan, *Molyneux's Question: Vision, Touch and the Philosophy of Perception*, Cambridge, Cambridge University Press, 1977, p. 33. For an examination of Enlightenment ideas about the blind see W.R. Paulson, *Enlightenment, Romanticism, and the Blind in France*, Princeton, NJ, Princeton University Press, 1987.

7 G. Révész, *Psychology and Art of the Blind*, H.A. Wolff, trans., London, Longmans, Green, and Co., 1950, pp. 175–83.

8 Ibid., p. 219.

9 Ibid., p. 328.

10 Ibid., pp. 218, 224–8.

11 Ibid., p. 205.

12 Ibid., p. 311.

13 R. Wollheim, "What the Spectator Sees," in N. Bryson, M.A. Holly, and K. Moxey, eds., *Visual Theory: Painting and Interpretation*, New York, Harper Collins, 1991, p. 101.

14 J.-P. Sartre, *Being and Nothingness: An Essay on Phenomenological Ontology*, H.E. Barnes, trans., New York, Philosophical Library, 1956, pp. 254–8.

15 N. Bryson, "The Gaze in the Expanded Field," in H. Foster, ed., *Vision and Visuality*, Seattle, WA, Bay Press, 1988. p. 89.

16 I follow Sartre here in using a man as the subject of my example, for one cannot speak of a woman's experience of an empty park without evoking a whole other discourse concerning women's fears of male violence.

17 J.M. Hull, *Touching the Rock: An Experience of Blindness*, New York, Pantheon, 1990, pp. 82–3.

18 Ibid., p. 82.

19 On the concept of the world as "soundscape" see R.M. Schafer, *The Tuning of the World*, New York, Knopf, 1977 and J.D. Porteous, *Landscapes of the Mind: Worlds of Sense and Metaphor*, Toronto, University of Toronto Press, 1990.

20 On Sartre's critique of vision see M. Jay, *Downcast Eyes: The Denigration of Vision in Twentieth-Century French Thought*, Berkeley, University of California Press, 1994, pp. 275–97.

21   Of course what *most often* manifests a look is the convergence of two ocular globes in my direction. But the look will be given just as well on occasion when there is a rustling of branches, or the sound of a footstep followed by silence . . .

           Sartre, *Being and Nothingness*, p. 257.

22 J.-P. Sartre, *The War Diaries of Jean-Paul Sartre: November 1939/March 1940*, New York, 1984, cited by Jay, *Downcast Eyes*, p. 276.

23 R. Hayman, *Sartre: A Life*, New York, Simon and Schuster, 1987, p. 459.

24 C. Fourier, *The Passions of the Human Soul, and Their Influence on Society and Civilization*, H. Doherty, trans., London, Hippolyte Baillière, 1851, vol. 2, pp. 316–17.

25 Ibid., p. 316.

26 The implicit notion here is that sight is so powerful that it can subsume the roles of all the other senses. Thus merely looking at a work of art becomes a multisensory experience. See, for example, H. Molesworth, "Before *Bed*," *October*, 1993, vol. 63, pp. 69–82. Interestingly, Leonardo da Vinci similarly thought that a painting could appeal to all the senses: "The mouth would like to swallow it bodily, the ear takes pleasure in hearing of its beauties, the sense of touch would absorb it through all its pores, the nose would inhale the air which continually emanates from it." Cited by L. Vinge, *The Five Senses: Studies in a Literary Tradition*, Lund, Sweden, Royal Society of Letters at Lund, 1975, p.73.

27 For a discussion of some of these different critical perspectives on the role of sight in culture see M. Jay, "Scopic Regimes of Modernity," in H. Foster, ed., *Vision and Visuality*, Seattle, WA, Bay Press, 1988, pp. 3–23.

28 See, for example, B.M. Stafford, "Redesigning the Image of Images: A Personal View," *Eighteenth-Century Studies*, vol. 28, no. 1 1994, pp. 9–16; D. Haraway, "The Persistence of Vision," in K. Conboy, N. Medina, and S. Stanbury, eds., *Writing on the Body: Female Embodiment and Feminist Theory*, New York, Columbia University Press, 1997, pp. 283–95.

29 Jay, *Downcast Eyes*, p. 591.

30 On the invention of the kaleidoscope by Brewster and its subsequent role as a symbol for "the multiplicity of life," see J. Crary, *Techniques of the Observer: On Vision and Modernity in the Nineteenth Century*, Cambridge, MA, MIT Press, 1994, pp. 113–16.

31 E. de Condillac, *Treatise on the Sensations*, G. Carr, trans., London, Favil, 1930.

32 As Laura grew up her faculties of taste and smell improved and her world expanded from one sense to three. M.S. Lamson, *Life and Education of Laura Dewey Bridgman*, Boston, MA, Houghton Mifflin, 1881, p. 107.

33 Ibid., p. 26.

34 Ibid., p. 75.

35 Ibid., pp. 167–8.

36 Ibid., p. 294.

37 Ibid., p. 185; M. Howe and F.H. Hall, *Laura Bridgman: Dr. Howe's Famous Pupil and What He Taught Her*, Boston, Little, Brown and Company, 1903, pp. 175, 307.

38 Ibid., p. 320; Lamson, *Laura Dewey Bridgman*, pp. 255, 259, 360.

39 Ibid., p. 303. In *Physiological Aesthetics* Grant Allen presents a highly visualist understanding of poetry:

     Poetry is mainly pictorial, and much of its art is, to use the well-chosen modern phrase, word-painting. . . . Touches yield so little pleasure or pain [?], and taste and [smell] are so little revivable, that they hardly occupy any appreciable place in the colour-box of the versifier.

G. Allen, *Physiological Aesthetics*, London, Henry S. King, 1877, p. 258.

40 L.H. Sigourney, "Laura Bridgman," cited by Lamson, *Laura Dewey Bridgman*, p. 83.

41 Howe and Hall, *Laura Bridgman*, pp. 157, 287. Charles Dickens describes his visit with Laura Bridgman in *American Notes*, New York, Charles Scribner's Sons, 1911, pp. 33–52.

42 C. Rocheleau, *Hors de sa prison: Extraordinaire histoire de Ludivine Lachance, l'infirme des infirmes, sourde, muette et aveugle*, Montreal, Arbour and Dupont, 1927, p. 123.

43 H. Keller, *The World I Live In*, New York, Century, 1909, p. 7.

44 J.M. Kennedy, *Drawing and the Blind: Pictures to Touch*, New Haven, CT, Yale University Press, 1993, pp. 286–7.

45 Ibid., pp. 57–283.

46 Ibid., p. 255.

47 Cited by Morgan, *Molyneux's Question*, p. 48.

48 B.W. White, F.A. Saunders, L. Scadden, P. Bach-y-rita, and C.C. Collins, "Seeing with the Skin," *Perception and Psychophysics*, 1970, vol. 7, no. 1, pp. 23–7.

49 Ibid.

50 R. Arnheim, *Visual Thinking*, Berkeley, University of California Press, 1969, p. 18.

51 See, for example, the varied collection of small aesthetic objects catalogued in A.H. Eaton, *Beauty for the Sighted and the Blind*, New York, St. Martin's Press, 1959.

52 Keller, *World I Live In*, pp. 6–7.

53 See J. Fisher, "Museums and Mediation: Locating the Exhibition Experience," MA thesis, Montreal, Concordia University, 1988.

54 L. Heschong, *Thermal Delight in Architecture*, Cambridge, MA, MIT Press, 1990, pp. 16–17.

55 G. Vorreiter, "Theatre of Touch," *The Architectural Review*, 1989, no. 185, pp. 66–9; M. Wagner, "Theater of Touch," *Interiors*, 1989, no. 149, pp. 98–9.

56 R. Arnheim, "Perceptual Aspects of Art for the Blind," in R. Arnheim *To the Rescue of Art: Twenty-Six Essays*, Berkeley, University of California Press, 1992, p. 136.

57 Keller, *World I Live In*, p. 65.

58 J.-K. Huysmans, *Against Nature*, R. Baldick, trans., Harmondsworth, England, Penguin, 1959, p. 119.

59 Cited by E. Starkie, *Baudelaire*, London, Faber and Faber, 1933, p. 235.

60 G.E. Lessing, *Laocoon: An Essay upon the Limits of Painting and Poetry*, E. Frothingham, trans., New York, Noonday Press, 1957, p. 167.

61 W. Hooper, ed., *All My Road Before Me: The Diary of C.S. Lewis, 1922–1927*, San Diego, CA, Harcourt Brace Jovanovich, 1991, p. 344.

62 "Most people" wrote Helen Keller, "are smell-blind-and-deaf." *World I Live In*, p. 76.

63 C. Classen, D. Howes, and A. Synnott, *Aroma: The Cultural History of Smell*, London, Routledge, 1994.

64 Ibid., p. 78.

65 Ibid., p. 72.

66 Ibid., p. 69.

67 John Macy, cited in H. Keller, *The Story of My Life*, New York, Grosset and Dunlap, 1902, p. 293.

68 P. Süskind, *Perfume: The Story of a Murderer*, J.E. Woods, trans., New York, Alfred A. Knopf, 1986.

69 Lamson, *Laura Dewey Bridgman*, p. xxi.

70 Keller, *World I Live In*, p. 76.

71   What one of the manual arts or trades taught in the school for the blind is conducive either to aesthetic appreciation or to aesthetic expression? . . . Weaving has no pattern of tactual beauty and simplicity. . . . Basketry, reedwork, and caning are still more unpleasant.

T.D. Cutsforth, *The Blind in School and Society*, New York, American Foundation for the Blind, 1951, p. 177.

72   P. Villey, *The World of the Blind: A Psychological Study*, New York, Macmillan, 1930, p. 319.

73   W.B. Carpenter, *Principles of Mental Physiology*, London, Henry S. King and Co., 1874, p. 141.

74   In his philosophy of art Johann Gottfried Herder imagined haptic sensations to offer the original sensory ground necessary for a visual aesthetics. The art historian Alois Reigl presented a sensory evolution of art, with ancient Egyptian aesthetics being haptic, ancient Greek aesthetics haptic-visual, and Christian European aesthetics visual. Révész, *Psychology and Art of the Blind*, pp. 287–8.

75   V. Lowenfeld, *The Nature of Creative Activity*, O.A. Oeser, trans., London, Routledge and Kegan Paul, 1959, p. 139.

76   On Viktor Lowenfeld's theories of tactile art see R. Arnheim, "Victor Lowenfeld and Tactility," in R. Arnheim, *New Essays on the Psychology of Art*, Berkeley, University of California Press, 1986.

77   See C. Classen and D. Howes, "Making Sense of Culture: Anthropology as a Sensual Experience," *Etnofoor*, 1996, vol. 9, no. 2, pp. 86–95; D. Howes, ed., *The Varieties of Sensory Experience: A Sourcebook in the Anthropology of the Senses*, Toronto, University of Toronto Press, 1991.

78   F. Schiller, *On the Aesthetic Education of Man*, E.M. Wilkinson and L.A. Willoughby, eds. and trans., Oxford, Clarendon, 1982, p. 195. Comparisons of the role of touch across cultures abound. See, for example, A. Synnott, *The Body Social: Symbolism, Self and Society*, London, Routledge, 1993, pp. 170–3.

79   V. de l'Isle-Adam, *Tomorrow's Eve*, R. Martin Adams, trans., Urbana, University of Illinois Press, 1982, p. 15.

80   See, for example, G. Greer, *The Obstacle Race: The Fortunes of Women Painters and Their Work*, London, Secker and Warburg, 1979; R. Parker and G. Pollock, *Old Mistresses: Women, Art and Ideology*, London, Routledge and Kegan Paul, 1981.

81   J. Chicago, *The Dinner Party: A Symbol of Our Heritage*, Garden City, NY, Doubleday, 1979, p. 12. For other examples see R. Parker and G. Pollock, eds., *Framing Feminism: Art and the Women's Movement, 1970–1985*, London, Pandora, 1987.

82   *Tactile*, Quebec City, Musée du Québec, 1978, p. 12.

83   C. de Zegher, "Cecilia Vicuña's Ouvrage: Knot a Not, Notes as Knots," in G. Pollock, ed., *Generations and Geographies in the Visual Arts: Feminist Readings*, London, Routledge, 1996, p. 206.

84   F.T. Marinetti, "Tactilism," in R.W. Flint, ed., *Marinetti: Selected Writings*, R.W. Flint and A.A. Coppotelli, trans., New York, Farrar, Straus, and Giroux, 1972, p. 110.

85   Ibid., pp. 117–20.

86   F.T. Marinetti, *The Futurist Cookbook*, L. Chamberlain, ed., S. Brill, trans., San Francisco, CA, Bedford Arts, 1989, p. 77.

87   Ibid., pp. 172–3.

88   J. Hendricks, ed., *The Fluxus Codex*, New York, The Gilbert and Lila Silverman Fluxus Collection in association with Harry N. Abrams, 1988.

89   See, for example, J. Fisher, "Relational Sense: Towards a Haptic Aesthetics," *Parachute*, 1997, no. 87, pp. 4–11; J. Drobnick, "Reveries, Assaults and Evaporating Presences: Olfactory Dimensions in Contemporary Art," *Parachute*, 1998, no. 89, pp. 10–19.

90 F.T. Marinetti, "Electrical War," in R.W. Flint, ed., *Marinetti: Selected Writings*, R.W. Flint and A.A. Coppotelli, trans., New York, Farrar, Straus, and Giroux, 1972, p. 106. Marinetti went so far as to imagine "the possibility of broadcasting nutritious radio waves" in future years. *Futurist Cookbook*, p. 67.

91 For example, M. Merleau-Ponty, *Phenomenology of Perception*, C. Smith, trans., London, Routledge and Kegan Paul, 1996, pp. 227–30.

92 T. Eagleton, *The Ideology of the Aesthetic*, Oxford, Basil Blackwell, 1990.

93 G. Lista, *Futurism*, C.L. Clark, trans., New York, Universe Books, 1986, p. 24. The Fascists, of course, would also prove to be unreceptive to new artistic practices.

94 J. Kristeva, "Julia Kristeva in Conversation with Rosalind Coward," in L. Appignansesi, ed., *Desire*, London, Institute of Contemporary Arts, 1984, p. 23.

95 G.L. Ullmer, *Applied Grammatology: Post(e)-Pedagogy from Jacques Derrida to Joseph Beuys*, Baltimore, MD, Johns Hopkins University Press, 1985, pp. 34–5, 248.

96 The succession of visual logics within modern Western cultural history is examined in P. Virilio, *The Vision Machine*, J. Rose, trans., Bloomington, Indiana University Press, 1994 and B.M. Stafford, "Presuming Images and Consuming Words: The Visualization of Knowledge From the Enlightenment to Post-modernism," in J. Brewer and R. Porter, eds., *Consumption and the World of Goods*, London, Routledge, 1993, pp. 462–77.

97 On the displacement of touch in contemporary "technovisualism" see K. Robins, *Into the Image: Culture and Politics in the Field of Vision*, London, Routledge, 1996, pp. 29–33.

Bibliography

Albert, J.-P., *Odeurs de sainteté: la mythologie chrétienne des aromates*, Paris, Editions de l'Ecole des Hautes Etudes en Sciences Sociales, 1990.

Allen, G., *Physiological Aesthetics*, London, Henry S. King, 1877.

Allen, P., *The Concept of Woman: The Aristotelian Revolution, 750 BC–AD 1250*, Montreal, Eden Press, 1985.

Allen, P. and Salvatore, F., "Lucrezia Marinelli and Woman's Identity in Late Italian Renaissance," *Renaissance and Reformation*, 1992, vol. 28, no. 4, pp. 5–39.

Argüelles, J.A., *Charles Henry and the Formation of a Psychophysical Aesthetic*, Chicago, University of Chicago Press, 1972.

Aristotle, *Generation of Animals*, A.L. Peck, trans., Cambridge, MA, Harvard University Press, 1963.

Arnheim, R., *Visual Thinking*, Berkeley, University of California Press, 1969.

—— "Victor Lowenfeld and Tactility," in R. Arnheim, *New Essays on the Psychology of Art*, Berkeley, University of California Press, 1986.

—— "Perceptual Aspects of Art for the Blind," in R. Arnheim, *To the Rescue of Art: Twenty-Six Essays*, Berkeley, University of California Press, 1992, pp. 133–43.

Arnold, T., ed., *Select English Works of John Wyclif*, 3 vols., Oxford, Clarendon, 1869.

Astell, M., "Letter to John Norris of Bemerton," in R. Perry, *The Celebrated Mary Astell: An Early English Feminist*, Chicago, University of Chicago Press, 1986.

Atchley, E., *A History of the Use of Incense in Divine Worship*, London, Longmans, Green, and Co., 1909.

Babbitt, I., *The New Laokoon: An Essay on the Confusion of the Arts*, Boston, MA, Houghton Mifflin, 1910.

Bacci, P., *The Life of St. Philip Neri*, 2 vols., F. Antrobus, trans., London, Kegan Paul, Trench, Trubner, and Co., 1902.

Baer, R.A., *Philo's Use of the Categories Male and Female*, Leiden, E.J. Brill, 1970.

Bailey, M.L., *Milton and Jakob Boehme: A Study of German Mysticism in Seventeenth-Century England*, New York, Haskell House, 1964.

Bakhtin, M., *Rabelais and His World*, H. Iswolsky, trans., Bloomington, Indiana University Press, 1984.

Balakian, A., *Literary Origins of Surrealism: A New Mysticism in French Poetry*, New York, New York University Press, 1947.

—— *The Symbolist Movement: A Critical Appraisal*, New York, New York University Press, 1977.

Baldick, R., *The Life of J.-K. Huysmans*, Oxford, Clarendon Press, 1955.

Balla, G., "The Futurist Universe," in U. Apollonio, ed., *Futurist Manifestos*, London, Thames and Hudson, 1973.

Balzac, H. de, *Seraphita*, K. Prescott Wormeley, trans., Boston, Roberts Brothers, 1889.

Barbey D'Aurevilly, J., *Les Bas-bleus*, Paris, Société Générale de Librairie Catholique, 1878.

Barker-Benfield, G.J., *The Culture of Sensibility: Sex and Society in Eighteenth-Century Britain*, Chicago, University of Chicago Press, 1992.

Barthes, R., *Sade, Fourier, Loyola*, R. Miller, trans., Berkeley, University of California Press, 1989.

Baudelaire, C., "L'Art romantique," in C. Baudelaire, *Curiosités esthétiques: l'art romantique, et autres ouevres critiques*, Paris, Editions Garnier Frères, 1962.

—— *Artificial Paradise: On Hashish and Wine as Means of Expanding Individuality*, E. Fox, trans., New York, Herder and Herder, 1971.

—— *Selected Poems*, J. Richardson, trans., Harmondsworth, England, Penguin, 1975.

—— *The Painter of Modern Life and Other Essays*, New York, Garland, 1978.

—— *Les Fleurs du mal*, Paris, Classiques Garnier, 1994.

Beauvais, P. de, *A Medieval Book of Beasts*, G.R. Mermier, trans., Lampeter, Wales, Edwin Mellen Press, 1992.

Beecher, J., *The Visionary and His World*, Berkeley, University of California Press, 1986.

Benjamin, W., "The Work of Art in the Age of Mechanical Reproduction," in W. Benjamin, *Illuminations*, H. Zohn, trans., New York, Schocken Books, 1968.

Berleant, A., "Toward a Phenomenological Aesthetics of Environment," in D. Ihde and H. Silverman, eds., *Descriptions*, Albany, State University of New York Press, 1985, pp. 112–28.

Bernard of Clairvaux, *On the Song of Songs*, 4 vols., K. Walsh, trans., Spencer, MA, Cistercian Publications, 1971.

Bernheimer, C., "Huysmans: Writing Against (Female) Nature," in S.R. Suleiman, ed., *The Female Body in Western Culture*, Cambridge, MA, Harvard University Press, 1986, pp. 373–86.

Bertocci, A.P., *From Symbolism to Baudelaire*, Carbondale, Southern Illinois University Press, 1964.

Bloch, R.H., *Medieval Misogyny and the Invention of Western Romantic Love*, Chicago, University of Chicago Press, 1991.

Boccaccio, G., *The Corbaccio*, A.K. Cassell, ed. and trans., Urbana, University of Illinois Press, 1975.

Boccioni, U., "Futurist Painting and Sculpture," in U. Apollonio, ed., *Futurist Manifestos*, London, Thames and Hudson, 1973.

Boccioni, U., Carrà, C., Russolo, L., Balla, G., and Severini, G., "Manifesto of the Futurist Painters," in U. Apollonio, ed., *Futurist Manifestos*, London, Thames and Hudson, 1973.

Bodin, J., *De la démonomanie des sorciers*, Paris, Iacques du Puys, 1580.

Boehme, J., *The Three Principles of the Divine Essence*, J. Sparrow, trans., London, John M. Watkins, 1910.

—— *The Signature of All Things*, London, J.M. Dent, 1934.

—— *The Aurora*, J. Sparrow, trans., London, John M. Watkins and James Clarke, 1960.

—— *Mysterium Magnum*, J. Sparrow, trans., London, John M. Watkins, 1965.

Boer, P.A.H. de, "Job 39:25," in P. Ackroyd and B. Lindars, eds., *Words and Meaning: Essays Presented to David Winston Thomas*, Cambridge, Cambridge University Press, 1968.

Bordo, S., *The Flight to Objectivity: Essays on Cartesianism and Culture*, Albany, State University of New York Press, 1987.

Bowerbank, S., "The Spider's Delight: Margaret Cavendish and the 'Female' Imagination," in K. Farrell, E.H. Hageman, and A.F. Kinney, eds., *Women in the Renaissance: Selections from English Literary Renaissance*, Amherst, MA, University of Massachusetts Press, 1971.

Bowers, F., *Scriabin: A Biography of the Russian Composer*, 2 vols., Tokyo, Kodansha, 1969.

Bowlby, R., *Just Looking: Consumer Culture in Dreiser, Gissing and Zola*, New York, Methuen, 1985.

Bradstreet, A., "The Prologue," in A. Stanford, ed., *The Women Poets in English*, New York, McGraw-Hill, 1972.

Brant, C. and Purkiss, D., eds., *Women, Texts and Histories: 1575–1760*, London, Routledge, 1992.

Breton, A., *What Is Surrealism?*, D. Gascoyne, trans., London, Faber and Faber, 1936.

—— *Anthologie de l'humour noir*, Montreuil, SIP, 1966.

—— "Second Manifesto of Surrealism," in A. Breton, *Manifestos of Surrealism*, R. Seaver and H.R. Lane, trans., Ann Arbor, University of Michigan Press, 1969.

—— *Ode to Charles Fourier*, K. White, trans., London, Cape Goliard, 1969.

—— "Genesis and Perspective of Surrealism in the Plastic Arts," in F. Rosemont, ed., *What is Surrealism?*, London, Pluto Press, 1978.

Brodey, W., "Sound and Space," *New Outlook for the Blind*, 1965, vol. 59, no. 1, pp. 1–4.

Bruyn, L. de, *Woman and the Devil in Sixteenth-Century Literature*, Tisbury, England, Compton Press, 1979.

Bryson, N., *Vision and Painting: The Logic of the Gaze*, New Haven, CT, Yale University Press, 1983.

—— "The Gaze in the Expanded Field," in H. Foster, ed., *Vision and Visuality*, Seattle, WA, Bay Press, 1988, pp. 87–108.

Buckberrough, S.A., *Robert Delaunay: The Discovery of Simultanaeity*, Ann Arbor, MI, UMI Research Press, 1982.

Buffon, G.L.L., *Natural History of Man, the Globe, and of Quadrupeds*, New York, Leavitt and Allen, 1857.

Bullough, V.L. *The Development of Medicine as a Profession*, Basil, S. Karger, 1966.

Burke, P., *Popular Culture in Early Modern Europe*, London, Temple Smith, 1978.

Burns, E.J., *Bodytalk: When Women Speak in Old French Literature*, Philadelphia, University of Pennsylvania Press, 1993.

Burtt, E.A, *The Metaphysical Foundations of Modern Physical Science*, rev. edn, London, Routledge and Kegan Paul, 1950.

Bynum, C.W., *Holy Feast and Holy Fast: The Religious Significance of Food to Medieval Women*, Berkeley, University of California Press, 1987.

Calvin, J., *Commentary on the Book of the Prophet Isaiah*, vol. 1, J. Pringle, trans., Grand Rapids, MI, Baker Book House, 1981.

Camden, C., *The Elizabethan Woman*, Mamaroneck, NY, Paul P. Appel, 1975.

Camporesi, P., *The Incorruptible Flesh: Bodily Mutilation and Mortification in Religion and Folklore*, T. Croft-Murray and H. Elsom, trans., Cambridge, Cambridge University Press, 1988.

—— *Bread of Dreams: Food and Fantasy in Early Modern Europe*, D. Gentilcore, trans., Cambridge, Polity Press, 1989.

—— *Fear of Hell: Images of Damnation and Salvation in Early Modern Europe*, L. Byatt, trans., Cambridge, Polity Press, 1991.

—— *The Anatomy of the Senses: Natural Symbols in Medieval and Early Modern Europe*, A. Cameron, trans., Cambridge, Polity Press, 1994.

Carnandet, J., ed., *Acta Sanctorum*, vol. 11, Paris, Victor Palmé, 1866.

Carpenter, W.B., *Principles of Mental Physiology*, London, Henry S. King and Co., 1874.

Carrà, C., "The Painting of Sounds, Noises and Smells," in U. Apollonio, ed., *Futurist Manifestos*, London, Thames and Hudson, 1973.

Carrière, J.-C., *The Secret Language of Film*, J. Leggatt, trans., New York, Pantheon Books, 1994.

Carrington, L., *The Hearing Trumpet*, New York, St. Martin's Press, 1974.

—— *The Stone Door*, New York, St. Martin's Press, 1976.

—— *Down Below*, Chicago, Black Swan Press, 1983.

—— "As They Rode Along the Edge," in L. Carrington, *The Seventh Horse and Other Stories*, K. Talbot and A. Kerrigen, trans., London, Virago, 1989.

Catherine of Genoa, "The Spiritual Dialogue," in *Catherine of Genoa*, S. Hughes, trans., New York, Paulist Press, 1979.

Catherine of Siena, *The Dialogue*, S. Noeffke, trans., New York, Paulist Press, 1980.

Cavendish, M., "A True Relation of my Birth, Breeding and Life," in M. Cavendish, *The Life of William Cavendish*, C.H. Firth, ed., London, George Routledge and Sons, n.d., pp. 155–78.

—— *The Life of William Cavendish*, C.H. Firth, ed., London, George Routledge and Sons, n.d.

—— *The Philosophical and Physical Opinions*, London, J. Martin and J. Allestrye, 1655.

—— *The World's Olio*, London, J. Martin and J. Allestrye, 1655.

—— *Nature's Pictures Drawn by Fancies Pencil to the Life*, London, J. Martin and J. Allestrye, 1656.

—— *Orations of Divers Sorts*, London, n.p., 1662.

—— *Playes*, London, John Martyn, James Allestry and Tho. Dicas, 1662.

—— *Philosophical Letters*, London, n.p., 1664.

—— *Grounds of Natural Philosophy*, London, A. Maxwell, 1668.

—— *Plays, Never Before Printed*, London, A. Maxwell, 1668.

—— *Observations Upon Experimental Philosophy*, London, A. Maxwell, 1668.

—— *Sociable Letters*, Menston, England, Scolar Press, 1969.

—— *Poems and Fancies*, Menston, England, Scolar Press, 1972.

—— *The Description of A New World Called The Blazing World*, K. Lilley, ed., London, William Pickering, 1992.

Caws, M.A., "Ladies Shot and Painted: Female Embodiment in Surrealist Art," in S. Rubin Suleiman, ed., *The Female Body in Western Culture*, Cambridge, MA, Harvard University Press, 1985.

Chadwick, W., *Women Artists and the Surrealist Movement*, Boston, Little, Brown, 1985.

—— *Women, Art, and Society*, rev. edn, London, Thames and Hudson, 1996.

Chicago, J., *The Dinner Party: A Symbol of Our Heritage*, Garden City, NY, Doubleday, 1979.

Cixous, H. and Clément, C., *The Newly Born Woman*, B. Wing, trans., Minneapolis, MN, University of Minnesota Press, 1986.

Classen, C., *Worlds of Sense: Exploring the Senses in History and Across Cultures*, London, Routledge, 1993.

Classen, C. and Howes, D., "Making Sense of Culture: Anthropology as a Sensual Experience," *Etnofoor*, 1996, vol. 9, no. 2, pp. 86–95.

Classen, C., Howes, D., and Synnott, A., *Aroma: The Cultural History of Smell*, London, Routledge, 1994.

Cloud of Unknowing, The, J. Walsh, ed., New York, Paulist Press, 1981.

Clough, R.T., *Futurism*, New York, Philosophical Library, 1961.

Cobham Brewer, E., *A Dictionary of Miracles*, Detroit, MI, Gale Research Company, 1966.

Colgrave, B. and Mynors, R., eds., *Bede's Ecclesiastical History of the English People*, Oxford, Clarendon, 1969.

Condillac, E. de, *Treatise on the Sensations*, G. Carr, trans., London, Favil, 1930.

Conger, S.M., *Mary Wollstonecraft and the Language of Sensibility*, Rutherford, NJ, Farleigh Dickinson University Press, 1994.

Conybeare, F.C., *Myth, Magic and Morals: A Study of Christian Origins*, London, Watts and Co., 1910.

Corbin, A., *The Foul and the Fragrant: Odor and the French Social Imagination*, M. Kochan, R. Porter, and C. Prendergast, trans., Cambridge, MA, Harvard University Press, 1986.

Corradini, B. and Settimelli, E., "Weights, Measures and Prices of Artistic Genius," in U. Apollonio, ed., *Futurist Manifestos*, London, Thames and Hudson, 1973.

Coudert, A.P., "The Myth of the Improved Status of Protestant Women: The Case of the Witchcraze," in J.R. Brink, A.P. Coudert, and M.C. Horowitz, eds., *The Politics of Gender in Early Modern Europe*, Kirksville, MS, Sixteenth Century Journal Publishers, 1989, pp. 61–90.

Crary, J., *Techniques of the Observer: On Vision and Modernity in the Nineteenth Century*, Cambridge, MA, MIT Press, 1994.

Cutsforth, T.D., *The Blind in School and Society*, New York, American Foundation for the Blind, 1951.

Cytowic, R.E., *Synesthesia: A Union of the Senses*, New York, Springer-Verlag, 1989.

—— *The Man Who Tasted Shapes*, New York, Warner Books, 1993.

Dauphiné, C., *Rachilde*, Paris, *Mercure de France*, 1991.

Derrida, J., *Memoirs of the Blind: The Self-Portrait and Other Ruins*, P.-A. Brault and M. Naas, trans., Chicago, University of Chicago Press, 1993.

Detienne, M., *The Gardens of Adonis: Spices in Greek Mythology*, J. Lloyd, trans., Atlantic Highlands, NJ, The Humanities Press, 1977.

Dickens, C., *American Notes*, New York, Charles Scribner's Sons, 1911.

Dionysius the Areopagite, *The Mystical Theology and the Celestial Hierarchies*, Surrey, England, The Shrine of Wisdom, 1965.

Drobnick, J., "Reveries, Assaults and Evaporating Presences: Olfactory Dimensions in Contemporary Art," *Parachute*, 1998, no. 89, pp. 10–19.

Duncan, S.J., "An Impossible Ideal," in S.J. Duncan, *The Pool in the Desert*, Harmondsworth, England, Penguin, 1984.

Eagleton, T., *The Ideology of the Aesthetic*, Oxford, Basil Blackwell, 1990.

Easlea, B., *Witch Hunting, Magic and the New Philosophy: An Introduction to Debates of the Scientific Revolution 1450–1750*, Sussex, England, The Harvester Press, 1980.

Eaton, A.H., *Beauty for the Sighted and the Blind*, New York, St. Martin's Press, 1959.

Eliot, T.S., *Essays: Ancient and Modern*, New York, Harcourt, Brace, and Company, 1936.

Ellis, H., *Studies in the Psychology of Sex*, vol. 1, New York, Random House, 1942.

England, G., ed., *The Towneley Plays*, London, Oxford University Press for Early English Text Society, 1897.

Etiemble, R., *Le Sonnet des voyelles*, Paris, Gallimard, 1968.

Eusebius, *Ecclesiastical History*, R.J. Deferrari, trans., New York, Fathers of the Church, 1953.

Evenden Nagy, D., *Popular Medicine in Seventeenth-Century England*, Bowling Green, OH, Bowling Green State University Popular Press, 1988.

Feldman, J.R., *Gender on the Divide: The Dandy in Modernist Literature*, Ithaca, NY, Cornell University Press, 1993.

Fisher, J., "Museums and Mediation: Locating the Exhibition Experience," MA thesis, Montreal, Concordia University, 1988.

—— "Relational Sense: Towards a Haptic Aesthetics," *Parachute*, 1997, no. 87, pp. 4–11.

Flanagan, S., *Hildegard of Bingen: A Visionary Life*, London, Routledge, 1990.

Flaubert, G., *Salammbô*, Paris, Librairie Armand Colin, 1960.

Foster, H., ed., *Vision and Visuality*, Seattle, WA, Bay Press, 1988.

Foucault, M., *The Birth of the Clinic: An Archaeology of Medical Perception*, A.M. Sheridan Smith, trans., New York, Random House, 1975.

Fourier, C., *The Passions of the Human Soul, and Their Influence on Society and Civilization*, 2 vols., H. Doherty, trans., London, Hippolyte Baillière, 1851.

—— *Oeuvres complètes*, Paris, Editions Anthropos, 1967.

Fournival, R. de, *Master Richard's Bestiary of Love and Response*, J. Beer, trans., Berkeley, University of California Press, 1986.

Francis de Sales, *The Love of God: A Treatise*, V. Kerns, trans., Westminster, England, The Newman Press, 1962.

Friedlander, M., ed., *The Commentary of Ibn Ezra on Isaiah*, vol. 1, New York, Philip Feldheim, 1873.

Friedrich, C.J. and Blitzer, C., *The Age of Power*, Ithaca, NY, Cornell University Press, 1957.

Galen, *On the Usefulness of the Parts of the Body*, M.T. May, trans., Ithaca, NY, Cornell University Press, 1968.

Galileo Galilei, *Dialogue Concerning the Two Chief World Systems – Ptolemaic and Copernican*, S. Drake, trans., Berkeley, University of California Press, 1962.

Gauthier, X., *Surréalisme et sexualité*, Paris, Gallimard, 1971.

Gay, P., *The Enlightenment: An Interpretation. The Rise of Modern Paganism*, New York, Alfred Knopf, 1967.

Gerrish Nunn, P., *Victorian Women Artists*, London, The Women's Press, 1987.

Gibson, M., *The Symbolists*, New York, Harry N. Abrams, 1988.

Gilbert S.M. and Gubar, S., *The Madwoman in the Attic: The Woman Writer and the Nineteenth-Century Literary Imagination*, New Haven, CT, Yale University Press, 1979.

Ginzburg, C., *The Cheese and the Worms: The Cosmos of a Sixteenth-Century Miller*, J. Tedeschi and A. Tedeschi, trans., Harmondsworth, England, Penguin Books, 1987.

Goldwater, R., *Symbolism*, New York, Harper and Row, 1979.

Gould, S.J., *The Flamingo's Smile: Reflections in Natural History*, New York, W.W. Norton, 1985.

Grant, D., *Margaret the First*, London, Rupert Hart-Davis, 1957.

Greenberg, C., "On the Role of Nature in Modernist Painting," in C. Greenberg, *Art and Culture: Critical Essays*, Boston, MA, Beacon Press, 1965, pp. 171–83.

Greer, G., *The Obstacle Race: The Fortunes of Women Painters and Their Work*, London, Secker and Warburg, 1979.

Grosz, E., *Volatile Bodies: Towards a Corporeal Feminism*, Bloomington, Indiana University Press, 1994.

Guerin, P., ed., *Les Petites Bollandistes: Vies des saints*, 17 vols., Paris, Bloud et Barral, 1878.

Guillory, J., "Dalila's House: *Samson Agonistes* and the Sexual Division of Labor," in M.W. Ferguson, M. Quilligan, and N.J. Vickers, eds., *Rewriting the Renaissance: The Discourses of Sexual Difference in Early Modern Europe*, Chicago, University of Chicago Press, 1986, pp. 106–22.

Hale, R.D., "'Taste and See, for God is Sweet': Sensory Perception and Memory in Medieval Christian Mystical Experience," in A.C. Barlett, ed., *Vox Mystica: Essays on Medieval Mysticism*, Rochester, NY, D.S. Brewer, 1995, pp. 3–14.

Hallisey, M., *Venemous Woman: Fear of the Female in Literature*, New York, Greenwood Press, 1987.

Haraway, D., "The Persistence of Vision," in K. Conboy, N. Medina, and S. Stanbury, eds., *Writing on the Body: Female Embodiment and Feminist Theory*, New York, Columbia University Press, 1997, pp. 283–95.

Harry, M., *Trois Ombres: J.-K. Huysmans, Jules Lemaître, Anatole France*, Paris, Ernest Flammarion, 1932.

Harvey, S.A., "Incense Offerings in the Syriac *Transitus Mariae*: Ritual and Knowledge in Ancient Christianity," in A. Malherbe, F. Norris, and J. Thompson, eds., *The Early Church in its Context: Studies in Honor of Everett Ferguson*, Leiden, E.J. Brill, 1998.

——"Olfactory Knowing: Signs of Smell in the *Vitae* of Simeon Stylites," in G.J. Reinink and A.C. Klugkist, eds., *Change and Continuity in Syriac Christianity: A Festschrift for H.J.W. Drijvers*, Louvain, Peeters Press, forthcoming.

—— "St. Ephrem on the Scent of Salvation," *Journal of Theological Studies*, 1998, vol. 49, no. 1.

Hassig, D., *Medieval Bestiaries: Text, Image, Ideology*, Cambridge, Cambridge University Press, 1995.

Hawthorne, M.C., "*Monsieur Venus*: A Critique of Gender Roles," *Nineteenth-Century French Studies*, 1987/88, vol. 16, nos. 1 and 2, pp. 162–79.

Hayman, R., *Sartre: A Life*, New York, Simon and Schuster, 1987.

Hebreo, L., *Diálogos de Amor*, M. de Burgos Núñez, ed., "El Inca" Garcilaso de la Vega, trans., Seville, Padilla Libros, 1992.

Helland, J., "Daughter of the Minotaur," Ph.D. Dissertation, Victoria, BC, University of Victoria, 1984.

—— "Surrealism and Esoteric Feminism in the Paintings of Leonora Carrington," *Canadian Art Review* 1989, 16, pp 53–61.

—— *The Studios of Frances and Margaret Macdonald*, Manchester, Manchester University Press, 1996.

Hendricks, J., ed., *The Fluxus Codex*, New York, The Gilbert and Lila Silverman Fluxus Collection in association with Harry N. Abrams, 1988.

Hendricks, M. and Parker, P., eds., *Women, "Race," and Writing in the Early Modern Period*, London, Routledge, 1994.

Herrick, R., *The Poetical Works of Robert Herrick*, L.C. Martin, ed., Oxford, Clarendon, 1956.

Herz, D.M., *The Tuning of the Word: The Musico-Literary Poetics of the Symbolist Movement*, Carbondale and Edwardsville, Southern Illinois University Press, 1987.

Heschong, L., *Thermal Delight in Architecture*, Cambridge, MA, MIT Press, 1990.

Hildegard of Bingen, *Liber simplicis medicinae*, in J.-P. Migne, ed., *Patrologiae cursus completus: series latina*, vol. 197, Paris, Migne, 1864, pp. 1125–1352.

—— *Causae et curae*, P. Kaiser, ed., Leipzig, 1903.

—— *Scivias*, B. Hozeski, trans., Santa Fe, NM, Bear and Company, 1986.

—— *Book of Divine Works with Letters and Songs*, M. Fox, ed., Santa Fe, NM, Bear and Company, 1987.

—— *Symphonia: A Critical Edition of the Symphonia armonie celestium revelationum*, B. Newman, ed., Ithaca, NY, Cornell University Press, 1988.

—— *The Book of the Rewards of Life*, B. Hozeski, trans., New York, Garland, 1994.

Hill, B., *Women, Work, and Sexual Politics in Eighteenth-Century England*, Montreal, McGill-Queen's University Press, 1994.

Hindsley, L., *Margaret Ebner: Major Works*, New York, Paulist Press, 1993.

Hippocrates, *Airs, Waters, Places*, W.H.S. Jones, trans., Cambridge, MA, Harvard University Press, 1923.

Hippolytus, *Philosophumena*, vol. 2, F. Legge, trans., London, Society for Promoting Christian Knowledge, 1921.

Hooper, W., ed., *All My Road Before Me: The Diary of C.S. Lewis, 1922–1927*, San Diego, Harcourt Brace Jovanovich, 1991.

Horkheimer, M. and Adorno, T.W., *Dialectic of Enlightenment*, J. Cumming, trans., New York, Herder and Herder, 1972.

Howe, M. and Hall, F.H., *Laura Bridgman: Dr. Howe's Famous Pupil and What He Taught Her*, Boston, Little, Brown, and Company, 1903.

Howes, D., "Controlling Textuality: A Call for a Return to the Senses," *Anthropologica*, 1990, vol. 32, no. 1, pp. 55–73.

——, ed., *The Varieties of Sensory Experience: A Sourcebook in the Anthropology of the Senses*, Toronto, University of Toronto Press, 1991.

Hughes, M.J., *Women Healers in Medieval Life and Literature*, Freeport, NY, Books for Libraries Press, 1943.

Huizinga, J., *The Waning of the Middle Ages*, F. Hopman, trans., London, Edward Arnold, 1948.

Hull, J.M., *Touching the Rock: An Experience of Blindness*, New York, Pantheon, 1990.

Hull, S.W., *Chaste, Silent and Obedient: English Books for Women, 1475–1640*, San Francisco, Huntingdon Library, 1982.

Hulten, P., ed., *Futurism and Futurisms*, New York, Abbeville, 1986.

Hunter, J., ed., *Milton's Samson Agonistes and Lycidas*, London, Longmans, Green, and Co., 1872.

Huntingdon, E., *The Character of Races*, New York, Scribner, 1925.

Huysmans, J.-K., *Saint Lydwine of Schiedam*, A. Hastings, trans., London, Kegan Paul, Trench, Trubner, and Co., 1923.

—— *The Cathedral*, C. Bell, trans., London, Kegan Paul, Trench, Trubner, and Co., 1925.

—— *Against Nature*, R. Baldick, trans., Harmondsworth, England, Penguin, 1959.

—— *Down Stream, and Other Works*, S. Putman, trans. and ed., New York, Howard Fertig, 1975.

Hyde, H.M., *Oscar Wilde*, New York, Farrar, Straus, and Giroux, 1975.

Ignatius of Loyola, *The Spiritual Exercises*, J. Morris, trans., London, Burns and Oates, 1952.

Imbert-Gourbeyre, A., *La Stigmatisation*, J. Bouflet, ed., Grenoble, France, Editions Jérôme Millon, 1996.

Irigaray, L., "Interview avec Luce Irigaray," in M.-F. Hans and G. Lapouge, eds., *Les Femmes, la pornographie et l'érotisme*, Paris, Editions du Seuil, 1978, pp. 43–58.

—— *Speculum of the Other Woman*, G.C. Gill, trans., Ithaca, NY, Cornell University Press, 1985.

—— *This Sex Which Is Not One*, C. Porter and C. Burke, trans., Ithaca, NY, Cornell University Press, 1985.

Isler, W., *Walter Pater: The Aesthetic Moment*, Cambridge, Cambridge University Press, 1987.

Jacquart, D. and Thomasset, C., *Sexuality and Medicine in the Middle Ages*, Princeton, NJ, Princeton University Press, 1988.

Janson, H.W., *Apes and Ape Lore in the Middle Ages and the Renaissance*, London, The Warburg Institute, 1952.

Jarocinski, S., *Debussy: Impressionism and Symbolism*, R. Myers, trans., London, Eulenburg Books, 1976.

Jarry, A., "Les Cinq sens," in A. Jarry, *Les Minutes de sable mémorial, Oeuvres complètes*, vol. 1, Paris, Gallimard, 1972, pp. 206–9.

Jay, M., "Scopic Regimes of Modernity," in H. Foster, ed., *Vision and Visuality*, Seattle, WA, Bay Press, 1988, pp. 3–23.

—— *Downcast Eyes: The Denigration of Vision in Twentieth-Century French Thought*, Berkeley, University of California Press, 1994.

Jean, M., *The History of Surrealist Painting*, S. Watson Taylor, trans., New York, Grove Press, 1960.

Jerome, St., "Life of St. Hilarion," in R.J. Deferrari, ed., *Early Christian Biographies*, Washington, DC, Fathers of the Church, Catholic University of America Press, 1952.

John of the Cross, "Spiritual Canticle," in *The Complete Works of Saint John of the Cross*, vol. 2, D. Lewis, trans., London, Longmans, Green, and Co., 1864.

Jones, A.R., "Writing the Body: Toward an Understanding of *l'Ecriture féminine*," in E. Showalter, ed., *The New Feminist Criticism: Essays on Women, Literature, and Theory*, New York, Pantheon, 1985, pp. 361–77.

—— "Surprising Fame: Renaissance Gender Ideologies and Women's Lyric," in N.K. Miller, ed., *The Poetics of Gender*, New York, Columbia University Press, 1986, pp. 74–95.

Jonson, B., *Epicoene or The Silent Woman*, L.A. Beaurline, ed., Lincoln, University of Nebraska Press, 1966.

Jordan, C., *Renaissance Feminism: Literary Texts and Political Models*, Ithaca, NY, Cornell University Press, 1990.

—— "Renaissance Women and the Question of Class," in J.G. Turner, ed., *Sexuality and Gender in Early Modern Europe: Institutions, Texts, Images*, Cambridge, Cambridge University Press, 1993, pp. 90–106.

Jordan, W.D., *White Over Black: American Attitudes Toward the Negro, 1550–1812*, Chapel Hill, University of North Carolina Press, 1968.

Jordanova, L., *Sexual Visions: Images of Gender in Science and Medicine between the Eighteenth and Twentieth Centuries*, New York, Harvester Wheatsheaf, 1989.

Jullian, P., *Prince of Aesthetes: Count Robert de Montesquiou, 1855–1921*, J. Haylock and F. King, trans., New York, The Viking Press, 1965.

—— *Dreamers of Decadence: Symbolist Painters of the 1890s*, R. Baldick, trans., New York, Praeger Publishers, 1971.

Kandinsky, W., *Concerning the Spiritual in Art and Painting in Particular*, M. Sadleir, trans., New York, George Wittenborn, 1947.

Kant, I., *Anthropology From a Pragmatic Point of View*, V.L. Dowdell, trans., Carbondale and Edwardsville, Southern Illinois University Press, 1978.

Kaplan, J., *The Art of Gustave Moreau: Theory, Style, and Content*, Ann Arbor, MI, UMI Research Press, 1982.

Kaplan, J.A., *Unexpected Journeys: The Art and Life of Remedios Varo*, New York, Abbeville Press, 1988.

Kaptainis, A., "Can the Band Play On?" *The Gazette*, Montreal, February 24, 1996.

Katz, B., "The Women of Futurism," *Woman's Art Journal*, 1986/7, vol. 7, pp. 3–13.

Keats, J., *The Poems of John Keats*, M. Allott, ed., London, Longman, 1970.

Keller, E.F., *Reflections on Gender and Science*, New Haven, CT, Yale University Press, 1985.

Keller, E.F. and Grontkowski, C.R., "The Mind's Eye," in S. Harding and M.B. Hintikka, eds., *Discovering Reality: Feminist Perspectives on Epistemology, Metaphysics, Methodology and Philosophy of Science*, Dordrecht, Netherlands, D. Reidel, 1983.

Keller, H., *The Story of My Life*, New York, Grosset and Dunlap, 1902.

—— *The World I Live In*, New York, Century, 1909.

Kelso, R., *Doctrine for the Lady of the Renaissance*, Urbana, University of Illinois Press, 1956.

Kempis, T. à, *St. Lydwine of Schiedam*, V. Scully, trans., London, Burns and Oates, 1912.

Kendall R. and Pollock, G., eds., *Dealing With Degas: Representations of Women and the Politics of Vision*, New York, Universe, 1992.

Kennedy, J.M., *Drawing and the Blind: Pictures to Touch*, New Haven, CT, Yale University Press, 1993.

Kern, S., "Olfactory Ontology and Scented Harmonies: On the History of Smell," *Journal of Popular Culture*, 1974, vol. 7, no. 4, pp. 816–24.

Keynes, G. *The Life of William Harvey*, Oxford, Clarendon Press, 1966.

King, M., "The Sacramental Witness of Christina *Mirabilis*: The Mystic Growth of a Fool for Christ's Sake," in L.T. Shank and J.A. Nichols, eds., *Medieval Religious Women II: Peaceweavers*, Kalamazoo, MI, Cistercian Publications, 1987, pp. 145–64.

Kingcaid, R.A., *Neurosis and Narrative: The Decadent Short Fiction of Proust, Lorrain and Rachilde*, Carbondale and Edwardsville, University of Illinois Press, 1992.

Kneller, J., "Discipline and Silence: Women and Imagination in Kant's Theory of Taste," in H. Hein and C. Korsmeyer, eds., *Aesthetics in Feminist Perspective*, Bloomington, Indiana University Press, 1993, pp. 179–92.

Knox, J., *The Political Writings of John Knox*, M.A. Breslow, ed., Washington, Folger Books, 1985.

Kramer, H. and Sprenger, J., *The Malleus Maleficarum of Heinrich Kramer and James Sprenger*, M. Summers, ed. and trans, Salem, NH, Ayer, 1948.

Kristeva, J., "Julia Kristeva in Conversation with Rosalind Coward," in L. Appignansesi, ed., *Desire*, London, Institute of Contemporary Arts, 1984.

Kuenzli, R.E., "Surrealism and Misogyny," in M.A. Caws, R.E. Kuenzli, and G. Raaberg, eds., *Surrealism and Women*, Cambridge, MA, MIT Press, 1991.

Labé, L., "To Mademoiselle Clémence de Bourges of Lyon," in K.M. Wilson, ed., *Women Writers of the Renaissance and Reformation*, Athens, University of Georgia Press, 1987.

Labriolle, R. de, *Benoîte la bergère de Notre-Dame du Laus*, Gap, France, Louis-Jean, 1977.

Lamson, M.S., *Life and Education of Laura Dewey Bridgman*, Boston, MA, Houghton Mifflin, 1881.

Laqueur, T., *Making Sex: Body and Gender from the Greeks to Freud*, Cambridge, MA, Harvard University Press, 1990.

Lawrence, S.C., "Educating the Senses: Students, Teachers and Medical Rhetoric in Eighteenth-Century London," in W.F. Bynum and R. Porter, eds., *Medicine and the Five Senses*, Cambridge, Cambridge University Press, 1993, pp. 154–78.

Lea, H.C., *Materials Toward a History of Witchcraft*, 3 vols., New York, Thomas Yoseloff, 1957.

Le Breton, D., *Anthropologie du corps et modernité*, Paris, Presses Universitaires de France, 1990.

Le Chapelain, A., *The Art of Courtly Love*, J.J. Parry, trans., New York, Frederick Ungar, 1941.

Le Double, A.-F., *Rabelais: Anatomiste et physiologiste*, Paris, Ernest Leroux, 1899.

Leppert, R., *The Sight of Sound: Music, Representation and the History of the Body*, Berkeley, University of California Press, 1993.

Lessing, G.E., *Laocoon: An Essay upon the Limits of Painting and Poetry*, E. Frothingham, trans., New York, Noonday Press, 1957.

Leuba, J.H., *The Psychology of Religious Mysticism*, New York, Harcourt, Brace, and Company, 1925.

Levin, D.M., ed., *Modernity and the Hegemony of Vision*, Berkeley, University of California Press, 1993.

Lingua, in W.C. Hazlitt, ed., *A Select Collection of Old English Plays*, New York, Benjamin Bloom, 1964.

L'Isle-Adam, V. de, *Tomorrow's Eve*, R. Martin Adams, trans., Urbana, University of Illinois Press, 1982.

Lista, G., *Futurism*, C.L. Clark, trans., New York, Universe Books, 1986.

Lloyd, G., *The Man of Reason: "Male" and "Female" in Western Philosophy*, London, Methuen, 1984.

Lowenfeld, V., *The Nature of Creative Activity*, O.A. Oeser, trans., London, Routledge and Kegan Paul, 1959.

Lukacher, M., *Maternal Fictions: Stendhal, Sand, Rachilde, and Bataille*, Durham, NC, Duke University Press, 1994.

Luther, M., "The Magnificat," in *Luther's Works*, vol. 21, J. Peliken, ed., A. Steinhaeuser, trans., St. Louis, MI, Concordia, 1956.

—— "The Table Talk," in *Luther's Works*, vol. 54, T.G. Tappert, trans. and ed., Philadelphia, PA, Fortress Press, 1967.

MacCarthy, B.G., *The Female Pen: Women Writers and Novelists, 1621–1818*, New York, New York University Press, 1994.

McCulloch, F., *Medieval Latin and French Bestiaries*, Chapel Hill, University of North Carolina Press, 1962.

McDannell, C. and Lang, B., *Heaven: A History*, New Haven, CT, Yale University Press, 1988.

McGrath, F.C., *The Sensible Spirit: Walter Pater and the Modernist Paradigm*, Tampa, University of South Florida Press, 1986.

Maclean, I., *The Renaissance Notion of Woman: A Study in the Fortunes of Scholasticism and Medical Science in European Intellectual Life*, Cambridge, Cambridge University Press, 1980.

Mallarmé, S., "Crisis in Poetry," in *Mallarmé: Selected Prose, Poems, Essays, and Letters*, B. Cook, trans., Baltimore, MD, Johns Hopkins University Press, 1956.

Manilius, *Astronomica*, G.P. Goold, trans., London, William Heinemann, 1977.

Malory, T., *Le Morte d'Arthur*, M. Oskar Sommer, ed., London, D. Nutt, 1889.

Marcus, J., "Still Practice, A/Wrested Alphabet: Toward a Feminist Aesthetic," in S. Benstock, ed., *Feminist Issues in Literary Scholarship*, Bloomington, Indiana University Press, 1987, pp. 79–97.

Marinetti, F.T., "Against *Amore* and Parliamentarianism", in R.W. Flint, ed., *Marinetti: Selected Writings*, R.W. Flint and A.A. Coppotelli, trans., New York, Farrar, Straus, and Giroux, 1972.

—— "Electrical War," in R.W. Flint, ed., *Marinetti: Selected Writings*, R.W. Flint and A.A. Coppotelli, trans., New York, Farrar, Straus, and Giroux, 1972.

—— "Let's Murder the Moonshine," in R.W. Flint, ed., *Marinetti: Selected Writings*, R.W. Flint and A.A. Coppotelli, trans., New York, Farrar, Straus, and Giroux, 1972.

—— "Tactilism," in R.W. Flint, ed., *Marinetti: Selected Writings*, R.W. Flint and A.A. Coppotelli, trans., New York, Farrar, Straus, and Giroux, 1972.

—— "Destruction of Syntax – Imagination Without Strings – Words-In-Freedom," in U. Apollonio, ed., *Futurist Manifestos*, London, Thames and Hudson, 1973.

—— "The Founding and Manifesto of Futurism," in U. Apollonio, ed., *Futurist Manifestos*, London, Thames and Hudson, 1973.

—— "Geometric and Mechanical Splendour and the Numerical Sensibility," in U. Apollonio, ed., *Futurist Manifestos*, London, Thames and Hudson, 1973.

—— "The Variety Theatre," in U. Apollonio, ed., *Futurist Manifestos*, London, Thames and Hudson, 1973.

—— "Nous renions nos maîtres les symbolistes, derniers amants de la lune," in F.T. Marinetti, *Le Futurisme*, Lausanne, L'Age D'Homme, 1980.

—— *The Futurist Cookbook*, L. Chamberlain, ed., S. Brill, trans., San Francisco, Bedford Arts, 1989.

—— Settimelli, E. and Corra, B., "The Futurist Synthetic Theatre," in U. Apollonio, ed., *Futurist Manifestos*, London, Thames and Hudson, 1973.

Markham, G., *The English Housewife*, M.R. Best, ed., Montreal, McGill-Queens University Press, 1986.

Marks, L.E., *The Unity of the Senses: Interrelations among the Modalities*, New York, Academic Press, 1978.

Martensen, H.L., *Jacob Boehme*, T. Rhys Evans, trans., New York, Harper and Brothers, 1949.

Martensen, R., "The Transformation of Eve: Women's Bodies, Medicine and Culture in Early Modern Europe," in R. Porter and M. Teich, eds., *Sexual Knowledge, Sexual Science: The History of Attitudes to Sexuality*, Cambridge, Cambridge University Press, 1994, pp. 107–33.

Martin, L.C., ed., *The Poetical Works of Robert Herrick*, Oxford, Clarendon, 1956.

Martin, M.W., *Futurist Art and Theory: 1909–1915*, New York, Hacker Art Books, 1978.

Masham, D., *Occasional Thoughts In Reference to a Vertuous or Christian Life*, London, Black-Swan, 1705.

Mazzoni, C., *Saint Hysteria: Neurosis, Mysticism, and Gender in European Culture*, Ithaca, NY, Cornell University Press, 1996.

Meaney, A.L., "The Anglo-Saxon View of the Causes of Illness," in S. Campbell, B. Hall, and D. Klausner, eds., *Health, Disease and Healing in Medieval Culture*, New York, St. Martin's Press, 1992, pp. 12–33.

Ménagier de Paris, Le, Geneva, Slatkin Reprints, 1966.

Mendelson, S.H., *The Mental World of Three Stuart Women: Three Studies*, Amherst, MA, University of Massachusetts Press, 1987.

Merchant, C., *The Death of Nature: Women, Ecology and the Scientific Revolution*, New York, Harper and Row, 1980.

Merkel, I., "*Aurora*; or The Rising Sun of Allegory: Hermetic Imagery in the Work of Jakob Böhme," in I. Merkel and A.G. Rebus, eds., *Hermeticism and the Renaissance*, Washington, DC, Folger, 1988.

Merleau-Ponty, M., *Phenomenology of Perception*, C. Smith, trans., London, Routledge and Kegan Paul, 1996.

Messaris, P., *Visual "Literacy": Image, Mind, and Reality*, Boulder, CO, Westview, 1994.

Meyer-Baer, K., *Music of the Spheres and the Dance of Death: Studies in Musical Iconology*, Princeton, NJ, Princeton University Press, 1970.

Miles, M., *Image as Insight: Visual Understanding in Western Christianity and Secular Culture*, Boston, MA, Beacon Press, 1985.

Miller, J., "The Humours of Oxford", in H.W. Wells, ed., *Three Centuries of English and American Plays: England, 1500–1800*, vol. 3, New York, Redex Microprint Corporation, 1963.

Miller, N.K., "Arachnologies: The Woman, the Text, and the Critic," in N.K. Miller, ed., *The Poetics of Gender*, New York, Columbia University Press, 1986, pp. 270–93.

Milner, J., *Symbolists and Decadents*, London, Studio Vista, 1971.

Milton, J., *Milton's Samson Agonistes and Lycidas*, J. Hunter, ed., London, Longmans, Green, and Co., 1872.

Minowski, W.L., "Physician Motives in Banning Medieval Traditional Healers," *Women and Health*, 1994, vol. 21, no. 1, pp. 84–96.

Molesworth, H., "Before *Bed*," *October*, 1993, vol. 63, pp. 69–82.

Molière, *Les Femmes savantes*, Boston, D.C. Heath, 1896.

Montesquiou, R. de, *Pays des aromates*, Saint-Cloud, France, Imprimerie Belin Frères, 1903.

—— *Le Chef des odeurs suaves*, Paris, Georges Richard, 1907.

—— *Les Pas effacés: mémoires*, 3 vols., Paris, Emile-Paul Frères, 1923.

Moore, T., *The Planets Within: Marsilio Ficino's Astrological Psychology*, London, Associated University Presses, 1982.

More Roper, M., "A Devout Treatise upon the 'Pater Noster'," in K.M. Wilson, ed., *Women Writers of the Renaissance and Reformation*, Athens, University of Georgia Press.

Morgan, M.J., *Molyneux's Question: Vision, Touch and the Philosophy of Perception*, Cambridge, Cambridge University Press, 1977.

Morton, J., *The Ancren Riwle: A Treatise on the Rules and Duties of Monastic Life*, New York, Johnson Reprint Corporation, 1968.

Mulvey, L., *Visual and Other Pleasures*, London, Macmillan, 1989.

Munhall, E., *Whistler and Montesquiou: The Butterfly and the Bat*, New York and Paris, The Frick Collection/Flammarion, 1995.

Munro, J.M., *Arthur Symons*, New York, Twayne, 1969.

Nettesheim, A. von, *De Occulta Philosophia*, Graz, Austria, Akademische Druck, 1967.

—— "Female Pre-eminence," in *The Feminist Controversy of the Renaissance*, Delmar, NY, Scholars' Facsimiles and Reprints, 1980.

Newall, V., "The Jew as Witch Figure," in V. Newall, ed., *The Witch Figure*, London, Routledge and Kegan Paul, 1973.

Newman, B., *Sister of Wisdom: St. Hildegard's Theology of the Feminine*, Berkeley, University of California Press, 1987.

—— "Introduction," in Hildegard of Bingen, *Symphonia: A Critical Edition of the Symphonia armonie celestium revelationum*, B. Newman, ed., Ithaca, NY, Cornell University Press, 1988.

Nicholl, D., "St. Bede," in J. Walsh, ed., *Pre-Reformation English Spirituality*, New York, Fordham Press, 1985, pp. 1–14.

Nicolson, M.H., *The Breaking of the Circle: Studies in the Effect of the "New Science" upon Seventeenth-Century Poetry*, rev. edn, New York, Columbia University Press, 1962.

—— *Science and the Imagination*, Ithaca, NY, Great Seal Books, 1963.

—— *Newton Demands the Muse: Newton's Optiks and the Eighteenth Century Poets*, Princeton, NJ, Princeton University Press, 1966.

Nihell, E., *A Treatise on the Art of Midwifery*, London, A. Morley, 1760.

Nordau, M., *Degeneration*, New York, D. Appleton and Company, 1900.

Nordenfalk, C., "The Sense of Touch in Art," in K.-L. Selig and E. Sears, eds., *The Verbal and The Visual: Essays In Honor of William Sebastian*, New York, Italica Press, 1990, pp. 109–32.

Norris, J., *Reflections Upon the Conduct of Human Life*, London, Awnsham and John Churchill, 1696.

Nussbaum, F.A., *The Brink of All We Hate: English Satires on Women: 1660–1750*, Lexington, University Press of Kentucky, 1984.

Odorisio, G.C., *Donna e societa' nel seiciento*, Rome, Bulzoni editore, 1979.

O'Faolain, J. and Martines, L., eds., *Not in God's Image*, San Francisco, Harper and Row, 1973.

Oldenburg, H., "The Publisher to the Reader," in R. Boyle, *Experiments and Considerations Touching Colours*, in R. Boyle, *The Works*, T. Birch, ed., Hildesheim, Germany, Georg Olms, 1965.

Onians, R., *The Origins of European Thought about the Body, the Mind, the Soul, the World, Time and Fate*, Cambridge, Cambridge University Press, 1951.

Orenstein, G.F., "Manifestations of the Occult in the Art and Literature of Leonora Carrington," in F. Luanne, ed., *Literature and the Occult: Essays in Comparative Literature*, Arlington, University of Texas Press, 1977.

—— "Leonora Carrington's Visionary Art for the New Age," *Chrysalis*, 1978, vol. 3, pp. 65–77.

—— *The Reflowering of the Goddess*, New York, Pergamon Press, 1990.

Origo, I., *The World of San Bernardino*, New York, Harcourt, Brace, and World, 1962.

Owens, C., "The Discourse of Others: Feminists and Postmodernism," in H. Foster, ed., *The Anti-Aesthetic: Essays on Postmodern Culture*, Port Townsend, WA, Bay Press, 1983, pp. 57–82.

Pagel, W., *Paracelsus: An Introduction to Philosophical Medicine in the Era of the Renaissance*, Basel, Karger, 1958.

Paladilhe, J. and Pierre, J., *Gustave Moreau*, B. Wadia, trans., London, Thames and Hudson, 1972.

Palmer, R., "In Bad Odour: Smell and Its Significance in Medicine from Antiquity to the Seventeenth Century," in W.F. Bynum and R. Porter, eds., *Medicine and the Five Senses*, Cambridge, Cambridge University Press, 1993, pp. 61–8.

Paracelsus, *The Hermetic and Alchemical Writings*, A.E. Waite, ed., London, James Elliot, 1894.

Parker, R., *The Subversive Stitch: Embroidery and the Making of the Feminine*, London, The Women's Press, 1984.

Parker, R. and Pollock, G., *Old Mistresses: Women, Art and Ideology*, London, Routledge and Kegan Paul, 1981.

—— eds., *Framing Feminism: Art and the Women's Movement 1970–1985*, London, Pandora, 1987.

Pater, W., "Poems by William Morris," *Westminster Review*, 1868, vol. 90, pp. 300–12.

Paulson, W.R., *Enlightenment, Romanticism, and the Blind in France*, Princeton, NJ, Princeton University Press, 1987.

Phillips, J.A., *Eve: The History of an Idea*, San Francisco, Harper and Row, 1984.

Philo, *Questions and Answers on Genesis*, R. Marcus, trans., Cambridge, MA, Harvard University Press, 1961.

Pico della Mirandola, G., *Heptaplus or Discourse on the Seven Days of Creation*, J.B. McGraw, trans., New York, Philosophical Library, 1977.

Pierrot, J., *The Decadent Imagination: 1880–1900*, D. Coltman, trans., Chicago, University of Chicago Press, 1981.

Pieterse, J.N., *White on Black: Images of Africa and Blacks in Western Popular Culture*, New Haven, CT, Yale University Press, 1992.

Pina-Cabral, J. de, "Cults of Death in Northwestern Portugal," *Journal of the Anthropological Society of Oxford*, 1980, vol. 11, no. 1, pp. 1–14.

Pizan, C. de, *The Book of the City of Ladies*, E.J. Richards, trans., New York, Persea Books, 1982.

—— *A Medieval Woman's Mirror of Honor: The Treasury of the City of Ladies*, M.P. Cosman, ed., C.C. Willard, trans., New York, Persea Books, 1989.

Plato, *Timaeus*, B. Jowett, trans., New York, The Liberal Arts Press, 1949.

Plutarch, *De Iside et Osiride*, Swansea, University of Wales Press, 1970.

Pollock, G., *Vision and Difference: Femininity, Feminism, and Histories of Art*, London, Routledge, 1988.

Ponnelle, L. and Bordet, L., *St. Philip Neri and the Roman Society of his Times*, R. Kerr, trans., London, Sheed and Ward, 1937.

Porteous, J.D., *Landscapes of the Mind: Worlds of Sense and Metaphor*, Toronto, University of Toronto Press, 1990.

Porter, R., "The Rise of Physical Examination," in W.F. Bynum and R. Porter, eds., *Medicine and the Five Senses*, Cambridge, Cambridge University Press, 1993, pp. 179–97.

Poullain de la Barre, F., *The Equality of the Two Sexes*, D. Frankforter and P.J. Morman, trans., Lampeter, Wales, Edwin Mellen Press, 1989.

Prampolini, E., "Chromophony – the Colours of Sounds," in U. Apollonio, ed., *Futurist Manifestos*, London, Thames and Hudson, 1973.

Praz, M., *The Romantic Agony*, A. Davidson, trans., London, Oxford University Press, 1970.

Ptolemy, *Tetrabiblos*, F.E. Robbins, ed. and trans., Cambridge, MA, Harvard University Press, 1980.

Rachilde, *Monsieur Venus*, Paris, Ernest Flammarion, 1926.

—— *Madame Adonis*, Paris, J. Ferenczi et Fils, 1929.

—— *The Marquise de Sade*, L. Heron, trans., Sawtry, England, Dedalus, 1994.

Rahner, K., "La Doctrine des 'sens spirituels' au moyen-age," in *Revue d'ascétique et de mystique, 1933*, Brussels, Culture et Civilisation, 1964, pp. 263–99.

Rémy, N., *Demonolatry*, E.A. Ashwin, trans., London, John Rodker, 1930.

Révész, G., *Psychology and Art of the Blind*, H.A. Wolff, trans., London, Longmans, Green, and Co., 1950.

Reynolds, M., *The Learned Lady in England: 1650–1760*, Gloucester, MA, Peter Smith, 1964.

Ribera, F. de, *Vida de Santa Teresa de Jesús*, Barcelona, Gustavo Gili, 1908.

Robins, K., *Into the Image: Culture and Politics in the Field of Vision*, London, Routledge, 1996.

Rocheleau, C., *Hors de sa prison: extraordinaire histoire de Ludivine Lachance, l'infirme des infirmes, sourde, muette et aveugle*, Montreal, Arbour and Dupont, 1927.

Rojas, F. de, *Celestina*, D. Sherman Severin, ed., J. Mabbe, trans., Warminster, England, Aris and Phillips, 1987.

Rowland, B., *Animals with Human Faces: A Guide to Animal Symbolism*, Knoxville, University of Tennessee Press, 1973.

Roy, B., "La Belle e(s)t la bête: aspects du bestiaire féminin au moyen âge," *Etudes françaises*, 1974, vol. 10, no. 3, pp. 320–34.

Russolo, L., "The Art of Noises," in U. Apollonio, ed., *Futurist Manifestos*, London, Thames and Hudson, 1973.

Sackville-West, V., *The Eagle and the Dove: A Study in Contrasts, St. Teresa of Avila, St. Thérèse of Lisieux*, London, Sphere, 1988.

Sadler, J., *The Sick Womans Private Looking-Glasse*, Amsterdam, Theatrum Orbis Terrarum, 1977.

Saint-Point, V., "Manifesto of the Futurist Woman," in B. Katz, "The Women of Futurism," *Woman's Art Journal*, 1986/7, vol. 7, p. 12.

—— "Futurist Manifesto of Lust," in B. Katz, "The Women of Futurism," *Woman's Art Journal*, 1986/7, vol. 7, p. 13.

Salvaggio, R., *Enlightened Absence: Neoclassical Configurations of the Feminine*, Urbana, University of Illinois Press, 1988.

Sankovitch, T.A., *French Women Writers and the Book*, Syracuse, NY, Syracuse University Press, 1988.

Sartre, J.-P., *Being and Nothingness: An Essay on Phenomenological Ontology*, H.E. Barnes, trans., New York, Philosophical Library, 1956.

Schafer, R.M., *The Tuning of the World*, New York, Knopf, 1977.

Schiebinger, L., *The Mind Has No Sex? Women in the Origins of Modern Science*, Cambridge, MA, Harvard University Press, 1989.

—— *Nature's Body: Gender in the Making of Modern Science*, Boston, MA, Beacon Press, 1993.

Schiesari, J., "The Face of Domestication: Physiognomy, Gender Politics, and Humanism's Others," in M. Hendricks and P. Parker, eds., *Women, 'Race,' and Writing in the Early Modern Period*, London, Routledge, 1994, pp. 55–70.

Schiller, F., *On the Aesthetic Education of Man*, E.M. Wilkinson and L.A. Willoughby, eds. and trans., Oxford, Clarendon, 1982.

Schlieker, A., "Introduction," in A. Schlieker, ed., *Leonora Carrington: Paintings, Drawings and Sculptures*, London, Serpentine Gallery, 1991.

Schloezer, B. de, *Scriabin: Artist and Mystic*, N. Slonimsky, trans., Berkeley, University of California Press, 1987.

Schor, N., *Breaking the Chain: Women, Theory and French Realist Fiction*, New York, Columbia University Press, 1985.

Schrader, L., *Sensación y sinestesia*, Madrid, Editorial Gredos, 1975 .

Scot, R., *The Discoverie of Witchcraft*, London, Centaur Press, 1964.

Scriptores Historiae Augustae, The, 3 vols., D. Magie, trans., London, William Heinemann, 1922.

Seaman, D.W., *Concrete Poetry in France*, Ann Arbor, MI, UMI Research Press, 1981.

Sears, E., "Sensory Perception and its Metaphors in the Time of Richard of Fournival," in W.F. Bynum and R. Porter, eds., *Medicine and the Five Senses*, Cambridge, Cambridge University Press, 1993.

Ségalen, V., "Les Synesthésies et l'école symboliste," *Mercure de France*, 1902, vol. 4, pp. 57–90.

Severini, G., "The Plastic Analogies of Dynamism," in U. Apollonio, ed., *Futurist Manifestos*, London, Thames and Hudson, 1973.

Sharp, J., "Sounds, Noises, and Smells: Sensory Experience in Futurist Art," in A. Coffin Hanson, ed., *The Futurist Imagination*, New Haven, CT, Yale University Art Gallery, 1983.

Shattuck, R., *The Banquet Years: The Origins of the Avant-Garde in France, 1885 to World War I*, Salem, NH, Ayer Company, 1984.

Shelley, P.B., *The Complete Poetical Works of Shelley*, G.E. Woodberry, ed., Boston, MA, Houghton Mifflin, 1901.

Solterer, H., "Seeing, Hearing, Tasting Woman: Medieval Senses of Reading," *Comparative Literature*, 1991, vol. 16, no. 2, pp. 129–45.

Soranus, *Gynecology*, O. Temkin, trans., Baltimore, MD, Johns Hopkins University Press, 1956.

Spencer, M.C., *Charles Fourier*, New York, Twayne, 1981.

Spratt, T., *History of the Royal Society*, J.I. Cope and H.W. Jones, eds., St. Louis, MO, Washington University Press, 1966.

Stafford, B.M., *Body Criticism: Imaging the Unseen in Enlightenment Art and Medicine*, Cambridge, MA, MIT Press, 1991.

—— "Presuming Images and Consuming Words: The Visualization of Knowledge From the Enlightenment to Post-modernism," in J. Brewer and R. Porter, eds., *Consumption and the World of Goods*, London, Routledge, 1993, pp. 462–77.

—— "Redesigning the Image of Images: A Personal View," *Eighteenth-Century Studies*, 1994, vol. 28, no. 1, pp. 9–16.

Stallybrass, P. and White, A., *The Politics and Poetics of Transgression*, Ithaca, NY, Cornell University Press, 1986.

Starkie, E., *Baudelaire*, London, Faber and Faber, 1933.

Stopp, E., *St. Francis de Sales: A Testimony by St. Chantal*, London, Faber and Faber, 1967.

Süskind, P., *Perfume: The Story of a Murderer*, J. E. Woods, trans., New York, Alfred A. Knopf, 1986.

Swedenborg, E., *Heaven and its Wonders and Hell*, J.C. Ager, trans., New York, Swedenborg Foundation, 1930.

Swift, J., "The Lady's Dressing Room," in H. Davis, ed., *Poetical Works*, London, Oxford University Press, 1967.

Swinburne, A.C., *The Poems of Algernon Charles Swinburne*, vol. 1, London, Chatto and Windus, 1912.

Synnott, A., *The Body Social: Symbolism, Self and Society*, London, Routledge, 1993.

Tactile, Quebec City, Musée du Québec, 1978.

Talbot, C.H., ed. and trans., *The Life of Christina of Markyate: A Twelfth-Century Recluse*, Oxford, Clarendon Press, 1959.

Taylor, H.O., *The Medieval Mind: A History of the Development of Thought and Emotion in the Middle Ages*, vol. 1, Cambridge, MA, Harvard University Press, 1962.

Teresa de Jesús, *Libro de las fundaciones*, in *Obras completas*, E. de la Madre de Dios and O. Steggink, eds., Madrid, Biblioteca de Autores Cristianos, 1972.

—— *Libro de la vida*, in *Obras completas*, E. de la Madre de Dios and O. Steggink, eds., Madrid, Biblioteca de Autores Cristianos, 1972.

Tester, S.J., *A History of Western Astrology*, Woodbridge, England, Boydell Press, 1987.

Thompson, C., *Mystery and Lure of Perfume*, London, John Lane, The Bodley Head, 1927.

Thorndike, L., *A History of Magic and Experimental Science*, 8 vols., New York, Columbia University Press, 1934.

Thurston, H., *The Physical Phenomena of Mysticism*, J.H. Crehan, ed., London, Burns and Oates, 1952.

Todd, J., *The Sign of Angellica: Women, Writing and Fiction 1660–1800*, London, Virago, 1989.

Topsell, E., *The History of Four-Footed Beasts and Serpents and Insects*, vol. 1, New York, Da Capo, 1967.

Trollope, A., *Can You Forgive Her?*, London, Oxford University Press, 1975.

Trombley, S., *"All that Summer She was Mad": Virginia Woolf and Her Doctors*, London, Junction Books, 1981.

Trotula of Salerno, *The Diseases of Women*, E. Mason-Hohl, trans., Los Angeles, Ward Ritchie Press, 1940.

Ullmer, G.L., *Applied Grammatology: Post(e)-Pedagogy from Jacques Derrida to Joseph Beuys*, Baltimore, MD, Johns Hopkins University Press, 1985.

Vallas, L., *The Theories of Claude Debussy*, M. O'Brien, trans., New York, Dover Publications, 1967.

Varo, B., *Remedios Varo: En el centro del microcosmos*, Mexico City, Fondo de Cultura Económico, 1990.

Vauchez, A., *La Sainteté en Occident aux derniers siècles du Moyen Age*, Rome, Ecole Française du Rome, 1981.

Veith, I., *Hysteria: The History of a Disease*, Chicago, University of Chicago Press, 1965.

Villey, P., *The World of the Blind: A Psychological Study*, New York, Macmillan, 1930.

Vinge, L., *The Five Senses: Studies in a Literary Tradition*, Lund, Sweden, Royal Society of Letters at Lund, 1975.

Virilio, P., *The Vision Machine*, J. Rose, trans., Bloomington, Indiana University Press, 1994.

Vives, J.L., "Formación de la mujer cristiana," in *Obras completas*, vol. 1, L. Riber, ed., Madrid, M. Aguilar, 1947.

Voragine, J. de, *The Golden Legend*, G. Ryan and H. Ripperger, trans., London, Longmans, Green, and Co., 1941.

Vorreiter, G., "Theatre of Touch," *The Architectural Review*, 1989, no. 185, pp. 66–9.

Vriesen, G. and Imdahl, M., *Robert Delaunay: Light and Color*, New York, Harry N. Abrams, 1967.

Waelti-Walters, J., *Feminist Novelists of the Belle Epoque*, Bloomington, Indiana University Press, 1990.

Wagner, M., "Theater of Touch," *Interiors*, 1989, no. 149, pp. 98–9.

Wallas, A., *Before the Bluestockings*, London, George Allen and Unwin, 1929.

Walpole, H., *Horace Walpole's Correspondence with the Countess of Upper Ossory*, vol. 33, W.D. Wallace and A.D. Wallace, eds., New Haven, CT, Yale University Press, 1965.

Walsh, D., *The Mysticism of Innerworldly Fulfillment: A Study of Jacob Boehme*, Gainesville, University of Florida Press, 1983.

Warner, M., *Monuments and Maidens: The Allegory of the Female Form*, New York, Atheneum, 1985.

—— "Introduction," in L. Carrington, *The Seventh Horse and Other Stories*, K. Talbot and A. Kerrigen, trans., London, Virago, 1989.

—— "Leonora Carrington's Spirit Bestiary; or the Art of Playing Make-Believe," in A. Schlieker, ed., *Leonora Carrington: Paintings, Drawings and Sculptures*, London, Serpentine Gallery, 1991.

Warren, A., "William Law: Ascetic and Mystic," in W. Law, *A Serious Call to a Devout and Holy Life, The Spirit of Love*, P.G. Stanwood, ed., New York, Paulist Press, 1978.

Weinstein, D. and Bell, R.M., *Saints and Society: The Two Worlds of Western Christendom, 1000–1700*, Chicago, University of Chicago Press, 1982.

Weisner, M.E., *Women and Gender in Early Modern Europe*, Cambridge, Cambridge University Press, 1993.

Wenk, A.B., *Claude Debussy and the Poets*, Berkeley, University of California Press, 1976.

White, B.W., Saunders F.A., Scadden, L., Bach-y-rita, P., and Collins, C.C., "Seeing with the Skin," *Perception and Psychophysics*, 1970, vol. 7, no. 1, pp. 23–7.

White, T.H., ed. and trans., *The Bestiary*, New York, G.P. Putnam's Sons, 1960.

Whitehead, A.N., *Science and the Modern World*, New York, Mentor, 1925.

Williams, G., *The Age of Agony: The Art of Healing 1700–1800*, London, Constable, 1975.

Wilson, K.M., ed., *Women Writers of the Renaissance and Reformation*, Athens, University of Georgia Press, 1987.

Wollheim, R., "What the Spectator Sees," in N. Bryson, M.A. Holly and K. Moxey, eds., *Visual Theory: Painting and Interpretation*, New York, Harper Collins, 1991, pp. 101–50.

Wollstonecraft, M., *A Vindication of the Rights of Woman*, New York, Source Book Press, 1971.

Woolf, V., *A Room of One's Own*, London, Chatto and Windus, 1984.

Woolley, H., *The Queen-like Closet or Rich Cabinet*, 5th ed., London, R. Chiswel, 1684.

Zayas, M. de, *Amorous and Exemplary Novels*, H.P. Boyer, trans., Berkeley, University of California Press, 1990.

Zegher, C. de, "Cecilia Vicuña's Ouvrage: Knot a Not, Notes as Knots," in G. Pollock, ed., *Generations and Geographies in the Visual Arts: Feminist Readings*, London, Routledge, 1996.

Zoa, S.M., "Maria de Zayas y Sotomayor: Sibyl of Madrid (1590?-1661?)," in J.R. Brink, ed., *Female Scholars: A Tradition of Learned Women Before 1800*, Montreal, Eden Press, 1980, pp. 54–67.

Index